Social goals and social organization
Essays in memory of Elisha Pazner

Elisha A. Pazner, 1941–1979. (Photo by June Flanders.)

Social goals and social organization
Essays in memory of Elisha Pazner

Edited by
LEONID HURWICZ   *University of Minnesota*
DAVID SCHMEIDLER   *Tel-Aviv University*
HUGO SONNENSCHEIN   *Princeton University*

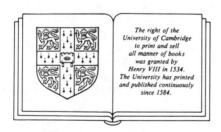

The right of the
University of Cambridge
to print and sell
all manner of books
was granted by
Henry VIII in 1534.
The University has printed
and published continuously
since 1584.

CAMBRIDGE UNIVERSITY PRESS

Cambridge
London   New York   New Rochelle
Melbourne   Sydney

Published by the Press Syndicate of the University of Cambridge
The Pitt Building, Trumpington Street, Cambridge CB2 1RP
32 East 57th Street, New York, NY 10022, USA
10 Stamford Road, Oakleigh, Melbourne 3166, Australia

First published 1985

Printed in the United States of America

Library of Congress Cataloging in Publication Data
Main entry under title:
Social goals and social organization.
Bibliography: p.
Includes index.
1. Welfare economics – Addresses, essays, lectures.
2. Distributive justice – Addresses, essays, lectures.
3. Pazner, Elisha, 1941–1979. I. Pazner, Elisha, 1941–1979. II. Hurwicz,
Leonid. III. Schmeidler, David, 1939–. IV. Sonnenschein, Hugo.
HB846.S65 1985   330.15′5   85-6668
ISBN 0 521 26204 6

ACKNOWLEDGMENTS FOR THE REPRINTED ARTICLES BY
ELISHA PAZNER

"A Difficulty in the Concept of Fairness" (with David Schmeidler), *Review of Economic
Studies*, *41*(3), 441–443 (1974). Reprinted by permission of the Society for Economic
Analysis Ltd.

"Recent Thinking on Economic Justice," *Journal of Peace Science*, *2*(1), 143–153 (1976).
Reprinted by permission of the Journal of Peace Studies.

"Social Contract Theory and Ordinal Distributive Equity" (with David Schmeidler), *Journal of Public Economics*, *5*(3–4), 261–268 (1976). Reprinted by permission of the North-
Holland Publishing Company.

"Pitfalls in the Theory of Fairness," *Journal of Economic Theory*, *14*(2), 458–466 (1977).
Reprinted by permission of the Journal of Economic Theory.

"Cheatproofness Properties of the Plurality Rule in Large Societies" (with Eugene
Wesley), *Review of Economic Studies*, *45*(1), 85–91 (1978). Reprinted by permission
of the Society of Economic Analysis Ltd.

"Egalitarian Equivalent Allocations: A New Concept of Economic Equity" (with David
Schmeidler), *Quarterly Journal of Economics*, *92*(4), 671–687 (1978). Reprinted by
permission of John Wiley and Sons, Inc.

Contents

vi   **Contents**

Elisha A. Pazner

Elisha A. Pazner was born on April 16, 1941, in Geneva, Switzerland, and died on March 28, 1979, in Jerusalem. He arrived in Israel in 1953, but left soon after for Argentina because of his father's foreign service position. His compulsory service in the Israeli Defense Force extended from May 1960 until October 1962. Elisha began his study of economics at the Hebrew University of Jerusalem (B.A. 1966) and did graduate work at Harvard University (M.A. 1969, Ph.D. 1971). He was a member of the Department of Economics at Tel-Aviv University from October 1971 until his sudden death. During this time he spent over two years as a visitor at Northwestern University, Evanston, Illinois.

Elisha's interests in economics were quite broad. Although most of his research was in theory and mainly microtheory, he did work in macro-theory, including applications to the Israeli economy. He belonged to the minority of the members of his department who could quote the recent economic indicators of the Israeli economy.

Elisha's main research efforts were devoted to topics in public finance, public economics, general equilibrium analysis, welfare economics, social choice, incentives, and industrial organization. A large share of these works followed a research plan that was only slightly adjusted over the years. He was interested in the welfare evaluation of economic activity. The basic neoclassical premise that an agent's welfare depends only on his own consumption seemed to Elisha too restrictive, and his work on economic equity has helped us to understand how we can reach further. Elisha also emphasized the issue of procedural justice, which had been neglected by most of the profession. This was a major stimulus to his interest in decentralization and allocation mechanisms. As he put it in nonscientific terms, "It matters not only what you get but how you get it." Those who knew Elisha personally are not surprised that he made this point. Many will agree that the "how" is important for human motivation. Elisha believed that it can and should be part of welfare economics and it was the main topic on his research agenda at the time of his death.

PUBLICATIONS AND RESEARCH PAPERS OF
ELISHA A. PAZNER

I   Published titles and journal articles (in English)

Pazner, Elisha A. [1972]. "Merit Wants and the Theory of Taxation." *Public Finance*, 27:460–472.

Pazner, Elisha A., and David Schmeidler [1974]. "A Difficulty in the Concept of Fairness." *Review of Economic Studies*, 41(3):441–443. [Chapter 10, this book]

Pazner, Elisha A., and Assaf Razin [1974]. "Welfare Aspects of Exchange-Rate Uncertainty.." *Econometrica*, 11(163):256.

Pazner, Elisha A., and Assaf Razin [1974]. "A Model of Investment under Interest Rate Uncertainty." *International Economic Review*, 15:798–802.

Pazner, Elisha A. [1974]. "Economic Principles and Environmental Quality." *Quarterly Review of Economics*, 21:202–206.

Pazner, Elisha A. [1975]. "Quality Choice and Monopoly Regulation," Chapter 1 in *Regulating the Product*, edited by Richard E. Caves and Marc J. Roberts, The Brookings Institution, pp. 3–16. Cambridge, Mass.: Ballinger.

Pazner, Elisha, A. [1975]. "Optimal Pricing and Income Distribution," Chapter 10 in *Regulating the Product*, edited by Richard E. Caves and Marc J. Roberts, The Brookings Institution, pp. 201–219. Cambridge, Mass.: Ballinger.

Pazner, Elisha A., and Richard E. Caves [1975]. "Value of Options, Value of Time and Local Airline Subsidy," Chapter 12 in *Regulating the Product*, edited by Richard E. Caves and Marc. J. Roberts, The Brookings Institution, pp. 249–268. Cambridge, Mass.: Ballinger.

Pazner, Elisha A., and Assaf Razin [1975]. "Expected Present value vs. Expected Future Value." *The Journal of Finance*, 30(3):875–877.

Pazner, Elisha A., and Assaf Razin [1975]. "Industry Equilibrium under Random Demand." *European Economic Review*, 6(4):387–395.

Pazner, Elisha A., and David Schmeidler [1975]. "Competition Analysis under Complete Ignorance." *International Economic Review 16* (February):246–257.

Pazner, Elisha A. [1976]. "Recent Thinking on Economic Justice," *Journal of Peace Science*, 2(1):143–153. [Chapter 11, this book]

Pazner, Elisha A. [1976]. "Inflation, Resource Allocation and Income Distribution." *Quarterly Review of Economics*, 23:417–423 (in Hebrew).

Pazner, Elisha A., and David Schmeidler [1976]. "Social Contract Theory and Ordinal Distributive Equity." *Journal of Public Economics*, 5(3–4):261–268. [Chapter 12, this book]

Pazner, Elisha A., Ehud Kalai, and David Schmeidler [1976]. "Collective Choice Correspondences as Admissible Outcomes of Social Bargaining Processes." *Econometrica*, 44(2):233–240.

Pazner, Elisha A., Alex Cukierman, and Assaf Razin [1977]. "A Macroeconomic Model of the Israeli Economy: 1956–1974." *Bank of Israel Economic Review*, 44:29–64.

Pazner, Elisha A. [1977]. "Pitfalls in the Theory of Fairness." *Journal of Economic Theory*, 14(2):458–466. [Chapter 13, this book]

Pazner, Elisha A. [1977]. "Comprehensive Income Taxation, Equity and Efficiency." *The Israeli Tax Review*, *37–38*:135–138 (in Hebrew).

Pazner, Elisha A., and Eugene Wesley [1977]. "Stability of Social Choices in Infinitely Large Societies." *Journal of Economic Theory*, *14*(2):252–262.

Pazner, Elisha A. [1978]. "Wage Indexation to Prices and Output: A Proposal." *Quarterly Review of Economics*, *25*:188–191 (in Hebrew).

Pazner, Elisha A., and Eugene Wesley [1978]. "Cheatproofness Properties of the Plurality Rule in Large Societies," *Review of Economic Studies*, *45*(1): 85–91. [Chapter 14, this book]

Pazner, Elisha A., and David Schmeidler [1978]. "Decentralization, Income Distribution and the Role of Money in Socialist Economies." *Economic Inquiry*, *16*(2):257–264.

Pazner, Elisha A., and David Schmeidler [1978]. "Egalitarian Equivalent Allocations: A New Concept of Economic Equity." *Quarterly Journal of Economics*, *92*(4):671–687. [Chapter 15, this book]

Pazner, Elisha A. [1978]. "Individual Rationality and the Concept of Social Welfare." *Theory and Decision 10*(1–4):281–292.

Pazner, Elisha A. [1979]. "Equity, Nonfeasible Alternatives and Social Choice: A Reconsideration of the Concept of Social Welfare." *Aggregation and Revelation of Preferences*, edited by Jean-Jacques Laffont, pp. 161–173. Amsterdam: North Holland.

Pazner, Elisha A. [1979]. "The Characterization of Implementable Choice Rules." *Aggregation and Revelation of Preferences*, edited by Jean-Jacques Laffont, pp. 349–350. Amsterdam: North Holland.

Pazner, Elisha A., and Assaf Razin [1980]. "Competitive Efficiency in an Overlapping Generation Model with Endogenous Population." *Journal of Public Economics*, *13*(2):249–258.

Pazner, Elisha A., and Efraim Sadka [1980]. "Excess-Burden and Economic Surplus as Consistent Welfare Indicators." *Journal of Public Finance*, *35*(2): 249–258.

Pazner, Elisha A., and Richard A. Musgrave [1980]. "Liability Rules, Equity and Efficiency." *Journal of Public Finances*, *35*(1):1–12.

Pazner, Elisha A., and Efraim Sadka [1981]. "Welfare Criteria for Tax Reforms-Efficiency Aspects." *Journal of Public Economics*, *16*:113–122.

Pazner, Elisha A. [1981]. "On Indexation and Macroeconomic Stability," in *Development in an Inflationary World*, edited by M. June Flanders and Assaf Razin. Sapir Institution, pp. 155–161. New York: Academic Press.

II   Unpublished reports

Pazner, Elisha A., and David Schmeidler [1974]. "Just Saving and the Golden Rule." The Foerder Institute for Economic Research, T.R. 38, 8 pages.

Pazner, Elisha A. [1975]. "Distributive Justice, Entitlement Principles and the Original Position." 20 pages.

Editors' preface

Soon after Elisha Pazner's death, the editors of this book gathered together to plan a tribute to his memory. Rather than deciding to give Elisha's many friends the opportunity to provide a paper on a subject of their choice, we decided on a more ambitious undertaking. Our idea was to solicit a collection of surveys on subjects closely associated with Elisha's interest in the design and evaluation of economic mechanisms. We approached some of the people who we felt were making the most outstanding contributions in those areas. Because we believed that bargaining theory and the economics of competitive bidding were especially ripe for surveys, we extended our boundaries to include those topics as well, despite the fact that they fall marginally outside of Elisha's own research interests. We could not be more pleased with the result. It is a tribute to Elisha that so many busy people were willing to put aside their research to prepare these surveys. No areas of economic theory are more active today than those surveyed here; similarly, none are concerned with more basic issues. We have tried to honor Elisha with a book that he would have wanted to have on hand and use for his lectures.

The surveys are preceded by "A Perspective" by Leo Hurwicz. It contains a systematic account of the development of the literature on mechanism design and thus provides a context for both the surveys and the six published papers authored or coauthored by Elisha that follow.

L. H.
D. S.
H. S.

Contributors

Claude d'Aspremont
Center for Operations Research
  and Econometrics
Université Catholique de Louvain

Leonid Hurwicz
Department of Economics
University of Minnesota

Ehud Kalai
Graduate School of Management
Northwestern University

Eric S. Maskin
Department of Economics
Harvard University

Paul R. Milgrom
Department of Economics
Yale University

Eitan Muller
School of Business Administration
University of Jerusalem

Roger B. Myerson
Graduate School of Management
Northwestern University

Andrew Postlewaite
Department of Economics
University of Pennsylvania

Mark A. Satterthwaite
Graduate School of Management
Northwestern University

William Thomson
Department of Economics
University of Rochester

Hal R. Varian
Department of Economics
University of Michigan

CHAPTER 1

A perspective

Leonid Hurwicz

Because this volume is dedicated to the memory of Elisha Pazner, let me start with two reminiscences. I first met Elisha sometime in 1969 or 1970 when I was visiting at Harvard. Elisha consulted with me on problems related to his dissertation. Initially, we did not find it easy to communicate, but I was impressed by his original insights and depth. Then, after 1971, I was back at Minnesota and he was visiting at Northwestern. By that time we shared the interest in problems of implementation. We had conversations on several occasions, including at least one visit by Elisha to Minneapolis. He was, I remember, particularly concerned about the relationship of the positive "free rider" results due to Groves and Ledyard to my earlier negative results concerning incentive compatibility (extended to public goods by Ledyard and Roberts [1974]). I feel indebted to Elisha both for the stimulation to pursue this issue and clarification of many essential points.

Subsequently, Elisha's interests moved toward the implementation of rules satisfying criteria of fairness as well as efficiency in environments involving production, especially in the presence of a nontransferable endowment such as labor. His pathbreaking contributions in this area are discussed and references given in two essays of the present book (Varian and Thomson; Postlewaite).

All the essays in this book qualify under the rubric of *normative economics*: they go beyond the *positive economics* designed to explain the observed economic phenomena and aim at the development of criteria to be used in judging economic policies and systems. Normative economics, in turn, has focused on two major issues: one examining the logic and merits of the various welfare criteria in terms of which the consequences

This research was partially supported by National Science Foundation Grant No. SES-8208378.

1

of economic actions may be judged, and the other examining – in the light of such criteria – the workings of various policies and mechanisms.

Among the essays in this volume, two – focused on welfare criteria (d'Aspremont; Varian and Thomson) – are of the first category; four – devoted to problems of implementation – are of the second category. Of the latter, one (Myerson) is devoted to Bayesian implementation, one (Muller and Satterthwaite) to dominance implementation, and two (Maskin; Postlewaite) to Nash implementation. Two essays (Kalai; Milgrom) are devoted to problems (bargaining, bidding) that are outside the present framework.

The first category of studies has led to the development of the concepts of orderings and other attributes of social welfare, social welfare functions, and performance (or: social choice) functions or correspondences (rules). Among the orderings of social states, the Pareto criterion is the best known and most frequently used. More recently, different notions of fairness, so important in Pazner's work, have come to play an important role. Among social welfare functions, those associated with the names of Bergson, Samuelson, and Arrow are of prime importance. Performance functions were perhaps first formalized and their importance stressed by Reiter and Mount in the context of informationally oriented models, and by Maskin in a game-theoretic (incentive-respecting) framework.[1]

In the earlier literature (Bergson [1938], Lange [1942], Lerner [1944], Arrow [1951], Koopmans [1957], Debreu [1959], Arrow and Hahn [1971]), the central question asked was whether certain mechanisms (especially the competitive or monopoly mechanism) generated Pareto-optimal allocations, and – if so – for what categories of economic environments. Subsequently, the question was reversed: instead of regarding the mechanism as given and seeking the class of environments for which it works well, one seeks mechanisms that will work well for a given class of environments. Initially, in part because of the nature of Hayek, Mises, Lange, Lerner debates concerning the feasibility of socialism, the emphasis was on the informational (as distinct from incentival) aspects of economic mechanisms. One question posed was whether, for "classical"[2] environments, there exist mechanisms with the same optimality proper-

---

[1] Among related precursor concepts one should mention that of a social choice function $C(S)$ in Arrow [1951, 1963] and the notion of the choice function $C(S, R)$ in Sen [1970]. It is important to note that, in its contemporary version, the social performance correspondence need not be derived from any maximization process, and that its domain is a class of environments (n-tuples of individual characteristics) rather than merely feasible sets and preference profiles. In particular, the status quo (e.g., initial endowment) may be part of the specification of the environment. The idea of a more general concept of a social choice function is suggested in Arrow ([1963], footnote 34, p. 104).

[2] Satisfying the assumptions of convexity, divisibility, and so forth as, for instance, in Koopmans's [1957] Propositions 4 and 5.

ties as perfect competition but, in some sense, informationally more efficient than (or as efficient as) perfect competition. It was shown (Mount and Reiter [1974], Hurwicz [1977], Osana [1978]) that no mechanisms with a smaller message space would guarantee optimality. Analogous results for the Lindahl mechanism were obtained by Sato [1981]. A uniqueness result for the Walrasian mechanism was obtained by Jordan [1982] under the additional postulate of individual rationality.

But not everyone was satisfied with the analysis of performance of various mechanisms restricted to classical environments and to their purely informational properties. In particular, incentive properties in two types of nonclassical environments had engaged the economists' attention for a long time: technologies with increasing returns, and public goods. Indeed, in each of these areas alternative mechanisms had been suggested to supplement, or substitute for, the competitive market: for increasing returns, marginal cost pricing; for public goods, the Lindahl solution. (See Lindahl [1919], Hotelling [1938], Lange [1938], Lerner [1944].)

Each of these remedies was shown to have certain defects, and the analysis of these defects led to important theoretical developments. For our purposes, the problem of public goods serves as an excellent example.

Public goods

To begin with, standard theorems concerning the optimality properties of competitive equilibria assume the absence of public goods. Indeed, it is not obvious how the competitive equilibrium in an economy with public goods is to be defined. It seems clear, however, that any reasonable definition of a competitive market would not yield Pareto optimality in the presence of public goods. On the other hand, Lindahl equilibrium (this term is formally defined below) in public goods economies is well defined and, under the customary assumptions of convexity and so on, Pareto optimal (Foley [1970], Milleron [1972]). But, as pointed out by Samuelson [1954, 1955], it may be unrealistic to expect the behavior required of individuals in order that a Lindahl equilibrium prevail.

To understand the problem, let us illustrate the Lindahl equilibrium in Lindahl's own simple setting. In one scenario representing the Lindahl mechanism, there is an "auctioneer" proposing shares p_i $(i = 1, \ldots, n)$, $\Sigma_{i=1}^{n} p_i = 1$, of the aggregate cost of a public service to be borne by the n participants; in turn, the ith participant responds by specifying the level y_i of the public service that would maximize his or her utility given p_i; agent i would then contribute $p_i y_i$ to cover the costs of public service. Equilibrium obtains when the shares p_i are so chosen that all agents desire the same level of public service, that is, $y_1 = \cdots = y_n$.

Let the ith agent's utility function in an economy, with two goods be $\overset{\circ}{u}{}^i(x^i, y)$ where x^i is the amount of private good X held by i (after taxes) and y is the level of public service Y provided to every agent. Assume furthermore, as is often done, that Y can be produced by using X as the input; that the production function is one of constant returns; and that the units of measurement are chosen so that one unit of X produces one unit of Y. If the contribution of X (tax paid) by agent i is denoted by t^i, we have $x^i = \bar{x}^i - t^i$ where $\bar{x}^i$ is the initial X-endowment of agent i. Assuming zero initial endowment of Y and production efficiency feasibility, we obtain the balance requirement

$$y = \sum_{i\text{-}1}^{n} t^i .$$

A *Lindahl equilibrium* for the economy $\overset{\circ}{e} = (\overset{\circ}{e}{}^1, \ldots, \overset{\circ}{e}{}^n)$, $\overset{\circ}{e}{}^i = (\overset{\circ}{u}{}^i, \bar{x}^i)$ may be defined as a vector

$$(x^{*1}, \ldots, x^{*n}, y^*; p^{*1}, \ldots, p^{*n})$$

such that

$$\sum_{i=1}^{n} p_i^* = 1$$

$$y^* = \sum_{i=1}^{n} (\bar{x}^i - x^{*i});$$

and for each $i = 1, \ldots, n$,

$$p^{*i} \geq 0, \qquad (x^{*i}, y^*) \text{ is individually feasible,}^3$$

$$p_i^* y^* + x^{*i} = \bar{x}^i$$

and

$$\overset{\circ}{u}{}^i(x^{*i}, y^*) \geq \overset{\circ}{u}{}^i(x^i, y)$$

for each individually feasible (x^i, y) satisfying the budget equality $p_i^* y + x_i = \bar{x}^i$.

The preceding defines the *Lindahl allocation correspondence* L on the class E of economies by

$$L(e) = \{(x^1, \ldots, x^n, y): \text{ for some } (p^1, \ldots, p^n), \text{ the vector}$$
$$(x^1, \ldots, x^n, y; p^1, \ldots, p^n) \text{ is a Lindahl equilibrium}$$
$$\text{for } e\},$$

for every e in E. [Here, again, $e = (e^1, \ldots, e^n)$, $e^i = (u^i, \bar{x}^i)$.]

---

[3] That is, (x^{*i}, y^*) is in the ith agent's consumption set C^i, often chosen as the non-negative quadrant.

The Lindahl scenario assumes that each agent treats the proposed shares p_i parametrically (i.e., as given) and that the agent's response y_i is based on the maximization of the agent's *true* utility function. But, as stressed by Samuelson, agents might find it to their advantage to respond with a value of y_i that does not maximize their true utility functions. That is, they might benefit by misrepresenting their preferences. Consequently, the Lindahl mechanism may fail to produce Pareto-optimal outcomes. If it does fail, is there another mechanism that would succeed where the Lindahl mechanism fails? In searching for such a mechanism, how is the problem to be formalized?

One answer is to be found in the theory of noncooperative games.[4] Specifically, one may consider rules prescribing resource allocation behavior (such as Lindahl, or competitive profit maximization, or marginal cost pricing) as equivalent to direct-revelation mechanisms, giving rise to a special class of games (Hurwicz [1972]). But the terms "mechanism" and "direct revelation" must be defined.

A *mechanism* is defined by endowing each of the n participants with a *strategy domain*, with S^i denoting the domain of the ith agent, and the *outcome function* (also called strategy outcome function or game form) denoted by h; this outcome function h specifies the resource allocation $(x^1, \ldots, x^n, y)$ resulting from any n-tuple of strategy choices. Thus the outcome function specifies the rules of the game; for the economy described previously, it may be written as follows:

$$(x^1, \ldots, x^n, y) = h(s^1, \ldots, s^n), \qquad s^i \in S^i, \quad i = 1, \ldots, n.$$

Formally, a mechanism is the ordered pair (S, h), $S = S^1 \times \cdots \times S^n$. The space of outcomes containing the range of h will be noted by Z.

Now consider an economy $e = (e^1, \ldots, e^n)$ where e^i has the utility function u^i, and a mechanism $m = (S, h)$, $S = S^1 \times \cdots S^n$. Let Γ denote the noncooperative game $(S, \varphi_{m,e})$ where the ith agent's payoff function is given by $\varphi^i_{m,e}(s) = u^i(h(s))$ for all s in S. Denote by $\nu_m(e)$ the set of Nash equilibria of the game Γ for the economy e.[5] We say that the mechanism $m = (S, h)$ *Nash implements* a performance correspondence $F: E \longrightarrow Z$ on E if it is the case that for every e in E, (1) the set $\nu_m(e)$ is

[4] An important role in the development of public goods theory was played by the pioneering contributions of Drèze and de la Vallée Poussin [1969], Malinvaud [1969], and the subsequent dynamics-oriented literature. Unfortunately, I am unable to cover this work in the present essay.

[5] $(s^{*1}, \ldots, s^{*n}) = s^*$ in S is a *Nash equilibrium* of the game $\Gamma = (S, \varphi)$, $S = S^1 \times \cdots \times S^n$, if, for every $i = 1, \ldots n$, it is the case that $\varphi^i(s^*) \geqq \varphi^i(i, s^i/s^*)$ for all s^i in S^i, where $i, s^i/s^*$ denotes the n-tuple s^* with its ith entry s^{*i} replaced by s^i.

not empty, and (2) $h(v_m(e)) \subseteq F(e)$. (This is sometimes called "weak" implementation.)

The general problem of designing a mechanism that yields Pareto-optimal outcomes in a given range E of environments can now be formally stated as that of finding a mechanism implementing the Pareto correspondence $P : E \twoheadrightarrow Z$ on E where $P(e)$ is the set of allocations that are Pareto optimal for e.

A *direct-revelation mechanism* in $E = E^1 \times \cdots \times E^n$ may be defined by the following property: $S^i = E^i$, where E^i is the class of a priori admissible characteristics of agent i ($i = 1, \ldots n$).

A *natural*[6] direct-revelation *mechanism* in $E = E^1 \times \cdots \times E^n$ for the performance correspondence $F : E \twoheadrightarrow Z$ may then be defined as a direct-revelation mechanism in E such that, for $s = e$ [i.e., for $(s^1, \ldots, s^n) = (e^1, \ldots, e^n)$], the outcome $h(s)$ is an element of $F(e)$; that is, $h(s)|_{s=e} \in F(e)$. In particular, when F is a (single-valued) function and the mechanism m is natural for F, it is the case that $h(s)|_{s=e} = F(e)$. That is to say, in a natural direct-revelation mechanism, the outcome is one that would be desirable according to the performance function F if the agents were truthful. The corresponding game $\Gamma = (E, \varphi_{m,e})$ is called a *natural* direct-revelation *game* for F.

In such a natural direct-revelation game for F one would wish that the (unique) n-tuple of Nash equilibrium strategies be *truthful*; the mechanism is then called *straightforward*. This requirement can be written as

$$v_\Gamma(e) = \{e\} .$$

For clearly, in this case, Γ Nash implements F. (It does not follow that a mechanism must be straightforward to implement F.) A natural direct-revelation mechanism whose Nash equilibria are truthful is called *incentive compatible*.

Now it turns out (d'Aspremont and Gérard-Varet [1979b], Thm. 1; Dasgupta, Hammond, and Maskin [1979], Thm. 7.1.1) that if a mechanism is incentive compatible, its Nash equilibria are also dominance equilibria. But it is also known that, generally speaking, there do not exist mechanisms guaranteeing dominance equilibria for sufficiently broad classes of environments when F is Pareto optimal (i.e., a subcorrespondence of the Pareto correspondence).[7] Hence the aim of constructing

---

[6] The term *natural* is introduced to focus attention on the postulated property of the outcome function.

[7] For economies with transferable utilities (of the form $u^i(x^i, y) = x + v_i(y)$) this nonexistence follows (roughly) from the following results. (1) If for a given mechanism dominance equilibria exist, then there is an "equivalent" natural direct mechanism with

incentive-compatible equilibria in the sense of the preceding definition is too ambitious. (This is true not only for public goods economies, but also for private goods pure exchange economies. See the subsequent discussion.)

The recognition of this fact can lead to several alternative compromises. One might sacrifice Pareto optimality or postulate probabilistic (Bayesian) beliefs. This latter approach was pioneered by Harsanyi [1967, 1968]; its economic applications include contributions by d'Aspremont and Gérard-Varet [1979a,b] and Arrow [1977]. (See the essay by Myerson, this volume.) But we shall confine ourselves here to the study of another compromise, sacrificing the dominance equilibrium property. We shall still ask for Pareto optimality and Nash implementability but no longer in a natural direct-revelation game. Thus there is no longer any necessary relationship between S^i and E^i and no requirement corresponding to $h(s)|_{s=e} \in F(e)$. (In fact, if the game is not of direct-revelation type, $s = e$ no longer makes sense.)

In this broader class of games, the Nash implementation of a Pareto-optimal performance correspondence is no longer impossible. This was shown by Groves and Ledyard who were the first to construct a mechanism (not of direct-revelation type) that yielded Pareto-optimal Nash allocations in public goods environments. However, the performance correspondence of the Groves−Ledyard mechanism was not individually rational. It became, therefore, natural to ask whether some Pareto optimal individually rational correspondence could be Nash implemented. Since the Lindahl performance is both Pareto optimal and individually rational, the question could be answered affirmatively by showing that the Lindahl correspondence is Nash implementable. As it turned out, it is

---

truth as everyone's dominant strategy (Dasgupta, Hammond, and Maskin [1979], Thm. 4.1.1). (2) On "smoothly connected" domains V^i of valuation functions v_i, any mechanism with truthful dominance equilibria is a "Groves mechanism" (Green and Laffont [1977, 1979]; Holmström [1979], Thm. 1). (3) A Groves mechanism is generically unbalanced (Green and Laffont [1979], Walker [1980], Thm. 1). (4) An unbalanced mechanism is not Pareto optimal.

Note that the case of transferable utilities is somewhat special. In this case there is a unique interior Pareto-optimal level $\hat{y}$ of the public service, defined for differentiable utility functions by the Samuelson condition $\Sigma_{i=1}^{n} v_i'(\hat{y}) = 1$. (Uniqueness of $\hat{y}$ follows from the fact that v_i' is assumed strictly decreasing.) For such economies it is possible to design incentive-compatible mechanisms that will yield a Pareto-optimal level $\hat{y}$ of the public service (Clarke [1971], Groves [1970], Groves and Loeb [1975], Green and Laffont [1979]). However, the balance condition cannot in general be satisfied, hence the resulting allocation, say $(x^1, \ldots, x^n, \hat{y})$ is not, in general, Pareto optimal.

not difficult to construct mechanisms that Nash implement the Lindahl correspondence (Hurwicz [1979], Walker [1981]).[8]

For balanced implementation of the Lindahl correspondence when there are three or more agents, *smooth* mechanisms ignoring the individual feasibility condition were constructed by Hurwicz [1979s][9] and Walker [1981].[10] The former has price-quantity proposals as strategic messages; that is, $m_i = (p_i, y_i)$, and uses a circular arrangement of participants so that each agent i is an auctioneer for his neighbor, say agent $i + 1$. Walker's arrangement is analogous but using a message space of smaller dimensions. Specifically, in a two-good, n-agent world with constant returns, the Walker strategy space is of dimension n while the Hurwicz strategy space is of dimension $2n$. Clearly, the Walker mechanism minimizes the dimensionality of the message space.

A (discontinuous) balanced mechanism with profile type strategy spaces where individual feasibility conditions *are* satisfied is constructed in Hurwicz, Maskin, and Postlewaite [1980]. Subject to additional conditions on the preferences, a Constrained Lindahl correspondence is feasibly implemented.

The mechanisms just mentioned are balanced, in the sense that, for every s in S, the balance requirement

$$y = \sum_{i=1}^{n} t^i$$

is satisfied.[11] But the requirement of individual feasibility [i.e., that $(x^i, y) \geqq 0$] might have been violated. (The same problem arose in Schmeidler's [1976] and Hurwicz's [1979] mechanisms Nash implementing the Walrasian correspondence.) However, as shown in Hurwicz, Maskin, and Postlewaite [1980], mechanisms analogous to those in Maskin [1977] can be constructed to Nash implement Lindahl, Walras, and various other correspondences without violating either the balance or the individual feasibility requirements.

These findings raise the more general question: Which correspondences are Nash implementable without violating the feasibility (individual and balance) requirements? To a considerable extent the question

---

[8] The trailblazing contribution to the analogous problem in private goods economies is due to Schmeidler [1976], who constructed a mechanism Nash implementing the Walrasian correspondence. However, see the subsequent text concerning the individual feasibility requirement.

[9] A two-good economy (one public, one private) and constant returns technology.

[10] Extended to arbitrarily many public and private goods and more general technologies.

[11] More explicitly, write $(t^1, \ldots, t^n, y) = h(s) = (T^1(s), \ldots, T^n(s), Y(s))$; then the balance requirement is that $Y(s) = \sum_{i=1}^{n} T^i(s)$ for all $s \in S$.

was answered in Maskin [1977] for cases where the feasible outcome set is a priori known to the designer of the mechanism. Maskin showed that (1) a Nash-implementable correspondence must be monotone;[12] and (2) if there are at least three agents, any correspondence that is monotone and has the "no-veto power"[13] property is Nash implementable.

Analogous Nash-implementability conditions for cases where the feasible set is not a priori known to the designer are given in Hurwicz, Maskin, and Postlewaite [1980].[14]

It is to be noted that the implementability results in Maskin [1977] and Hurwicz, Maskin, and Postlewaite [1980] are proved by constructive methods. Thus, for example, when the feasible set is a priori known to the designer and the correspondence to be implemented is monotone and has the "no-veto power" property, Maskin's proof of Nash implementability shows how to construct the outcome functions using preference profiles as the players' strategic variables. In Hurwicz, Maskin and Postlewaite, the profiles $(e^1, \ldots, e^n)$, where e^i involves endowments and/or production sets as well as preferences of the i agent, are used as the strategic variables.

Economists are particularly interested in implementing correspondences that are Pareto optimal[15] and either individually rational or envy free (i.e., fair). Let F be Pareto optimal and individually rational. Somewhat surprisingly, it turns out (Hurwicz [1979b]) that if (i) F is Pareto optimal, individually rational, and continuous, (ii) E is sufficiently broad, and (iii) F is Nash implementable over E, then (a) in public goods economies $F \supseteq L$, while (b) in private goods pure exchange economies, $F \supseteq W$ (where W is the Walrasian correspondence).

An analogous result for private goods pure exchange economies concerning fairness is due to Thomson [1979], who showed that if (i) F is Pareto optimal, envy free, and continuous, (ii) E is sufficiently broad, and (iii) F is Nash implementable over E, then $F \supseteq W_{I(w)}$. [Here $W_{I(w)}$ is

---

[12] F is monotone when the following holds: if an outcome z is F-desirable for a preference profile **R**, and another profile **R**' is no less favorable to z than **R** was, then z is also F-desirable for **R**' (Maskin [1977]). ("z is F-desirable for the environment e" means that z is an element of $F(e)$; "**R**' is no less favorable to z than **R** was" means that zR_iz' implies $zR_i'z'$ for all i and all z'.)

[13] F has the "no-veto power" property when the following holds: if an outcome z is the most preferred one for at least $n - 1$ agents then z is F-desirable (Maskin [1977]).

[14] In particular, an example due to Postlewaite (Hurwicz, Maskin, and Postlewaite [1980]) shows that in environments where boundary equilibria can occur, the Walras correspondence is not monotone and must be replaced by its "constrained" counterpart.

[15] That is, correspondences F such that $F(e) \ P(e)$ for all e in E where $P(e)$ is the set of Pareto-optimal outcomes in the environment e, and E is the class of environments over which implementation is sought.

the Walrasian correspondence from the equal initial endowment point $I(w)$ obtained by the redistribution of $w = (w^1, \ldots, w^n)$; w^i is i's initial endowment vector.[16]

Two-agent economies

It is worth noting that special difficulties arise with regard to balanced Nash implementation when there are only two agents ($n = 2$). Most mechanisms referred to in the preceding sections work only for three or more persons. It is possible,[17] however, to Nash implement Walrasian and Lindahl correspondences when $n = 2$ by balanced (but discontinuous) outcome functions (Hurwicz [1979c], Miura [1982][18]). That this cannot be done by *smooth* functions is shown in Reichelstein [1984]. (An analogous result for the Pareto-optimal correspondence has recently been obtained by Hurwicz and Hans Weinberger.)

Implementation through profiles as strategies (as in Maskin [1977] and Hurwicz, Maskin, and Postlewaite [1980]) has the disadvantage of using huge (indeed, infinite-dimensional) strategy domains, and discontinuous outcome functions. But it should be understood that the profile approach provides not merely the implementation of a particular performance correspondence but, rather, an *algorithm* for constructing outcome functions implementing a large class of performance correspondences.

When the specific correspondence to be implemented is known, it may be possible to do much better. In particular, for a pure exchange private goods economy, with three or more agents, and with endowments a priori known to the designer, Postlewaite and Wettstein [1983] have constructed a mechanism with a *continuous* outcome function where each agent's strategy domain is of finite dimension (equal to $2l + 1$ where l is the number of goods), a mechanism that Nash implements the Constrained Walrasian correspondence.

For *smooth* balanced mechanisms[17] Reichelstein [1982] has found minimal dimensions of strategy spaces for Nash implementing the Walrasian correspondence in two-good economies with three or more

---

[16] That is, for $e = (e^1, \ldots, e^n)$, $e^i = (u^i, w^i)$, $i = 1, \ldots, n$, we have $z \in W_{I(w)}(e)$ if and only if z is the Walrasian allocation in an economy with the same preferences $(u^1, \ldots, u^n)$ but with each agent's initial endowment equalized to $I(w) = \Sigma_{i=1}^{n} w^i/n$.

[17] Ignoring the individual feasibility condition.

[18] Miura points out an error in Hurwicz's [1979c] Lindahl-implementing outcome function; his modified outcome function does implement the Lindahl correspondence for two or more agents.

traders.[19] (As mentioned previously, when there are only two traders, smooth implementation of the Walrasian correspondence is altogether impossible.)

Private goods economies

Although the problem of designing an incentive-compatible mechanism was particularly obvious in economies with public goods, it also arises in private goods economies. Thus it was shown in Hurwicz [1972, Ch. 14] that in simple (two-person, two-good) pure exchange economies there exist no natural incentive-compatible mechanisms guaranteeing Pareto optimality and individual rationality. An analogous result in Dasgupta, Hammond, and Maskin [1979], Thm. 4.4.1, replaces the requirement of individual rationality by that of nondictatorship and broadens the class of admissible preferences so as to permit nonsmoothness and even discontinuities.[20]

In [1983], Hurwicz and Walker show, without postulating individual rationality, that dominance-equilibrium mechanisms are generically non-optimal. This is a counterpart of the result in Walker [1980] for public goods economies and was conjectured by Walker in [1980].

Pure exchange economies were also studied by Satterthwaite [1976] and in Satterthwaite and Sonnenschein [1981]. It was shown that "regular," "nonbossy" direct-revelation mechanisms that are strategy-proof and defined on an open set of utility functions are serially dictatorial. In certain economies with production this may generate nonoptimality.

It should be noted that the parallelism of the impossibility results, as between economies with and without public goods, breaks down in "large" economies: in private goods economies the incentive to misrepresent dwindles as the economy increases, but this is not the case for public goods economies (J. Roberts [1976], J. Roberts and Postlewaite [1976]).

Economies with production

Private goods economies with production provided some of the original stimulus for the study of alternative mechanisms and incentive-compatibility games. Thus, for instance, in a socialist economy of the

---

[19] This minimal dimension is lower than that used in smooth balanced mechanisms implementing the Walrasian correspondence in Hurwicz [1979].

[20] It appears that a strengthening of assumptions made in Dasgupta, Hammond, and Maskin [1979] is required when the number of agents exceeds two (Sonnenschein and Satterthwaite [1981], and a private communication from Eric Maskin).

Lange–Lerner type, if the environment is "classical," each manager of a production unit is supposed to choose a profit-maximizing input–output vector *treating prices parametrically*.[21] (The result is a competitive equilibrium.) But if, for instance, the firm has a monopoly of its product, higher profits could be attained by exploiting the monopoly power – that is, by *not* treating prices parametrically. Now suppose the manager's reward is an increasing function of profits. This creates an incentive to misrepresent the firm's production function in such a way that a level of output that maximizes monopoly profits for the true production function is presented as the competitive profit-maximizing output for a false production function (Hurwicz [1973]). Thus, in an economy with a finite number of firms, the competitive mechanism is not incentive compatible if the decision maker's rewards increase with profits and informational decentralization prevails.[22] But, again, it is possible to design mechanisms implementing a wide class of performance correspondences (Hurwicz, Maskin, and Postlewaite [1980]). These mechanisms use (as strategies) the profiles $(Y^1, \ldots, Y^n)$ of production possibility sets, similarly to the use of preference profiles in Maskin [1977]. This problem is somewhat analogous to that arising in economies in which endowments may be destroyed by agents. The analysis of the latter problem was pioneered by Postlewaite [1979].

It may be noted that the presence of production creates difficulties in reconciling efficiency with certain notions of fairness (e.g., in the sense of being envy free). Much of Pazner's work was devoted to this problem.

By now the literature dealing with economic mechanisms is huge. The present notes do no more than pursue a few topics that seem of particular importance in the earlier stages of development of this area. Most workers in the field are far from satisfied with the accomplishments to date. There are differences of opinion as to the appropriateness of different game-theoretic models. There is a need for better integration of incentive and informational aspects of our models. Also, the issue of combining fairness with efficiency is still before us. Elisha Pazner's pioneering insights in this area will continue to illuminate the path for future explorers.

---

[21] More generally, when the production function is not assumed concave, the requirement is that the input–output vector yield the equality of output prices and marginal costs, again with all prices treated parametrically.

[22] It is of particular interest to note that imposing rules of behavior (such as profit maximization) where actions are prescribed as functions of the agents' characteristics, and with the center acting on the assumption that these rules are honestly obeyed, is equivalent to operating a natural direct-revelation game!

REFERENCES

Arrow, K. J. [1951]. "An Extension of the Basic Theorems of Welfare Economics," in *Proceedings of the Second Berkeley Symposium on Mathematical Statistics and Probability* edited by G. Neyman, pp. 507–532. Berkeley: University of California Press.

Arrow, K. J. [1951, 1963]. *Social Choice and Individual Values*. New York: Wiley, 1951. New Haven: Yale University Press, 1963.

Arrow, K. J. [1977]. "The Property Rights Doctrine and Demand Revelation under Incomplete Information." IMSSS Technical Report no. 243, Stanford University.

Arrow, K. J., and F. Hahn [1971]. *General Competitive Analysis*. San Francisco: Holden-Day.

Bergson, A. [1938]. "A Reformulation of Certain Aspects of Welfare Economics." *Quarterly Journal of Economics*, 52:310–334.

Clarke, E. H. [1971]. "Multipart Pricing of Public Goods." *Public Choice*, 2:19–33.

Dasgupta, P., P. Hammond, and E. Maskin [1979]. "The Implementation of Social Choice Rules: Some General Results on Incentive Compatibility." *Review of Economic Studies*, 46:181–216.

d'Aspremont, C., and L.-A. Gérard-Varet [1979a]. "On Bayesian Incentive Compatible Mechanisms," in *Aggregation and Revelation of Preferences*, edited by J.-J Laffont, Ch. 22, pp. 269–288. Amsterdam: North Holland.

d'Aspremont, C., and L.-A. Gérard-Varet [1979b]. "Incentives and Incomplete Information," *Journal of Public Economics*, 11:25–45.

Debreu, G. [1959]. *Theory of Value*. New York: Wiley.

Drèze, J., and D. de la Vallée Poussin [1969]. "A Tâtonnement Process for Guiding and Financing an Efficient Production for Public Goods," CORE paper, 1969. (*RES*, 38 [1971], pp. 133–150.)

Foley, D. K. [1970]. "Lindahl's Solution and the Core of an Economy with Public Goods." *Econometrica*, 38:66–72.

Green, J., and J.-J. Laffont [1977]. "Characterization of Satisfactory Mechanisms for the Revelation of Preferences for Public Goods." *Econometrica*, 45: 427–438.

Green, J., and J.-J. Laffont [1979]. *Incentives in Public Decision-Making*. Amsterdam: North Holland.

Groves, T. [1970]. "The Allocation of Resources under Uncertainty." Unpublished Ph.D. dissertation, University of California, Berkeley.

Groves, T., and J. Ledyard [1977]. "Optimal Allocation of Public Goods: A Solution to the 'Free Rider' Problem." *Econometrica*, 45(4):783–811.

Groves, T., and J. Ledyard [1980]. "The Existence of Efficient and Incentive Compatible Equilibria with Public Goods." *Econometrica*, 48:1487–1506.

Groves, T., and M. Loeb [1975]. "Incentives and Public Inputs." *Journal of Public Economies*, 4(3):211–226.

Harsanyi, J. [1967–68]. "Games with Incomplete Information Played by Bayesian Players." *Management Science 14*:159–82, 320–34, 486–502.

von Hayek, F.A. [1945]. "The Use of Knowledge in Society." *American Economic Review*, 35:519–530.

Holmström, B. [1979]. "Groves Scheme on Restricted Domain." *Econometrica*, 47: 1137–1144.

Hotelling, H. [1938]. "The General Welfare in Relation to Problems of Taxation and of Railway and Utility Rates." *Econometrica*, 6:242–269.

Hurwicz, L. [1972]. "On Informationally Decentralized Systems," in *Decision and Organization (Volume in Honor of J. Marschak)*, edited by R. Radner and C. B. McGuire, pp. 297–336. Amsterdam: North Holland.

Hurwicz, L. [1973]. "The Design of Mechanisms for Resource Allocation." *American Economic Review*, 63:1–30, esp. pp. 25–26.

Hurwicz, L. [1977]. "On the Dimensional Requirements of Informationally Decentralized Pareto-Satisfactory Processes," in *Studies in Resource Allocation Processes*, edited by K. J. Arrow and L. Hurwicz, pp. 413–424. Cambridge: Cambridge University Press.

Hurwicz, L. [1979a]. "Outcome Functions Yielding Walrasian and Lindahl Allocations at Nash Equilibrium Points." *Review of Economic Studies*, 46(2): 217–225.

Hurwicz, L. [1979b]. "On Allocations Attainable through Nash Equilibria." *Journal of Economic Theory*, 21, (1):140–165; also in: *Aggregation and Revelation of Preferences*, edited by J.-J. Laffont, Ch. 22, pp. 397–419. Amsterdam: North Holland.

Hurwicz, L. [1979c]. "Balanced Outcome Functions Yielding Walrasian and Lindahl Allocations at Nash Equilibrium Points for Two or More Agents," in *General Equilibrium, Growth, and Trade*, edited by R. Green and J. A. Scheinkman. New York: Academic Press.

Hurwicz, L., E. Maskin, and A. Postlewaite [1980]. "Feasible Implementation of Social Choice Correspondences by Nash Equilibria." Mimeo. [Abbreviated as HMP.]

Hurwicz, L., and M. Walker [1983]. "On the Generic Non-Optimality of Dominant-Strategy Mechanisms with an Application to Pure Exchange." Research Paper No. 250, circulated by the Economic Research Bureau, State University of New York at Stonybrook.

Johansen, L. [1963]. "Some Notes on the Lindahl Theory of Determination of Public Expenditure," *International Economic Review*, 4:346–358.

Jordan, J. S. [1982]. "The Competitive Allocation Process Is Informationally Efficient Uniquely." *Journal of Economic Theory*, 28:1–18.

Koopmans, T. C. [1957]. "Allocation of Resources and the Price System," in *Three Essays on the State of Economic Science*. New York: McGraw-Hill.

Lange, O., and F. M. Taylor [1938]. *On the Economic Theory of Socialism*. Minneapolis: University of Minnesota Press.

Lange, O. [1942]. "The Foundations of Welfare Economics." *Econometrica*, 10:215–228.

Ledyard, J. [1977]. "Incentive Compatible Behavior in Core-Selecting Organizations." *Econometrica*, 45(7):1607–1621.

Ledyard, J., and J. Roberts [1974]. "On the Incentive Problems with Public Goods." Discussion Paper No. 116, CMSEMS, Northwestern University, Evanston, Ill.

Lerner, A. P. [1944]. *Economics of Control*. New York: Macmillan.

Lindahl, E. [1919]. "Just Taxation – A Positive Solution," in *Classics in the Theory of Public Finance*, edited by R. A. Musgrave and A. T. Peacock, London: Macmillan, 1964, pp. 168–176. (Also, New York: St. Martin's Press, 1964.)

Malinvaud, E. [1969]. "Procédures pour la détermination d'un programme de consommation collective." Paper presented at the Brussels meeting of the Econometric Society, September 1969. Mimeo.

Maskin, E. [1977]. "Nash Equilibrium and Welfare Optimality." Working paper, October 1977, Massachusetts Institute of Technology; scheduled to appear in *Mathematics of Operations Research*.

Milleron, J.-C. [1972]. "Theory of Value with Public Goods: A Survey Article." *Journal of Economic Theory*, 5:419–477.

Miura, Rei [1982]. "Counter-Example and Revised Outcome Function Yielding the Nash-Lindahl Equivalence for Two or More Agents." Keio University, Tokyo. Privately circulated paper.

Mount, K., and S. Reiter [1974]. "The Informational Size of Message Spaces." *Journal of Economic Theory*, 8(3):161–192.

Osana, H. [1978]. "On the Informational Size of Message Spaces for Resource Allocation Processes." *Journal of Economic Theory*, 17:66–78.

Postlewaite, A. [1979]. "Manipulation via Endowments." *Review of Economic Studies*, 46:255–262.

Postlewaite, A., and D. Wettstein [1983]. "Implementing Constrained Walrasian Equilibria Continuously." CARESS Working Paper #83-24, University of Pennsylvania.

Reichelstein, S. [1982]. "On the Informational Requirements for the Implementation of Social Choice Rules." Handout for the Decentralized Conference, May.

Reichelstein, S. [1984]. "Smooth versus Discontinuous Mechanisms." February, privately circulated paper.

Reiter, S. [1977], "Information and Performance in the (New)[2] Welfare Economics." *American Economic Review*, 67(1):226–234.

Roberts, J. [1976]. "The Incentives for Correct Revelation of Preferences and the Number of Consumers." *Journal of Public Economics*, 6:359–374.

Roberts, J., and A. Postlewaite [1976]. "The Incentives for Price-Taking Behavior in Large Economies." *Econometrica*, 44:115–128.

Samuelson, P. [1954]. "The Pure Theory of Public Expenditure." *The Review of Economics and Statistics*, 36:387–389.

Samuelson, P. [1955]. "Diagrammatic Exposition of a Theory of Public Expenditure." *The Review of Economics and Statistics* 37:350–356.

Sato, F. [1981]. "On the Informational Size of Message Spaces for Resource Allocation Processes in Economies with Public Goods," *Journal of Economic Theory*, 24(1):48–69.

Satterthwaite, M. [1976]. "Straightforward Allocation Mechanisms." Discussion Paper no. 253, CMSEMS, Northwestern University, Evanston, Ill. October.

Satterthwaite, M., and H. Sonnenschein [1981]. "Strategy Proof Allocation Mechanisms at Differentiable Points." *Review of Economic Studies*, 48: 587–597.

Schmeidler, D. [1976]. "A Remark on a Game Theoretic Interpretation of Walras Equilibria." University of Minnesota, Minneapolis. Mimeo.

Schmeidler, D. [1980]. "Walrasian Analysis via Strategic Outcome Functions." *Econometrica*, 48:1585–1594.

Schmeidler, D. [1982]. "A Condition Guaranteeing that the Nash Allocation Is Walrasian." *Journal of Economic Theory*, 28:376–378.

Sen, A. K. [1970]. *Collective Choice and Social Welfare*. San Francisco: Holden-Day.

Thomson, W. [1979]. "Comment on L. Hurwicz: On Allocations Attainable through Nash Equilibria," in *Aggregation and Revelation of Preferences*, edited by J.-J. Laffont, pp. 420–431. Amsterdam: North Holland.

Walker, M. [1980]. "On the Nonexistence of a Dominant Strategy Mechanism for Making Optimal Public Decisions." *Econometrica*, *48*(6):1521–1540.

Walker, M. [1981]. "A Simple Incentive Compatible Scheme for Attaining Lindahl Allocations." *Econometrica*, *49*:65–73.

PART I
THE SURVEYS

CHAPTER 2

Axioms for social welfare orderings

Claude d'Aspremont

1   Introduction

The theoretical literature on social organizations has always been concerned with the determination of effective institutions or common decision criteria that integrate, in some way or another, the different participating units. In fact this "aggregation problem" has become the fundamental subject of the formal analysis of political and economic organizations. This is clear in the considerable development of the theory of social choice, as initiated by K. Arrow [1951, 1963]. But this problem is also at the foundation of the theory of games, which has grown extensively since the book of J. von Neumann and O. Morgenstern [1947]. Furthermore it motivates essentially the revival of interest in a "formal" approach to ethics that has been recently stimulated by Rawls's [1972] criticism of utilitarianism and by Harsanyi's [1965, 1977] defense of this doctrine.

The intention of this essay is to give an introduction to that part of social choice theory that has strong ethical implications. This part is particularly related to the area of economics that is called, after Pigou [1920], welfare economics. It is less directly related to the area of political science, which analyzes the various methods of election.

As a deductive system, social choice theory has made clear the difficult issues that the various interpretations of its basic terms introduce. It has made clear that for each particular "model" a specific set of axioms should be constructed. My objective is thus to discuss the specific conditions that determine the welfare interpretation of social choice theory.

I am much obliged to Louis Gevers, Peter Hammond and John Weymark for helpful comments and suggestions.

The results surveyed in the following are only representative of this welfare model.[1]

In welfare terms, the aggregation problem can be formulated as the problem of deriving, for some collectivity of individuals and some set of social alternatives, a social judgment about those alternatives, which is based on their evaluation by each individual. In other words, the social evaluation of the different alternatives should be determined by their "utility" for each individual. The basic terms involved are the individuals themselves, their utilities, and the social alternatives together with their social evaluation. Even in welfare economics these terms have been understood quite differently and the relevance of the results presented thereafter depends crucially on these differences.

1.1   *Utility and social alternatives*

The term *utility* appeared in the eighteenth-century moral philosophy, characterized by its concern for human "happiness" and fundamentally inspired by the success of the natural sciences. It is as an integrated part of this general effort to develop a social science oriented toward human happiness that the "classical utilitarianism" doctrine was built up. This doctrine probably starts with Hutcheson [1725] but is best known through Bentham [1789]. As well emphasized by Little ([1957], p. 7), the notion of utility was then seen as an intrinsic property of objects, that of generating satisfaction. Thus the happiness of an individual was simply the sum of his satisfactions and the happiness of society the sum total of the happiness of all the individuals in society. In the utilitarian approach the set of social alternatives is usually taken to be very comprehensive. At a first level, where we shall speak of "social states," it may include the level of all sorts of goods, not only economic goods and services, but, to take a Rawlsian terminology, all "social primary goods" including "rights and liberties, powers and opportunities, income and wealth." However, adopting a consequentialist viewpoint, the set of alternatives may also be defined at a higher level and comprise all individual actions resulting in some more or less good social state (see Sen [1979a]). At even higher levels one may introduce the institutions or rules governing these actions or, in a more subtle way, the patterns of motivations or personal dispositions that are most useful to obtain some social states. These different interpretations of the set of social alternatives give rise successively to different kinds of utilitarianism: outcome utilitarianism, act utilitarianism, rule utilitarian-

---

[1] Some more general results are given in K. Roberts thesis (or K. Roberts [1980a−c]). See also Sen [1977a] and Blackorby, Donaldson, and Weymark [1984] and Moulin [1982]. A general survey of social choice theory can be found in Sen [1979b].

ism, motive utilitarianism, and so on. The reason for this comprehensiveness is to maintain the project of a unified scientific approach to the understanding of mankind, both for descriptive and prescriptive purposes, and, hence, to take the principle of "the greatest amount of happiness on the whole" (Sidgwick [1907]) as the objective criterion for morality and to base on such a maximum principle the edification of a *mécanique sociale*, which "may one day take her place along with *mécanique céleste*" (Edgeworth [1881]).[2]

Contrary to this unifying utilitarian project, another tendency has been to try to separate economics and other social sciences from ethics in some way or another. This other tendency was already present at the rise of the utilitarian doctrine, but it received its main impetus from Pigou [1920], for whom the economics of welfare were to be distinguished from ethics since it was a scientific discipline dealing with measurable quantities. These measurable quantities were the individual utilities or "satisfactions," namely that part of total welfare which "can be brought directly or indirectly into relation with the measuring rod of money" (Pigou [1920]).[3] More than a reinterpretation of the notion of utility, this represents a limitation imposed on the set of social alternatives: welfare economics should only be concerned with social states differing in the amount of goods and services relevant to describe the production and exchange process. A reinterpretation of the notion of utility was definitely involved though in the development of what has been called later the new welfare economics (Stigler [1943], Samuelson [1947]) and which centered on the collective optimality concept introduced by Pareto [1909]. This has led to the conclusion that utility should only be an ordinal representation of an individual preference defined on some set of possibilities. These preferences should in turn be determined by reference to some (hypothetical) choice situation; an individual prefers some possibility to some other if he would choose it rather than the other. In other words, an individual utility is based on his (hypothetical) behavior, which is supposed to respect some general consistency conditions. No underlying notion of satisfaction or happiness is now required. More generally, the motivations underlying the choices (e.g., to get some pleasure, to do his duty, etc.) are not relevant as long as these choices are consistent.[4] A characteristic of

---

[2] See the 1967 Reprint p. 1, quoted in Little [1957], p. 8.

[3] See the 1962 Reprint p. 11.

[4] However, if the ordinality of the utility representation is combined with some limitation imposed on the set of alternatives (quantities of goods, for example) then notions like satisfactions, tastes, and needs can still be used, but more as a way to describe "expected" experiences then ex-post feelings.

this new approach was the avoidance, or for some authors like Robbins [1932] the rejection, of any sort of interpersonal comparisons of utilities. The Pareto optimality conditions — as also developed by Lerner [1934], Barone [1935], Hotelling [1938] and others — were realized to be valid even if interpersonal comparisons were not possible. Moreover, later on the great multiplicity of Pareto-optimal points was emphasized and "compensation tests" were devised[5] to extend Pareto's definition of an increase in social welfare without making interpersonal comparisons and thus avoid ethical considerations. It is the merit of Bergson's [1938] and Samuelson's [1947] concept of social welfare function to have made clear

> that it is not literally true that the new welfare economics is devoid of *any* ethical assumptions. Admittedly, however, its assumptions are more general and less controversial, and it is for this reason that it gives incomplete necessary conditions, whose full significance emerges only after one has made interpersonal assumptions. To refuse to take the last step renders the first two steps nugatory; like pouring out a glass of water and then refusing to drink. . . (Samuelson [1947], p. 249).

We shall return subsequently to this concept of social welfare function. In fact, one may argue that Arrow's [1951, 1963] theorem on the impossibility of a social welfare function may be viewed, in some sense, as the explicit formalization of Samuelson's statement, leading to the same negative conclusion concerning the compensation principle.

1.2   *Interpersonal comparisons and the identity of individuals*

It is not because the introduction of interpersonal comparisons reinforces the ethical character of the presuppositions involved in any kind of welfare judgment, that these comparisons should be denied any empirical significance. As stressed by Little [1957], interpersonal comparisons do rest on observation or introspection. In fact many economists have attempted to measure marginal utility. The early methods were criticized by Vickrey [1945]:

> Most attempts to determine marginal utility hitherto have been based on the assumptions first that some utility function can be found that will thus make the marginal utility of some commodity independent of the quantities of all other commodities, and second that this function when found has some special validity for the purposes at hand. The

---

[5] These were given by Kaldor [1939], Hicks [1939], Scitovsky [1941−42]. See also Baumol [1946], Little [1957], and Samuelson [1947]. For a survey see Graaff [1957].

methods suggested by Irving Fisher [1927], and the isoquant, quantity-variation, and translation methods of Ragnar Frisch [1932] all involve such assumptions.

Hence these methods do not seem to lead to a plausible way of making interpersonal comparisons. Arrow [1951, 1963] criticizes three different analytic approaches to derive empirically (and ethically) meaningful interpersonal comparisons. The first is due to Dahl [1956] and bases an interpersonal measure of preference intensity on the disutility of the act of voting. The second is due to Goodman and Markowitz [1952] and uses the psychological notion of "just-noticeable-difference" between alternatives: each individual has a finite number of indifference levels called levels of discretion and "a change from one level to the next represents the minimum difference which is discernible to an individual" (p. 259). Their fundamental assumption then is to use, for every individual, the number of discernible discretion levels between a pair of alternatives as the common measure of the strength of his preference. With this assumption and other conditions that are very similar to conditions used by Milnor [1954] and to conditions that shall be introduced below to characterize utilitarianism, they obtain that the social evaluation of an alternative is the sum of the individual utilities associated to that alternative. However, the difficulty in using levels of discretion as a means for interpersonal comparisons is well put in an example given by Luce and Raiffa [1957]:

> Consider two individuals, s_1 and s_2 who have to select one of two candidates A_1 or A_2; candidate A_1 is preferred by s_1 and A_2 by s_2. To resolve the strength of preference problem, these voters are also asked to rank some nonavailable candidates, $A_3, A_4, \ldots, A_{100}$. Voter s_2 is very discerning, and he ranks the candidates A_2 over A_3 over $A_4 \ldots$ over A_{99} over A_{100} over A_1. On the other hand, voter s_1 is dedicated to a single issue and he divides all candidates into two camps, namely, those who are "for" it and those who are "against" it; he is indifferent among the "for's" and indifferent among the "against's". In this case s_2 will have his way since he can discern 99 difference levels between A_2 and A_1, whereas s_1 can only discern one indifference level between them. But who is to say that s_2 feels more strongly than s_1. (pp. 347−348)

The discussion has been pursued recently by Ng [1975]. He argues that empirical studies have shown that thresholds for various feelings almost coincide for different individuals and that the number of just-noticeable-differences should not vary too much from one to the other. This argument, however, does not provide a fundamental reason to use his method. Such a reason may better be looked for in his attempt to ground his conventions on an approach in terms of expected utility.[6] This type of justification, based on assumptions about rational behavior in the face of risk (or uncertainty) has been advocated by several authors and will be discussed in Section 4. This type of justification is also linked to the third approach, purporting to found interpersonal comparisons mentioned by Arrow, which has received much attention. This is based on a principle of "extended sympathy" (Suppes [1966], Sen [1970], Chs. 9 and 9*). The idea is to adopt an individual viewpoint and consider comparisons of the form: I prefer to be in the position of individual j under alternative x than of individual k under alternative y. As we immediately see, this amounts to expand the set of alternatives on which all individuals can, hypothetically, exert their capacity for choice. Hence it is compatible with the choice interpretations of individual utility. However, this approach amounts to making interpersonal comparisons from the point of view of a single person. In other words, the difficulty of such comparisons is brought back again to the difficulty of measuring a single individual utility, but of a new kind. In addition, if the viewpoint of a single individual is adopted, then we must assume some special status for the individual (such as being an ethical observer) or, more fundamentally, we must introduce some way of identifying the viewpoints of all individuals (each being considered as a different ethical observer). This could be based either on the ethical justification of an "identity principle" for the moral person or on the ethical recognition of a "principle of cooperation" leading to some sort of consensus. Here the work of Pazner [1979] should be recalled. He well stressed the fact that the Arrow impossibility theorem was also applicable at the level of extended preferences. Indeed he showed (among other things) that reasonable conditions analogous to Arrow's conditions would imply a dictatorial ethical observer. And as he said, "even dictatorship in the present sense is troublesome, especially if one wishes to interpret extended sympathy orderings in terms of value judgments of a higher order" (p. 164, fn. 2).

Moreover, this identity (or consensus) problem is present in any empirical approach to the measurement of individual utility (be it of the

---

[6] Historically the approach based on discrimination levels can be traced back to Borda [1781] and Edgeworth [1881]. It was analyzed more extensively by Armstrong [1951]. See also the discussion in Rothenberg [1961] and Arrow ([1951, 1963], p. 115). Concerning the discussion (and references) on the expected utility approach and the problem of measuring a single person's von Neumann–Morgenstern utility function, see Luce and Raiffa ([1957], p. 34). For a critique and an alternative model see Kahneman and Tversky [1979].

first kind or of the second kind) and any attempt at solving it should be related to the use this measurement is to have. This is due to the fact that in all empirical studies only "typical" individuals can be considered. Whatever the method of interpersonal comparison used — whether the ones of Fisher and Frisch or the just-noticeable-difference method or, to take another example, the use of "proxies" like suicide rates, proposed by Simon [1974] — it is always assumed, for practical reasons, that the individuals are "representative individuals" or "average individuals" in some relevant classes.[7] That this identity problem should arise in any empirical study is even clearer if one realizes that, practically, the difficulty of the interpersonal comparisons is not very different from the difficulty of the comparisons of a single individual utility at various times (i.e., intrapersonal but intertemporal comparisons).[8]

In spite of this problem it seems that the "extended sympathy" approach has been formally the most fruitful. In Section 3, I introduce Sen's concept of "social welfare functional" and the related concept of "social welfare ordering," which may be viewed as particular formal representations of such an extended preference. In Section 3 various types of interpersonal comparisons are defined for this concept of social welfare ordering. Finally, in Section 4, I come back to the present discussion by considering the ethical theories of Rawls and Harsanyi. What is needed for the presentation is to start from a single extended preference. The examination of some aspects of these two, essentially distinct, theories will eventually lead to some ethical justification for such a procedure.

2   Welfarism

Since Arrow's [1951, 1963] particular formalization of the concept of social welfare functions, several other formalizations have been proposed. In this section we shall review some of these and try to relate them to the original Bergson—Samuelson concept. This review will provide some understanding of the issues involved in basing social welfare judgments on individual utility alone which, by definition, forms the welfarist point of view.

---

[7] On this point see Vickrey [1960], p. 522, or Little [1957], p. 49. It seems that it is also for practical purposes that Rawls introduces the notion of representative individual (see Rawls [1972], p. 128). Notice that Little is also conscious that this notion may help to solve the intertemporal and intergenerational problem. On this last problem and in relation to Rawls see Arrow [1973b], Dasgupta [1974], and Solow [1974].

[8] See the recent discussion of Mirrlees [1982] and his notion of isomorphic individuals.

2.1   *From constitutions to social welfare orderings*

We start with Arrow's definition of a social welfare function, which, following his suggestion, we shall call a "constitution." First we are given a (finite) set of individuals $N = \{1, 2, \ldots, i, \ldots, n\}$ and a set X of possible social alternatives. For our purpose we shall assume that the number of individuals is at least two and the number of alternatives at least three. A priori, however, the set of social alternatives is not more specified, but we shall see that some of the conditions introduced later imply some additional restrictions concerning X. Second we consider all possible preference orderings $\Re$ over X and the set $\Re^N$ of all n-tuples $(R_1, R_2, \ldots, R_n)$ of preference orderings in $\Re$, called the set of "individual preference profiles." As usual (see Sen [1970], Ch. 1), a preference ordering R in $\Re$ will be assumed to be a reflexive, transitive, and complete binary relation on X. Also, for any $R, R', \bar{R}, \ldots$, in $\Re$, we shall denote by $P, P', \bar{P}, \ldots$, the associated strict preference relation and by $I, I', \bar{I}, \ldots$, the associated indifference relation. Then a *constitution* is a function F from some subset of $\Re^N$ to $\Re$, associating to each admissible individual profile some admissible ordering called the social ordering. This definition can be weakened to take into account the fact that the social choice of some alternative among a finite set of social alternatives does not require a social ordering of X. Indeed, the range of the function F has only to be the set of reflexive, complete, and acyclic preference relations on X, and F is then called a *social decision function* (Sen [1970], Ch. 1).

The second definition I want to introduce with the view to formalizing social welfare functions is due to Sen [1970]; it is motivated by the need to consider interpersonal comparisons. It reintroduces in social choice individual utility functions. More precisely, instead of considering a domain in the set $\Re^N$ of all individual preference profiles it considers a domain in the set $\mathcal{U}$ of all real-valued functions on $X \times N$. Accordingly, for each i in N, the real-valued function $U(\cdot, i)$ defined on X is to be interpreted as i's utility function, and any U in $\mathcal{U}$ may be called an "individual utility profile." Also a *social welfare functional* (SWFL) can be simply defined to be a function F from some subset of $\mathcal{U}$ to $\Re$. Finally, as before, if the range of F may include any reflexive, complete, and acyclic preference relation, then F is called a *social decision functional*.

To the extent that individual preference orderings can be represented by individual utility functions (i.e., xR_iy if and only if $U(x, i) \geqslant U(y, i)$), Sen's framework contains Arrow's approach to social welfare functions. Hence the conditions imposed on constitutions can be formulated in terms of SWFLs. However, to be equivalent to Arrow's original conditions some precision should be given about the significance of the individual utility indicators. This question is taken up in the next section.

To simplify the analysis performed here, we want to impose some basic conditions on the SWFLs. These conditions are very similar to some of Arrow's conditions. The first is a condition of

Unrestricted domain for SWFLs (UD): The SWFL F is defined for every U in $\mathcal{U}$.

This condition is broad and imposes implicitly some restriction on X. For instance, if we suppose that X is the distribution of some fixed total income, then it may seem unreasonable to assume, for some individual i in N, that his utility is decreasing with the income level. However one might adopt a more abstract viewpoint, from which the investigation is not limited to a specific social choice problem with some given particular set of social alternatives. Then X may be any set of social alternatives and no individual utility profile can be discarded a priori.

The next condition is the key condition for introducing the simplifying approach to be used in the following. The main justification for this restriction is practical. All the results that will be surveyed here were obtained under conditions as restrictive or nearly as restrictive as this one. This condition says that the evaluation of some social alternative x should be based on its corresponding welfare vector $(U(x, 1), U(x, 2), \ldots, U(x, n))$ and should not take into account nonwelfare characteristics of the alternatives themselves. More precisely, we define[9]

Strong neutrality (SN): For any U^1 and U^2 in $\mathcal{U}$ and any two pairs of social alternatives $\{a, b\}$ and $\{c, d\}$ if

$$(U^1(a, 1), U^1(a, 2), \ldots, U^1(a, n)) = (U^2(c, 1), U^2(c, 2), \ldots, U^2(c, n))$$

and

$$(U^1(b, 1), U^1(b, 2), \ldots, U^1(b, n)) = (U^2(d, 1), U^2(d, 2), \ldots, U^2(d, n))$$

then aR^1b if and only if cR^2d, where $R^1 = F(U^1)$ and $R^2 = F(U^2)$.

To illustrate the strength of this condition, Sen [1979a] considers the following example. He considers a utility matrix involving the evaluation of two social outcomes by two individuals:

---

[9] Strong neutrality is defined here as in Sen [1977]. On neutrality see G. Th. Guilbaud [1952], May [1952], Guha [1972], and Blau [1976]. In relation to welfarism see also Sen [1979c] and Ng [1981].

	Outcome 1	Outcome 2
Individual r	10	8
Individual p	4	7

In a first case individual 1 is a rich person r and individual 2 a poor person p, outcome 2 is a social state b where some redistributive taxation is adopted (but r remains richer), and outcome 1 the status quo, say state a. Now for the second case, Sen gives the following short parable.

> Let r be the rider of a motor cycle − joyful, rich, in good health and resilient − while p is a pedestrian − morose, poor, ill in health and frustrated. In state d (outcome 1 here) the rider gleefully goes by; in state c (outcome 2) he falls inadvertently into a ditch, breaking his bike and getting bruised badly. The rider is worse off in c than in d, while the pedestrian, who has not caused the accident in any way, thoroughly enjoys the discomfiture and discomfort of the rider (I could kill myself laughing looking at that crestfallen Angel!). The utility values of r and p are the same in this case. . ." (p. 477).

Strong neutrality would imply that b (taxation) should be socially preferred to a (no taxation) if and only if d (accident) is socially preferred to c (no accident). However the moral intuition of many people could be hurt by the pedestrian taking pleasure from the rider's discomfiture and discomfort. The argument against the condition is that some nonutility information should be used to assert the morality of outcomes. Moreover, this nonutility information should not be introduced simply to replace utility information when this one is insufficient, but to bring in essential elements like personal motivations and values (liberty, historical rights) or general moral principles. This argument concerns directly the way the utility functions are interpreted and the determination of the sets of social outcomes that are to be ranked. Clearly, the more the utility measures are interpreted in descriptive terms (introducing such notions as "pleasure" or "desires") − as opposed to normatively constrained interpretations − and the more arbitrary is the set X of admissible social states, the stronger will this argument be.[10]

We shall return to this issue later and analyze now the consequences of these basic conditions. Indeed, a third formalization of the concept of social welfare functions results from these basic conditions. Specifically, the following theorem shows that a SWFL satisfying UD and SN gener-

---

[10] For instance, Sen [1979a] excludes the definition of X as a set of actions, or rules of actions (the use of a SWFL is not to establish the "rightness" of actions), but he insists on the descriptive content the utility measures should have.

ates an ordering on the Euclidean space E^N of welfare vectors (E denotes the real line and E^N the n-dimensional space indexed by the names of the individuals). Such an ordering has been called by Gevers [1979] a *social welfare ordering*. Formally we shall identify *welfarism* to the existence of such a social welfare ordering. This is justified by the following theorem (see also Theorem 2.3 below).

Theorem 2.1 (welfarism theorem): *Let F be a* SWFL *satisfying* UD *and* SN. *Then there is a social welfare ordering R^* such that, for all x and y in X and U in $\mathcal{U}$,*

   uR^*v *if and only if* xRy

where $u = (U(x, 1), U(x, 2), \ldots, U(x, n))$, $v = (U(y, 1), U(y, 2), \ldots, U(y, n))$, and $R = F(U)$.

Proof: By UD, for any u and v in E^N there are U in $\mathcal{U}$, a and b in X such that $u = (U(a, 1), U(a, 2), \ldots, U(a, n))$ and $v = (U(b, 1), U(b, 2), \ldots, U(b, n))$. Hence, we let uR^*v if and only if aRb, for $R = F(U)$. However, by SN, for any other V in $\mathcal{U}$ and any c and d in X, such that $(V(c, 1), V(c, 2), \ldots, V(c, n)) = u$, $(V(d, 1), V(d, 2), \ldots, V(d, n)) = v$ and $R' = F(V)$, we have $cR'b$ if and only if aRb if and only if uR^*v. Hence R^* is well defined. The fact R^* is reflexive and complete results immediately from the reflexivity and completeness of $F(U)$ (for any U). To prove transitivity take any u, v and w in E^N such that uR^*v and vR^*w. By UD, there are a, b, and c in X and U in $\mathcal{U}$ such that $u = (U(a, 1), U(a, 2), \ldots, U(a, n))$, $v = (U(b, 1), U(b, 2), \ldots, U(b, n))$, $w = (U(c, 1), U(c, 2), \ldots, U(c, n))$, and, letting $R = F(U)$, aRb and bRc. Since R is an ordering we get aRc and, hence, uR^*w. The result follows.   Q.E.D.

2.2   *The single-profile approach*

If we come back now to the original concept of a Bergson–Samuelson social welfare function, Arrow's constitution may be directly related to this concept, if interpreted as being a social ordering of X. Indeed a constitution may be viewed as associating to each individual preference profile a certain Bergson–Samuelson social welfare function. Furthermore, if we write the Bergson–Samuelson function as it is sometimes, but ambiguously, written: $W = f(U_1, U_2, \ldots, U_n)$ then the SWFL or the SWO formalization seems to be adequate. As explained by Sen [1977]

If W and U_i are taken not be welfare *numbers* but *functions* defined over X, then welfarism is not, in fact, implied. (Indeed the $f(\cdot)$ will be very like a social welfare *functional* SWFL defined [above], with W being a real-valued representation of the social R determined by a SWFL.) However, it appears that this "functional" interpretation of $f(\cdot)$ was not intended in the formulations in question (see the operations of Samuelson (1947, p. 246, Eq. (31)) and Graaff (1957, p. 51, Fig. 7(b)). And if $(U_1, \ldots, U_n)$ is simply a vector of individual utilities, then welfarism will follow. . . . (p. 1,566)

However the usefulness of these formalizations has been greatly contested by some authors (see recently Samuelson [1977]). These authors insist on the fact that traditional (new) welfare economics are only dealing with social choice for only one given individual preference profile (a utility profile): "it could be *any* one, but it is *only* one" (Samuelson [1967], p. 49). Therefore all conditions imposed on either constitutions or SWFLs that involve comparisons for different individual profiles and are at the basis of most major results in social choice theory, and, above all, Arrow's impossibility theorem, should be rejected. In particular the SN condition is not admissible and therefore the welfarism theorem is not relevant. The conclusion seems to be rather ambiguous: in some way the welfarist formalism appears to be very close to welfare economics presentations and in another it has inadmissible foundations.

A new perspective in this debate has been brought by contributions of Parks [1976], Kemp and Ng [1976], Hammond [1976b], Roberts [1977], and Pollak [1979]. They developed a social choice theory within a single-profile approach obtaining, for instance, analogues to Arrow's [1951, 1963] impossibility theorem, Sen's [1970] theorem characterizing the Pareto extension rule, and May's [1952] theorem characterizing majority voting. In particular this development provides a basis to come back to welfarism, even if we want to restrict it to a single individual profile, by giving conditions similar to conditions UD and SN. The idea is to strengthen the structural implications of these conditions on the set of admissible social alternatives. (For other arguments, see Rubinstein [1979] and Bordes [1980].) Now the term *single profile* is somewhat misleading if we talk about individual utility profile. In that case utility functions are taken as representations of individual preferences and they are unique up to some admissible transformation. For example, in the ordinal setup of the new welfare economists, each individual utility function is unique up to a strictly monotone transformation. In general to any individual utility profile $\bar{U}$ in $\mathcal{U}$ one can associate the set $[\bar{U}]$ of all individual utility profiles that are to be considered as equivalent representations, so that $F(U) = F(\bar{U})$ for all U in $[\bar{U}]$. We shall return to this unicity problem later. For the moment the problem is to impose conditions on some SWFL that are relative to some particular given individual utility profile $\bar{U}$ in $\mathcal{U}$. Following Roberts [1977] we define UP.

Unrestricted individual utility profile (UP): The individual utility profile $\bar{U}$ in $\mathcal{U}$ is such that, for any u, v and w in E^N there exist distinct x, y, and z and X for which

$$(U(x, 1), U(x, 2), \ldots, U(x, n)) = u$$

$$(U(y, 1), U(y, 2), \ldots, U(y, n)) = v$$

and

$$(U(z, 1), U(z, 2), \ldots, U(z, n)) = w \quad \text{for some } U \text{ in } [\bar{U}].$$

It is clear that the satisfaction of this condition depends on the nature of the social alternatives considered in a particular situation. In an ordinal context this is denoted U^{*3} by Pollak [1979], who provides the following examples.

> if we think of social states as "social consumption vectors" specifying (among other things) the quantity of one or more continuously divisible goods that each selfish individual is to receive then U^{*3} is highly plausible. But neither selfishness, the presence of many consumption goods, nor their continuous divisibility is required for U^{*3}. For example, if there is a subset of social states that differ only in each individual's consumption of a single good, and if each individual's allotment of that good can assume at least three distinct values (small, medium, and large), and if each individual's ordering of the states within the subset depends only on his own consumption, then U^{*3} is automatically satisfied.

The other condition is the analogue of SN, but here it is relative to $\bar{U}$, the given individual utility profile. Hence the SWFL has only to be defined on $[\bar{U}]$.

Relative neutrality (RN): Given $\bar{U}$ in $\mathcal{U}$, for any U in $[\bar{U}]$ and any two pairs of social alternatives $\{a, b\}$ and $\{c, d\}$ if

$$(\bar{U}(a, 1), \bar{U}(a, 2), \ldots, \bar{U}(a, n)) = (U(c, 1), U(c, 2), \ldots, U(c, n))$$

and

$$(\bar{U}(b, 1), \bar{U}(b, 2), \ldots, \bar{U}(b, n)) = (U(d, 1), U(d, 2), \ldots, U(d, n)),$$

then $a\bar{R}b$ if and only if cRd, where $\bar{R} = F(\bar{U}) = F(U)$.

This condition is subject to the same kind of objections as strong neutrality in the multiprofile approach. The interesting fact, proved below, about these conditions is that given some $\bar{U}$ in $\mathcal{U}$ and some SWFL F defined and constant on $[\bar{U}]$ and a set of social alternatives such that UP and RN are both satisfied then it is possible to extend F in a natural way such that both UD and SN are satisfied (for this and related results, see Roberts [1977, 1980c]). This result in turn allows to construct a SWO R^* on E^N by application of the welfarism theorem.

Theorem 2.2: *Suppose $\bar{U}$ in $\mathcal{U}$ and a SWFL $\bar{F}$ defined on $[\bar{U}]$ such that $\bar{F}(U) = \bar{F}(\bar{U}) = \bar{R}$ for all U in $[\bar{U}]$. Assume UP and RN are satisfied. For any U in $\mathcal{U}$ and any x and y in X let xRy and $F(U) = R$ if and only if, for some V in $[\bar{U}]$ and a and b in X,*

$$(U(x, 1), U(x, 2), \ldots, U(x, n)) = (V(a, 1), V(a, 2), \ldots, V(a, n))$$

$$(U(y, 1), U(y, 2), \ldots, U(y, n)) = (V(b, 1), V(b, 2), \ldots, V(b, n))$$
$$\text{and} \quad a \, \bar{R} \, b.$$

Then F satisfies UD and SN and $F(U) = \bar{F}(U)$ for all U in $[\bar{U}]$.

Proof: We start by showing that for any U in $\mathcal{U}$, for which $F(U) = R$ is defined, then R is an ordering of X. To prove the transitivity of R take any x, y, z in X such that xRy and yRz. Then there are a, b, c in X and V in $[\bar{U}]$ such that

$$(U(x, 1), \ldots, U(x, n)) = (V(a, 1), \ldots, V(a, n))$$

$$(U(y, 1), \ldots, U(y, n)) = (V(b, 1), \ldots, V(b, n))$$

$$(U(z, 1), \ldots, U(z, n)) = (V(c, 1), \ldots, V(c, n))$$

$$a \, \bar{R} \, b \quad \text{and} \quad b \, \bar{R} \, c.$$

By the transitivity of $\bar{R}$ we get $a\bar{R}c$ and, hence, xRy. Completeness and reflexivity can be proved similarly. Now UP implies directly that for any U in $\mathcal{U}$, any x and y in X, there is some V in $[\bar{U}]$ and some a and b in X such that

$$(U(x, 1), \ldots, U(x, n)) = (V(a, 1), \ldots, V(a, n))$$

and

$$(U(y, 1), \ldots, U(y, n)) = (V(b, 1), \ldots, V(b, n))$$

Hence F is a SWFL defined on all of $\mathcal{U}$; that is, it satisfies UD. To see that it satisfies SN, take any U^1 and U^2 in $\mathcal{U}$, and any two pairs $\{a, b\}$ and $\{c, d\}$ satisfying the antecedent of this condition. Then by construction of F there is V in $[\bar{U}]$ and $\bar{a}$ and $\bar{b}$ in X such that

$$(U^1(a, 1), \ldots, U^1(a, n)) = (U^2(c, 1), \ldots, U^2(c, n)) =$$
$$(V(\bar{a}, 1), \ldots, V(\bar{a}, n)),$$

$$(U^1(b, 1), \ldots, U^1(b, n)) = (U^2(d, 1), \ldots, U^2(d, n)) =$$
$$(V(\bar{b}, 1), \ldots, V(\bar{b}, n)),$$

and $a R^1 b$ if and only if $\bar{a} \bar{R} \bar{b}$ if and only if $c R^2 d$.

Therefore aR^1b if and only if cR^2d and the result follows.   Q.E.D.

This theorem is interesting not only because it brings us back to welfarism but also because it shows how properties or conditions imposed in a single-profile SWFL approach have their analogues in the multiprofile SWFL approach, which in turn have their analogues in the social welfare ordering approach. As another example take the Pareto condition as used by Arrow. In the single-profile approach it can be stated as follows.

Weak Pareto (for a single profile $\bar{U}$): For any x and y in X, if $\bar{U}(x, i) > \bar{U}(y, i)$, for all i in N, then $x\bar{P}y$, for $\bar{P}$ associated to $\bar{R} = F(\bar{U})$.
Whereas in the SWFL approach it becomes the following.

Weak Pareto (WP): For any U in $\mathcal{U}$ and any x and y in X, if $U(x, i) > U(y, i)$, for all i in N, then xPy, for P associated to $R = F(U)$.
The analogous condition for SWOs will be given in the next section.

2.3   *Neutrality reconsidered*

Now let us return to the debate on Bergson–Samuelson social welfare functions. In a reply to Kemp and Ng [1976], Samuelson [1977] asserts that the Bergson–Samuelson social welfare function reflects the judgment of an ethical observer and that Arrow's constitution notion should only be considered as an attempt to formalize the design of political processes. In other words, "mathematical politics" should be clearly separated from "mathematical ethics." As well explained in Pollak [1979], Samuelson's final objection against most of social choice theory is not so much that it is limited to a multiprofile approach, since it can be reformulated in a single-profile approach, but that this reformulation requires a neutrality condition. Hence there is a convergence of opinions against neutrality: Samuelson, like Sen, considers that nonwelfare characteristics should intervene in a crucial way in the judgments of an ethical observer.

And this, of course, goes against the implications of strong neutrality and unrestricted domain as shown by Theorem 2.1. Moreover, under unrestricted domain, strong neutrality is equivalent to two other conditions which have been extensively used in social choice theory.[11] These conditions for SWFLs are as follows.

Pareto indifference (PI): For any U in $\mathcal{U}$ and any x and y in X, if $U(x, i) = U(y, i)$, for all i in N, then xIy, for I associated to $R = F(U)$.

Independence of irrelevant alternatives for pairs (IR): For any U^1 and U^2 in $\mathcal{U}$ and any *pair* x and y in X, if $U^1(x, i) = U^2(x, i)$ and $U^1(y, i) = U^2(y, i)$, for all i in N, then xR^1y if and only if xR^2y, where $R^1 = F(U^1)$ and $R^2 = F(U^2)$.

In Sen [1977], it is shown that, under UD and PI, for SWFLs, IR is equivalent to SN. Here we prove the following (logically close) statement.

Theorem 2.3: *For any* SWFL *satisfying* UD, *the conditions* PI *and* IR *hold if and only if* SN *holds.*

Proof: That SN implies PI and IR is easy to see. Indeed, for PI, it is enough to take, in SN, $U^1 = U^2$, $a = d = x$ and $b = c = y$. For IR it is enough to put $a = c$ and $b = d$ in SN.

To prove the converse, suppose U^1 and U^2 in $\mathcal{U}$ and two pairs $\{a, b\}$ and $\{c, d\}$ (not necessarily distinct) are such that

$$(U^1(a, 1), \ldots, U^1(a, n)) = u = (U^2(c, 1), \ldots, U^2(c, n))$$
$$(U^1(b, 1), \ldots, U^1(b, n)) = v = (U^2(d, 1), \ldots, U^2(d, n)).$$

Since UD holds and $|X| \geqslant 3$, we may take e in X, and U^3, U^4 and U^5 in $\mathcal{U}$ such that if $\{a, b\} = \{c, d\}$ then $a \neq e \neq b$, and

$$(U^3(a, 1), \ldots, U^3(a, n)) = (U^3(e, 1), \ldots, U^3(e, n)) = u,$$
$$(U^3(b, 1), \ldots, U^3(b, n)) = v;$$

$$(U^4(c, 1), \ldots, U^4(c, n)) = (U^4(e, 1), \ldots, U^4(e, n)) = u,$$
$$(U^4(d, 1), \ldots U^4(d, n)) = v;$$

$$(U^5(e, 1), \ldots, U^5(e, n)) = u,$$

$$(U^5(b, 1), \ldots, U^5(b, n)) = (U^5(d, 1), \ldots, U^5(d, n)) = v.$$

Then, assuming IR, we get

---

[11] For example, for PI, Samuelson [1947] (condition (5), p. 223): "If any movement leaves an individual on the same indifference curve, then the social welfare function is unchanged. . . ." For IR, see Arrow [1951, 1963].

aR^1b if and only if aR^3b, cR^2d if and only if cR^4d,

eR^3b if and only if eR^5b, and eR^4d if and only if eR^5d.

Also, assuming PI, we have

$a\ I^3\ e$, cI^4e, and bI^5d.

Combining all these relations, finally we get

$a\ R^1\ b$ if and only if $c\ R^2\ d$. Q.E.D.

This result means that the welfarist approach amounts to imposing the conditions of unrestricted domain, Pareto indifference, and independence of irrelevant alternatives on SWFLs.

Roberts [1980b], in a similar approach, does not impose Pareto indifference and hence allows SWFLs for which nonwelfare characteristics may play a role. However, since he still imposes UD, IR, and WP, his results still have strong "welfarist" implications. In fact he proves that under these conditions, a "weak neutrality" property holds. This is done by introducing, for an admissible SWFL, a notion of "strong strict social preference" over pairs of social alternatives that cannot be affected by nonwelfare characteristics in the same way as, with Pareto indifference, the whole social ordering could not be affected. Then, as we shall do in the following, but with strong neutrality, he analyzes the possibilities for social orderings under different informational bases.

On the other hand, the negative implications for social choice of the neutrality features underlying the weak Pareto conditions, combined with unrestricted domain, seem to be already explicitly and extensively exploited in the social choice literature. Indeed these features play a crucial role for two well-known paradoxes: Arrow's [1951, 1963] theorem on *the impossibility of a social welfare function* and Sen's [1970] theorem on *the impossibility of a Paretian liberal*. Since we shall return to the former theorem in the next section, let us now examine the latter as well as the extensive discussion it has triggered. However, this we shall do briefly; for a complete reappraisal of the paradox, see Sen [1976a].

2.4 *The Paretian liberal and the multiplicity of social choice problems*

The "Paretian liberal" paradox is due to the consideration of social alternatives that should be viewed as belonging to some individual personal domain of decisions. For instance, if two social alternatives differ from each other only in some matter that is considered part of individual *i*'s privacy − for example, that *i* sleeps on his back or on his belly − then the respect of his liberty would require that *i* alone should decide in the choice between *x* and *y*. More specifically, Sen [1970] introduces a "weak libertarianism" condition requiring that for each individual *i* there is at least one pair of social alternatives *x* and *y* such that if *i* prefers *x* to *y* (resp. *y* to *x*), then society should prefer *x* to *y* (resp. *y* to *x*). Formally Sen [1970] has established the impossibility of finding a social decision function satisfying simultaneously the conditions (as stated for social decision functions) of unrestricted domain, weak Pareto, and weak libertarianism. We shall not prove this theorem. However, the essence of this paradox is well explained by Sen's original example.

There are three social alternatives involving the reading of a copy of D.H. Lawrence's book *Lady Chatterley's Lover* by a "prude" Mr. A or by a "lascivious" Mr. B or by neither. A prefers most that no one read the book but would rather read it himself than let B read it. On the other hand, B enjoys above all that A read this book and, of course, prefers to read it himself than having no one reading it. Hence, by weak libertarianism, B reading the book should be socially preferred to no one reading it. Now both prefer A to read the book rather than B so that, by weak Pareto, A reading the book should be socially preferred to B reading it. Finally, since A prefers no one reading the book to reading it himself, if one applies weak libertarianism again then one gets a social preference cycle.

Many authors have discussed this paradox and proposed some way out of the difficulty by relaxing one condition or another. Sen [1980] argues that the plurality of the possible solutions "shows how a variation of non-utility description can precipitate different moral judgments" and that "this is, of course, contrary to the essence of welfarism. Nonutility information relating to *how* 'personal' the choices are, what *motivation* the persons have behind their utility rankings, whether the interdependence arises from liking or disliking the others' physical acts (in this case the reading of the book) or from the *joys and sufferings* of the others, etc. . . . , may well be found to be relevant in deciding which way to resolve the conflict." It seems, though, that more fundamentally it is the question of the plurality of the interpretation of the "aggregation problem" itself that is concerned. Even if one restricts one's interpretation to social welfare evaluation, several particular models of social choice can be studied involving different sets of alternatives.

This interpretation question is typically involved in Nozick's [1974] proposed solution, where the set of alternatives is so restricted that individual rights are already taken into account: "Rights do not determine a social ordering but instead set the constraints within which a social choice is to be made, by excluding certain alternatives, fixing others, and so on. . ." (p. 165). This suggests that, contrary to the universality of the original utilitarian project, one should introduce the problem of social choice at different levels, the choices made at some level being the norms constraining the choices to be made at the next. The levels would be determined by the nature of the social alternatives. In any case the importance of the nature of the set of alternatives is already explicit in Sen's starting distinction between choices that are personal and those that are not, and justifies Seidl's [1975] criticism of the existential form of the libertarianism condition. This is also explicit in one of Farrell's [1976] proposed solutions, by which the set of social alternatives is partitioned into socially equivalent subsets of alternatives differing in matters that are private to some individual.

However, it is not only the nature of the alternatives that is involved; the nature of the preferences or the interpretation of the individual utilities is also essential. This kind of paradox arises because the preferences of individuals are such that "the individuals are meddling in each other's affairs"—to use Blau's [1975] terminology − or from "one person's taking a perverse interest in the affairs of another" (Gibbard [1974], p. 398). Hence to solve the conflict one may on the one hand, as Blau and Gibbard do, consider that libertarian rights are alienable in some way or another.[12] On the other hand, one may consider either that the preferences themselves should be amended (an alternative solution of Farrell [1976]) or that only some part of it should count (Sen [1976a]). However, to choose between these two types of solutions seems to be more than to choose between accepting and rejecting the welfarist implications of the Pareto condition. It indicates the fundamental difficulty of a unified and universal approach to social choice.

3   Axioms for social welfare orderings

We have seen that, under some conditions, the derivation of a collective preference ordering over the set X, from the knowledge of individual utility functions, can be adequately simplified by the introduction of a social ordering on the n-dimensional Euclidean space E^N indexed by the name of the individuals. Thus instead of introducing axioms on SWFLs and then showing their equivalent formulation for SWOs, we shall introduce them directly for SWOs. It should be kept in mind, however, that

---

[12] See also Suzumura [1980] for a critical analysis of the related Gibbard [1974] and Kelly [1976] system of alienable rights.

this simplification can be avoided and even should be avoided if non-welfare considerations are to be introduced.

3.1   *A first approach to utilitarianism and leximin*

As mentioned in the introduction, the most traditional rules to evaluate alternative economic policies are utilitarian, even though the justifications for such rules have greatly evolved in parallel to the evolution of the concept of utility. Given following is the definition of classical utilitarianism as a particular kind of SWOs.

Utilitarianism: The *pure utilitarian* SWO R^* is such that, for any u and v in E^N, uR^*v if and only if $\sum_{i=1}^{n} u_i \geq \sum_{i=1}^{n} v_i$.

Even though Rawls's theory of justice seems to be rather in opposition to the present pure welfarist approach, it remains that the "difference principle" it advocates can be expressed in similar terms.

The difference principle: For any u and v in E^N, if $\min_i u_i > \min_i v_i$ then uP^*v.

However, this principle, known also as the maximin rule, does not give as such a SWO. Instead we shall concentrate on Sen [1970] proposed modification, as an alternative SWFL, which is simply a lexicographic completion of it. Before presenting it, as a SWO, we need the following notation. For any $u \in E^N$, let us define a function $i(\cdot)$ from N to itself such that, for every h and k in N,

$$u_{i(h)} < u_{i(k)} \text{ implies } h < k.$$

In other terms, for every $u \in E^N$, we have a particular function $i(\cdot)$ such that

$$u_{i(1)} \leq u_{i(2)} \leq \cdots \leq u_{i(n)};$$

that is, the function $i(\cdot)$ gives the ranking of the components of u. When there are ties, they may be broken arbitrarily. Note that $i(k)$ does not necessarily denote the same individual in u and in v. We may now write the leximin rule.

The leximin rule: Let R^* be the SWO such that, for any u and v in E^N, uP^*v if and only if

for some k in N, $u_{i(k)} > v_{i(k)}$

for all $h < k$, $u_{i(h)} = v_{i(h)}$.

In the first part of Section 3 we shall mainly concentrate on these two rules and reserve for the end the introduction of other rules. We start by examining the basic properties of such SWOs. Only such an examination could give some kind of justification for using one of these principles as an evaluation procedure for social choice. The first set of properties that can be introduced is very general and the properties will not allow discrimination between these two rules. We shall see that they are pure ordinal properties. The first is the weakest and we stated it for SWFLs.

Weak Pareto (WP*): For any u and v in E^N, if, for all i in N, $u_i > v_i$, then uP^*v.

In words, this says that if some welfare vector u strictly dominates some other welfare vector v, with respect to every individual component, than it should be strictly preferred by the collectivity. A stronger form of this Paretian principle, which corresponds to the Pareto-dominance concept used by most economists, is the following.

Strong Pareto (SP*): For any u and v in E^N, if for all i in N, $u_i \geqslant v_i$, then uR^*v; if, in addition, $u_j > v_j$, for some j in N, then uP^*v.

On the other hand, once welfarism is accepted the two axioms seem reasonable. Indeed, if it is granted that utility indices take into account all elements that should (or should not) influence social choice (and, for some, these would include interpersonal feelings as envy and pity, or even moral considerations about fairness, liberty, equality, or all kinds of rights), then the concomitant betterment of all such indices should be admitted as a collective improvement.

In the same spirit, we may state another property of the two foregoing rules as acceptable. It is a separability condition which says that the ordering of two welfare vectors should be independent of the welfare of all unconcerned individuals, namely those individuals who have the same utility level in the two vectors. Formally we get a strong property first proposed by Fleming [1952] in his characterization of utilitarianism (see Young [1974], Strasnick [1975], and Arrow [1977]).

Separability (SE*): For any u^0, v^0, u^1 and v^1 in E^N, if every individual i in M, a subset of N, is such that $u_i^0 = u_i^1$ and $v_i^0 = v_i^1$ but if every other individual j in $N \backslash M$ is such that $u_j^0 = v_j^0$ and $u_j^1 = v_j^1$, then $u^0 R^* v^0$ if and only if $u^1 R^* v^1$.

This first set of properties does not raise any question concerning the comparability of the utility measurements. However utilitarianism and leximin as such do raise this kind of question. In particular they raise the question of interpersonal utility comparisons because they treat all the individual symmetrically. Indeed, both satisfy an axiom of anonymity.

Anonymity (A*): If σ is a permutation of N (i.e., a bijection from N to itself) and if u and v in E^N are such that $u_i = v_{\sigma(i)}$, $i = 1, 2, \ldots, n$, then uI^*v.

Further, they both satisfy a condition that is a generalization both of A* and SP* and which was proposed by Suppes [1966] as follows.

The grading principle: For any u and v in E^N, if for some permutation σ of N and for all i in N, $u_i \geq v_{\sigma(i)}$, then uR^*v; and if, moreover, $u_j > v_{\sigma(j)}$ for some j, then uP^*v.

It is important to note that the grading principle implies a partial ordering of utility vectors. A more general formulation of this principle which we shall use later is the following.

The m-person grading principle: A SWO R^* satisfies the m-grading principle, $1 \leq m \leq n$, if, for every subset M of m individuals and all u and v in E^N, with $u_h = v_h$ for every h not in M, and for any permutation σ of M,

$$uR^*v \text{ whenever } u_i \geq v_{\sigma(i)} \text{ for all } i \text{ in } M,$$

and

$$uP^*v \text{ whenever } u_i \geq v_{\sigma(i)} \text{ for all } i \text{ in } M \text{ and } u_j \geq v_{\sigma(j)}$$

$$\text{for some } j \text{ in } M.$$

This will permit us to demonstrate a characteristic of this principle that is true of many other equity principles and that we shall use recurrently in the sequel: to require it in general it is sufficient to require it in situations where only two persons are nonindifferent. Paraphrasing Sen [1979b], for the leximin, we may state the following lemma (see Hammond [1979]).

Lemma 3.1.1 (The grading principle from inch to ell): *The 2-grading principle implies* A* *and* SP* *that imply the m-grading principle*, $1 \leq m \leq n$.

Proof: Suppose u and v in E^N are such that $u_i = v_{\sigma(i)}$, for all i in N and some permutation σ of N. Now a result on permutations permits the assertion of the existence of a sequence of pairs $N_1, N_2, \ldots, N_p$ in N, a sequence of permutations $\sigma_1, \sigma_2, \ldots, \sigma_p$ on N and a sequence of welfare vectors $u^1, u^2, \ldots, u^p$ in E^N such that, for $1 \leq k \leq p$,

$\sigma_k(i) = i$ for i not in N_k,

$\sigma_p(\sigma_{p-1}(\ldots (\sigma_1(i)) \ldots)) = \sigma(i)$,

$u^0 = u$, $u_i^{k-1} = u_{\sigma_k(i)}^k$ for all i in N.

Hence, applying the 2-grading principle p times, we get

$$u = u^0 \, I^* u^1 I^* \ldots I^* \, u^p = v.$$

So that A^* holds.

To prove SP*, take any u and v in E^N such that $u_i \geqslant v_i$ for all i in N (consider simultaneously the eventuality that, in addition, $u_j > v_j$ for some j). Take $v^0, v^1, \ldots , v^n$ such that $v^0 = v$, $v_k^k = u_k$ and $v_i^k = v_i^{k-1}$, for all $i \neq k$ and $k = 1,2, \ldots , n$. Then, by the 2-grading principle, $v^k R^* v^{k-1}$ (and $v^k P^* v^{k-1}$ if $u_k > v_k$) and by transitivity $u R^* v$ (and eventually $u P^* v$), since $v^n = u$.

Hence the 2-grading principle implies A^* and SP*. To prove that A^* and SP* implies the m-grading principle, for $1 \leqslant m \leqslant n$, consider any u and v in E^N such that $u_i = v_i$, for $m < i \leqslant n$, and for some permutation σ of $\{1,2, \ldots ,m\}$, $u_i \geqslant v_{\sigma(i)}$, $1 \leqslant i \leqslant m$. Clearly, if $u_i = v_{\sigma(i)}$ for all i in $\{1,2, \ldots ,m\}$, then $u I^* v$ by A^*, since we can extend σ to a permutation τ of N for which $\tau(i) = i$, $m < i \leqslant n$. Otherwise we may define w in E^N such that $w_i = v_{\tau(i)}$, for all i in N. Then we get, by A^*, $w I^* v$ and, by SP*, $u P^* w$. Hence $u P^* v$ and the proof is complete.   Q.E.D.

However many authors have proposed to reformulate utilitarianism in a generalized form so that it does not imply anonymity. For an $S \subset N$, let $E_+^S = \{u \text{ in } E^S: u_i \geqslant 0, \text{ all } i \text{ in } S \text{ and } u \neq 0\}$.

Generalized utilitarianism: For λ in E_+^N, a *utilitarian* SWO R^* is such that: for any u and v in E^N,

$$u R^* v \text{ if and only if } \sum_{i=1}^{n} \lambda_i u_i \geqslant \sum_{i=1}^{n} \lambda_i v_i.$$

Hence a pure utilitarian SWO is simply a utilitarian SWO for which λ has all its components equal to the same positive number. However, the choice of the weights to assign to each individual utility index remains and, so, the problem of interpersonal comparability. This is linked also to the measurement scale that is used for each individual utility. The way to specify these measurability-comparability requirements is to determine the class of numerical transformations of the utility indices that leave the SWO invariant. This invariance reflects the type of measurement used to quantify all individual information that is available. It is therefore very crucial to notice that utilitarian rules as well as leximin are not compatible with any kind of informational base. More generally the type of invariance that is associated to the available information determines drastically the type of SWOs that are possible.

In the context of this discussion one way to interpret Arrow's impossibility theorem ([1951, 1963]) is particularly interesting. First Arrow used a property much weaker than anonymity that remains ordinal and involves no interpersonal comparisons.

Nondictatorship (ND*): There is no i in N such that: for any u and v in E^N, if $u_i > v_i$ then uP^*v.

Second if one wants to keep the requirements of the new welfare economics, where utility indices are to be interpreted ordinally as reflecting the preferences of the individuals as they would be expressed by some choice behavior, then these utility indices would have meaning only up to a monotone transformation. This gives our first invariance axiom.

Ordinality and noncomparability (ON*): Let $\varphi_1, \varphi_2, \ldots, \varphi_n$ be any strictly increasing numerical functions. Then, for any u and v in E^N,

$$uR^*v \quad \text{if and only if} \quad \varphi(u)R^*\varphi(v),$$

where $\varphi(u) = (\varphi_1(u_1), \varphi_2(u_2), \ldots, \varphi_n(u_n))$, and $\varphi(v) = (\varphi_1(v_1), \varphi_2(v_2), \ldots, \varphi_n(v_n))$.

However, in a welfarist approach, such a property appears to be prohibitively restrictive as it is well known[13] from Arrow's theorem

Theorem 3.1: *If a SWO satisfies WP* and ND* then it cannot satisfy ON*.*

Therefore to build up some SWO having even the weakest Paretian property and the minimal egalitarian property of nondictatorship, an ordinal information base, which excludes interpersonal comparisons, is insufficient. In the next section we introduce different informational bases allowing for more discrimination.

3.2   *Invariance axioms*

The axioms we are going to list (nonexhaustively) below all restrict the kind of transformations that can be applied to the individual utility

---

[13] A proof for this theorem will be provided below (p. 52). For versions of this theorem with specific economic domains see Kalai, Muller, and Satterthwaite [1979] and Border [1983]. This last author, as Wilson [1972], drops the Pareto condition.

indices without affecting the social ordering. The analysis of the implications of these informational hypotheses for the equity content of collective choice was initiated by Sen. With respect to ON*, either cardinality or some interpersonal comparability is introduced.

The first introduces only cardinality by allowing all positive affine transformations

Cardinality and noncomparability (CN):* Let $a_1, a_2, \ldots, a_n$ be any numbers and $b_1, b_2, \ldots, b_n$ be any positive numbers. Then, for any u and v in E^N, uR^*v if and only if

$$(a_1 + b_1u_1, a_2 + b_2u_2, \ldots, a_n + b_nu_n)R^*(a_1 + b_1v_1, a_2 + b_2v_2, \ldots, a_n + b_nv_n).$$

However, in the present welfarist framework the introduction of cardinality does not change the situation for the following reason.[14]

Lemma 3.2.1: *A SWO R^* satisfies CN* if and only if it satisfies ON*.*

Proof: We shall only prove that CN* implies ON*, the other direction being trivial. Suppose u and v in E^N are such that uR^*v. Consider n strictly increasing numerical functions $\varphi_1, \varphi_2, \ldots, \varphi_n$. We have to show that, by CN*, $\varphi(u)R^*\varphi(v)$, where $\varphi(u) \equiv (\varphi_1(u_1), \ldots, \varphi_n(u_n))$ and $\varphi(v) \equiv (\varphi_1(v_1), \ldots, \varphi_n(v_n))$. However it is simple to find $a \in E^N$ and $b \in E^N_+$ such that $b_i > 0$,

$$a_i + b_iu_i = \varphi_i(u_i) \quad \text{and} \quad a_i + b_iv_i = \varphi_i(v_i), \qquad i = 1, 2, \ldots, n.$$

Hence $\varphi(u) = (a_1 + b_1u_1, \ldots, a_n + b_nu_n)$, $\varphi(v) = (a_1 + b_1v_1, \ldots, a_n + b_nv_n)$ and the result follows.   Q.E.D.

The same kind of result holds also when the origin of all individual utility functions is common while the scale factors may vary from individual to individual; that is,

Cardinality and origin comparability (COC):* Let a and $b_1 > 0$, $b_2 > 0, \ldots, b_n > 0$ be $n + 1$ numbers. Then, for any u and v in E^N, uR^*v if and only if $(a + b_1u_1, \ldots, a + b_nu_n)R^*(a + b_1v_1, \ldots, a + b_nv_n)$.

Lemma 3.2.2.: *A SWO R^* satisfies CN* if and only if it satisfies COC*.*

---

[14] See d'Aspremont and Gevers [1977]. This cardinality statement was first considered by Sen [1970] but in a limited case (for binary independence of irrelevant alternatives).

Proof: Again we need only prove that COC* implies CN*. Suppose u and v in E^N such that uR^*v and choose $a, b \in E^N$, $b > 0$. We have to show that, by COC*, $(a_1 + b_1u_1, \ldots, a_n + b_nu_n)R^*(a_1 + b_1v_1, \ldots, a_1 + b_nv_n)$. Choose, for that purpose, $\beta \in E_+^N$ and $\theta \in E$ such that

$$a_1 - \frac{b_1}{\beta_1} = a_2 - \frac{b_2}{\beta_2} = \cdots = a_n - \frac{b_n}{\beta_n} = \theta < \min_i a_i.$$

Then, by COC*, $u^1R^*v^1$ with $u_i^1 = 1 + \beta_iu_i$ and $v_i^1 = 1 + \beta_iv_i$, $i = 1, 2, \ldots, n$. Also, by COC*, $u^2R^*v^2$ with $u_i^2 = \theta + (a_i - \theta)u_i^1$ and $v_i^2 = \theta + (a_i - \theta)v_i^1$, $i = 1, 2, \ldots, n$. The result follows since, by construction, for every i in N

$$u_i^2 = a_i + b_iu_i \quad \text{and} \quad v_i^2 = a_i + b_iv_i \qquad \text{Q.E.D.}$$

Using Lemma 3.2.1 (resp. Lemma 3.2.2) we immediately get the following generalization of Theorem 3.1 first given by Sen [1970].

Theorem 3.2: *If a SWO satisfies WP* and ND* then it cannot satisfy CN* (resp. COC*).*

It seems that, in order to get possibility results, we need to introduce more comparability. Of course this can be done simply by supposing

Co-cardinality (or cardinality and comparability) (CC*): Let a and $b > 0$ be two numbers. Then, for any u and v in E^N, uR^*v if and only if $(a + bu) R^* (a + bv)$.

Here both individual units and individual origins of the utility indices are common. Hence both interpersonal comparisons of welfare gains and interpersonal comparisons of welfare levels are permitted. Although this is not the strongest informational setup, it is already very demanding. Some would argue that even if interpersonal comparisons are introduced, an ordinal approach should be kept. This leads to the axiom of co-ordinality.

Co-ordinality (or ordinality and comparability) (OC*): Let φ be a strictly increasing numerical function. Then, for any u and v in E^N, uR^*v if and only if

$$(\varphi(u_1), \varphi(u_2), \ldots, \varphi(u_n))R^*(\varphi(v_1), \varphi(v_2), \ldots, \varphi(v_n)).$$

If the ordering R^* results from some SWFL F defined on $X \times N$, this property means that U is simply an ordinal representation of a social preference over pairs (x, i) in $X \times N$. To say that a pair (x, i) is to be preferred to a pair (x, j) is to say that individual i is better off in state x than individual j in state y. Hence, in utility terms, welfare levels are comparable but not the welfare gains. The reverse situation is obtained by the property of

Cardinality and unit-comparability (CU*): Let $a_1, a_2, \ldots, a_n$ and $b > 0$, be $n + 1$ numbers. Then, for any u and v in E^N, uR^*v if and only if

$$(a_1 + bu_1, \ldots, a_n + bu_n) \, R^* \, (a_1 + bv_1, \ldots, a_n + bv_n).$$

This invariance axiom, allowing only for a common utility unit, may be linked to the utilitarian tradition. There the importance was attached to interpersonal comparisons of *marginal utilities* in a context of income distribution: does an additional unit of income increase more the welfare of individual i than the welfare of individual j? This is why invariance with respect to individual origins of utility was indifferent. However, even this may appear to be too strong a restriction to decide on some welfare issues, like a normative analysis of poverty or of population size. Making the origin both common and nonarbitrary is achieved through

Ratio scale and comparability (RC*): Let b be any positive number. Then, for any u and v in E^N, uR^*v if and only if buR^*bv.

As well noted by Blackorby and Donaldson [1982] "this restriction allows negative and positive utilities to be treated in a qualitatively different way. Thus the origin may represent an interpersonally significant welfare position such as a poverty line" (p. 253).

On the other hand it may also be interesting from a welfare point of view to distinguish between an increase in everyone's welfare and a simple reduction of the unit of measurement of each utility index. But this would mean that it is possible to define a "natural" unit of measurement. In that case one could enunciate an axiom of

Difference comparability (DC*): Let a be any number. Then, for any u and v in E^N, uR^*v if and only if $(u + \bar{a}) \, R^* \, (v + \bar{a})$ where $\bar{a} = (a, a, \ldots, a) \in E^N$.

Of course to combine (RC*) with (DC*) would amount to reduce invariance to nothing, but would be extremely demanding with respect to welfare information: it would require having both a "natural" origin and a "natural" unit of measurement.

The last invariance axiom we shall define is given here to show how one can multiply the possibilities by varying the combinations and because it will be used in the sequel. It is called by Gevers [1979]

Almost co-cardinality (ACC*): Let $a_1, a_2, \ldots, a_n$ and $b > 0$ be any numbers and let φ be any strictly increasing numerical function. Then, for any u and v in E^N, uR^*v if and only if $u^1R^*v^1$, where, for every i in N, $u_i^1 = a_i + bu_i$, $v_i^1 = a_i + bv_i$ and also $u_i^1 = \varphi(u_i)$ and $v_i^1 = \varphi(v_i)$.

This axiom combines OC* with CU* and as such prohibits interpersonal comparisons of utility gains within a particular utility vector.

3.3   A characterization of utilitarian rules and lexical individual dictatorship

After examining alternative information bases for social choice we shall return now to the two rules introduced earlier, namely utilitarianism and leximin. The axiomatization we shall review here will put forward the fact that it is mainly the type of discrimination that is admitted in the ordering of all utility vectors that determines the type of welfare rule that is admissible. In this section we present an axiomatic characterization of utilitarianism and as a by-product a proof of Arrow's theorem as stated previously. In the next we shall do the same exercise for leximin. In both cases the presentation will be much simplified by the welfarist approach we have adopted. For both rules we shall proceed in two steps: first we show that if the rule holds for utility vectors where only two persons are concerned then it holds for all utility vectors; second we characterize the rule for two-person situations. The approach we adopt here is, in some sense, intermediate between two basic approaches to utilitarianism already known in decision theory, one represented by Blackwell and Girschik [1954] and the other by Milnor [1954]. These are far from being the only axiomatic elucidation of utilitarianism. Others will be discussed in subsequent sections.

In order to proceed this way for utilitarianism we need some more definitions:

Generalized m-person utilitarianism: A SWO R^* is called *m-utilitarian*, $1 \leq m \leq n$, if for every subset M of m individuals there is some λ in E_+^M such that, for all u and v in E^N with $u_h = v_h$ for every h not in M,

$$uR^*v \text{ if and only if } \sum_{i \in M} \lambda_i u_i \geq \sum_{i \in M} \lambda_i v_i.$$

Weak m-person utilitarianism: A SWO R^* is called *weakly m-utilitarian*, $1 \leq m \leq n$, if for every subset M of m individuals there is some λ in E_+^M such that, for all u and v in E^N with $u_h = v_h$ for every h not in M,

$$\sum_{i \in M} \lambda_i u_i > \sum_{i \in M} \lambda_i v_i \text{ implies } uP^*v.$$

Then, again paraphrasing Sen [1977], we may state

Lemma 3.3.1: (Utilitarianism from inch to ell): *If a SWO is 2-utilitarian, then it is m-utilitarian for all m, $1 < m \leqslant n$.*

Proof: The argument goes by induction. More precisely, it is enough to show that 2-utilitarianism and m-utilitarianism for some m, $2 < m < n$, implies $(m + 1)$-utilitarianism. Without loss of generality take $M = \{1, 2, \ldots, m\}$. By m-utilitarianism we may associate to M some λ^0 in E_+^M and some j in M such that $\lambda_j^0 > 0$. By 2-utilitarianism we may associate to $\{j; m + 1\}\lambda^1$ in $E_+^{\{j,m+1\}}$ and suppose λ^0 is appropriately normalized (λ_j^1 must be positive, otherwise a contradiction would arise on u and v such that $u_h = v_h$, $h \neq j$), so that $\lambda_j^0 = \lambda_j^1$. Let λ in $E_+^{M \cup \{m+1\}}$ be equal to $(\lambda_1^0, \lambda_2^0, \ldots, \lambda_m^0, \lambda_{m+1}^1)$ and take any u and v in E^N such that $u_h = v_h$ for $h = m + 2, m + 3, \ldots, n$. We may easily find w in E^N such that

$$\lambda_j w_j + \lambda_{m+1} w_{m+1} = \lambda_j u_j + \lambda_{m+1} u_{m+1}$$

$$w_{m+1} = v_{m+1}$$

$$w_k = u_k, \, j \neq k \neq m + 1.$$

By 2-utilitarianism, wI^*u; by m-utilitarianism wR^*v if and only if $\Sigma_{i=1}^m \lambda_i w_i \geqslant \Sigma_{i=1}^m \lambda_i v_i$. Equivalently we get uR^*v if and only if $\Sigma_{i=1}^{m+1} \lambda_i u_i = \Sigma_{i=1}^{m+1} \lambda_i w_i \geqslant \Sigma_{i=1}^{m+1} \lambda_i v_i$. The result follows.   Q.E.D.

Lemma 3.3.2: (Weak utilitarianism from inch to ell): *If a SWO is weakly 2-utilitarian, then it is weakly m-utilitarian for all m, $1 < m \leqslant n$.*

Proof: As above take $M = \{1, 2, \ldots, m\}$ and λ^0 in E_+^M with $\lambda_j > 0$, $j \in N$, such that weak m-utilitarianism applies. Consider, first, the case where, as above we may associate to $\{j, m + 1\}$ some λ^1 in $E_+^{\{j,m+1\}}$ with $\lambda_j^1 > 0$ and appropriately normalized so that $\lambda_j^1 = \lambda_j^0$. Then, similarly, we define $\lambda = (\lambda_1^0, \lambda_2^0, \ldots, \lambda_m^0, \lambda_{m+1}^1)$ in $E_+^{M \cup \{m+1\}}$ and, for any u and v in E^N with $u_h = v_h$, $h > m + 1$, and $\Sigma_{i=1}^{m+1} \lambda_i u_i - \Sigma_{i=1}^{m+1} \lambda_i v_i > 0$, we may construct w in E^N such that, for some k in $\{1, 2, \ldots, m\}$,

$$\lambda_j w_j + \lambda_{m+1} w_{m+1} = \lambda_j u_j + \lambda_{m+1} u_{m+1} - \varepsilon, \text{ for } 0 < \varepsilon < \sum_{i=1}^{m+1} \lambda_i (u_i - v_i)$$

$$w_{m+1} = v_{m+1}$$

$$w_h = u_h, \quad j \neq h \neq m + 1$$

By weak 2-utilitarianism, uP^*w; moreover, by construction

$$\sum_{i=1}^{m+1} \lambda_i w_i = \sum_{i=1}^{m+1} \lambda_i u_i - \varepsilon > \sum_{i=1}^{m+1} \lambda_i v_i$$

and, since $w_{m+1} = v_{m+1}$, we get

$$\sum_{i=1}^{m} \lambda_i w_i > \sum_{i=1}^{m} \lambda_i v_i$$

which, by weak m-utlitarianism, implies wP^*v and hence uP^*v.

A trickier case arises when $\lambda_j^0 > \lambda_j^1 = 0$ (hence, $\lambda_{m+1}^1 > 0$). In this case we take $\lambda = (0, 0, \ldots, 0, \lambda_{m+1}^1)$ in $E_+^{M \cup \{m+1\}}$. Indeed, for any u and v in E^N, with $u_h = v_h$, $h > m + 1$, and $u_{m+1} > v_{m+1}$, there exist $\varepsilon > 0$ sufficiently small and w in E^N such that

$$\sum_{i=1}^{m} \varepsilon\lambda_i^0 u_i + \lambda_{m+1}^1 u_{m+1} > \sum_{i=1}^{m} \varepsilon\lambda_i^0 v_i + \lambda_{m+1}^1 v_{m+1}$$

$$w_{m+1} = v_{m+1}$$

$$\varepsilon\lambda_j^0 w_j + \lambda_{m+1}^1 w_{m+1} = \varepsilon\lambda_j^0 u_j + \lambda_{m+1}^1 u_{m+1}$$

$$w_h = u_h, \quad j \neq h \neq m + 1.$$

Then, by weak 2-utilitarianism, uP^*w (since $u_{m+1} > w_{m+1}$); also,

$$\sum_{i=1}^{m} \varepsilon\lambda_i^0 w_i + \lambda_{m+1}^1 w_{m+1} = \sum_{i=1}^{m} \varepsilon\lambda_i^0 u_i + \lambda_{m+1}^1 u_{m+1}$$

$$> \sum_{i=1}^{m} \varepsilon\lambda_i^0 v_i + \lambda_{m+1}^1 v_{m+1}$$

which implies $\sum_{i=1}^{m} \varepsilon\lambda_i^0 w_i > \sum_{i=1}^{m} \varepsilon\lambda_i^0 v_i$. Therefore, by weak m-utilitarianism, wP^*v and, hence, uP^*v.   Q.E.D.

The following theorem is a weaker version of Blackwell and Girschik [1954], Theorem 4.3.1, (see also Theorem 2 by Roberts [1980b]).

Theorem 3.3.3: *A SWO R^* is weakly n-utilitarian whenever* SP* *and* CU* *are satisfied.*

Proof: Take any SWO R^* satisfying SP* and CU*. By Lemma 3.3.2 we only have to show that it is weakly 2-utilitarian. Consider the space $\bar{E}^2 = \{u \in E^N : u_i = 0, \ 1 \neq i \neq 2\}$. By CU* it is clear that we only have to show that, for some $\lambda \in E_+^2$, if u and v in $\bar{E}^2$ are such that

$\lambda_1 u_1 + \lambda_2 u_2 > \lambda_1 v_1 + \lambda_2 v_2$ then uP^*v. We shall distinguish two cases.

Case 1: There exist u^0 and v^0 in $\tilde{E}^2$ such that $u^0 \, I^* \, v^0$ and $u^0 \neq v^0$. Suppose without loss of generality that $u_1^0 - v_1^0 > 0$. So, by SP*, $u_2^0 - v_2^0 < 0$ and, by CU*, $w^0 \, I^* \, \mathbf{0}$, for $w^0 = (u^0 - v^0)$ and $\mathbf{0} = (0, \ldots, 0) \in \tilde{E}^2$. Take $\lambda^0 \in E_+^2$ such that $\lambda_1^0 w_1^0 + \lambda_2^0 w_2^0 = 0$. Then

$$\left(1, -\frac{\lambda_1^0}{\lambda_2^0}, 0, \ldots, 0\right) = \left(\frac{w_1^0}{w_1^0}, \frac{w_2^0}{w_1^0}, 0, \ldots, 0\right) I^* \mathbf{0},$$

using CU*. Also for any u in $\tilde{E}^2$ such that $u_1 > 0$, $u_2 \leq 0$, and $\lambda_1^0 u_1 + \lambda_2^0 u_2 = 0$, we must have $uI^*\mathbf{0}$. Otherwise we would have either $\mathbf{0}P^*$ $(u_1, u_2, 0, \ldots, 0)$ or $(u_1, u_2, 0, \ldots, 0)P^*\mathbf{0}$. Since $(1, - \lambda_1^0/\lambda_2^0) = (u_1/u_1, u_2/u_1)$ this is equivalent, by CU*, of having $\mathbf{0}P^*$ $(1, - \lambda_1^0/\lambda_2^0, 0, \ldots, 0)$ or $(1, - \lambda_2^0/\lambda_2^0, 0, \ldots, 0)$ $P^*\mathbf{0}$, which gives us a contradiction. Moreover, for any u in $\tilde{E}^2$ such that $u_1 < 0$, $u_2 > 0$ and $\lambda_1^0 u_1 + \lambda_2^0 u_2 = 0$, we get $-uI^*\mathbf{0}$ and, by CU*, $\mathbf{0}I^*u$. Also, for any v in $\tilde{E}^2$, if $\lambda_1^0 v_1 + \lambda_2^0 v_2 > 0$ then there is u in $\tilde{E}^2$ such that $u_1 < v_1$, $u_2 < v_2$ and $\lambda_1^0 u_1 + \lambda_2^0 u_2 = 0$, so that $uI^*\mathbf{0}$ and, by SP*, $vP^*\mathbf{0}$. Similarly, for any v in $\tilde{E}^2$, if $\lambda_1^0 v_1 + \lambda_2^0 v_2 < 0$, $\mathbf{0}P^*v$. In other terms for any u and v in $\tilde{E}^2$ such that $\lambda_1^0 u_1 + \lambda_2^0 u_2 > \lambda_1^0 v_1 + \lambda_2^0 v_2$, we get $(u - v)P^*\mathbf{0}$ or, by CU*, uP^*v. In this first case we even have more than we need since if $\lambda_1^0 u_1 + \lambda_2^0 u_2 = \lambda_2^0 v_1 + \lambda_2^0 v_2$, then $(u - v)I^*\mathbf{0}$, or, by CU*, uI^*v. We get 2-utilitarianism.

Case 2: For any distinct u and v in $\tilde{E}^2$ either uP^*v or vP^*u. Define in $\tilde{E}^2$ the line $L = \{u \in \tilde{E}^2 : u_1 - u_2 = 1\}$ and two subsets of this line: $I_1 = \{u \in L : uP^*\mathbf{0}\}$ and $I_2 = \{u \in L : \mathbf{0}P^*u\}$. Each of these subsets is a connected subset of L, since if u is in I_1 (resp. is in I_2) and v in L is such that $v_1 > u_1$ (resp. $v_1 < u_1$) then, by SP*, v must also belong to I_1 (resp. to I_2). Moreover, for any u in L, SP* implies that $uP^*\mathbf{0}$, whenever $u_1 \geq 0$ and $u_2 \geq 0$, and $\mathbf{0}P^*u$ whenever $u_1 \leq 0$ and $u_2 \leq 0$. Therefore there must be a point u^0 in L, $u_1^0 \geq 0$, $u_2^0 \leq 0$, such that, for all u in L: either $uP^*\mathbf{0}$ whenever $u_1 \geq u_1^0$ and $\mathbf{0}P^*u$ otherwise or $uP^*\mathbf{0}$ whenever $u_1 > u_1^0$ and $\mathbf{0}P^*u$ otherwise.

Accordingly define λ^0 in E_+^2 to be such that $\lambda_1^0 u_1^0 + \lambda_2^0 u_2^0 = 0$. Suppose first that $u^0 P^*\mathbf{0}$. Then, by arguments similar to Case 1, for any u in $\tilde{E}^2$ such that $u \neq \mathbf{0}$ and $\lambda_1^0 u_1 + \lambda_2^0 u_2 = 0$, we must have $uP^*\mathbf{0}$ whenever $u_1 \geq 0$ and $u_2 \leq 0$ (and $\mathbf{0}P^*u$ whenever $u_1 \leq 0$ and $u_2 \geq 0$). Similarly if we have $\mathbf{0}P^*u^0$, then for any u in $\tilde{E}^2$ such that $\lambda_1^0 u_1 + \lambda_2^0 u_2 = 0$ and $u \neq \mathbf{0}$, we must have $\mathbf{0}P^*u$ whenever $u_1 \geq 0$ and $u_2 \leq 0$ (and $uP^*\mathbf{0}$ whenever $u_1 \leq 0$ and $u_2 \geq 0$). Moreover, for any v in $\tilde{E}^2$ with $v_1 \geq 0$, $v_2 \leq 0$ and $\lambda_1^0 v_1 + \lambda_2^0 v_2 > 0$, there is λ^1 in E_+^2 and w in L such that

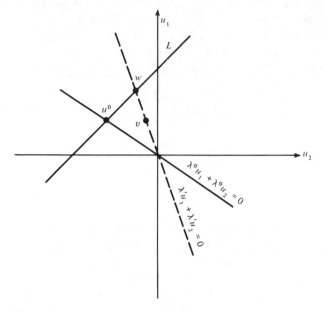

Figure 1

$\lambda_1^1 v_1 + \lambda_2^1 v_2 = \lambda_1^1 w_1 + \lambda_2^1 w_2 = 0$ (see Figure 1) and, since $w_1 > u_1^0$, we must have $wP^*\mathbf{0}$. Hence by the same reasoning as above $vP^*\mathbf{0}$. Similarly, for any v in $\bar{E}^2$ with $v_1 \geqslant 0$, $v_2 \leqslant 0$ and $\lambda_1^0 v_1 + \lambda_2^0 v_2 < 0$ we must have $\mathbf{0}P^*v$. All v in $\bar{E}^2$ such that $v_1 \leqslant 0$ and $v_2 \geqslant 0$ can be treated in the same way since, by CU*, we may simply consider $-v$. Any other v in $\bar{E}^2$, $v \neq 0$, is either such that $v_1 \geqslant 0$ and $v_2 \geqslant 0$ or such that $v_1 \leqslant 0$ and $v_2 \leqslant 0$; by SP* we get either $vP^*\mathbf{0}$ or $\mathbf{0}P^*v$. In conclusion we see that, in this second case, we obtain the following: for any u and v in $\bar{E}^2$, if $\lambda_1^0 u_1 + \lambda_2^0 u_2 > \lambda_1^0 v_1 + \lambda_2^0 v_2$ then uP^*v. The SWO R^* satisfying SP* and CU* is weakly 2-utilitarian.   Q.E.D.

The first version of Theorem 3.3.3., given by Blackwell and Girschick [1954], rests on a weaker Pareto condition and its proof is based on a supporting hyperplane theorem (also proved in their book).

However in the proof just given it is interesting to consider each of the two cases. The second case is the more particular. It occurs when R* is a simple order on $\bar{E}^2$. This simple order is completely described in the proof and can be of two types: one that privileges the first individual, along the lines determined by the coefficients λ_1^0, λ_2^0, and one that privileges the other individual along these lines.

The first case considered in the proof can be obtained under very reasonable conditions, since it only requires that there be two indifferent vectors in $\bar{E}^2$. Such a condition is anonymity and we then obtain a characterization of pure utilitarianism.

Theorem 3.3.4: *A SWO R^* is pure utilitarian if and only if it satisfies* SP*, CU* *and* A*.

Proof: For any u^0 in $\bar{E}^2$ such that $u_1^0 \neq u_2^0$, if $v^0 = (u_2^0, u_1^0, 0, \ldots, 0)$ then $v^0 I^* u^0$. Therefore in the proof of Theorem 3.3.3 we may consider only Case 1 and instead of using Lemma 3.3.2, use Lemma 3.3.1 and A*. The converse is easy to verify.   Q.E.D.

Another proof of this theorem can be based on an argument used by Milnor [1954] in the characterization of the Laplace criterion. However to characterize n-utilitarianism a much weaker condition than anonymity can be used such as the following.

Weak anonymity: For all i and j in N, there are u and v in E^N such that $u_i > v_i$, $u_j < v_j$, $u_h = v_h$, $i \neq h \neq j$, and uI^*v.

By exactly the same reasoning we get the following alternative to Theorem 3.3.4.

Theorem 3.3.5: *A SWO R^* is n-utilitarian if and only if it satisfies* SP*, CU* *and* WA*.

Note however that weak anonymity is still stronger than nondictatorship. We shall now return to nondictatorship and replace CU* by CN* (or ON*). Since all transformations allowed by CU* are allowed by CN* all the arguments in the proof of Theorem 3.3.3 still hold. This permits us to consider a particular aspect of Theorem 3.3.3. Indeed as such, weak utilitarianism does not satisfy ND*: it suffices to let $\lambda_i > 0$ for some i in N and $\lambda_j = 0$ for all $j \neq i$, which gives us dictatorship of individual i. However dictatorship of some individual is not sufficient to specify completely R^*. The following specification and the resulting theorem were suggested by Luce and Raiffa [1957] (as based on the result by Blackwell and Girschick).

Lexical individual dictatorship: There exists a permutation σ of N such that for any u and v in E^N,

$$uP^*v \text{ if and only if } u_{\sigma(j)} > v_{\sigma(j)} \text{ for some } j \text{ in } N$$

$$u_{\sigma(i)} = v_{\sigma(i)} \text{ for all } i < j.$$

As well stated by Gevers [1979], "this aggregation principle thus rests on an exogenously given hierarchy among individuals, which hinges only on their names, and social preference always endorses the strict preference of the individual who stands highest in the hierarchy."

Theorem 3.3.6: *A SWO* R^* *is lexical individual dictatorship if and only if* SP* *and* CN* *(or* ON*) *holds.*

Proof: Since CN* implies CU*, we may use Theorem 3.3.3; i.e., there exists λ^1 in E_+^N such that, for all u and v in E^N,

$$\sum_{i \in N} \lambda_i^1 u_i > \sum_{i \in N} \lambda_i^1 v_i \text{ implies } uP^*v \text{ and } \lambda_{i_1}^1 > 0 \text{ for some } i_1 \text{ in } N.$$

Consider some $\bar{u}$ and $\bar{v}$ in E^N such that $\bar{u}_{i_1} > \bar{u}_{i_1}$, $\bar{u}_i < \bar{v}_i$, $i \neq i_1$, and $\Sigma_{i \in N} \lambda_i^1 (\bar{u}_i - \bar{v}_i) > 0$. Hence $\bar{u} P^* \bar{v}$ and, by CN*, for every positive scalar c,

$$\lambda_{i_1}^1 (\bar{u}_{i_1} - \bar{v}_{i_1}) \geq c \sum_{i \neq i_1} \lambda_i^1 (\bar{v}_i - \bar{u}_i) > 0$$

which gives a contradiction unless $\lambda_i^1 = 0$ for all $i \neq i_1$.

Now considering again the argument of the proof of Theorem 3.3.3 and Lemma 3.3.2, we may repeat the argument for the set of all u in E^N with u_{i_1} maintained fixed. Then we get $(n - 1)$-weak-utilitarianism, and there exists λ^2 in $E_+^{N \setminus \{i_1\}}$ such that, for all u and v in E^N with $u_{i_1} = v_{i_1}$, $\Sigma_{i \neq i_1} \lambda_i^2 u_i > \Sigma_{i \neq i_1} \lambda_i^2 v_i$ implies uP^*v, $\lambda_{i_2}^2 > 0$ for some i_2 in N, $i_2 \neq i_1$. Then by the same argument as above, $\lambda_i^2 = 0$ for all i, $i_1 \neq i \neq i_2$. Repeating this procedure n times we construct a sequence $\lambda_{i_1}^1, \lambda_{i_2}^2, \ldots, \lambda_{i_n}^n$ of positive scalars such that $\{i_1, i_2, \ldots, i_n\} = N$ and such that, for any j, $1 \leq j \leq n$, and any u and v in $E^{N \setminus \{i_1, i_2, \ldots, i_{j-1}\}}$ with $u_i = v_i$ for all i in $\{i_1, i_2, \ldots, i_{j-1}\}$ we get: $\lambda_{i_j} u_{i_j} > \lambda_{i_j} v_{i_j}$ implies uP^*v.

This gives lexical individual dictatorship. The reverse direction is left to the reader.   Q.E.D.

This theorem appears to imply a weaker version of Arrow's theorem, where WP* would be replaced by SP*. In Gevers [1979], Theorem 3.3.6 is proved as an implication of the following theorem.

Theorem 3.3.7: *If* R^* *satisfies* SP* *and* ACC*, *there exists a partition of* N *in* s *subsets* $S_1, S_2, \ldots, S_s$ *with strictly positive associated weights* λ^1, $\lambda^2, \ldots, \lambda^s$, *respectively in* $E^{S_1}, E^{S_2}, \ldots, E^{S_s}$ *such that, for any* v *and* w *in* $\{u \in E^N: i < j \text{ implies } u_i < u_j\}$, *if, for some integer* $r \leq s$, $v_i = w_i$ *for all* i *in* S_p, $p < r$, *and*

$$\sum_{i \in S_r} \lambda_i^r (v_i - w_i) > 0$$

then uP^*w. Moreover, if R^* also satisfies OC^*, the partition of N consists only of singletons.

Proof: See Gevers [1979].

The last statement in the theorem uses the condition OC^*. In the following section we shall analyze the consequences of this invariance axiom more extensively.

3.4   *A characterization of leximin and rank dictatorship*

We shall now give an axiomatic presentation of leximin. In fact this presentation which, as above, will proceed in two steps — first leximin "from inch to ell" and, second, a characterization of leximin for two-person situations — leads to several of the numerous axiomatic derivations of leximin that have been considered. This is the approach adopted in Strasnick [1976], Sen [1977, 1979], and Hammond [1976a, 1979].

To confine the application of leximin to situations where only a small number of persons are nonindifferent seems to respond to an objection often raised. It consists of considering the case where an improvement (possibly enormous) in the welfare of a great number of persons should be rejected because of a deterioration (possibly almost imperceptible) of the worst off. However, this response appears to be insufficient as we shall see. First we introduce m-person leximin.

m-Person leximin: A SWO R^* is called *m-leximin*, $1 \leq m \leq n$, if, for every subset M of m individuals and all u and v in E^N with $u_h = v_h$ for every h not in M, uP^*v if and only if

$$u_{i(k)} > v_{i(k)} \text{ for some } k \text{ such that } i(k) \text{ is in } M.$$

$$u_{i(h)} = v_{i(h)} \text{ for all } h < k.$$

Lemma 3.4.1: (Leximin from inch to ell): *If a SWO is 2-leximin, then it is m-leximin for all m, $1 \leq m \leq n$.*

Proof: First we may verify that 2-leximin implies the 2-grading principle. Indeed take any u and v in E^N such that $u_h = v_h$, for $i \neq h \neq j$, and some i and j in N. Suppose either

$$u_i \geq v_i \text{ and } u_j \geq v_j$$

or

$$u_i \geqslant v_j \text{ and } u_j \geqslant v_i.$$

In both cases 2-leximin implies uR^*v and if, in addition, one inequality is strict, then uP^*v.

Thus, by Lemma 3.1.1, we know that A^* and SP^* hold and so 1-leximin is immediate. To derive m-leximin ($m \geqslant 3$), suppose a contrario that $(m - 1)$-leximin, $(m - 2)$-leximin, ..., 1-leximin hold but that m-leximin does not. Using A^*, this means that we can find u and v in E^N such that

$$u_h = v_h, \quad m < h \leqslant n$$

$$u_1 \leqslant u_2 \leqslant \cdots \leqslant u_m$$

$$v_1 \leqslant v_2 \leqslant \cdots \leqslant v_m$$

$$u_1 > v_1 \text{ and } u_h \neq v_h, \quad 1 < h \leqslant m$$

and

$$vR^*u.$$

By SP^*, there must be some k in $\{2, 3, \ldots, m\}$ such that $u_k < v_k$ (otherwise we would have a contradiction). Now if $v_2 = v_1$, then $u_2 > v_2$ and taking w in E^N such that $w_1 = v_1$ and $w_h = u_h$, for $h \neq 1$, one gets uP^*w, by SP^*, and wP^*v, by $(m - 1)$-leximin (since $w_h = v_h$ for $h = 1$, $m + 1$, $m + 2, \ldots, n$ and $w_m \geqslant w_{m-1} \geqslant w_2 > v_2 \leqslant v_3 \leqslant \ldots \leqslant v_m$). Or, if $v_2 > v_1$ then we may construct w in E^N such that $w_k = u_k$, $v_1 < w_1 < \min \{v_2, u_1\}$ and $w_h = v_h$, $1 \neq h \neq k$. Then again we get uP^*w, but this time using $(m - 1)$-leximin (since $w_h = u_h$ for $h = k$, $m + 1$, $m + 2, \ldots, n$ and $w_m \geqslant w_{m-1} \geqslant \cdots \geqslant w_{k+1} \geqslant w_{k-1} \geqslant \cdots \geqslant w_2 = v_2 > w_1 < u_1 \leqslant u_2 \leqslant \cdots \leqslant u_{k-1} \leqslant u_{k+1} \leqslant \cdots \leqslant u_m$) and wP^*v, by 2-leximin. In both cases ($v_2 = v_1$ and $v_2 > v_1$) we obtain a contradiction, i.e., uP^*vR^*u. The result follows.   Q.E.D.

This lemma allows us to prove a theorem, which by Lemma 3.1.1, is equivalent to Theorem 5 in Hammond [1979] and which leads to an alternative proof of Theorem 7.2 in Hammond [1976a]. All these theorems are based on a strong equity condition concerning two-person situations and which Hammond introduced with the objective of generalizing the "weak equity axiom" introduced by Sen [1973] for the case of income distribution.

Two-person equity (Hammond's equity: HE*): If u and v in E^N are such that, for some i and j and all h in N, $i \neq h \neq j$,

$v_i < u_i < u_j < v_j$ and $u_h = v_h$

then uR^*v.

Theorem 3.4.2: *A SWO R^* is leximin if and only if it satisfies* SP*, A*, *and* HE*.

Proof: We know that leximin satisfies SP* and A* and it is easy to see that it satisfies HE*. So, by the preceding lemma, it remains to show that SP*, A*, and HE* imply 2-leximin. For that purpose take any u and v in E^N such that, for some i and j in N, $u_h = v_h$, $i \neq h \neq j$. By A*, we may suppose that $\{i, j\} = \{1, 2\}$ and that $u_1 \leqslant u_2$ and $v_1 \leqslant v_2$. Clearly, if $u_1 = v_1$, then uRv if and only if $u_2 \geqslant v_2$. So consider the case where $u_1 > v_1$. If $u_2 \geqslant v_2$ then uP^*v by SP*. Therefore it remains only the subcase where $v_2 > u_2 \geqslant u_1 > v_1$. For that take w in E^n such that

$$w_h = u_h = v_h, \quad 1 \neq h \neq 2$$

and

$$v_2 > u_2 \geqslant u_1 > w_2 > w_1 > v_1$$

By SP*, uP^*w and, by HE*, wR^*v (since $v_2 > w_2 > w_1 > v_1$). Hence uP^*v. The result follows by Lemma 3.4.1.   Q.E.D.

The characterization of leximin provided by this theorem does not rely explicitly on any invariance axiom. We shall now turn to this problem. As it is stressed by Rawls in his book, an advantage of the difference principle (and of leximin) is that it requires only an ordinal informational basis: "it suffices that the least favored person can be identified and his rational preference determined" (see Rawls [1971], p. 77). It is therefore natural to consider first co-ordinality. The other characterization we shall offer relies strongly on the following interesting lemma, based on both OC* and SE*.

Lemma 3.4.3 (Equity−inequity lemma): *Suppose a SWO R^* satisfies* SP*, A*, SE*, *and* OC*. *Then one and only one of the following two conditions arises.*

(i) *If u and v in E^N are such that, for some i and j and all h in N, $i \neq h \neq j$,*

   $v_i < u_i < u_j < v_j$ *and* $u_h = v_h$

   then uP^*v.

(ii) *If u and v in E^N are such that, for some i and j and all h in N,
$i \neq h \neq j$,*

$$v_i < u_i < u_j < v_j \quad and \quad u_h = v_h$$

then vP^*u.

Proof: Consider u^0, u^1, v^0 and v^1 in E^N such that

for some i and j, $v_i^0 < u_i^0 < u_j^0 < v_j^0$ and $u_h^0 = v_h^0$,
   $i \neq h \neq j$,

for some k and l, $v_k^1 < u_k^1 < u_l^1 < v_l^1$ and $u_h^1 = v_h^1$,
   $k \neq h \neq l$.

We want to show first that $u^0 R^* v^0$ if and only if $u^1 R^* v^1$. Clearly, there exist u^2 and v^2 in E^N and a permutation σ of N such that

$$u_h^2 = u_{\sigma(h)}^1 \text{ and } v_h^2 = v_{\sigma(h)}^1, \text{ for all } h \text{ in } N, \text{ and both } \sigma(i) = k$$
$$\text{and } \sigma(j) = l.$$

Then, by A*, we know that $u^2 I^* u^1$ and $v^2 I^* v^1$. Now, using OC*, we may construct a strictly increasing function φ such that

$$u_i^0 = \varphi(u_i^2), \quad u_j^0 = \varphi(u_j^2), \quad v_i^0 = \varphi(v_i^2), \text{ and } v_j^0 = \varphi(v_j^2).$$

Taking u^3 and v^3 in E^N such that $u_h^3 = \varphi(u_h^2)$ and $v_h^3 = \varphi(u_h^3)$, for all h in N, we get $u^3 I^* u^2$ and $v^3 I^* v^2$, by OC*. Since, also, $u_i^3 = u_i^0$, $u_j^3 = u_j^0$, $v_i^3 = v_i^0$, $v_j^3 = v_j^0$, $u_h^3 = v_h^0$ and $u_h^3 = v_h^3$, $i \neq h \neq j$, we may apply SE* and get $u^0 R^* v^0$ if and only if $u^3 R^* v^3$, which is equivalent to $u^0 R^* v^0$ if and only if $u^1 R^* v^1$.

To complete the proof there remains to eliminate the possibility of indifference. Suppose, a contrario, that $u^0 I^* v^0$ and take u^1 and v^1 in E^N such that

$$v_i^0 < u_i^1 < u_i^0 \text{ and } u_h^1 = u_h^0, \text{ all } h \neq i, \text{ but } v^1 \equiv v^0.$$

Then, by above, $u^1 I^* v^1$; that is, $u^1 I^* v^0$. Hence $u^0 I^* u^1$, which contradicts SP*. Therefore we must have $u^0 P^* v^0$ or $v^0 P^* u^0$ and the result follows.
                                                            Q.E.D.

It is interesting to remark the similarity of condition (i) in the lemma with HE*. In fact condition (i) is stronger than HE*, but also satisfied by leximin. So in Theorem 3.4.2 we could replace HE* by condition (i). Moreover condition (ii) appears as an "inequity condition" dual to condition (i): the better-off individual wins in all two-person situations of the kind described. Applying the reasoning of Theorem 3.4.2 in an obvious way we get a SWO that is dual to leximin and may be called *leximax*. It says that, if the best-off individual is nondifferent, then let him decide; but, if he is indifferent, then let the second best-off individual decide; and so on. We may take as a condition the negation of condition (ii), namely minimal equity.

Minimal equity (ME*): For some u and v in E^N and i and j in N,

$$v_i < u_i < u_j < v_j, \quad u_h = v_h, \quad i \neq h \neq j, \quad \text{and } uR^*v.$$

Then we get the following results (from Lemma 3.4.3 and Theorem 3.4.2).

Theorem 3.4.4: *A SWO R^* satisfying* SP*, A*, SE*, *and* OC* *is either the leximin or the leximax.*

Theorem 3.4.5: *A SWO R^* is the leximin if and only if it satisfies* SP*, A*, SE*, OC*, *and* ME*.

This last theorem is another characterization of the leximin where HE* has been replaced by three conditions SE*, OC*, and ME*. It is now interesting to compare Theorem 3.4.5 to Theorem 3.3.4. Since SE* and ME* are clearly satisfied by pure utilitarianism we arrive at the disturbing conclusion that the difference between this SWO and leximin can be entirely explained by invariance axioms. So we are led to require even more discrimination than the one allowed by either CU* or OC*. This we do in the next section. However, before that, one may wonder what type of SWO would result from the three conditions SP*, A*, and OC*. First, in our welfarist approach it is clear that, once the anonymity condition A* has been introduced, individual names do not matter, as such, anymore to compare any two welfare vectors. Only the ranking position of the individual components (as given by the function $i(\cdot)$ defined in Section 3.1) are important. Focusing on ranks we see that the difference principle, the leximin and the leximax have a common property: they privileged one rank (the worst-off position or the best-off position). This allows us to extend the notion of dictatorship from individuals to ranks and to state the following theorem (see Gevers [1979] or Roberts [1977]).

Theorem 3.4.6 (The rank-dictatorship theorem): *If a SWO R^* satisfies* SP*, A*, *and* OC*, *then there exists an integer r in $\{1, 2, \ldots, n\}$, that is, a rank, such that, for any u and v in E^N,*

$$u_{i(r)} > v_{i(r)} \text{ implies } uP^*v.$$

This is in a co-ordinal, anonymous (and welfarist) framework an analogue to Arrow's theorem.

However leximin and leximax go further. They both define a hierarchy of the set of ranks, such that each rank becomes a "dictator" whenever all lower ranks in the hierarchy are indifferent. In other words we should extend lexical individual dictatorship to lexical rank dictatorship. As shown by Gevers [1979], this is implied by SP*, A*, and OC* only on the subset W of vectors in E^N such that no two individual components are equal (i.e., $u \in W$ if and only if $u_i \neq u_j$, all i and j in N). Gevers [1979] provides a counterexample for welfare vectors in which there are ties.

Theorem 3.4.7 (Lexical rank-dictatorship theorem): *If a SWO R^* satisfies SP*, A*, and OC*, there exists a permutation σ of $\{1,2, \ldots ,n\}$ such that, for any u and v in W, uP^*v if and only if*

$$u_{i(\sigma(k))} > v_{i(\sigma(k))} \text{ for some } k \text{ in } \{1,2, \ldots ,n\}$$

and

$$u_{i(\sigma(h))} > v_{i(\sigma(h))} \text{ for all } h \text{ in } \{1,2, \ldots ,k-1\}.$$

Proof: The proof of this theorem is based on Lemma 3.1.1 and Theorem 3.3.7.

3.5   *Other social welfare orderings and inequality measures*

The purpose of this section is to investigate the class of SWOs that result from other types of invariance allowing for more discrimination than either CU* or OC*. Most of the results will be presented without proofs.

3.5.a   *Joint characterization of utilitarianism and leximin*

The first type of invariance that it seems natural to introduce now is co-cardinality: it allows both comparisons of individual welfare levels and comparisons of individual welfare gains. The first result we state in this respect is due to Roberts [1980b].

Theorem 3.5.1: *If a SWO R^* satisfies WP* and CC* then there exists a numerical function g, homogeneous of degree 1, such that for any u and v in E^N,*

$$\bar{u} + g(u - \bar{u}) > \bar{v} + g(v - \bar{v}) \text{ implies } uP^*v$$

where

$$\bar{u} = \frac{1}{n} \sum_{i=1}^{n} u_i \quad and \quad \bar{v} = \frac{1}{n} \sum_{i=1}^{n} v_i.$$

Roberts [1980b] gives the following interesting example of such a numerical function g. Let

$$g(u) \stackrel{\text{def}}{=} \alpha \min_{i \in N} u_i, \quad u \in E^N, \quad 0 \leqslant \alpha \leqslant 1.$$

Then the SWO R^* is such that for any u and v in E^N

$$\bar{u} + \alpha \min_{i \in N} \{u_i - \bar{u}\} > \bar{v} + \alpha \min_{i \in N} \{v_i - \bar{v}\} \text{ implies } uP^*v.$$

This ordering is then weakly utilitarian for $\alpha = 0$ and satisfies the difference principle for $\alpha = 1$. When α is between 0 and 1 then R^* satisfies a combination of these two principles with respective weights $(1 - \alpha)$ and α.

However, the preceding result still gives a large class of possible SWOs. The following theorem due to Deschamps and Gevers [1978] introduces more conditions and restricts considerably the class of possible SWOs.

Theorem 3.5.2: *For $n \geqslant 3$, a SWO R^* satisfying* SP*, A*, ME*, *and* CC* *is either the leximin or weakly utilitarian.*

This theorem gives, a posteriori, some argument, in addition to the historical reasons, for our focusing on utilitarianism and leximin in our structural investigation of SWOs. It is clear also that the role played by minimal equity (ME*) is to discard leximax. Now if the other conditions are coupled with the condition of continuity (C^*), then using Debreu's [1960] theorem on additive separability, Maskin [1978] shows that leximin and leximax are both discarded and the SWO must be pure utilitarianism.[15]

Theorem 3.5.3: *For $n \geqslant 3$, a SWO R^* satisfying* SP*, A*, C*, *and* CC* *is pure utilitarian.*

---

[15] This argument may also be founded on Myerson [1978] approach based on either a linearity or a concavity condition. Even more different arguments are given in Yaari [1981] and Pazner and Schmeidler [1976].

3.5.b   *Global means and Kolm−Pollak functions*

The two other types of invariance properties we shall investigate, and which introduce still more comparability than co-cardinality does, are ratio-scale comparability and difference comparability. As stressed by Blackorby and Donaldson [1982], the crucial question resulting from ratio-scale comparability is the interpretation of the interpersonally significant welfare level taken as origin. Consequently, negative and positive utilities belong to two different categories separated by an interpersonally recognized norm, such as a "poverty line." To avoid the difficulties involved by this natural origin, a way to proceed is to restrict utilities to the nonnegative orthant of E^N. For SWFLs this would amount to the introduction of some domain restriction. Such an approach is used by Roberts [1980b] and can be justified by taking the contractualist viewpoint adopted by the theory of bargaining. In this theory, the origin may be interpreted as a "status quo" or a "disagreement point" that obtains only if the negotiation breaks down. In this context SWOs, as restricted to the nonnegative orthant of E^N, may be viewed as "arbitration schemes."[16] The next chapter of this volume is devoted to the bargaining problem.

The first of the results that we shall quote and which are due to Blackorby and Donaldson [1982], does not, however, introduce any domain limitation.

Theorem 3.5.4: *For $n \geq 3$, a SWO R^* satisfying SP*, C*, SE*, and RC* is defined by a global mean of order $r > 0$. Namely, for any u and v in E^N, uR^*v, if and only if, for some $r > 0$, $G_r(u) \geq G_r(v)$ where, for any $w \in E^N$,*

$$G_r(w) = \left[\sum_{i=1}^{n} \frac{\alpha(w_i)}{\alpha^+} |\beta_i(w_i)w_i|^r \right]^{1/r} \quad if \quad \sum_{i=1}^{n} \alpha(w_i) \mid \beta_i(w_i)w_i|^r \geq 0$$

$$= - \left[\sum_{i=1}^{n} \frac{\alpha(w_i)}{\alpha^-} |\beta_i(w_i)w_i|^r \right]^{1/r} \quad if \quad \sum_{i=1}^{n} \alpha(w_i) \mid \beta_i(w_i)w_i|^r \leq 0$$

---

[16] However, here interpersonal comparisons are introduced, which is not the case, for instance, in Nash's bargaining theory [1950]. Moreover, through the welfarist approach, we assume implicitly some kind of independence of irrelevant alternatives that is clearly violated in Nash's theory (e.g., see the discussion in Sen [1974a]). However, from another viewpoint, as well stressed by Pazner [1979], the extended sympathy framework can be presented (by Arrow [1951, 1963], p. 135) as one type of use of irrelevant alternatives ("irrelevant" because it is not feasible for someone to become somebody else).

with $\alpha^+ > 0$, $\alpha^- < 0$, $\beta_i(.)$ *positive and constant both for all* $w_i \geq 0$ *and all* $w_i < 0$,

$$\alpha(w_i) = \alpha^+ \quad \textit{if } w_i \geq 0 \,,$$
$$= \alpha^- \quad \textit{if } w_i < 0 \,,$$

and all these parameters chosen so that $G_r(1, 1, \ldots , 1) = -G_r(-1, -1, \ldots , -1) = 1$.

The second result simplifies a lot the foregoing description of the SWO involved by restricting its domain to $\bar{E}_+^N$ (the nonnegative orthant of E^N).

Theorem 3.5.5: *For* $n \geq 3$, *a SWO* R^* *with its domain restricted to* $\bar{E}_+^N$ *and satisfying there* SP*, C*, SE*, *and* RC* *is defined by a generalized mean of order r. Namely, for any u and v in* $\bar{E}_+^N$, uR^*v, *if and only if* $g_r(u) \geq g_r(v)$ *where, for any* $w \in \bar{E}_+^N$

$$g_r(w) = \left[\sum_{i=1}^{n} \alpha_i w_i^r \right]^{1/r} \quad \textit{if } r \neq 0$$

$$= \prod_{i=1}^{n} w_i^{\alpha_i} \quad \textit{if } r = 0$$

with every $\alpha_i > 0$ *and* $\Sigma_{i=1}^{n} \alpha_i = 1$.

The proofs of these theorems are based on results on functional equations of Eichhorn [1978]. It is interesting to note that g_0 in the Theorem 3.5.5 coincides with the nonsymmetric Nash solution to the bargaining problem.

Turning now to difference comparability and using exponential transformations of the expressions in Theorem 3.5.5, the SWO involved becomes now what Blackorby and Donaldson [1980] have called a Kolm–Pollak function.[17] This is

Theorem 3.5.6: *For* $n \geq 3$, *a SWO* R^* *satisfying* SP*, C*, SE*, *and* DC* *is defined by a Kolm–Pollak function. Namely, for any u and v in* E^N, uR^*v, *if and only if* $K_r(u) \geq K_r(w)$, *where, for any* $w \in E^N$,

---

[17] Blackorby and Donaldson ([1980a], p. 116) show that the reference-level free absolute index suggested by Kolm [1976a,b] coincides with the index derived from a social evaluation function that is additively separable and homothetic to minus infinity in the sense of Chipman and Pollak.

$$K_r(w) = \frac{1}{r} \log \left[\sum_{i=1}^{n} \alpha_i e^{rw_i} \right] \quad r \neq 0$$

$$= \sum_{i=1}^{n} \alpha_i w_i \qquad\qquad r = 0$$

with every $a_i > 0$ and $\Sigma_{i=1}^{n} \alpha_i = 1$.

Letting every $\alpha_i = 1/n$, then we may compute that, for $r = 0$, K_r becomes pure utilitarianism and that for r approaching $-\infty$, K_r approaches the maximin function.[18]

An important application of these SWOs is the justification of various measures of economic inequality. The next subsection provides some remarks concerning the relationship between inequality measures and social welfare orderings.

3.5.c   *Social welfare functions and inequality indices*

The measurement of inequality, and more specifically the measurement of inequality of income distribution by a single index, has been the object of many economic studies. Early in this century several economists had already proposed various ways to evaluate the change in economic inequality resulting from changes in the distribution of incomes. The Lorenz curve, the Gini coefficient, as well as contributions by Pigou and by Dalton are well-known examples. (On this subject see the book by Sen [1973].) The problem in measuring inequality is that indices that look reasonable — for example the relative mean deviation, the variance, the coefficient of variation, or the relative mean difference — may give contradictory indications. It is therefore crucial to study the various properties and the ethical implications of the indices one wants to use. One way to achieve this objective is to relate each inequality measure to the social welfare function, which may be viewed as being implicit in this measure. This idea, which can be traced back to Dalton [1920], has recently been given precise formulation with the notion of an *equally distributed equivalent income* (see Kolm [1969], Atkinson [1970], and Sen [1973]). This notion can be easily presented in our welfarist framework and so we shall

---

[18] See Blackorby and Donaldson ([1980a], p. 117, fn. 9) and Atkinson [1970]. This is analogous to the result of Arrow ([1973], pp. 256–257), who presents it to show that the maximin criterion may appear as the limiting case of average utilitarianism. This argument is debated in Sen [1974a], where an analogous result is presented (under CC* though).

do, introducing simultaneously the distinction between relative and absolute inequality indices — or "rightist" and "leftist" indices to use Kolm's [1976] terminology. This distinction is analogous to the two different comparability conditions analyzed in the previous subsection.

In our framework a *social welfare function* can be defined simply as real-valued function defined on the utility space E^N. A social welfare function can be used to define a SWO. The resulting SWO is then *represented* by the given social welfare function. We have done this several times in the preceding, using for instance the various utilitarian social welfare functions or, in the previous subsection, characterizing the social welfare functions defined as global (or generalized) means, on the one hand, and the Kolm—Pollak social welfare function, on the other.

As a first case take a continuous SWO R^* restricted to $\bar{E}_+^N$ and satisfying ratio-scale comparability. Then it can be represented by, and only by, a homothetic social welfare function W (see Theorem 3.5.5.). Thus we may write, for any $u \in \bar{E}_+^N$,

$$W(u) = \varphi(\widetilde{W}(u))$$

where φ is an increasing transformation and $\widetilde{W}$ a social welfare function that is positively homogeneous of degree 1. The *equally distributed equivalent utility level* is a $w_u \in E$ such that

$$W(w_u, w_u, \ldots, w_u) = W(u)$$

or $\qquad \widetilde{W}(w_u, w_u, \ldots, w_u) = \widetilde{W}(u)$

$$w_u = \frac{\widetilde{W}(u)}{\widetilde{W}(\mathbf{1})} \quad \text{with } \mathbf{1} = (1, 1, \ldots, 1) \in \bar{E}_+^N.$$

Note that $\widetilde{W}$, and hence w, are both social welfare functions representing the same SWO as W. Now, letting $\bar{u} \underset{\text{def}}{=} (1/n)\Sigma u_i$, the social welfare function

$$I(u) \underset{\text{def}}{=} (\bar{u} - w_u)/\bar{u}$$

is called the *relative index of inequality corresponding* to W. It is a relative index since it is homogeneous of degree zero. Moreover, it is zero for any vector of equal utilities.[19]

---

[19] Blackorby and Donaldson [1978] show how to generate a family of reasonable indices of relative inequality (continuous, homogeneous of degree zero, and S-concave) from any social welfare function that is continuous, increasing along rays and S-concave. Conversely, from any reasonable index of relative inequality one may generate at least one social welfare function with the foregoing properties.

Example 1: As an example take the Gini index of relative inequality

$$I_G(u) = \frac{1}{2n^2\bar{u}} \sum_{i=1}^{n} \sum_{j=1}^{n} |u_i - u_j| , \quad u \in \bar{E}_+^N$$

or, as shown in Sen [1973], p. 31,

$$I_G(u) = 1 + \frac{1}{n} - \frac{2}{n^2\bar{u}} [n u_{i(1)} + (n-1)u_{i(2)} + \cdots + u_{i(n)}], \quad u \in \bar{E}_+^N$$

where $i(\cdot)$ is defined in Section 3.1.

Then, as shown by Donaldson and Weymark [1980],

$$\widetilde{W}_G(u) = \sum_{k=1}^{n} [2(n-k)+1]u_{i(k)} , \quad u \in \bar{E}_+^N.$$

Since the coefficients in this function look arbitrary, they propose to consider a larger class of social welfare functions given by

$$W_\gamma(u) = \sum_{k=1}^{n} a_k u_{i(k)} , \quad u \in \bar{E}_+^N ,$$

where $a_k > 0$, $k = 1, \ldots n$, and $a_1 \geq a_2 \geq \cdots \geq a_n$. (This is axiomatized in Gevers [1979]).

Corresponding to this function, we get the following relative index

$$I_\gamma(u) = 1 - \frac{\displaystyle\sum_{k=1}^{n} a_k u_{i(k)}}{\displaystyle\bar{u} \sum_{k=1}^{n} a_k} , \quad u \in \bar{E}_+^N.$$

This is called the generalized Gini relative index.

As a second case, take now a continuous SWO R^* satisfying difference comparability. Then it can be represented by, and only by, a translatable social welfare function W (see Theorem 3.5.6). In other words we may write, for an $u \in E^N$

$$W(u) = \varphi(\widetilde{\widetilde{W}}(u))$$

where φ is an increasing transformation and $\widetilde{\widetilde{W}}$ is a social welfare function that is unit-translatable; for any scalar b

$$\widetilde{\widetilde{W}} (u + \mathbf{1} b) = \widetilde{\widetilde{W}}(u) + b, \quad \text{with } \mathbf{1} = (1,1, \ldots ,1) \in E^N.$$

Again we have for w_u the equally distributed equivalent utility level

$$\widetilde{\widetilde{W}} (\mathbf{1} w_u) = \widetilde{\widetilde{W}}(u) , \quad u \in E^N$$

and, since $\widetilde{\widetilde{W}}$ is unit-translatable, we get

$$w_u = \widetilde{\widetilde{W}}(u) - \widetilde{\widetilde{W}}(\mathbf{0}), \quad \text{with } \mathbf{0} = (0,0, \ldots ,0) \in E^N.$$

We may now define an *absolute index of inequality corresponding to W*:

$$A(u) = \bar{u} - w_u, \quad u \in E^N$$

It is an absolute index since it is invariant to any translation.[20]

Example 2: We can define the Gini index of absolute inequality by

$$A_G(u) = \bar{u} - \frac{1}{n^2} \sum_{k=1}^{n} [2(n - k) + 1]u_{i(k)}, \quad u \in E^N.$$

Similarly we may write the generalized Gini absolute index:

$$A_\gamma (u) = \bar{u} - \frac{\sum\limits_{k=1}^{n} a_k\, u_{i(k)}}{\sum\limits_{k=1}^{n} a_k}, \quad u \in E^N,$$

where $a_k > 0$, $k = 1, \ldots , n$, and $a_1 \geqslant a_2 \geqslant \cdots \geqslant a_n$.

The example of the Gini indices was good to take since every W_γ is both homothetic and translatable.

4   Conclusion: two fundamental justifications

In this concluding section I would like to come back to the main difficulty, which is linked to the extended sympathy approach I have used as the basis for this presentation. As Elisha Pazner justly noted, "it seems natural to presume that there is a limit to one's ability to put oneself into somebody else's shoes. The implication of such a limit is that interpersonal orderings become a subjective matter and will generally differ for different individuals" ([1979], p. 163). How, then, can one justify, on ethical grounds, the use, at any level of social choice, of a single social welfare ordering? The theories of Harsanyi and Rawls may be viewed as providing two such justifications, albeit rather distinct ones.

---

[20] In Blackorby and Donaldson [1980a] it is shown that any well-behaved social welfare function can generate a family of absolute indices of inequality. Conversely for each absolute index there exists a family of social welfare functions that imply this index and that represent the same SWO whenever they are translatable.

4.1   *Expected utility and the fundamental preference*

Both theories may be seen as theories of justice based on a notion of "fairness." This notion is inseparable from the construction of some sort of procedure. The fairness of the result can only be secured by the reasonable character of the rules defining the procedure. Applications of such a constructivist approach are numerous in normative economics and in game theory. A well-known example is the procedure of fair division. The simplest case of it is when two individuals have to divide a cake. The fair solution is presented as the one resulting from the procedure consisting in asking the first individual to divide the cake into two parts, and the second individual to choose the part that pleases him most (i.e., the biggest). However, the most important application of this idea, from the present viewpoint, is the one developed by Lerner [1944], Vickrey [1945, 1960], and Harsanyi [1953, 1955, 1977]. Because the most systematic development of this application is due to Harsanyi, we shall concentrate on his procedure.

The objective of Harsanyi is to build up a "general theory of rational behavior" divided in two main parts. The first part is the theory of rational behavior of the individual, respectively under certainty, risk, and uncertainty. The second part concerns rational behavior in a social setting and is developed at two levels. At the first level, the game-theoretic one, each individual pursues his own self-interest and is moved according to personal preferences. At the second level, where the ethical norms constraining the first level have to be chosen, each individual pursues the interests of society as a whole and is moved according to social (or moral) preferences. The fairness procedure is introduced to determine these moral preferences. In this procedure each individual, who has to judge different possible situations for society, is to adopt an impartial view, and this he may achieve by acting *as if* "he simply did not know in advance what his own social position would be in each social situation" ([1977], p. 49). For that purpose, the moral preference of every individual should be based on complete information not only about the objective social situation of every other individual but also about the subjective attitudes characterizing their personal preferences. To understand this distinction, let us return to Harsanyi's example. Suppose a society consists of two individuals, and consider two possible social situations, one in which fish is the main item of everyone's diet and the other in which everyone's diet consists mainly of meat. Suppose in addition that the first individual has a mild personal preference for fish and the second a strong distaste for fish. The requirement is that if some individual, say the first, wants to order socially the two situations, he must take into account not only the objective diet characterizing them (meat or fish) but also his own personal taste and the other individual's taste. It seems then that, socially, he would prefer the meat diet. Thus, in Harsanyi's theory, the social preference is defined on the set of "extended" social alternatives that are alternatives of the kind: "being in social alternative x with the objective position and the subjective attitude of individual i." The fairness or impartiality of the moral preference of an individual comes from the fact that it is determined in a hypothetical situation where, for each social alternative, the individual supposes that he has an *equal chance* of being in the objective position and of adopting the subjective attitude of any of the individuals. Then assuming that, in such an "original position," the individual's moral preference would satisfy the conditions imposed in the theory of rational behavior in the face of risk, and assuming that, whenever he adopts some other individual's subjective attitudes, he thereby adopts the personal preference of this other individual, Harsanyi is led to infer that the individual's moral preference can be represented by a von Neumann–Morgenstern utility function. This is simply, here, the average of the utilities representing the personal preferences of all individuals.

More precisely, consider a society of n individuals and a set X of social alternatives $a, b, c, \ldots$ etc. Then the hypothetical decision problem for the individual in the original position may be presented in the following table.

	1	2	3	$\cdots$	n
a	C_{1a}	C_{2a}	C_{3a}	$\cdots$	C_{na}
b	C_{1b}	C_{2b}	C_{3b}	$\cdots$	C_{nb}
c	C_{1c}	C_{2c}	C_{3c}	$\cdots$	C_{nc}
etc.					

This table summarizes a decision problem in the face of risk, where the decisions to be chosen are the social alternatives $a, b, c, \ldots$, and the "states of the world" are the individuals $1, 2, \ldots, n$. In addition each consequence C_{iz}, resulting from some decision z in state i, is a complete description of the objective situation and of the subjective attitude of individual i in the social situation z, say $C_{iz} = (x_i, p_i)$, where x_i and p_i are the respective vectors of "objective" and "subjective" characteristics of individual i. Finally the probability attached to every state of the world is simply $1/n$. Then using the axioms of decision theory under risk one gets that the chosen alternative should maximize on X:

$$\sum_{i=1}^{n} \frac{1}{n} u(C_{ix}) = \sum_{i=1}^{n} \frac{1}{n} u(x_i, p_i)$$

where u is some (cardinal utility) function defined on the set of consequences. By the assumption that to adopt some individual subjective attitude is to adopt his personal preferences (as they are embodied at the game-theoretic level of behavior) we may identify

$$u(x_i, p_i) = U_i(x)$$

where $U_i(\cdot)$ is individual i's personal utility. Therefore the objective of an individual in the original position becomes

$$\sum_{i=1}^{n} \frac{1}{n} U_i(x)$$

which, in the context of a fixed population, is simply pure utilitarianism.

Of course the crucial step, from our viewpoint, is the identification of $u(C_{ix})$ to $U_i(x)$ for every i, since this is where the interpersonal judgment is introduced. On this basis any individual who would put himself in the original position would end up with the same social preference. This step has been often criticized. First, each individual solving the problem in the original position may have what is called in decision theory a different "risk attitude" (see the detailed discussion in Pattanaik [1968]). Second, the utilities introduced are representations that are not unique; their unit and origins may be arbitrarily changed. As we have seen in the preceding text, some invariance condition must be used and justified. To such questions Harsanyi provides a general answer that has been called the "theory of fundamental preference."[21] In such a theory the subjective attitudes characterizing each individual (including his risk attitude) may be reduced to the same list of parameters the value of which may vary from individual to individual. This is based on the presumption that

> the different individuals choice behavior and preferences are at least governed by the *same basic psychological laws*. For in this case each individual's preferences will be determined by the same general causal variables. Thus the differences we can observe between different people's preferences can be predicted, at least in principle, from differences in these causal variables, such as differences in their biological inheritance, in their past life histories, and in their current environmental conditions. (Harsanyi [1977], p. 58)

---

[21] For an analysis of different possible formal presentations of Harsanyi's theory, see Blackorby, Donaldson, and Weymark [1980b].

In the notation of this chapter this means that for a sufficient a priori specification of the subjective attitudes of the individuals, both the variables x_i and the variables p_i appearing in the function u are in some sense "objective." Hence, by taking as part of the decision problem, all those causal variables that explain individual differences, we may eventually obtain one single fundamental social preference that would be, in the words of Kolm [1972], a formal expression for the notion of human nature.

4.2   Contractualism and social unity

Although Rawls's theory of justice also relies on a notion of fairness resulting from the original position procedure, he insists that "the unity of society and the allegiance of its citizens to their common institutions rest not on their espousing one rational conception of the good but on an agreement as to what is just for free and equal persons with different and opposing conceptions of the good" ([1982], p. 160). Despite the universal character of the principles of justice, they should not reduce the incommensurability of the different individual conceptions of the good. In Kant's view this is the compatibility of the universal character of the categorical imperative ("Act always on such a maxim as thou canst at the same time will to be a universal law") with the principle of the autonomy of the will. The moral person cannot be governed by maxims, even if they can be taken as universal laws, since he would then be reduced to a simple mean. He himself, as a reasonable being, should be the legislator. For Rawls, this universality and this autonomy should both be realized through the procedure of the original position. Universality is warranted by such a procedure since every individual should be represented in this hypothetical situation and because each representative individual should be "behind a veil of ignorance"; that is, he should not know his place in society, his class position, his endowment in natural assets and abilities, his psychological propensities, and even his own conception of the good. Autonomy is implied because the parties in the original position are supposed to be moved by "their highest-order interests" to promote the understanding and the realization of a conception of justice and of a conception of the good (whatever it is). However as representatives, they should only possess the "minimum adequate powers of moral personality" ([1980], p. 529). This should only be enough to make possible the deliberation procedure through which an agreement on the principles of justice may be reached.

Rawls, in defining the original position, not only specifies the (artificial) personality of the representative individuals, but also the subject of their deliberation, that is, the social alternatives. These are limited to be the various ways of providing and distributing the "primary goods" that is the goods that are under the control of the major social, political and economic institutions (as opposed to natural goods). More precisely Rawls gives the following list:

(a)   First, the basic liberties as given by a list, for example: freedom of thought and liberty of conscience; freedom of association; and the freedom defined by the liberty and integrity of the person, as well as by the rule of law; and finally the political liberties;

(b)   Second, freedom of movement and choice of occupation against a background of diverse opportunities;

(c)   Third, powers and prerogatives of offices and positions of responsibility, particularly those in the main political and economic institutions;

(d)   Fourth, income and wealth; and

(e)   Finally, the social bases of self-respect. (Rawls ([1982], p. 162)

To arrive at an agreement, the parties in their original deliberation are supposed to have a preference ordering on the set of alternatives which can be derived from this list of primary goods. This preference is represented by a utility function or more precisely by "an index of primary goods" and this index is supposed to be the same for everyone. However here this identical index is not to be founded on some understanding of the "basic psychological laws" but is part of the agreement in the original position. The identity of the index does not result from some conception of a "human nature" but is agreed upon by representatives of free and equal persons (having incommensurable conceptions of the goods). If this identity may be viewed as a form of fundamentalism, it is a contractual fundamentalism (as opposed to a natural fundamentalism). Here I should quote Rawls again:

> To clarify this contrast, we can write the function which represents interpersonal comparisons in questions of justice made by citizens in the well-ordered society of justice as fairness: $g = f(x_i, \bar{p})$. Here g is the index of primary goods (a real number), f is the function that determines the value of g for individual i, and x_i is the vector of primary goods held or enjoyed by individual i. The vector y, which in $w = u(x, y)$ includes entries for all features of the person which may affect satisfaction, is here replaced by a constant vector $\bar{p}$ which has entries only for the characteristics of free and equal moral persons presumed to be fully cooperating members of society over a complete life. This vector is constant since all citizens are taken to possess these features to the minimum sufficient degree. Thus the same function holds for all citizens and interpersonal comparisons are made accordingly. The difference between the functions f and u expresses the fact that in justice as fairness individuals'

different final ends and desires, and their greater or less capacities for satisfaction, play no role in determining the justice of the basic structure. They do not enter into $\bar{p}$. (Rawls [1982], p. 178, fn. 21)

In the terminology of the preceding subsection, $\bar{p}$ would be a subvector of p, common to every individual i, which characterizes the basic common subjective attitude making social unity possible.

Once it is assumed that the parties in the original position will agree on a common index of primary goods, Rawls is led to argue in favor of an explicit rule, which is the negotiated solution to this particular form of the social choice problem and which has to be defined for every such index. This rule is described by a list of three principles – the principles of justice – which should be taken in hierarchical order. The first is a *principle of equal liberty*: the basic liberties should be distributed equally and the (equal) share of every individual should be the largest possible. The second principle in this hierarchy is a *principle of equal opportunity*: the offices and positions considered should be fairly and equally open to every individual. These first two principles take care, respectively, of the distribution of the two first categories of primary goods (see (a) and (b) above). The third and last principles in this hierarchy is the already mentioned *difference principle*, which is to be applied to all the remaining primary goods: the allocation of all these should be to the greatest benefit of the least advantaged.

This will conclude our sketchy presentation of Rawls's fundamental justification for social unity. In contrast to Harsanyi's natural fundamentalism, which leads to some form of pure utilitarianism, this contractual fundamentalism leads to some rule of the maximin type. However Rawls's (nonaxiomatic) approach, by introducing a hierarchy of principles, takes explicitly into account the nature of the social alternatives which are defined in terms of primary goods. From the viewpoint of social choice theory, this may be taken again as a strong indication of the need to develop axiomatics for welfare models that would essentially diverge from a universal application of welfarism.

REFERENCES

Armstrong, W. E. [1951]. "Utility and the Theory of Welfare." *Oxford Economic Papers*, 3:257–271.

Arrow, K. J. [1963] (1st ed. [1951]). *Social Choice and Individual Values*, 2nd ed. New Haven, Conn.: Yale University Press.

Arrow, K. J. [1973a]. "Some Ordinalist Utilitarian Notes on Rawls's Theory of Justice." *Journal of Philosophy*, 70(9).

Arrow, K. J. [1973b]. "Rawls's Principle of Just Saving." *The Swedish Journal of Economics*, 75:323–335.

Arrow, K. J. [1977]. "Extended Sympathy and the Possibility of Social Choice." *American Economic Review*, 67(1).

Atkinson, A. B. [1970]. "On the Measurement of Inequality." *Journal of Economic Theory*, 2:244–263.

Barone, E. [1935]. "The Ministry of Production in the Collectivist State." in *Collective Economic Planning*, edited by F. A. von Hayek London: Routledge.

Baumol, W. J. [1946]. "Community Indifference." *Review of Economic Studies*, 14:44–48.

Bentham, J. [1789]. *An Introduction to the Principle of Morals and Legislation*. Payne, 1789. Oxford: Clarendon Press, 1907.

Bergson, A. [1938]. "A Reformulation of Certain Aspects of Welfare Economics." *Quarterly Journal of Economics*, 52:310–334.

Blackorby, C., and D. Donaldson [1978]. "Measures of Relative Equality and Their Meaning in Terms of Social Welfare." *Journal of Economic Theory*, 18:59–80.

Blackorby, C., and D. Donaldson [1980]. "A Theoretical Treatment of Indices of Absolute Inequality." *International Economic Review*, 21(1):107–136.

Blackorby, C., and D. Donaldson [1982]. "Ratio-Scale and Translation-Scale Full Interpersonal Comparability without Domain Restrictions: Admissible Social-Evaluation Functions." *International Economic Review*, 23(2):249–268.

Blackorby, C., D. Donaldson, and J. A. Weymark [1980]. "On John Harsanyi's Defences of Utilitarianism." CORE Discussion Paper 8013, Université Catholique de Louvain.

Blackorby, C., D. Donaldson, and J. A. Weymark [1984]. "Social Choice with Interpersonal Utility Comparisons: A Diagrammatic Introduction." *International Economic Review*, 25(2):327–356.

Blackwell, D., and M. A. Girshick [1954]. *Theory of Games and Statistical Decisions*. New York: Wiley.

Blau, J. H. [1976]. "Neutrality, Monotonicity and the Right of Veto: A Comment." *Econometrica*, 44:603.

Border, K. C. [1983]. "Social Welfare Functions for Economic Environments with and without the Pareto Principle." *Journal of Economic Theory*, 29:205–216.

Bordes, G. [1980]. "Individualisme, ordinalisme et bien-être social." Discussion Paper of the Laboratoire d'analyse et de recherche économiques, Faculté des Sciences économiques, Université de Bordeaux I.

Dahl, R. A. [1956]. *A Preface to Democratic Theory*. Chicago: University of Chicago Press.

Dalton, H. [1920]. "The Measurement of the Inequality of Incomes." *Economic Journal*, 30.

Dasgupta, P. [1974]. "On Some Problems Arising from Professor Rawls' Conception of Distributive Justice." *Theory and Decision*, 4:225–344.

d'Aspremont, C., and L. Gevers [1977]. "Equity and the Informational Basis of Collective Choice." *Review of Economic Studies*, 44:199–209.

de Borda, J. C. [1781]. "Mémoire sur les élections au scrutin." *Mémoires de l'Académie Royale des Sciences* (English translation by A. de Grazia, Isis, 1953).

Debreu, G. [1960]. "Topological Methods in Cardinal Utility Theory." in *Mathematical Methods in the Social Sciences*. edited by K. J. Arrow, S. Karlin, and

P. Suppes. Stanford, Calif.: Stanford University Press.

Deschamps, R., and L. Gevers [1977]. "Separability, Risk-Bearing and Social Welfare Judgments." *European Economic Review*, *10*:77−94.

Deschamps, R., and L. Gevers [1978]. "Leximin and Utilitarian Rules: A Joint Characterization." *Journal of Economic Theory*, *17*:143−163.

Donaldson, D., and J. A. Weymark [1980]. "A Single-Parameter Generalization of the Gini Indices of Inequality." *Journal of Economic Theory*, *22*(1):67−86.

Edgeworth, F. Y. [1881]. *Mathematical Psychics*. London: Kegan Paul: 1881; New York: A. M. Kelly, 1967.

Eichhorn, W. [1978]. *Functional Equations in Economics*. Reading, Mass.: Addison-Wesley.

Farrell, M. J. [1976]. "Liberalism in the Theory of Social Choice." *Review of Economic Studies*, *43*:3−10.

Fisher, I. [1927]. "A Statistical Method for Measuring Marginal Utility and Testing the Justice of a Progressive Income Tax," in *Economic Essays in Honor of J. B. Clark*. New York: Macmillan.

Fleming, M. [1952]. "A Cardinal Concept of Welfare." *The Quarterly Journal of Economics*, *66*:366−384.

Frisch, R. [1932]. *New Methods of Measuring Marginal Utility*. Tubingen: J. C. B. Mohr.

Gevers, L. [1979]. "On Interpersonal Comparability and Social Welfare Orderings." *Econometrica*, *47*:75−89.

Gibbard, A. [1974]. "A Pareto-consistent Libertarian Claim." *Journal of Economic Theory*, *7*:388−410.

Goodman, L. A., and H. Markovitz [1952]. "Social Welfare Function Based on Individual Rankings," *American Journal of Sociology*, *58*:257−262.

Graaff, J. de V. [1957]. *Theoretical Welfare Economics*. Cambridge: Cambridge University Press.

Guha, A.S. [1972]. "Neutrality, Monotonicity and the Right of Veto." *Econometrica*, *40*:821−826.

Guilbaud, G.-Th. [1952]. "Les théories de l'intérêt général et le problème logique de l'agrégation." *Economie Appliquée, 5*.

Hammond, P. J. [1976a], "Equity, Arrow's Conditions and Rawls' Difference Principle." *Econometrica*, *44*:793−804.

Hammond, P. J. [1976b]. "Why Ethical Measures of Inequality Need Interpersonal Comparisons", *Theory and Decision*, *7*:263−274.

Hammond, P. J. [1979]. "Equity in Two Person Situations: Some Consequences." *Econometrica*, *47*:1127−1135.

Harsanyi, J. C. [1953]. "Cardinal Utility in Welfare Economics and in the Theory of Risk-Taking." *Journal of Political Economy*, *61*:434−435.

Harsanyi, J. C. [1955]. "Cardinal Welfare, Individualistic Ethics and Interpersonal Comparisons of Utility." *Journal of Political Economy*, *63*.

Harsanyi, J. C. [1976]. *Essays on Ethics, Social Behavior and Scientific Explanation*. Dordrecht, Holland: D. Reidel.

Harsanyi, J. C. [1977]. *Rational Behavior and Bargaining Equilibrium in Games and Social Situations*. Cambridge: Cambridge University Press.

Hicks, J. R. [1939]. "Foundations of Welfare Economics." *Economic Journal*, *49*:696−712.

Hotelling, H. [1938]. "The General Welfare in Relation to Problems of Taxation and of Railway and Utility Rates." *Econometrica*, *6*:242−269.

Hutcheson, F. [1725]. *An Inquiry Concerning Moral Good and Evil*.

Kahneman, D., and A. Tversky [1979]. "Prospect Theory: An Analysis of Decision under Risk." *Econometrica*, *47*(2).

Kalai, E., E. Muller, and M. Satterthwaite [1979]. "Social Welfare Functions when Preferences are Convex, Strictly Monotonic and Continuous." *Public Choice*, *34*:87–97.

Kaldor, N. [1939]. "Welfare Propositions in Economics." *Economic Journal*, *49*.

Kelly, J. S. [1976]. "Rights Exercising and a Pareto-consistent Libertarian Claim." *Journal of Economic Theory*, *13*:138–153.

Kemp, M. C., and Y. K. Ng [1976]. "On the Existence of Social Welfare Functions, Social Orderings, and Social Decision Functions." *Economica*, *43*:59–66.

Kemp, M. C., and Y. K. Ng [1977]. "More on Social Welfare Functions: The Incompatibility of Individualism with Ordinalism." *Economica*, *44*:89–90.

Kolm, S. C. [1969]. "The Optimum Production of Social Justice," in *Public Economics*, edited by J. Margolis and H. Guitton. London: Macmillan.

Kolm, S. C. [1972]. *Justice et équité*. Paris: CNRS.

Kolm, S. C. [1976a,b]. "Unequal Inequalities 'I' and 'II' ". *Journal of Economic Theory*, *12*:416–442, and *13*:82–111.

Lerner, A. P. [1934a]. "The Concept of Monopoly and the Measure of Monopoly Power." *Review of Economic Studies*, *1*:157–175.

Lerner, A. P. [1934b]. "Economic Theory and Socialist Economy." *Review of Economic Studies*: *2*:51–61.

Lerner, A. P. [1944]. *The Economics of Control*. New York: Macmillan.

Little, I. M. D. [1952]. "Social Choice and Individual Values." *Journal of Political Economy*, *60*:422–432.

Little, I. M. D. [1957]. *A Critique of Welfare Economics*. (1st ed. [1950]). Oxford: Clarendon Press.

Luce, R. D., and H. Raiffa [1957]. *Games and Decisions*. New York: Wiley.

Maskin, E. [1978]. "A Theorem on Utilitarianism." *Review of Economic Studies*, *45*:93–96.

May, K. O. [1952]. "A Set of Independent Necessary and Sufficient Conditions for Simple Majority Decision." *Econometrica*, *20*:680–684.

Milnor, J. [1954]. "Games against Nature" in *Decision Processes*, edited by R. M. Thrall, C. H. Coombs, and R. L. Davis. New York: John Wiley.

Mirrlees, J. A. [1982]. "The Economic Uses of Utilitarianism" in *Utilitarianism and Beyond*, edited by A. Sen and B. Williams. Cambridge: Cambridge University Press Paris: la Maison des Sciences de l'Homme.

Moulin, H. [1982]. "Choix Social cardinal: résultats récents." Discussion Paper, Laboratoire d'Econométrie de l'Ecole Polytechnique, Paris.

Myerson, R. B. [1978]. "Linearity, Concavity and Scale Invariance in Social Choice Functions." Discussion Paper no. 321, Graduate School of Management, Northwestern University, Evanston, Ill.

Nash, J. F. [1950]. "The Bargaining Problem." *Econometrica*, *18*:155–162.

Ng, Y. K. [1975]. "Bentham or Bergson? Finite Sensibility, Utility Functions and Social Welfare Functions," *Review of Economic Studies*, *42*(4): 545–569.

Nozick, R. [1974]. *Anarchy, State and Utopia*. Oxford: Blackwell.

Pareto, V. [1909]. *Manuel d'Economie Politique*, (1st ed. [1897]). Paris: Giard.

Parks, R. P. [1976]. "An Impossibility Theorem for Fixed Preferences: A Dictatorial Bergson–Samuelson Welfare Function." *Review of Economic Studies*, *43*:447–450.

Pattanaik, P. K. [1968]. "Risk, Impersonality, and the Social Welfare Function." *Journal of Political Economy*, 76:1152−1169.

Pazner, E. A. [1979]. "Equity, Nonfeasible Alternatives and Social Choice: A Reconsideration of the Concept of Social Welfare." in *Aggregation and Revelation of Preferences*, edited by J. J. Laffont. Amsterdam: North Holland.

Pazner, E. A., and D. Schmeidler [1976]. "Social Contract Theory and Ordinal Distributive Equity." *Journal of Public Economics*, 5:261−268.

Pigou, A. C. [1920] (last reprint [1962]). *The Economics of Welfare*. London: Macmillan.

Pollak, R. A. [1979]. "Bergson-Samuelson Social Welfare Functions and the Theory of Social Choice." *The Quarterly Journal of Economics*:73−90.

Rawls, J. [1972]. *A Theory of Justice*. Oxford: Clarendon Press.

Rawls, J. [1980]. "Kantian Constructivism in Moral Theory. Rational and Full Autonomy." *The Journal of Philosophy*, 77(9):515−572.

Rawls, J. [1982]. "Social Unity and Primary Goods." in *Utilitarianism and Beyond*, edited by A. Sen and B. Williams. Cambridge: Cambridge University Press. Paris: la Maison des Sciences de l'Homme.

Robbins, L. [1932]. *An Essay on the Nature and Significance of Economic Science*. London: Macmillan.

Roberts, K. W. S. [1977]. *Welfare Theoretic Social Choice*. unpublished Ph.D. Thesis, Oxford University.

Roberts, K. W. S. [1980a]. "Possibility Theorems with Interpersonally Comparable Welfare Levels," *Review of Economic Studies*, 47:409−420.

Roberts, K. W. S. [1980b]. "Interpersonal Comparability and Social Choice Theory." *Review of Economic Studies*, 47:421−439.

Roberts, K. W. S. [1980c]. "Social Choice Theory: The Single-profile and Multi-profile Approaches." *Review of Economic Studies*, 47:441−450.

Rothenberg, J. [1961]. *The Measurement of Social Welfare*. Englewood Cliffs, N.J.: Prentice-Hall.

Rubinstein, A. [1979]. "The Single Profile Analogues to Multi Profile Theorems: Mathematical Logic's Approach." Discussion Paper of the International Centre for Economics and Related Disciplines, London School of Economics.

Samuelson, P. A. [1947]. *Foundations of Economic Analysis*. Cambridge, Mass.: Harvard University Press.

Samuelson, P. A. [1967]. "Arrow's Mathematical Politics." in *Human Values and Economic Policy: A Symposium*, edited by S. Hook. New York: New York University Press.

Samuelson, P. A. [1977]. "Reaffirming the Existence of 'Reasonable' Bergson−Samuelson Social Welfare Functions." *Economica*, 44:81−88.

Scitovsky, T. [1941]. "A Note on Welfare Propositions in Economics." *Review of Economic Studies*, 9:77−88.

Scitovsky, T. [1942]. "A Reconsideration of the Theory of Tariffs." *Review of Economic Studies*, 9:89−110.

Seidl, C. [1975]. "On Liberal Values." *Zeitschrift für Nationalökonomie*, 35:257−292.

Sen, A. K. [1970]. *Collective Choice and Social Welfare*. San Francisco: Holden-Day.

Sen, A. K. [1973]. *On Economic Inequality*. Oxford: Clarendon Press; and New York: Norton.

Sen, A. K. [1974a]. "Informational Bases of Alternative Welfare Approaches:

Aggregation and Income Distribution." *Journal of Public Economics*, *3*: 387–403.

Sen, A. K. [1974b]. "Rawls versus Bentham: An Axiomatic Examination of the Pure Distribution Problem." *Theory and Decision*:300–309.

Sen, A. K. [1976a]. "Liberty, Unanimity and Rights." *Economica*, *43*:217–245.

Sen, A. K. [1976b]. "Welfare Inequalities and Rawlsian Axiomatics." *Theory and Decision*, 7:243–262.

Sen, A. K. [1977]. "On Weights and Measures: Informational Constraints in Social Welfare Analysis." *Econometrica*, *45*:1539–1572.

Sen, A. K. [1979a]. "Utilitarianism and Welfarism." *The Journal of Philosophy*, 76(9):463–489.

Sen, A. K. [1979b]. "Social Choice Theory." forthcoming in *Handbook of Mathematical Economics*, edited by K. J. Arrow and M. Intriligator. Amsterdam: North-Holland.

Sen, A. K. [1979c]. "Personal Utilities and Public Judgments: or What's Wrong with Welfare Economics?" *The Economic Journal* 89:537–558.

Sen, A. K., and B. Williams (eds.) [1982]. *Utilitarianism and Beyond*. Cambridge: Cambridge University Press. Paris: La Maison des Sciences de l'Homme.

Sidgwick, H. [1907]. *The Methods of Ethics*. London: Macmillan.

Simon, J. L. [1974]. "Interpersonal Welfare Comparisons Can Be Made – and Used for Redistribution Decisions." *Kyklos*, 27:63–99.

Solow, R. M. [1974]. "Intergenerational Equity and Exhaustible Resources." *Review of Economic Studies*, Symposium.

Stigler, G. J. [1943]. "A Note on the New Welfare Economics." *American Economic Review*, 30.

Strasnick, S. L. [1975]. "Preference Priority and the Maximization of Social Welfare." Unpublished Ph.D. Dissertation, Harvard University, Cambridge, Mass.

Strasnick, S. L. [1976a]. "Social Choice and the Derivation of Rawls's Difference Principle." *The Journal of Philosophy*, 73(4):85–99.

Strasnick, S. L. [1976b]. "The Problem of Social Choice: Arrow to Rawls." *Philosophy and Public Affairs*, 5:241–273.

Suzumura, K. [1980]. "Liberal Paradox and the Voluntary Exchange of Rights Exercising." *Journal of Economic Theory*, 22:407–422.

Suppes, P. [1966]. "Some Formal Models of Grading Principles." *Synthese*, 6:284–306.

Vickrey, W. [1945]. "Measuring Marginal Utility by Reactions to Risk." *Econometrica*, *13*:319–333.

Vickrey, W. [1960]. "Utility, Strategy, and Social Decision Rules." *The Quarterly Journal of Economics*, 74(4):507–535.

von Neumann, J., and O. Morgenstern [1947]. *Theory of Games and Economic Behavior*. (1st ed. [1944]). Princeton, N.J.: Princeton University Press.

Wilson, R. [1972]. "Social Choice Theory without the Pareto Principle." *Journal of Economic Theory*, 5:478–486.

Yaari, M. E. [1981]. "Rawls, Edgeworth, Shapley, Nash: Theories of Distributive Justice Re-examined." *Journal of Economic Theory*, 24:1–39.

Young, H. P. [1974]. "An Axiomatization of Borda's Rule." *Journal of Economic Theory*, 9:52–53.

CHAPTER 3

Solutions to the bargaining problem

Ehud Kalai

1   Motivation and definition of the problem

The bargaining problem has received considerable attention over the last several years. New axiomatic solutions have emerged and new conditions, testing the performance of these solutions, have been suggested and studied. The problem is one of a choice of a unique feasible alternative by a group of people with possibly conflicting preferences in a cooperative environment. It may be viewed as a theory of consensus, because when it is applied it is often assumed that a final choice can be made if and only if every member of the group supports this choice.

Because this theory deals with the aggregation of peoples' preferences over a set of feasible alternatives, it bears close similarities to theories of social choice and the design of social welfare functions. However, there are two fundamental differences that enable us to reach a rich variety of positive results.

An important assumption made in bargaining theory that distinguishes it from other social choice theories is that there is a threat, or a disagreement, outcome. This is the outcome that would result if the bargainers fail to reach agreement. The existence of such an outcome makes the analysis of such situations easier because it enables us to start with a reference point from which comparisons of utility gains may be considered.

In bargaining theory, as in much of cooperative game theory, the physical outcomes involved in the bargaining process are ignored and only the resulting cardinal utility combinations of the players are considered. In other words the theory assumes that any two bargaining situations are the same if they yield the same set of feasible utility combinations.

A large portion of the literature dealing with this theory concentrates on the case in which the group of players consists of only two members.

77

For groups larger than two, this theory is irrelevant in many instances, since partial consensus, reached by intermediary coalitions (proper subsets of the entire group), may substantially effect the outcome chosen by the group as a whole. Bargaining theory deals with environments in which these partial gains are irrelevant or do not exist. However, the case of two individuals and the cases involving no profitable intermediary coalitions are important cases to solve and to gain intuition from before addressing the very general problem of solving general cooperative games. These games do allow and consider intermediary coalitions.

In this chapter we survey some of the axiomatic solutions that have been suggested in this theory and some of their properties. No attempt is made here for this survey to be complete, and some major contributions have been left out. We also made no attempt to give the strongest mathematical versions of the theorems that are presented. Our goal is to keep the presentation simple and unified, emphasizing more the later contributions. For more comprehensive coverage of this and related literature, the reader is referred to Luce and Raiffa [1957], Owen [1968], Schelling [1960], Harsanyi [1977], Schmitz [1977], Binmore [1980]. A very comprehensive coverage of the literature can be found in Roth [1979a]. For some references and results about experimental studies in bargaining we refer the reader to Rapoport and Perner [1974], Hoggatt et al. [1978], Nydegger and Owen [1975], O'Neill [1976], Heckathorn [1978], and Roth and Malouf [1979].

Some recent axiomatic generalizations of bargaining problem solutions to general cooperative games can be found in Aumann [forthcoming], Hart [1983] and Kalai and Samet [1985]. Generalizations to bargaining problems involving incomplete information can be found in Myerson [1984].

Formally we describe a two-person bargaining game by a pair (d, S) where $d \in \mathbb{R}^2$ (the two-dimensional Euclidean space) and $S \subseteq \mathbb{R}^2$. We assume that the pair (d, S) satisfies the following conditions:

1. $d \in S$.
2. S is compact and convex.
3. There is at least one $u \in S$ with $u > d$ ($u_i > d_i$ for $i = 1, 2$).

We let B be the set of all bargaining games satisfying these three conditions.

The intuitive interpretation of such a pair (d, S) is the following. The elements of S, the *feasible set*, are the utility pairs that the players can receive under cooperation if they reach a unanimous agreement. The *disagreement point* d (sometimes referred to as threat point or status quo point) is the utility pair that the players have for the state in which "negotiations have failed, proceed without attempting to reach unanimity."

A second interpretation is that S consists of all the compromises that an arbitrator deciding the case may choose where d stands for the utilities outcome of the situation if the arbitrator was not involved.

More precise interpretations of S and of d depend on the particular situation that is being modeled. For example, when the two bargainers represent a seller and a buyer of a certain item we may let d stand for the utilities of no exchange. S then represents all the feasible utilities that arise from all the possible exchanges between them.

Often the bargaining game is used to convert a noncooperative two-person strategic form game into a cooperative one. We then let S be the convex hull of all the utility pairs that may be obtained by correlating strategies in the noncooperative game where each of the two players commits himself to play his specific part of the correlated strategy. The disagreement point then is the pair of utilities resulting from non-cooperative (without commitment) private play, for example, a prespecified Nash equilibrium of the game.

A third type of application is for making social choices. Here we consider an organization that has to choose one state out of many feasible states. For example, S may represent the utilities arising from different agendas for running the organization, or S may represent utilities of different choices of public goods, or S may represent the individual utilities from different choices of a president, and so on. A certain state is the current one, and we let d represent the utilities of the participants for being in this state. In this case we may think of d as being a status quo point. S then represents the convex hull of the utility combinations resulting from all feasible choices.

The assumption that S is convex is reasonable in many applications and certainly when the players' utilities are of the von Neumann–Morgenstern (V–M) type. Convexity follows if we assume that randomizing among feasible alternatives is also a feasible choice since the V–M utilities are linear in probabilities.

There are two underlying questions motivating the study of solutions to the bargaining problem. The first type of a solution is a predictive one and attempts to answer the question of which feasible outcome would rational players arrive at on their own if commitments and signing contracts were possible. A second type of a solution is one that attempts to answer the question of which outcome should an arbitrator arbitrating the situation choose.

Our proposed solutions will be arrived at through axioms stating properties that a solution should satisfy. Thus, the relevancy of the various solutions to the question of predicting outcomes and to the question of arbitration may be tested by the reader through testing the underlying axioms against his or her intuition.

This axiomatic approach proves to be very useful, since it succeeds in choosing a unique solution through a small number of simple conditions. It saves us from having to get involved in the complicated process of bargaining that the players may be going through. Whatever this process is, the players will end up at our solution if our axioms are correct for their behavior. In the case of arbitration, the proposed axioms give the arbitrator a rationale on which to base a decision.

Given a bargaining pair (d, S) and a point $u \in \mathbb{R}^2$ we say that u is *individually rational* if $u \geq d$ ($u_i \geq d_i$ for $i = 1, 2$). u is *strongly individually rational* if $u > d$. We say that u is *Pareto optimal* if $u \in S$ and for every $w \in S$ if $w \geq u$ then $w = u$. We say that u is *weakly Pareto optimal* if for every $w \in S$, $w \not> u$.

A *solution* is a function $f: B \rightarrow \mathbb{R}^2$ such that for every $(d, S) \in B$, $f(d, S) \in S$.

2   Scale-independent solutions

The first type of solutions we consider are ones that do not depend on the scales of the utility functions that the players use to represent their preferences. The motivation for studying scale-independent solutions stems from an implicit assumption that the utilities under consideration are of the von Neumann−Morgenstern type. Since V−M utilities are determined only up to a choice of an affine scale if our solutions were scale dependent, then they may vary arbitrarily by the arbitrary choices of scales made to represent the problem by the individuals. In later sections I will bring forth criticism of this condition.

An *affine transformation of player* 1's *utility* is a function $T_1: \mathbb{R}^2 \rightarrow \mathbb{R}^2$ such that for some $a > 0$ and $b \in \mathbb{R}$, $T_1(u_1, u_2) = (au_1 + b, u_2)$. We similarly define affine transformations of player 2's utility.

Given a bargaining pair $(d, S) \in B$ and an affine transformation of player 1's utility T_1 we define $T_1(d, S) = (T_1(d), T_1(S))$, where $T_1(S) = \{T_1(u_1, u_2):$ for some $(u_1, u_2) \in S\}$. Similarly we define $T_2(d, S)$ for an affine transformation of player 2's utility. Thus $T_i(d, S)$ is a new bargaining pair that may be viewed as the old bargaining pair (d, S) but represented by a different utility scale of player i.

We say that a solution to the bargaining problem is *invariant under affine transformations of utility scale* if for every player i, for every bargaining pair (d, S), and for every affine transformation of utility scale T_i we have

$$T_i(f(d, S)) = f(T_i(d, S)).$$

If in the preceding definition we consider only T_i's for which $a = 1$ then we say that the solution *is invariant under additive transformations in utility scales*. If we consider only T_i's for which $b = 0$, then we say that the solution *is invariant under multiplicative transformations in utility scales*. Clearly a solution is invariant under affine transformations of utility scales if and only if it is invariant under both additive and multiplicative transformations.

A second condition that we may want to impose on a solution is that it always chooses a Pareto-optimal outcome. We say that a solution f is *(weakly) Pareto optimal* if for every $(d, S) \in B$, $f(d, S)$ is (respectively weakly) Pareto optimal. A solution f is (strongly) *individually rational* if for every $(d, S) \in B$, $f(d, S)$ is (respectively strongly) individually rational in S relative to d.

The next condition is one of symmetry. This condition guarantees that the outcome does not depend on the labeling of the players. Consider a bargaining pair (d, S) and its solution $f(d, S)$. Suppose we now change our modeling of the bargaining situation by calling player 1 player 2 and calling player 2 player 1. Since it is basically the same problem, we expect that the players with their new labeling receive the same utility as they did with their old labeling.

Formally let $\pi\colon \mathbb{R}^2 \to \mathbb{R}^2$ $\pi(x, y) = (y, x)$. A solution f is called *symmetric*[1] if for every $(d, S) \in B$ $\pi(f(d, S)) = f(\pi(d), \pi(S))$ where $\pi(S) = \{\pi(u)\colon u \in S\}$.

Another implication of the symmetry condition, to be discussed later, is that all the relevant characteristics of the two players are described by d and S and that only information which is described by this pair (d, S) may cause us to discriminate between them. In particular if (d, S) is a symmetric problem (that is, $d_1 = d_2$) and for every $(u_1, u_2) \in S$ we have $(u_2, u_1) \in S$, then $f_1(d, S)$ must equal to $f_2(d, S)$.

2.1   *The Nash solution*

The *Nash solution* is the function $\eta\colon B \to \mathbb{R}^2$, which selects the individually rational utility pair with a maximal *Nash product*, $(u_1 - d_1)$ $(u_2 - d_2)$. Formally for every bargaining pair (d, S), $\eta(d, S)$ is the feasible individually rational utility pair with the property that for every individually rational feasible utility pair $(w_1, w_2) \in S$

---

[1] Some authors refer to this condition as anonymity. They use the term *symmetry* for solutions that choose a symmetric outcome on symmetric problems.

$$[\eta_1(d, S) - d_1][\eta_2(d, S) - d_2] \geq (w_1 - d_1)(w_2 - d_2).$$

Thus the objective of the Nash solution is to maximize the product of the utility gains of the players. This maximization takes place over the individually rational outcomes. Since the Nash product and its square root attain their maximum at the same point we can also view the objective of the Nash solution as maximizing the geometric average of the utility gains of the bargainers.

It is easy to check that the maximum of the Nash product is attained at a unique point, because the feasible set is convex. Thus $\eta(d, S)$ is a unique feasible point for every bargaining pair $(d, S) \in B$.

Our next objective is to bring forth a rationale underlying the Nash solution. We say that a solution is *independent of irrelevant alternatives* (IIA) if for every two bargaining pairs (d, S) and (d, T) with $S \subseteq T$ if $f(d, T) \in S$ then $f(d, S) = f(d, T)$.

There are two ways to view the IIA condition. Starting with the pair (d, T) and its solution $f(d, T)$, imagine that the feasible set was reduced in size to S yet the solution $f(d, T)$ is still feasible. Then we require that it remains the solution in the smaller set. Thus if $f(d, T)$ was the "best choice" among the alternatives in T, then it is still the best choice among any subset of alternatives containing it.

A mathematically analogous way of viewing the IIA condition is the following. Starting with a feasible set of alternatives S and its solutions $f(d, S)$ and assuming that some new additional alternatives become available, we require that the choice in the new set be either $f(d, S)$, the old choice, or one of the new alternatives. In other words, we do not choose a different alternative among the old ones because of the availability of additional alternatives.

We can now state Nash's [1950] theorem.

Theorem 1: *A solution is Pareto optimal, symmetric, independent of irrelevant alternatives, and independent of affine transformations in utility scales if and only if it is the Nash solution.*

It is easy to see that the Nash solution satisfies these four properties. It is surprising that it is the only solution that satisfies them. Thus if we accept that a solution should satisfy these conditions, we must adopt the Nash solution and only it as our choice.

The axiomatization presented is the main rationalization of the Nash solution. Presented next is a second rationale underlying the Nash solution. Here we consider only one bargaining problem at a time and we do not apply any considerations relating the solution of one bargaining pair to another as is done by the IIA condition in Nash's axiomatization. Thus with this approach we could have defined the solution to one problem without considering a solution as a function of all bargaining pairs.

When the players attempt to compromise on an alternative (u_1, u_2) as the final outcome, two considerations may arise. They may want to maximize the total combined utility gains due to their cooperation and thus maximize the sum of $(u_1 - d_1) + (u_2 - d_2)$. They may also argue for equality and desire to have $u_1 - d_1 = u_2 - d_2$. Immediately two problems come to mind. The first difficulty is that these two different objectives may not lead to the same choice of (u_1, u_2). The second difficulty is that as we have written these objectives they depend on the scale of the utility functions used to represent the players' preferences. The Nash solution turns out to be the unique way to resolve these difficulties. Let (d, S) be any bargaining pair. Can we normalize the players' utilities in such a way that in the normalized utilities we are both maximizing the sum of the utility gains and preserving equality of gains? Formally consider the following problem.

Find $(u_1, u_2) \in S$ such that for some positive real numbers λ_1 and λ_2 we have

1. $\lambda_1(u_1 - d_1) = \lambda_2(u_2 - d_2)$, and
2. $\lambda_1(u_1 - d_1) + \lambda_2(u_2 - d_2) \geq \lambda_1(w_1 - d_1) + \lambda_2(w_2 - d_2)$
    for every $(w_1, w_2) \in S$.

The following theorem of Shapley [1969] answers our question.[2]

Theorem 2: (u_1, u_2) *solves the foregoing problem if and only if* (u_1, u_2) *is the Nash solution of* (d, S).

Because of the IIA condition the Nash solution depends on the feasible set through a neighborhood of the solution only. Formally we say that two problems (d, S) and (d, T) agree in a neighborhood of a point $x \in \mathbb{R}^2$ if there is a neighborhood O of x such that for every $u \in O$, $u \in S$ if and only if $u \in T$. We say that a solution f is *local* if for every $(d, S) \in B$ and for every $(d, T) \in B$ which agrees with (d, S) in a neighborhood of $f(d, S)$, $f(d, T) = f(d, S)$. It is easy to check that the Nash solution is local. Conversely, it can be shown that Theorem 1 is true with the condition that a solution be continuous and local replacing the IIA condition.

The next two solutions successively weaken the dependency of the

---

[2] There have been several generalizations of the Nash solution to general n-person characteristic function games in which this characterization plays a crucial role. An axiomatic generalization of this type was just developed by Aumann [forthcoming].

solution on the neighborhood of only one point. The Kalai–Smorodinsky solution depends crucially on three points in the feasible set and the Maschler–Perles solution depends on the entire Pareto frontier of the individually rational portion of the feasible set.

2.2   *The Kalai–Smorodinsky solution*

For every bargaining pair $(d, S) \in B$ we define the ideal point I of the pair by

$$I_1 = \text{Max } \{u_1\text{: for some } u_2 \in \mathbb{R} \ (u_1, u_2) \text{ is an individually}$$
$$\text{rational feasible point in } (d, S)\}.$$

We define I_2 similarly. The ideal utility levels have the interpretation that they are the most that the players can hope for assuming feasibility and individual rationality of their opponents.

The Kalai–Smorodinsky (KS) solution[3] is the function μ that chooses for every bargaining pair (d, S) the unique Pareto-optimal point (u_1, u_2) with $(u_1 - d_1)/(I_1 - d_1) = (u_2 - d_2)/(I_2 - d_2)$. Thus the players choose the best outcome subject to getting the same proportions of their ideal gains.

We can supply an axiomatic rationale for the KS solution as we did for the Nash solution. Here we would not accept the independence of irrelevant alternatives condition. We adopt instead a condition of individual monotonicity. This condition requires that if the feasible set is changed in favor of one of the players then this player should not end up losing because of it. For every bargaining pair (d, T) we say that u_2 *is a rational demand for player 2* if there is a pair (u_1, u_2) that is feasible and individually rational in (d, S).

We say that the bargaining pair (d, W) *is better for player 1 than* the bargaining pair (d, S) if the rational demands of player 2 are the same in both pairs, and for every such rational demand u_2 we have

$$\sup\{u_1\text{: } (u_1, u_2) \in W\} \geq \sup\{u_1\text{: } (u_1, u_2) \in S\}$$

In other words with every rational demand of his opponent, player 1 can get more in W than in S.

---

[3] There has been some confusion in the literature between this solution and a procedure suggested by Raiffa as an "ad hoc method" to do interpersonal comparisons of utilities for a given game (d, S). One of Raiffa's suggestions in Luce and Raiffa [1957] is to let $b = (b_1, b_2)$ be the highest levels of utilities in S that may be attained individually by the players, and $w = (w_1, w_2)$ be the lowest individual utilities that may occur in S. The players then choose the Pareto-optimal outcome $\bar{u}$ such that the line segment $(d, \bar{u})$ parallels the line segment (w, b).

We say that a solution f is *individually monotonic* for player 1 if whenever (d, W) is better for him than (d, S), then $f_1(d, W) \geq f_1(d, S)$. f is *individually monotonic* if the same property holds for both players.

A rationale behind the individual monotonicity condition is the following. Imagine the players facing a bargaining situation (d, S). Suppose that some additional resources are made available to player 1 as a function of his agreements with 2. Thus a new bargaining pair (d, W) is obtained in which player 1's feasible utility levels are increased. Player 1's outcome should not be made worse off than it was in the old situation.

The Nash solution does not satisfy this individual monotonicity condition. This is an immediate consequence of the following theorem (see Kalai and Smorodinsky [1975]).

Theorem 3: *A solution is symmetric, Pareto optimal, invariant under affine transformations of utility scale, and individually monotonic if and only if it is the Kalai–Smorodinsky solution.*

2.3 The Maschler–Perles solution

In this section we restrict our attention to a subset $B_0 \subseteq B$ of bargaining pairs $(d, S) \in B$ that satisfy the following additional properties.

1. For every $x \in S$, $x \geq d$; that is, S consists only of individually rational outcomes.
2. *Free disposal of utility*, if $x \in S$ and $d \leq y \leq x$ then $y \in S$.
3. *Existence of small utility transfers*, if $d < (u_1, u_2) \in S$, then there is a pair $(v_1, v_2) \in S$ with $v_1 > u_1$ and there is a pair $(w_1, w_2) \in S$ with $w_2 > u_2$.

Conditions 1 and 2 are self-explanatory. Condition 3 requires that for every feasible utility allocation that assigns both players positive gains, each one of the players can be made better off by some small amount (possibly at the expense of his opponent). This could be accomplished for example by any small transfer of money from one player to the other. This condition is also equivalent to the strong Pareto boundary being the same as the weak Pareto boundary of S. We denote this boundary by ∂S.

Consider a bargaining pair $(d, S) \in B_0$ and let $p = p(d, S) = (d_1, I_2(d, S))$ and $q = q(d, S) = (I_1(d, S), d_2)$, where I is the ideal point defined in the previous section. (See Figure 1.) The Maschler–Perles (MP) solution (see Perles and Maschler [1980]) is the unique point ϕ that satisfies

$$\int_p^\phi \sqrt{-du_1 du_2} = \int_\phi^q \sqrt{-du_1 du_2}$$

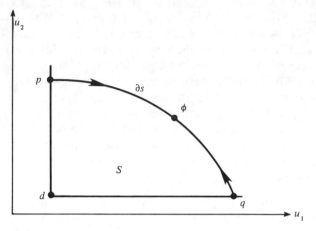

Figure 1

Where these are the line integrals taken along the corresponding arcs of ∂S.

Perles and Maschler propose two intuitive procedures that yield their solution.

Procedure 1: We imagine two points moving toward each other on ∂S starting from p and q, respectively. Each point moves in such a way that the products of its velocities in the u_1 and u_2 directions is a constant, say -1. ϕ is the point on the boundary where the two points meet. The integrals are the traveling time until the points meet.

Procedure 2: The players start from d on a continuous path that would lead them to ϕ. Each point on the path may be thought of as an intermediary agreement. These intermediary agreements preserve the balance of power in the following sense. If τ is on the path and we consider the new bargaining problem (τ, S), its outcome would also be ϕ. Consider a point τ on this status quo path and the two points v and w described by Figure 2. We let

$$t_1(v) = \sup \left\{ \frac{u_1 - v_1}{v_2 - u_2} : u \in S \text{ and } u_1 > v_1 \right\}.$$

$$t_2(w) = \sup \left\{ \frac{u_2 - w_2}{w_1 - u_1} : u \in S \text{ and } u_2 > w_2 \right\}.$$

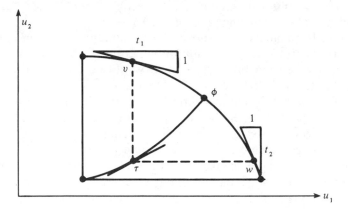

Figure 2

Notice that by the convexity of S it follows that the sup in the definition of t_1 is obtained as $u \to v$. Thus t_1 is the local rate of utility gain of player 1 per unit of utility loss of 2 at v. In other words t_1 may be thought of as the local ratio of utility transfers at v. t_2 has the symmetric interpretation. The status quo path turns out to have the property that at every such τ its slope is $(t_2/t_1)^{1/2}$. Thus along the status quo path the players' instantaneous ratio of utility gains equals the square root of the ratio of their per unit instantaneous exchanges at w and v.

The main rationale behind the MP solution comes from its axiomatic characterization. We say that a solution f is *superadditive* (see Myerson [1981]) if for every two bargaining pairs $(d, S), (d, T) \in B_0$ and for every $\lambda, 0 \le \lambda \le 1$,

$$f(d, \lambda S + (1 - \lambda)T) \ge \lambda f(d, S) + (1 - \lambda) f(d, T),$$

where

$$\lambda S + (1 - \lambda)T = \{\lambda u + (1 - \lambda)v : u \in S, v \in T\}.$$

The necessity of the superadditivity stems from the following argument. Suppose there is uncertainty about the bargaining problem to be played. For example it may be the case that a lottery is about to be performed in a way that with probability λ (d, S) will be played, and with probability $1 - \lambda$ (d, T) will be played. Before the lottery is performed, the players can make conditional agreement on what to choose in S and T under each of the two outcomes. If the players are risk neutral in the utilities (as is the case of von Neumann–Morgenstern) then their set of feasible utilities obtained by conditional agreements is exactly $\lambda S + (1 - \lambda)T$, and the bargaining problem that they face is $(d, \lambda S + (1 - \lambda)T)$.

On the other hand if they do not agree on conditional outcomes before the lottery is performed, then with probability λ, the outcome would be $f(d, S)$ and with probability $(1 - \lambda)$, it would be $f(d, T)$. Thus their expected outcome is $\lambda f(d, S) + (1 - \lambda)f(d, T)$.

It is a reasonable game-theoretic assumption that if binding agreements are possible, then binding conditional agreements should also be possible in a cooperative environment. Agreeing not to agree until after the lottery is performed is another feasible agreement. This may be thought of as the disagreement state at the stage prior to the performance of the lottery. Thus individual rationality would require that the outcome of the bargaining process at this stage should assign each player a utility not smaller than this expected utility outcome without an agreement at this stage. This is precisely the requirement of superadditivity.

A solution is *continuous in feasible sets* if for every $(d, S) \in B_0$ and every sequence $\{(d, S^i)\}_{i=1}^{\infty}$ of bargaining problems in B_0 if $S^i \to S$ in the Hansdorff metric then $f(d, S^i) \to f(d, S)$.

Theorem 4: *A solution defined on B_0 is symmetric, Pareto optimal, invariant under affine transformations of utility scales, superadditive, and continuous if and only if it is the Maschler–Perles solution.*

3   Scale-dependent solutions

The scale-independent condition used in the previous section is very appealing. The argument there is that it overcomes the difficulty presented by the indeterminacy of the scale in $V-M$ utility. However, while it accomplishes this task it brings about some other difficulties that make us question its validity as an undisputed axiom.

Consider for example the two bargainers 1 and 2 facing the following four possible allocations of money: ($0, $0), ($10, $0), ($0, $10), and ($0, $1,000). We assume that both bargainers are selfish (their utility for these allocations depend only on their own component) and that they have a monotonically increasing utility for money. We also assume for simplicity that their utility functions have been normalized so that for $i = 1, 2$, $u_i(\$0) = 0$ and $u_i(\$10) = 1$.

Now we will consider two bargaining pairs A and B. In both pairs the disagreement outcome is the ($0, $0) allocation resulting in the utility combination $(0,0)$. In A the feasible set consists of all the lotteries among the three outcomes ($0, $0), ($10, $0), and ($0, $10). In B the feasible set consists of all the lotteries between the three outcomes ($0, $0),

($10, $0), and ($0, $1,000). Thus the only difference between the two bargaining situations is that in B the alternative that is most attractive for player 2 was made much more attractive. Formally

$$A = [(0, 0), \text{Convex Hull } (\{(0, 0), (1, 0), (0, 1)\})].$$

$$B = [(0, 0), \text{Convex Hull } (\{(0, 0), (1, 0), (0, u_2(\$1000))\})].$$

We observe that the scale of player 2's utility can be changed by representing his utility with the function $w_2 = u_2/u_2(\$1,000)$. Then B is described by the bargaining pair

$$[(0, 0), \text{Convex Hull } (\{(0, 0), (1, 0), (0, 1)\})]$$

Thus, with the new scale of player 2's utility, B becomes identical to A. It follows from the axiom of invariance of utility scale that whatever lottery is the solution for A it should also be the solution for B. So for example if in A the players agree on an equal probability lottery between the two outcomes (0, $10) and ($10, 0), then by the scale-invariance axiom they must also agree on an equal probability lottery between the two outcomes (0, $1,000) and ($10, 0) in B.

It is not "axiomatically" obvious to us that these two situations are identical and would or should yield the same outcome. While an equal probability lottery is probably reasonable in A (especially if the players are "similar") it seems that in B player 1 could extract better than 0.50 probability for his good outcome. Imagine starting the negotiations in B with the equal probability proposal. Player 2 stands to lose significantly more than player 1 if this proposal fails and negotiations break off. Both players are aware of this fact, and it seems like a threat of player 1 to break the negotiation would have significant credibility behind it. Player 2 would have to compromise the equal probability position and suggest a new probability division, one that would make player 1 happier.

The argument just presented suggests that in bargaining situations interpersonal comparisons of utility may take place. For example, this can be detected in the statement "Player 2 stands to lose more than player 1." Many game theorists like to disregard theories involving these type of interpersonal comparisons on the ground that they cannot be done using von Neumann–Morgenstern utilities with their arbitrary scales. However, if one believes that interpersonal comparisons do take place in bargaining situations, then it would be a mistake to ignore them because they inconvenience us when put together with individual utility theory.

In this section of the chapter we will not rule out interpersonal comparisons by assuming invariance with respect to utility scale. We will consider two solution concepts of this type. I will show that conflicting axioms described in the previous section stop contradicting each other (in the sense of leading to different solution concepts) when this scale-invariance axiom is removed. New, appealing axioms can also be satisfied.

Although interpersonal comparison of utilities is not assumed in the rationales leading to these solution concepts, it does follow as a consequence of more primitive axioms. We will discuss how these solution concepts can be made useful despite their dependencies on the utility scales of the individuals.

In this section *we implicitly assume that every one of our players is using the same utility function with the same scale as we vary the bargaining pairs under consideration.* More precisely, consider two bargaining pairs (d, S) and (d, W) in B. For $u \in S$ and $w \in W$ if $u_1 > w_1$ then our implicit assumption implies that player 1 prefers the prize that gave rise to u over the prize that gave rise to w. Note that in the previous section this did not have to be the case, because the scales of the utilities that described (d, S) might have been different from the scales describing (d, W). The implications of axioms comparing different games (such that IIA and monotonicity) are clearer with this assumption because they compare only what they are intended to compare and do not involve comparisons of things that are not really comparable. Because we assume that the players' utility scales are fixed and because their choice may be arbitrary, it would make no sense to assume symmetry of the solution. The issue of symmetry will be discussed later in this section.

3.1   *The utilitarian solution*

The utilitarian solution has been discussed extensively in the social welfare literature. It was axiomatized and argued for extensively by Harsanyi [1975]. Harsanyi's arguments can be easily used in the bargaining context as well. Therefore, only a very short description of the solution is given here.

A solution will be called *utilitarian* if there are weights $\lambda = (\lambda_1, \lambda_2) \in \mathbb{R}_+^2$ such that for every bargaining pair (d, S)

$$f(d, S) = \arg\max [\lambda_1(u_1 - d_1) + \lambda_2(u_2 - d_2)]$$
$$= \arg\max [\lambda_1 u_1 + \lambda_2 u_2]$$

where the maximization takes place over the pairs (u_1, u_2) that are feasible individually rational elements of S.

Notice that the arg max in the preceding definition may not be unique. However we can restrict our attention to bargaining pairs (d, S) in which the Pareto surface of S is strictly concave and then uniqueness is guaranteed.

The interpretation of a given utilitarian solution (for a fixed (λ_1, λ_2)) is obvious. According to it, the right solution is the one that maximizes the sum of the utility gains. However, weights λ_1, λ_2 should be assigned to the utility scales of the two players, and then for every bargaining pair we would be maximizing the weighted sum of the utilities with the same (λ_1, λ_2) as weights. The question of how to determine these weights will be addressed later.

Notice that for a given utilitarian solution, with weights (λ_1, λ_2), if the scales that the players use were changed by defining new utility functions $\bar{u}_i = \lambda_i u_1$, then the objective of the utilitarian solution is to always choose the outcome that maximizes the symmetric sum of the gains in units of $\bar{u}_i$.

3.2   *The egalitarian solution*

In this section we restrict our discussion again to bargaining pairs belonging to B_0 as described in section 3.3.

A solution f is called *egalitarian*[4] (see Kalai [1977a]) if there are weights λ_1, $\lambda_2 > 0$ such that for every $(d, S) \in B$, $f(d, S)$ is Pareto optimal in S and satisfies

$$\lambda_1(f_1(d, S) - d_1) = \lambda_2(f_2(d, S) - d_2).$$

Thus an egalitarian solution is characterized by interpersonal weights λ and, for every bargaining pair, it chooses the highest level of utilities for the players subject to the constraint that their λ normalized gains are equal. Every choice of λ will uniquely determine an egalitarian solution; and, vice versa, every egalitarian solution defines uniquely the weights that it uses.

Let f be an egalitarian solution with some fixed weights λ_1 and λ_2. The reader can easily check that it satisfies the IIA condition of Nash, the individual monotonicity condition of Kalai−Smorodinsky, and the superadditivity condition of Maschler−Perles. Thus, whereas these conditions were contradictory in the presence of the scale-invariance condition, they are not contradictory when this condition is removed.

We next define two weak versions of the scale-invariance condition that the egalitarian solutions do satisfy. A solution f is *invariant under translations* if for every $a \in \mathbb{R}^2$ and every $(d, S) \in B_0$

$$f(a + d, \quad a + S) = a + f(d, S).$$

---

[4] These solutions were originally introduced under the name *proportional solutions*.

A solution f is *homogeneous* if for every $\alpha > 0$ and every $(0, S) \in B_0$

$$f(0, \alpha S) = \alpha f(0, S).$$

The invariance under translations guarantees that if each of the players receives a fixed prize regardless of reaching agreement and independently of the bargaining process, the prize will not affect the outcome of the bargaining.

The homogeneity condition guarantees that if the feasible set S is available but only with probability α (and disagreement payoff with probability $1 - \alpha$), then the players would still agree on the same outcome in S as they would in the case when S was available with certainty.[5]

A major justification of the egalitarian solution follows from an axiom of monotonicity that it satisfies. f is called *monotonic* if for every two bargaining pairs, (d, S) and (d, T), if $T \supseteq S$ then $f(d, S) \leqslant f(d, T)$. This condition is very appealing on normative grounds. If the opportunities of the players become greater, then none of them should be made worse off. However, aside from the normative issues, this condition must be satisfied in many bargaining situations by strategic considerations.

Let us recall our original interpretation of a bargaining pair (d, T). The elements of T are the utility combinations that may arise from prizes provided that both players agree to support these prizes. If $S \subseteq T$ and, for player i, it is the case that $f_i(d, S) > f_i(d, T)$, then player i can in effect block the alternatives giving rise to the utilities in $T - S$ and improve his outcome. Thus, viewing f as the outcome selected by an arbitrator, the monotonicity condition guarantees that none of the players will have an incentive to misrepresent his resources or to destroy some of them before coming to the arbitrator. Viewing f as a solution arrived at by the players, on their own, monotonicity follows from a general principle of individual rationality (Nash equilibrium) in the underlying noncooperative game that the players play in the process of negotiation.

Owen [1968] pointed out the incompatibility of the monotonicity condition with the utility scale invariance. However it was shown in Kalai [1977a] that, when scale invariance is not assumed, we obtain the following.

Theorem 5: *A solution satisfies Pareto optimality, strong individual rationality, translation invariance, homogeneity, and monotonicity if and only if it is egalitarian.*

---

[5] Allowing for $\alpha > 1$ will follow because if $\alpha > 1$, let $W = \alpha S$, then $S = (1/\alpha)W$ and the same conclusion follows.

A second rationale for the egalitarian solution was proposed by Kalai [1977a]. This is a condition requiring that the bargaining can be done in stages without affecting the final outcome. Mathematically, it is closely related to the monotonicity condition and it is often observed in actual processes of negotiations.

Suppose (d, S) and (d, T) are bargaining pairs with $S \subseteq T$. The players bargaining could break the process into two stages. In the first stage they would agree on an outcome in (d, S) and then use this outcome as a disagreement point for a second stage of negotiations where they may agree on a new alternative in $T - S$. We would like the final outcome of this two-stage process to be the same as the outcome resulting when the entire bargaining process is done in one step. A solution satisfying this property would have the appealing feature that the players would be willing to do the negotiations in stages addressing one small problem at a time. (Clearly, if a solution can be decomposed into two stages as described here, it can be decomposed into any finite number of stages by induction.)

A second appealing consequence of such a negotiation-by-stages condition is that it resolves many issues of uncertainty about future negotiations. If the players are uncertain at one point of time about which bargaining problems they may face in the future, they may hesitate in reaching agreement presently, thinking that their long-run outcome may be affected negatively by their present agreement. The condition discussed in the preceding will eliminate this type of consideration.

Formally, for every $(d, S), (d, T) \in B_0$ with $S \subseteq T$ and for a solution f, we define $R = (0, (T - f(d, S)) \cap \mathbb{R}_+^2)$.

Thus R is a bargaining pair whose threat point is 0 and whose feasible points are the individually rational net gains remaining after agreeing upon $f(d, S)$ in the first stage.

We say that a solution *decomposes into stages* if whenever $(d, S), (d, T)$ are as described previously and $R \in B_0$, then

$$f(d, T) = f(d, S) + f(R).$$

Theorem 6: *A solution satisfies Pareto optimality, strong individual rationality, translation invariance, homogeneity, and decomposes into stages if and only if it is egalitarian.*

3.3   *The uses of scale-dependent solutions*

Scale-dependent solutions may not be as useful as scale-independent solutions. If we consider them as solutions to the arbitrator's problem, then they do not resolve his problem in the sense that he still has to choose the appropriate λ_i's. As predictive solutions the same problem arises. How can we predict the outcome of the bargaining if we do not know the appropriate λ_i's? However they still provide us with a tremendous simplification of these two problems.

The arbitrator, in order to choose the appropriate λ_i's, can consider a simple hypothetical bargaining problem and think of the "right" outcome for it. For example he may try to think of two monetary prizes $A = (\$a, \$0)$ and $B = (\$0, \$b))$ for which an equal probability lottery would be "right." He can then set $\lambda_1 = 1/u_1(A)$ and $\lambda_2 = 1/u_2(B)$ as the appropriate weights for the scale-dependent solution and proceed to solve the original problem.

A similar simplification is possible when we try to use a scale-dependent solution for prediction. If these two players have bargained before we can compute their λ_i's from their past games and use them to predict the outcome of the new game. If past games are not available, we can again try to predict the outcome of a simpler hypothetical bargaining game and use the λ_i's obtained from it to predict the outcome of the game under consideration.

3.4   *An ordinal egalitarian solution*

In this section we depart from one of the underlying assumptions of this chapter. That is, we do not assume that the utilities of the players giving rise to bargaining pairs are cardinal. We make the weaker assumption that the player's utility functions are ordinal. This means that, if A is a set of possible outcomes and u_i: $A \to \mathbb{R}$, then u_i is a utility function for player i provided that $u_i(a) > u_i(b)$ if and only if player i prefers a to b. No assumption about preferences over lotteries on A, or any other assumptions giving rise to cardinal measurements, are made.

In such a situation, any other utility function w_i: $A \to \mathbb{R}$ is as meaningful as u_i provided that for every two outcomes $a, b \in A$

$$u_i(a) > u_i(b) \text{ if and only if } w_i(a) > w_i(b).$$

It can easily be shown that two utility functions of player i, u_i, and w_i, are equivalent in this sense if and only if there exists an order-preserving transformation g_i: $\mathbb{R} \to \mathbb{R}$ such that $w_i = g_i \circ u_i$ (for every outcome $a \in A$ $w_i(a) = g_i(u_i(a))$). What we mean by an order-preserving transformation is a strictly increasing function. Order-preserving transformations in ordinal utility theories play the same role as affine transformations (changes of scale) in the case of cardinal utilities. The idea is that if we start with a given utility function and apply an order-preserving transformation to it, we obtain a new utility function that expresses the exact same preferences as did the old one.

To ensure that we stay within the family of bargaining sets we restrict our attention to order-preserving transformations of utilities that are continuous. Thus we define an *order-preserving transformation of player i's utility* to be a strictly increasing continuous function g_i: $\mathbb{R} \to \mathbb{R}$.

With the foregoing interpretations in mind, Myerson [1977] defines a notion of ordinal egalitarian solution that operates on an appropriately defined set of bargaining pairs OB. A function f: $OB \to \mathbb{R}^2$ is an *ordinal egalitarian solution* if there are two order-preserving transformations g_i: $\mathbb{R} \to \mathbb{R}$ ($i = 1, 2$) such that, for every bargaining pair $(d, S) \in OB$, $f(d, S)$ is Pareto optimal and

$$g_1(f_1(d, S)) - g_1(d_1) = g_2(f_2(d, S)) - g_2(d_2).$$

Thus the ordinal egalitarian solutions capture in an ordinal setup the same idea as the egalitarian solutions do in a cardinal setup. It states that there is some appropriate individual normalization of the players' utilities under which, for every bargaining pair, the equal division would arise. This normalization is inter- and intrapersonal. Myerson then presents an ordinal version of Theorem 6. That is, if an ordinal solution decomposes into stages in the presence of a few other natural conditions, it must be an ordinal egalitarian solution.

4   Risk sensitivity of solutions

In this section we study the behavior of some of the solutions discussed earlier as one of the bargainers becomes more risk averse. We ask ourselves what happens to a player, say player 1, as his opponent, player 2, becomes more risk averse. One plausible expectation is that his final outcome would improve.

We break our analysis into two cases. In one case we restrict our attention to bargaining problems in which the individually rational Pareto-optimal payoffs all result from lotteries among individually rational pure outcomes. In this case it turns out that indeed player 1 should prefer a more risk-averse opponent. This is true if we assume the Nash solution, the Kalai–Smorodinsky solution, or the Maschler–Perles solution.

The second case is where some Pareto-optimal individually rational outcomes can only arise as a result of a lottery between pure outcomes that themselves are not individually rational (even though the lottery is). In this case, there is no definitive answer. Our analysis follows results of Kannai [1977], Kihlstrom, Roth, and Schmeidler [1981], and Roth and Rothblum [1982].

We first motivate our notion of risk-aversion comparisons based on the works of Pratt [1964], Arrow [1965], Yaari [1969], and Kihlstrom and Mirman [1974]. We consider a convex subset C of $\mathbb{R}^n$ and a von Neumann–Morgenstern utility function u defined on it (and on all the lotteries over it). For every pure outcome $c \in C$ we let

$$A_u(c) = \{m: m \text{ is a lottery with } u(m) \geq u(c)\}.$$

Thus $A_u(c)$ is the set of lotteries that are weakly preferred to the sure outcome c.

Now consider two utility functions u and w defined on C and which coincide on C (that is, for every $c, d \in C$ $u(c) > u(d)$ if and only if $w(c) > w(d)$). We say that w is *more risk averse than* u if for every $c \in C$ $A_w(c) \subseteq A_u(c)$. In other words, a player with a utility function u is willing to take more lotteries instead of c than a player with a utility function w. It was shown in Kihlstrom and Mirman [1974] that w is more risk averse than u if and only if there is an increasing concave function k such that $w = k \circ u$.

We consider first the set B_0 of bargaining problems defined in Section 3.3. Motivated by the preceding discussion, we define the following. For two bargaining problems (d, S) and $(\hat{d}, \hat{S})$ in B_1, we say that player 2 *is more risk averse in* $(\hat{d}, \hat{S})$ *than in* (d, S) if, for some increasing concave function $k: \mathbb{R} \to \mathbb{R}$, $(\hat{d}_1, \hat{d}) = (d_1, k(d_2))$ and

$$\hat{S} = \{(u_1, k(u_2)): (u_i, u_2) \in S\}.$$

Our interpretation is that the utility function of player 2 that gave rise to $(\hat{d}, \hat{S})$ is one that was obtained from his utility function in (d,S) but after he became more risk averse.

Given a solution to the bargaining problem f, defined on B_0, we say that *under* f, *player 1 prefers more risk-averse opponents* if

$$f_1(d, S) \geq f_1(\hat{d}, \hat{S})$$

whenever player 2 is more risk averse in $(\hat{d}, \hat{S})$ than in (d, S).

From Kihlstrom, Roth, and Schmeidler [1981] we obtain

Theorem 7: *Under the Nash, Kalai–Smorodinsky, and Maschler–Perles solutions player 1 (and 2) prefers more risk-averse opponents.*

From de Koster et al. [1983], it follows that preferences to bargain against risk-averse opponents follows from a property of a solution called twisting (see Thomson and Myerson [1980]).

For two bargaining problems (d, S) and (d, T) in B_0 and for a solution f defined on B_0 we say that T *is a twist of* S *in favor of player* 1 if

1. for every $(u_i, u_2) \in T - S$, $u_1 \geq f_1(d, S)$, and
2. for every $(u_1, u_2) \in S - T$, $u_1 \leq f_1(d, S)$.

An intuitive way of viewing twists is the following. Starting with the problem (d, S) and its solution $f(d, S)$ we compare it with (d, T). Every new allocation that is feasible in T but was not feasible in S is better for player 1 than the solution to S, and every allocation that was lost in the transition from S to T was worse for 1 than the solution to S.

We say that f is *monotonic in favorable twists for player 1* if whenever (d, T) is a player 1 favorable twist of (d, S) then $f_1(d, T) \geq f_1(d, S)$.

Lemma: *If f is monotonic in favorable twists for player 1 then under f player 1 prefers risk-averse opponents.*

It is easy to see that both the Nash solution and the Kalai–Smorodinsky solution are monotonic in favorable twists (see Thomson and Myerson [1980]), and hence one can prove the first two-thirds of Theorem 7 from this lemma.

Once we leave the class B_0 of bargaining problems, then there are no longer definitive answers (as in Theorem 7) to the question of how a solution performs with regard to risk aversion. An intuitive explanation for this is that now the risk involves also the disagreement point. More specifically a certain disagreement outcome may appear more favorable to a risk-averse opponent than a lottery that involves outcomes that are worse for him than the disagreement one. Thus in a relative sense his disagreement payoff is pushed up when he becomes more risk averse. As a result, in some instances he would have to be compensated in the final outcome for having a higher utility for disagreement. This issue is discussed in Roth and Rothblum [1982] and we illustrate it by an example.

Consider two bargaining pairs over a set of three outcomes: D, A, and B. D is the disagreement outcome. Suppose $u_1(D) = u_1(B) = 0$ and $u_1(A) = 2$. Now consider two possible utility functions, u_2 and $\hat{u}_2$ for player 2.

$$u_2(B) = \hat{u}_2(B) = 1 \quad u_2(D) = \hat{u}_2(D) = 0, \quad u_2(A) = -1 \quad \text{and}$$
$$\hat{u}_2(A) = -4.$$

It is clear that under $\hat{u}_2$ player 2 is more risk averse than under u_2. For example, under u_2 player 2 is indifferent between D and the lottery L, which chooses between A and B with equal probability. On the other hand, under $\hat{u}_2$ we have $\hat{u}_2(D) = 0$ and $\hat{u}_2(L) = -1.5$. If we let (d, S) and $(\hat{d}, \hat{S})$ be the bargaining pairs induced by the utility functions (u_1, u_2) and $(u_1, \hat{u}_2)$, respectively, we observe the following. In (d, S) both the

Nash solution and the Kalai−Smorodinsky solution assign player 1 an outcome with utility 1/2. In $(\hat{d}, \hat{S})$ both solutions assign him a utility of 1/5. Thus, bargaining against the more risk-averse $\hat{u}_2$ ended up in a loss of 0.3 in player 1's final outcome.

5   Generalizations to more than two players

Generalizations of solution concepts and various conditions discussed earlier to the cases of more than two players have been studied extensively. The Nash solution, the utilitarian solution, and the egalitarian solution generalize uniquely in a natural way. The Kalai−Smorodinsky solution can be generalized in several ways over different sets of bargaining problems. The axiomatization of the Maschler−Perles solution using the superadditivity condition cannot be generalized to n-person bargaining problems even when we make some restrictions on the class of problems (see Perles [forthcoming]).[6]

Two types of generalizations have been suggested. The first type are generalizations to a fixed number n of bargainers where $n \geq 2$. The second type are ones constructing solutions that solve the bargaining problems simultaneously for any finite group of players. The second approach allows for the possibility of making comparisons and imposing consistency conditions as we vary the set of players. We will refer to the first approach as n-person generalizations and to the second one as multiperson generalizations.

5.1   *n-Person generalizations*

We fix n to be a positive integer greater than 1, and we define the set of n-person bargaining pairs, B^n, in the same way as we did earlier but with $\mathbb{R}^2$ being replaced by $\mathbb{R}^n$. The definitions of individual rationality, Pareto optimality, solution, invariance under affine transformations of utility scale, symmetry, IIA, and monotonicity are all modified in the natural way by replacing $\mathbb{R}^2$ with $\mathbb{R}^n$. We also let B_1^n be the subset of B^n consisting of pairs (d, S) in which every element of S is individually rational and (d, S) allows for free disposal of utility (see Section 2.3.). We let B_0^n be the subset of B_1^n in which small transfers of utilities are possible (again, see Section 2.3).

---

[6] It is quite possible however that an n-person generalization of the second procedure in the description of the Maschler−Perles solution is possible.

The characterization of the Nash solution given by Theorem 1 carries over easily to the n-person case.

In general Theorem 1 and its (n-person generalization) can be strengthened by omitting the symmetry condition. An n-person *non-symmetric Nash solution* is the function $f: B^n \to \mathbb{R}$ such that for some $\alpha \in \mathbb{R}^n$ with $\alpha > 0$ we have the following: for every $(d, S) \in B^n$ $f(d, S)$ is the unique point in the individually rational part of S that maximizes the nonsymmetric Nash product $\Pi_{i=1}^n (u_i - d_i)^{\alpha_i}$ among all the individually rational utility allocations in S (see Harsanyi and Selten [1972]). Clearly the (symmetric) Nash solution is the special case of the nonsymmetric ones with $\alpha = (1, 1, \ldots, 1)$.

Theorem 8: *An n-person solution is Pareto optimal, strongly individually rational, independent of irrelevant alternative, and independent of affine transformations of utility scale if and only if it is a nonsymmetric Nash solution.*

An explanation of why nonsymmetric Nash solutions may arise was given in Kalai [1977b]. Consider a two-person bargaining problem $(d\ S)$ $\in B^2$. Now we would replicate player two to create a three-person bargaining problem $(\bar{d}, \bar{S})$ in which player 3 has identical interest to player 2. We define

$$\bar{d} = (d_1, d_2, d_2) \quad \text{and} \quad \bar{S} = \{(u_1, u_2, u_2) : (u_1, u_2) \in S\}$$

When the (symmetric) Nash solution is applied to $(\bar{d}, \bar{S})$ the solution is the $\mathrm{argmax}(u_1 - d_1)(u_2 - d_2)(u_3 - d_3)$. But $(u_3 - d_3) = (u_2 - d_2)$ in such a replicate game. Thus, in effect $(u_1 - d_1)(u_2 - d_2)^2$ is being maximized. Now consider the following scenario. Since player 2 and player 3 have identical interest in $(\bar{d}, \bar{S})$, player 3 gives player 2 a power of attorney to negotiate on his behalf. Now players 1 and 2 are playing the two-person game (d, S). If they use the symmetric two-person Nash solution, then $(u_1 - d_1)(u_2 - d_2)$ would be maximized and they would be worse off ($\mathrm{argmax}(u_1 - d_1)(u_2 - d_2)^2$ must give them a higher payoff) than if they played the three-person game.

The conclusion that we can draw from this example is that under the Nash philosophy, when a negotiator is representing m players with identical interest, then his weight in the Nash product must be raised to the mth power. Thus all the nonsymmetric Nash solutions with α's that have integer and even rational coordinates may be explained by situations where the bargainers represent unequal size constituencies to some underlying problems. In particular, it follows that if we have one player bargaining against another one, who represents the interest of m players, the first player will have to concede more and more as m gets larger. It is not clear whether this is a reasonable phenomenon. For example, in union negotiations it would suggest that as the number of workers gets larger they may individually get better conditions for themselves. What should we predict would happen if the number of stockholders gets larger? The reader can verify that the n-person Kalai–Smorodinsky solution, defined later, is invariant to replications of this type.

The utilitarian and the egalitarian solutions also generalize to the n-person case in one natural way. The rationales justifying these solutions as demonstrated by Harsanyi [1955] and by Kalai [1977a] (the analogues of Theorems 5 and 6) carry over easily to the n-person case.

Generalizations of the Kalai–Smorodinsky solution have been suggested by several authors with a variety of results. The reason for it is that the notion of individual monotonicity can be generalized in several ways. When applying one particular generalization over the bargaining problems in B^n, Roth [1979a] obtains an impossibility result. However, his notion of individual monotonicity is very strong, and the impossibility result relies strongly on the use of the full domain of problems in B^n. If one does not use as strong a notion of individual monotonicity and one is willing to be satisfied by solving the problems in B_0^n (accepting the availability of small utility transfers) then this difficulty disappears. Examples of such generalizations can be found in Heckathorn and Carlson [1980], Segal [1980], Peters and Tijs [1982], Imai [1983], as well as others.

Given an n-person bargaining pair $(d, S) \in B_1^n$ we define the ideal point $I \in \mathbb{R}^n$ by

$$I_i = \max \{u_i: u \text{ is an individually rational element of } S\}.$$

The n-person Kalai–Smorodinsky solution is then defined to be the unique weakly Pareto-optimal point in S, u, with the property that for every two bargainers, i and j, $(\mu_i - d_i)/(I_i - d_i) = (\mu_j - d_j)/(I_j - d_j)$. We observe that on B_1^n, μ always exists (because of the free disposal property) and that μ may be weakly and not strongly Pareto optimal for some pairs in B_1^n. Clearly this second difficulty would disappear if we restrict our attention to B_0^n.

5.2   *Multiperson generalizations*

We now take a more powerful approach to the multiperson problem suggested by Thomson [1983a]. We assume an infinite countable population of *potential bargainers* that we denote by $N = \{1, 2, 3, \ldots\}$. We let F be the set of *groups* of players that are finite nonempty subsets of N. The idea is that the solutions we will consider should assign an outcome for every potential group which may be involved in bargaining. This approach enables us to impose consistency and rationality conditions on a solution as we vary the group of participants. We will denote groups of players from F by a capital letter with the corresponding lowercase letter denoting the number of members of the group.

For every group $P \in F$ we let $\mathbb{R}^P$ denote the p-dimensional Euclidean space indexed by the members of P. For every $P \in F$ we define B^P, B_1^P and B_0^P as in the previous section to denote the set of bargaining problems in $\mathbb{R}^P$. We let B, B_1, and B_0 denote the collections of the B_i^P over the P's. A *solution* to the multiperson problem is a collection $f = \{f^P : P \in F\}$, where each f^P is a solution to the p-person problem. We say that f is a solution on B, B_1, and B_0 correspondingly to denote that each f^P is a solution on the corresponding B_i^P. We say that a solution f satisfies a given property if each of its f^P's satisfies the given property. We also define the Nash and the Kalai–Smorodinsky solution of the multiperson problem in the obvious way to be the collections of these solutions over the P's in F.

We first describe a multiperson characterization of the Nash solution suggested by Lensberg [1981]. The key condition used here is one requiring that the solution is stable with respect to negotiations by subgroups of the bargainers. More specifically let f be a multiperson solution and suppose that P and Q are groups of potential bargainers with $Q \underset{\neq}{\subseteq} P$. Given a bargaining pair $(d, S) \in B^P$ we define the set

$$(S: Q, f) = \{u \in \mathbb{R}^Q : \text{for some } w \in S, w \text{ coincides with } f(d, S) \text{ on } P - Q \text{ and with } u \text{ on } Q\}.$$

In other words, $(S: Q, f)$ are all the feasible allocations to the members of Q after meeting the demands of the members of $P - Q$ according to f. For $d \in \mathbb{R}^P$ we let d^Q be the restriction of d to $\mathbb{R}^Q$. We say that f is *stable for partial groups* if for every two groups P and Q in F with $Q \underset{\neq}{\subseteq} P$ and for every $(d, S) \in B_1^P$ if $(d^Q, (S: Q, f)) \in B_1^Q$ then $f^Q(d^Q, (S: Q, f))$ coincides with the restriction of $f^P(d, S)$ to the members of Q. The motivation for this condition is that in every subgroup of P that may be formed to renegotiate their part of the final agreement, no member has an incentive to deviate from the original agreement.

Theorem 9: *A solution defined on B_1 satisfies Pareto optimality, invariance with respect to affine transformations of scales of utility, symmetry, continuity, and stability for partial groups if and only if it is the multiperson Nash solution.*

A characterization of the multiperson Kalai–Smorodinsky solution was established by Thomson [1983a]. Thomson motivates his bargaining problems by considering problems of fair divisions of bundles of goods among n agents. Based on the results of Billera and Bixby [1973] we know that every bargaining pair $(d, S) \in B^n$ may be viewed as a bargaining over how to divide a fixed and finite bundle of goods among n agents. The point d is the von Neumann–Morgenstern utility image that the players have for the zero allocation, which we view as the disagreement, or status quo, outcome. The feasible set S represents the utilities induced by all the possible divisions of the given bundle among the n agents. Assuming monotonicity in every good, free disposal of goods, and concave utility functions, we generate bargaining problems in the class B_1^n. If we assume strict monotonicity in every good, then we generate bargaining problems in B_0^n.

With this interpretation of the pairs $(d, S) \in B_0^n$ in mind we may wish to impose the following condition on a solution f. Starting with a fixed bundle, a fixed set P of agents and their utility allocation $f^P(d, S)$, assume that another agent is added to the group to share the same original bundle. Now there is one more "mouth to feed" and we should expect that none of the old agents in P should become better off because of this extra partner to the division problem.

Given two bargaining pairs $(a,S) \in B_0^Q$ and $(b, T) \in B_0^P$ with $Q \subsetneq P$ we say that (b, T) is *derived* from (a, S) by *introducing* new agents if

1. $a_i = b_i$ for every $i \in Q$, and
2. $u \in S$ if and only if there is a $w \in T$ with $u_i = w_i$ for every $i \in Q$.

We say that a solution f is *monotonic in agents* if, for every $(a, S) \in B_0^Q$ and every $(b, T) \in B_0^P$ that is derived from (a, S) by introducing new agents, we have $f_i^Q(d, S) \leqslant f_i^P(b, T)$ for every $i \in Q$.

Theorem 10: *A solution defined on B_0 is Pareto optimal, symmetric, invariant with respect to affine transformations of scales of utility and monotonic in agents if and only if it is the Kalai–Smorodinsky solution.*

A multiperson solution f is *egalitarian* if for some sequence of positive numbers $\{\alpha_i\}_{i \in N}$, for every group of players $P \in F$, f^P is the p-person egalitarian solution with weights $\{\alpha_i\}_{i \in N}$. If all the α_i's are 1 then f is called the symmetric egalitarian solution. We can now present another characterization of the symmetric egalitarian solution due to Thomson [1983b].

Theorem 11: *A multiperson solution defined on B_1 is weakly Pareto optimal, independent of irrelevant alternatives, monotonic in agents, continuous, and symmetric if and only if it is the symmetric egalitarian solution.*

REFERENCES

Arrow, K. J. [1965]. *Aspects of the Theory of Risk-Bearing*. Helsinki: Yrgö Johnson Foundation.

Aumann, R. J. [forthcoming]. "An Axiomatization of the Non-transferable Utility Value." *Econometrica*.

Billera, L. J., and R. E. Bixby [1973], "Market Representations of *n*-person Games." *Bulletin of the American Mathematical Society*, *80* (3):522–526.

Binmore, K. [1980]. "Nash Bargaining Theory I, II, and III." International Centre for Economics and Related Disciplines, London School of Economics.

de Koster, R., H. J. M. Peters, S. H. Tijs, and P. Walker. [1983]. "Risk Sensitivity, Independence of Irrelevant Alternatives and Continuity of Bargaining Solutions." *Mathematical Social Sciences*, *4*:295–300.

Harsanyi, J. C. [1955]. "Cardinal Welfare, Individualistic Ethics, and Interpersonal Comparisons of Utility." *Journal of Political Economy*, *63*:309–321.

Harsanyi, J. C. [1977]. *Rational Behavior and Bargaining Equilibrium in Games and Social Situations*. Cambridge, Mass.: Harvard University Press.

Harsanyi, J. C., and R. Selten [1972]. "A Generalized Nash Solution for Two Person Bargaining Games with Incomplete Information." *Management Science*, *18*:80–106.

Hart, S. [1983]. "An Axiomatization of Harsanyi's Non-transferable Utility Solution." Northwestern University, Evanston, Ill.

Heckathorn, R. D. [1978]. "A Paradigm for Bargaining and a Test of Two Bargaining Models." *Behavioral Science*, *23*.

Heckathorn, R. D., and R. Carlson [1980]. "A Possibility Result Concerning *n*-person Bargaining Games." University of Missouri, Kansas City.

Hoggatt, A., R. Selten, D. Crockett, S. Gill, and J. Moor [1978]. "Bargaining Experiments with Incomplete Information," in *Contributions to Experimental Economics*, edited by H. Sauermann. Proceedings of the Second Conference on Experimental Economics.

Immai, H. [1983]. "Individual Monotonicity and Lexicographic Maxmin Solution." *Econometrica*, *51*:389–401.

Kalai, E. [1977a]. "Proportional Solutions to Bargaining Situations: Interpersonal Utility Comparisons." *Econometrica*, *45*:1623–1630.

Kalai, E. [1977b]. "Nonsymmetric Nash Solutions and Replications of Two-Person Bargaining." *International Journal of Game Theory*, *6*:129–133.

Kalai, E., and M. Smorodinsky [1975]. "Other Solutions to Nash's Bargaining Problem." *Econometrica*, *43*:513–518.

Kalai, E., and D. Samet. [1985]. "Monotonic Solutions to General Cooperative Games." *Econometrica*, *53*:307–327.

Kannai, Y. [1977]. "Concavifiability and Construction of Concave Utility Functions." *Journal of Mathematical Economics*, *4*.

Kihlstrom, R. E., and L. J. Mirman [1974]. "Risk Aversion with Many Commodities." *Journal of Economic Theory*, *8*:361–388.

Kihlstrom, R. E., A. E. Roth, and D. Schmeidler [1981]. "Risk Aversion and Nash's Solution to the Bargaining Problem," in *Game Theory and Mathematical Economics*, edited by O. Moeschlin and D. Pallaschke. Amsterdam: North Holland.

Lensberg, T. [1981]. "Stability of the Nash Bargaining Solution with Respect to

Partial Implementation." The Norwegian School of Economics and Business Administration, Bergen.

Luce, R. D., and H. Raiffa [1957]. *Games and Decisions*. New York: John Wiley and Sons.

Myerson, R. B. [1977]. "Two-Person Bargaining Problems and Comparable Utility." *Econometrica*, 45:1631–1637.

Myerson, R. B. [1981]. "Utilitarianism, Egalitarianism, and the Timing Effect in Social Choice Problems." *Econometrica*, 49:883–897.

Myerson, R. B. [1984]. "Two Person Bargaining Problems with Incomplete Information." *Econometrica*, 52:461–487.

Nash, J. F. [1950]. "The Bargaining Problem." *Econometrica*, 28:155–162.

Nydegger, R. V., and G. Owen [1975]. "Two Person Bargaining: An Experimental Test of Nash Axioms." *International Journal of Game Theory*, 3:239–249.

O'Neill, B. [1976]. "Variable Threat Bargaining: A Test of the Raiffa-Nash Theory." University of Michigan, Ann Arbor.

Owen, G. [1968]. *Game Theory*. Philadelphia: Saunders.

Perles, M. A. [Forthcoming]. "Non-existence of Super-additive Solutions for 3-person Games." *International Journal of Game Theory*.

Perles, M. A., and M. Maschler [1980]. "The Super-additive Solution for the Nash Bargaining Game." Report no. 1, The Institute for Advanced Studies, The Hebrew University, Jerusalem.

Peters, H. J. M., and S. H. Tijs [1982]. "Individually Monotonic Bargaining Solutions for *n*-person Bargaining Games." University of Nijmegen, The Netherlands.

Pratt, J. W. [1964]. "Risk Aversion in the Small and Large." *Econometrica*, 32:122–136.

Rapoport, A., and J. Perner [1974]. "Testing Nash's Solution of the Cooperative Game," in *Game Theory as a Theory of Conflict Resolution*, edited by A. Rapoport, Dordrecht, Holland: D. Reidel.

Roth, A. E. [1979a]. *Axiomatic Models of Bargaining*. New York: Springer Verlag.

Roth, A. E. [1979b]. "An Impossibility Result Concerning *n*-person Bargaining Games." *International Journal of Game Theory*, 8:129–132.

Roth, A. E., and M. K. Malouf [1979], "Game-Theoretic Models and the Role of Information in Bargaining." *Psychological Review*, 86:574–594.

Roth, A. E., and U. G. Rothblum [1982]. "Risk Aversion and Nash's Solution for Bargaining Games with Risky Outcomes." *Econometrica*, 50:639–647.

Schelling, T. C. [1960]. *The Strategy of Conflict*. Cambridge, Mass.: Harvard University Press.

Schmitz, N. [1977]. "Two Person Bargaining without Threats: A Review Note." Proceedings of the Operations Research Symposium, Aachen.

Segal, V. [1980]. "The Monotonic Solution of the Bargaining Problem." The Hebrew University, Jerusalem.

Shapley, L. S. [1969]. "Utility Comparison and the Theory of Games." *La Decision*, (edited by G. T. Guilband.) Paris: Editions du CNRS.

Thomson, W. [1983a]. "The Fair Division of a Fixed Supply among a Growing Population." *Mathematics of Operations Research*, 8:319–326.

Thomson, W. [1983b]. "Problems of Fair Division and the Egalitarian Solution." *Journal of Economic Theory*, *31*:211−226.

Thomson, W., and R. Myerson [1980]. "Monotonicity and Independence Axioms." *International Journal of Game Theory*, *9*:37−49.

Yaari, M. E. [1969]. "Some Remarks on Measures of Risk Aversion and on Their Uses," *Journal of Economic Theory*, *1*:315−329.

CHAPTER 4

Theories of justice based on symmetry

William Thomson and Hal R. Varian

The two issues, equity and efficiency, are at the center of any economic analysis. While the concept of economic efficiency is now well understood, there is still considerable debate concerning the appropriate definition of economic equity.

It is only since Foley [1967] that an ordinal concept of equity, the concept of an *envy-free* allocation, has been available for economic analysis. Since then, Foley's criterion has been the object of a number of studies. Its various properties and limitations have been examined and further refinements have been offered. In this chapter we will survey some of this literature on theories of equity based on considerations of *symmetry*.[1]

The essay is organized as follows. In Section 1 we study the central criterion of an envy-free allocation and several variants and extensions of the criterion as well as its main competitors. Section 2 is devoted to several formalizations of the notion of equality of opportunity. Economies with a large number of agents are examined in Section 3 and economies with production in Section 4. Questions of implementation are treated in Section 5 and applications in Section 6. A brief summary is given in Section 7.

---

[1] A note on terminology is in order. What we call *envy-free* allocations have also been referred to as "equitable" allocations (e.g., Varian [1974, 1975], Champsaur and Laroque [1981]) and also as "fair" allocations (Pazner [1977 (Chapter 13, this book)], Crawford [1977]). Similarly what we call *envy-free and efficient* allocations have been called "fair" allocations by others (e.g., Schmeidler and Yaari [1971], Varian [1974, 1975], Champsaur and Laroque [1981]). We have tried to be reasonably consistent in our own choice of terminology but have not always indicated the exact choices used by other authors. To do so would have only caused confusion.

1   Envy-free allocations and generalizations

Let us begin by considering the simplest problem of fair distribution: that of dividing a homogeneous commodity among n agents with equal claims on it. In this case there is no question of efficiency − as long as none of the resource is wasted − and we would argue that the appropriate solution is *equal division*.

Suppose now that there is more than one commodity. If all agents have identical tastes, equal division may still be an acceptable ethical norm. But if agents have different tastes, equal division is typically *(Pareto) inefficient*; that is, there will generally be some other allocation that all agents weakly prefer and at least one agent prefers to equal division.

Let us then seek a generalization of the idea of equal division that preserves the symmetry of this allocation, but has a chance of being compatible with efficiency. What makes equal division appealing is that no agent would want to exchange his bundle for anyone else's − since all bundles are the same. But there may well be other allocations that have this property. This observation leads us to the following definitions.

Definitions: Agent i *envies* agent j at the allocation x if he prefers agent j's bundle, x_j, to his own bundle x_i; in symbols: i envies j at x if $x_i \succ_i x_j$. An *envy-free* allocation is one in which no agent envies any other agent.

Since equal division is envy-free, the concept is not vacuous. But are there envy-free allocations that are also efficient? The following theorem provides an important element of an answer to this question.

Theorem (Foley [1967], Schmeidler and Vind [1972], Kolm [1972]): *Assume preferences are nonsatiated and let (p, x) be a Walrasian equilibrium with equal incomes. Then x is envy-free and Pareto efficient.*

Proof: Efficiency follows from the standard argument. Suppose that the allocation is not envy-free so that some agent i envies some agent j. Since each consumer is maximizing on his budget set, it must be that agent i cannot afford agent j's bundle. But all consumers have the same income, so what is affordable for j is also affordable for i.   □

This theorem shows that assumptions that guarantee the existence and the efficiency of Walrasian allocations also guarantee the existence of envy-free and efficient allocations. Even more interesting is the fact that under such assumptions, the theorem provides a constructive method for generating such allocations: simply divide the social endowment of goods

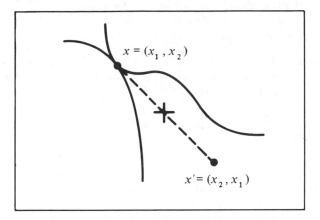

Figure 1. An envy-free allocation in an Edgeworth box.

equally among the agents and let them trade to a Walrasian allocation.

The major assumption typically used in proofs of existence of a Walrasian allocation is the convexity of preferences. However, as suggested by Schmeidler and Yaari [1971] and proved by Varian [1974], the existence of envy-free and efficient allocations can be established directly, without assuming convexity of preferences but only monotonicity of preferences and a mild regularity condition on the shape of the set of efficient allocations.

There is a simple geometric construction in the two-commodity, two-agent Edgeworth-box case that is worthy of some study. Given an allocation $x = (x_1, x_2)$ in the box, we determine its "swap" $x' = (x_2, x_1)$. This is simply the symmetric image of x with respect to the center of the box as depicted in Figure 1. Now we ask if either agent prefers the bundle he receives in the swapped allocation to the bundle he received originally. If the answer is *no* as in the case of Figure 1, then we have an envy-free allocation.

Several interesting facts concerning envy-free allocations can be illustrated with this Edgeworth-box apparatus. For example:

1. An allocation can be envy-free and efficient without necessarily Pareto-dominating equal division.
2. With convex preferences, any allocation Pareto-dominating equal division is envy-free.
3. Allocations may be in the core from equal division and yet not be envy-free, although this situation occurs in the two-person case

only if preferences are allowed to be nonconvex. An example with convex preferences and three agents was constructed by Feldman and Kirman [1974].

These results and others of a similar vein (Kolm [1972], Goldman and Sussangkarn [1978], Thomson [1982a]) indicate that the set of envy-free allocations does not have a particularly simple structure. (It is typically a disconnected union of closed sets.)

Several generalizations of the notion of envy-free allocations have been proposed.

One class of generalizations is based on the number of agents that each agent envies as compared to the number by which he is envied. Daniel [1975] proposes such a generalization, which will be considered in more detail in Section 4. Feldman and Weiman [1979] suggest using similar comparisons as a basis for defining a notion of class hierarchies.

An interesting result in this vein is the following relationship between envy and efficiency.

Theorem (Varian [1974]): *At any efficient allocation there is someone that no one envies and someone that envies no one.*

Proof: We prove only the first part since the two statements have similar proofs. Suppose instead that each agent envies some other agent. Agent 1 envies someone − say agent 2 − and agent 2 in turn envies someone − say agent 3. But because the number of agents is finite, there has to be a cycle: 1 envies 2, who envies 3, . . . , who envies k, who envies 1. Consider now the allocation obtained by giving each agent in the cycle the bundle of his neighbor, 1 getting 2's bundle, 2 getting 3's bundle . . . k getting 1's bundle. At this new allocation each agent in the cycle is better off, and the agents outside the cycle are no worse off. This contradicts the assumption of efficiency.   □

Thus at any efficient allocation there is a natural way to say which agents are "best off" (the agents that envy no one) and which agents are "worst-off" (the agents that no one envies). This result provides an appealing interpretation of Rawls's [1971] criterion of maximin welfare. Rawls argues that the most desirable social states are those that maximize the welfare of the worst-off individuals. This is generally interpreted as requiring some sort of interpersonal comparisons of utility. However, if we consider the worst-off agents to be the ones that no one envies, and we make them as well off as possible − that is, we ensure that they are envied by no one − we are led naturally to the criterion of an envy-free allocation, at which there are *no* envied agents. This interpretation yields a concept of equity that does not involve interpersonal comparisons of utility and yet is still in the spirit of Rawls's original idea.

One can also use the construction involved in the proof of this result to define various orderings of the agents. Such orderings have been suggested by Varian [1976] and examined in greater detail by Feldman and Weiman [1979].

A second generalization of the concept of envy-free allocations is that of a *coalitional envy-free allocation*. We can ask, for example, if any group of agents prefers the aggregate consumption bundle of any other group of agents of the same size, in the sense that they could distribute the other group's bundle among themselves in a way that they all prefer to their current holdings. If it is possible to do this, it is natural to say that one group envies the other. A related concept involves each group comparing its own average bundle to each other group's average bundle. Vind [1973] and Varian [1974] examined such concepts, while Jaskold-Gabszewicz [1975] considered similar ideas in a net-trade context. The most interesting results concerning these definitions are found in the case of large economies which we will discuss subsequently.

In other generalizations of the concept of envy-free allocations, Pazner [1977 (Chapter 13, this book)] proposed the weak requirement of Pareto *domination of equal division*, while Thomson [1982a] suggested the requirement that each agent *weakly prefers what he consumes to the average of what the others consume*.

A criterion in a somewhat different spirit is that of *egalitarian equivalence* (Pazner and Schmeidler [1978a (Chapter 15, this book)]). Let us say that an allocation (feasible or not), is *egalitarian* if the consumption bundles comprising this allocation are all identical. If commodities are not freely disposable, the only *feasible* egalitarian allocation is the equal division allocation. Then we say that a feasible allocation x is *egalitarian equivalent* if there exists a (possibly infeasible) egalitarian allocation e such that all agents are indifferent between what they receive at x and what they receive at e. Similarly, a feasible allocation is *envy-free equivalent* (Pazner [1977]) if there exists a (possibly infeasible) envy-free allocation with the same indifference property. Because these definitions were proposed mainly to deal with certain difficulties that arise in production economies, we postpone their discussion to Section 4.

2   Equality of opportunity

In the previous section we considered various interpretations of the idea of equitable allocations. We turn now to notions based on the idea of *equality of opportunities*. This idea can be understood in several ways.

One way to give substance to it is to let each agent choose his consumption from a common choice set. (This is advocated for example by Archibald and Donaldson [1979].) Since everyone has access to the bundles chosen by others, the list of consumption bundles obtained from this process will necessarily be envy-free. The difficulty is of course to find a choice set C such that the choices of all the agents are jointly feasible; that is, they constitute a feasible allocation. This requirement precludes that C be chosen once and for all. Instead one should have access to a whole family $\mathscr{C}$ of choice sets such that it can be guaranteed that for some member of $\mathscr{C}$ the aggregate feasibility condition can be met.

There is a well-known family that has this property, namely the family of budget sets with identical endowments. It is on this family that Varian [1976] based his notion of *opportunity-fair* allocations. An allocation is *opportunity-fair* if it is efficient and each agent weakly prefers his own bundle to any bundle in any other agent's budget set, where the budget sets are determined by the implicit prices supporting the allocation. It is not hard to see that if preferences are monotonic the only such opportunity-fair allocations are the equal-income Walrasian allocations.

But this is only one example of a family of choice sets that can be used to define notions of equality of opportunity. Is it the only such family? One can add certain sorts of choice sets to the family of budget sets just described if the number of agents is small, but it seems that, when the number of agents is arbitrary, a family of choice sets can be satisfactory only when it coincides with the family of Walrasian budget sets with equal incomes.

The notion of equal opportunity can also be interpreted as imposing certain restrictions on the transition from initial positions to final positions. Which transitions are desirable is specified by a choice correspondence, that is, a correspondence associating with each economy e in the initial position ω a set of final allocations $\phi(e, \omega)$. Our first requirement on ϕ is that the allocations in $\phi(e, \omega)$ be efficient. What other requirements should be imposed to formalize the idea of equal opportunity?

A minimum requirement is one of *anonymity*: agents should enter symmetrically in the description of ϕ. Another requirement is that *no agent be made worse off* by the operation of ϕ; that is, all allocations in $\phi(e, \omega)$ Pareto dominate the initial endowment ω. A third requirement is that the *set of allocations in $\phi(e, \omega)$ be "small"* relative to the set of all possible efficient allocations. The more specific the recommendation made by ϕ, the better it helps in the solution of the fair-division problem.

The Walrasian correspondence satisfies all of these requirements, and in fact is often advocated on that basis either formally, as in Schmeidler and Vind [1972], or informally, as in Nozick [1974].

Another example of particular interest is the correspondence associating to every economy in the initial position ω the set of efficient allocations attainable through an *envy-free trade*, defined as follows. Given agent i's initial endowment ω_i and his final bundle x_i, define $t_i = x_i - \omega_i$ to be agent i's net trade. Agent i's preference relation on final bundles x_i induces a preference relation on net trades t_i in the natural way: an agent prefers one net trade to another if he prefers the final bundle he ends up with in that net trade. A list of net trades is *envy-free* if no consumer prefers someone else's net trade to his own. Many properties of envy-free allocations have counterparts for net trades.

In particular, Schmeidler and Vind [1972], who introduced the concept, showed that Walrasian net trades are envy-free. They also proposed the stronger definition that *each agent prefers his net trade to any sum of integer multiples of the net trades of the others*, combining the equity notion behind the concept of an envy-free trade with a sort of strengthening of the anonymity requirement that agents should be able to enter the market any number of times.

Of course the fairness of a transition principle does not guarantee the equity of the final position, which will in general depend on the initial position. But how can we evaluate the equity of an initial position?

Once again, equal division is an appealing candidate. In fact, equal division seems to be a better candidate for an initial-state principle than for an end-state principle, since the inefficiencies of equal division will presumably be removed by the transition principle.

We could consider designing various theories of justice by formulating criteria to evaluate initial positions, as well as transitions and final positions. Of course, one of our prime concerns is to ensure consistency among these various criteria. But this may not be easy.

For instance, if we choose the envy-free criterion for both initial allocations and trades, we cannot expect this criterion to be met by final allocations. Indeed, Feldman and Kirman [1974] show by example that an envy-free trade from an envy-free allocation may lead to an allocation with envy. Goldman and Sussangkarn [1978] strengthen this result by showing that there are large classes of economies admitting of inefficient envy-free allocations that are Pareto dominated by no envy-free allocations, so that no Pareto-improving trade can lead from such an allocation to an efficient and envy-free allocation. Goldman and Sussangkarn [1980] also exhibit a three-person economy in which a sequence of envy-free net trades from equal division leads to an allocation in the core from equal division that is not envy-free. Finally, Thomson [1982a] shows that there are economies admitting of envy-free allocations from which no envy-free and efficient allocation can be reached through an envy-free trade.

Are there natural consistency requirements that one can impose to avoid these kinds of situations? Thomson [1983] argues that there are.

Given a transition principle ϕ, he first defines the consistency of initial-state and end-state principles *relative to* ϕ as follows: given a pair (ω, x) of an initial allocation and of a final allocation obtainable from ω through the operation of the transition principle, x is declared ϕ-equitable if permutations of the initial endowments followed by the operation of ϕ leave x unaffected. Similarly, ω is declared equitable if permutations of its components followed by the operation of ϕ can always lead to the allocation x.

Unfortunately, such a consistency criterion is not enough to rule out final allocations that seem manifestly unjust, for example, allocations at which one agent consumes strictly more of all commodities than some other agent.

For instance, if ϕ is the core correspondence C, one can easily construct a two-commodity, two-person economy such that for some allocation x with $x_1 > x_2$, x belongs to both $C(e, \omega)$ and $C(e, \omega')$, where ω and ω' are obtained from each other via a permutation of their components.

To prevent this sort of outcome, Thomson suggests that the test be extended by performing the permutation on the allocation x itself. This is in accord with the original motivation for the concept of no envy. In order to evaluate the equity of an efficient allocation x, it is natural to compare x to the permutations of x as required by the no-envy test. However, the allocations obtained by such permutations will typically be inefficient, so that this sort of comparison may be judged irrelevant if society's commitment to efficiency is strong enough. Instead it seems desirable to first remove the inefficiency of the permuted allocation by applying the transition principle, and then to compare x to the resulting allocation. We will call x a ϕ-*equitable final allocation* if it is invariant to this sequence of operations.

Of course the notion of equity obtained in this way for final allocations will typically depend on the transition principle that is used, as indicated by the notation. However, there is an inverse operation that allows one to derive transition principles from end-state principles. We have already seen how to derive the concept of an envy-free net trade from the concept of an envy-free allocation. More generally, given some end-state principle, one can obtain the corresponding transition principle by replacing in the formulation of the principle consumption bundles by trades and the preference relation over consumption bundles by the preference relation over net trades that it induces.

This allows us to complete the argument in an entirely internal way. Given some end-state principle, we derive the corresponding transition principle, and from it we obtain in turn the associated end-state principle. The final consistency requirement is that we end up where we started!

Are there examples for which this happens? Yes there are. Simply take no envy as both the end-state and the transition principles. Or take an equal-income Walrasian allocation as the end-state principle and Walrasian trade as the transition principle. We are not aware of other examples, which suggests that the envy-free allocations and the equal-income Walrasian allocations are truly central notions among the variety of possible definitions of equitable outcomes. This impression will be confirmed in other situations, particularly in Section 5, concerned with implementation questions.

3   Economies with a large number of individuals

We have shown above that equal-income Walrasian allocations are necessarily envy free and efficient under very mild assumptions. In general, there are many other envy-free and efficient allocations. However, under certain assumptions to be discussed, in "large" economies equal-income Walrasian allocations are the *only* envy-free allocations.

Consider the following heuristic argument. Suppose that there are many consumers and that tastes vary continuously in the population. Then if at some efficient allocation my neighbor has a higher implicit income than I do, and his tastes are very similar to mine, he will likely have purchased a bundle that I would prefer to my consumption bundle. Thus we might suspect that the *only* envy-free and efficient allocations in such an economy are those that involve equal implicit incomes.

This loose argument was first formalized by Varian [1976]. Let us develop it in somewhat greater detail. Assume that we can parameterize the set of agents by the open unit interval $(0, 1)$, so that an allocation is a map $x: (0, 1) \to R^k$ that assigns to each consumer t his consumption bundle $x(t)$. The utility function of consumer t is given by $u(x, t)$, which we assume to be a differentiable function of both arguments. This formalizes the notion that tastes vary smoothly across the population.

Let x be an envy-free and efficient allocation. This means that each consumer t weakly prefers his bundle to the bundle held by any other consumer s. Thus the function g defined by

$$g(s) = u(x(t), t) - u(x(s), t)$$

is nonnegative everywhere and reaches its minimum value of 0 at $s = t$. Hence the derivative of g(s) (assuming it exists) vanishes at $s = t$, which implies

$$Dg(t) = Du(x(t), t)Dx(t) = 0.$$

On the other hand x is efficient so that $Du(x(t), t) = \lambda(t)p$, for some price vector p. Substituting, we have

$$\lambda(t)pDx(t) = 0.$$

But this just says that the derivative of income with respect to t is zero. Hence it must be constant across consumers, and the result is proved.

The preceding argument required that both the utility function and the allocation be differentiable. It is easy to construct examples showing the necessity of assuming that the utility function be differentiable for this result to hold. The differentiability of the allocation itself is a bit subtler, as we now discuss.

Varian [1976] established that his parameterization and a convexity assumption on preferences implied that an envy-free and efficient allocation would be necessarily continuous. Subsequently, Kleinberg [1978, 1980] showed by way of an example that continuity was not enough to guarantee the equal-income property. However, he also showed that a minor strengthening of the regularity assumption on the allocation, namely that it satisfy a Lipschitz condition, would be sufficient for the result. Hence the differentiability of the allocation is not really needed. Analogous results were independently discovered by McLennan [1980] and Champsaur and Laroque [1981]. In the latter paper, the authors formulate assumptions on the primitive data defining the economy (the preferences) that guarantee the equal-income property. Yannelis [1981, 1982] and Mas-Colell [1982] investigated related questions in this area.

The equal-income theorem has an interesting interpretation in the incentive compatibility and self-selection literature that has been pointed out by several authors (Leffler, Long, and Russell [1979], Hammond [1979], and Champsaur and Laroque [1981]). In this framework it is typically the case that the no-envy condition must be satisfied by allocations obtained through an incentive-compatible mechanism. If each agent is choosing an action that is optimal for him and the other agents' choices are *feasible* for him, then clearly no agent can prefer any other agent's action to his own − that is, there must be no envy.

Another interesting aspect of large economies is the behavior of coalitional-fair allocations. Recall that an allocation is coalitional-fair if there is no group of agents that envies the per capita consumption bundle of any other group of agents. It is straightforward to show that equal-income Walrasian allocations are coalitional-fair, but in general there will be many other coalitional-fair allocations. However, in large economies, the equal-income Walrasian allocations are the *only* coalitional-fair allocations!

This result was originally established by Vind [1972] using a measure space approach. Subsequently, Varian [1974] generalized Vind's theorem and provided a new argument using constructions similar to those used in the core convergence theorem of Debreu and Scarf. Yaari [1982] also investigated this issue.

4   Symmetry theories involving production

The results of Section 1 concerning the existence and characterization of envy-free and efficient allocations in exchange economies are very appealing. It is important to consider how far they can be extended and in particular to ask how the no-envy criterion works in economic situations involving production. We might well be worried not only about a fair division of a cake, but also about a simultaneous fair division of the labor involved in baking the cake!

If all consumers have the same preferences but different productive capabilities, envy-free and efficient allocations continue generally to exist (Varian [1974]), for in this situation the consumption bundles in an envy-free allocation must be indifferent in terms of the common preferences. Thus to satisfy efficiency, we need only find an allocation with this property that is the highest in terms of these preferences. Similarly, if all consumers have the same productive capabilities but different preferences, envy-free and efficient allocations will typically exist. The problem arises when both tastes and abilities differ across the population. In this situation the demands for efficiency and equity may be in conflict.

Pazner and Schmeidler [1974 (Chapter 10, this book)] were the first to recognize this possibility. They presented a series of examples that demonstrated nonexistence in quite nonpathological cases. Obviously the original definition of an envy-free and efficient allocation is not appropriate for an economy involving production. What generalizations of the concept are appropriate?

Pazner and Schmeidler ([1978b], originally written in 1974) suggested one alternative that Varian [1974] later termed an *income-fair* allocation. This is simply an efficient allocation where the values of all agents' consumption−leisure bundles are the same. Thus all consumers have the same "implicit income" or "full income" given that each consumer's leisure is valued at its efficiency price. In the following pages we will refer to such allocations as being *full-income-fair*.

If we compared a more able to a less able person's consumption bundle at a full-income-fair allocation we would find that the more able person would likely consume less of his own (more expensive) leisure, while the less able person could afford to consume more of his own (less expensive) leisure.

Varian [1974] later suggested the concept of *wealth-fairness*. In a wealth-fair allocation it is required that each individual weakly prefers his consumption−output bundle to any other individual's consumption−output bundle. Thus an allocation at which one individual envies another's consumption of goods and leisure is not declared unfair *unless* the first individual is willing to match the other's *production* of output. Of course this definition is meaningful only if the aggregate output can be decomposed into outputs attributable to the individual agents.

A less restrictive definition can be obtained by requiring only that the envious individual produce output that has the same value at the supporting efficiency prices as the output of the other. However, the modified definition requires the existence of supporting prices and can therefore be applied only to efficient allocations.

If we compared a more able to a less able person's consumption bundles at a wealth-fair allocation, we would find that the more able person might well have a consumption that the less able person envies; but the less able person could not object to it, since he would be unwilling (or unable) to match the more able person's contribution to the social product.

It seems as though the less able are favored in a full-income-fair allocation and the more able are favored in a wealth-fair allocation. This impression is reinforced by a thought experiment suggested by Pazner and Schmeidler [1978b] and Varian [1974]. To prove the existence of envy-free and efficient allocations in an exchange economy, recall that we simply divided the social endowment equally and traded to a Walrasian allocation. What happens if we try the same technique in a production economy?

In order to answer this question we first have to decide what we mean by equal division. In particular what do we mean by equal division of ability? One possibility is to divide everyone's endowment of labor among everyone else. Thus each person gets a coupon entitling him to $1/n$th of each other person's labor time in addition to his endowment of $1/n$th of the social initial endowment of goods. We then trade to a Walrasian allocation, each person selling his endowment of goods and labor at the relevant prices. Clearly the resulting allocation is full-income-fair: everybody has *exactly* the same endowment — hence everybody must have the same value bundle in equilibrium.[2]

Alternatively we could consider dividing up equally the social initial endowment of goods only, not correcting at all for the distribution of abilities, and then trade to a Walrasian allocation. Varian [1974] showed that in this case the resulting allocation is wealth-fair (in fact this yields all the wealth-fair allocations according to the modified definition). The argument is again relatively straightforward: if I prefer your consumption–output bundle to my own — meaning that I am willing to produce output valued as highly as your output — then in equilibrium I would be able to earn as much as you earn. But then I could afford your consumption bundle in the first place.

Hence the full-income-fair notion *totally corrects* for the distribution of abilities, and the wealth-fair notion allows for *no correction* at all. Both of these views seem a bit extreme. Are there any other intermediate cases that one might consider?

Daniel [1975] suggested that if we cannot expect to have no envy, we might at least hope for a kind of balanced envy. Using quite general assumptions on preferences (in particular, no convexity assumptions are needed), he demonstrated the existence of efficient allocations at which each person is envied by the same number of people that he envies.

An appealing feature of this kind of balanced envy criterion is that when envy-free allocations exist, they have this property. Otherwise very little is known about the set of allocations that satisfy the Daniel criterion; however it may be consistent with situations in which the number of occurrences of envy is very large, as emphasized by Pazner [1977 (Chapter 13, this book)].

We also have the notion of an egalitarian-equivalent and efficient allocation mentioned earlier. Pazner and Schmeidler [1978b] show that such allocations exist under very general conditions, including economies involving production. (In fact efficient egalitarian-equivalent allocations will exist even if preferences are not convex; monotonicity and utility connectedness assumptions are enough.)

However, if no restriction is placed on the reference bundle, one can find economies with egalitarian-equivalent and efficient allocations where one agent consumes everything and the others nothing; and as showed by Postlewaite (quoted by Daniel [1978]), there are economies where the set of envy-free and efficient allocations is disjoint from the set of egalitarian-

---

[2] It is worthwhile noting, along with Pazner and Schmeidler [1978b] that the same argument may be used to show that under standard assumptions on preferences and technologies, any distribution of full income can be obtained at some Walrasian allocation.

equivalent and efficient allocations. If the reference bundle is required to be proportional to the average endowment, and there are only two agents both with convex preferences, Pazner and Schmeidler point out that any egalitarian-equivalent and efficient allocation will be envy-free as well. But if the restriction on the number of agents is relaxed, one can find economies admitting of egalitarian-equivalent and efficient allocations at which one agent consumes strictly more of every commodity as some other agent, in clear violation of moral intuition.

In another contribution, Otsuki [1980] suggested the concept of *distribution according to labor*, which is a generalization of Varian's notion of wealth-fair allocations in that it allows agents to gain from their own "labor ability set" while correcting for the distribution of other goods. Otsuki established that distributions according to labor exist under standard regularity conditions. However, it is not clear that each person should be allowed the entire gains from his labor ability set as Otsuki seems to imply. After all, the initial distribution of ability is as ethically arbitrary as the initial distribution of material resources. (Or is it?)

Although the idea of enlarging the range of admissible comparisons to arbitrary (feasible or not) lists of consumption bundles is conceptually interesting and has the advantage of yielding existence results, it has not yet yielded a fully convincing criterion for distributive justice.

So as of this date there does not seem to be an entirely satisfactory concept of equity in the case of a production economy. Perhaps this reflects an inherent difficulty with notions of justice based on symmetry. They seem to work well when everyone is similar, but if there are too many things that differ across individuals the demands of equity *and* efficiency become difficult to reconcile.

5   Information and incentives

Once an equity criterion has been selected, several questions of a more practical nature arise concerning the availability of the information on which the criterion is based. How much information is needed to determine whether a given allocation satisfies the criterion? How can allocations satisfying the criterion be found? Can all such allocations be found? What if agents behave strategically instead of truthfully supplying the information requested of them?

There is no unique way of evaluating and comparing the informational burdens of various equity criteria. In many of the examples of criteria described in the preceding it is natural simply to count the number of comparisons that have to be made: for instance $n(n - 1)$ comparisons are required to determine whether an allocation is envy-free, while only n

comparisons are needed to check that an allocation Pareto dominates equal division. This sort of consideration of informational simplicity was in fact an important motivation for Pazner's proposal of the latter criterion [1977 (Chapter 13, this book)].

In other cases more complicated operations have to be performed: the various criteria of coalitional equity require that a large number of blocking conditions be checked, while the criterion of egalitarian-equivalence is based on entire indifference surfaces. Perhaps the simplest criterion is that of full-income-fairness, which involves only local knowledge of indifference surfaces and the comparisons of the n agents' full incomes at the proposed allocation.

We now turn to a discussion of how to implement equitable allocations. Given some criterion ψ let us call a *realization mechanism for* ψ a set of rules describing how information is (i) generated, (ii) exchanged between the agents themselves and perhaps an "auctioneer" (an outside agent whose purpose is to help in coordinating the agents' activities), and (iii) processed, so as to yield some, or perhaps all, allocations satisfying the criterion. As an example let ψ be the envy-free and efficient criterion and the realization mechanism for ψ be the Walrasian mechanism from equal division. As we showed in Section 1, this will yield some, but not all, of the desired allocations.

It is interesting to note that the earliest papers devoted to problems of fair division centered on this realization question. The classical two-person divide-and-choose method (one agent divides and the other chooses) as well as the generalizations to n agents studied by Steinhaus [1948], Singer [1962], and Kuhn [1967] are operational methods of obtaining what these authors thought to be equitable outcomes, although the precise sense in which the outcomes could be described as equitable was left to Kolm [1972], Crawford [1977], Crawford and Heller [1979], and Samuelson [1980].

Given a realization mechanism for some criterion ψ, it is in general the case that, if all but one agent follow the rules of behavior assigned to them by the mechanism, the remaining agent will find it profitable not to behave as required. This observation opens up two lines of inquiry. What are the consequences of manipulation on realization mechanisms? Do there exist mechanisms that are robust against such attempts at manipulation?

These questions are best studied in a game-theoretic framework. We will discuss the latter question first. It can be more formally stated as follows: Given some equity criterion ψ, does there exist a game, that is, a list of strategy spaces, one for each agent, and an outcome function associating to each list of strategies some feasible allocation − such that the equilibrium allocations of the game are allocations that satisfy ψ? Such a game will be said to *implement* ψ.

For this question to be well posed, we need to make a few things more precise. What kind of strategic behavior is allowed? What information do the agents have about the other agents' preferences? How risk averse are they? Must the equilibrium allocations of the game be *all* the allocations satisfying ψ or only some nonempty subset?

We must also make precise the notion of equilibrium that is being used. What would be best of course is implementation in dominant strategies, strategies that are best for an agent no matter what strategies the other agents are choosing, but unfortunately this is not possible in general.

Because of this negative result many researchers have turned to implementation in Nash equilibria, defined by the property that each strategy is best against the particular strategies adopted by the other agents, and in this case several positive results were established. The most important of these, due to Maskin [1977], is that a correspondence is Nash implementable only if it satisfies the following condition of monotonicity.

Definition: Let e be an economy, x be an allocation in $\psi(e)$, and e' be an economy in which preferences are altered so that x does not fall in anyone's ordering. If x is necessarily in $\psi(e')$ then we say that ψ is *monotonic*.

Maskin shows that this definition is also sufficient for Nash implementation if there are at least three agents for any ψ satisfying "no-veto power," a condition that, in economic environments with private goods, as studied here, is vacuously satisfied. (The condition says that if an allocation is at the top of all but one of the agents' preferences in the economy e then the last agent cannot prevent it from being in $\psi(e)$.) By the theorem, the correspondence that associates with each economy its set of envy-free and efficient allocation is Nash implementable. The same is true of the Walrasian correspondence from equal division (ignoring boundary problems as we will here and in the following paragraphs.) On the other hand the egalitarian-equivalent and efficient correspondence is not monotonic as soon as there are more than two agents and is therefore not Nash implementable.

This result should be compared to an argument due to Thomson [1979] (adapted from Hurwicz [1979a]), which states that if ψ, defined over a "sufficiently large" domain, selects efficient and envy-free allocations, satisfies a mild continuity condition, and is Nash implementable, then it contains the Walrasian correspondence from equal division. The continuity condition can be replaced by the following property.

Property P: If equal division is efficient for e, then all allocations indifferent to equal division are in $\psi(e)$.

Property P is satisfied by all of the examples that we have reviewed. Therefore these two results of Maskin and Thomson together imply that under the preceding assumptions only supercorrespondences of the Walrasian correspondence from equal division can be Nash implemented.

Having settled the theoretical issue of the *possibility* of implementing equitable allocations, we turn to the question of actually constructing games to do it. Maskin [1977] described a general method for doing this, and other games implementing the Walrasian correspondence from equal division were provided by Hurwicz [1979b], Schmeidler [1980], and others.

The topic of implementation has also been considered by Crawford [1977, 1979, 1980] and Moulin [1981]. Crawford's starting point is the two-person divide-and-choose method, which he first shows to yield envy-free but possibly inefficient allocations (although they will be undominated by any other envy-free allocation.) He then shows that this drawback can be removed by having the divider present the chooser a choice between equal division and some other allocation x selected by him, the divider. This method yields an envy-free and efficient allocation but gives an advantage to the divider. If the role of the divider is auctioned off and the proceeds of the auction are equally distributed among the choosers, an egalitarian-equivalent and efficient allocation is obtained.

Unfortunately, the procedure may yield infeasible allocations out of equilibrium. Demange [1982] proposes a modification of Crawford's procedure that takes care of this problem.

Moulin [1981] studies the case of transferable utility economies (where preferences are representable by utility functions that are additively separable and linear in one commodity, the same for all agents) and proposes various procedures in the same spirit that yield egalitarian or Shapley-value allocations.

If a proposed equity criterion cannot be implemented by a game, then any mechanism that realizes it under truthful behavior will be manipulable in some manner. So the next question to consider is to what extent realization mechanisms will be vulnerable to manipulation. Of course, the answer to this question will depend on the particular criterion under consideration and on the particular mechanism used to realize it. However, there is an important class of mechanisms for which a large number of common results can be obtained. These are the *direct* realization mechanisms, in which each agent is asked simply to report his preferences. Thomson [1982b] studied this class of mechanisms in the context of a transferable utility economy and established the following results.

Let us consider the *manipulation game associated with a criterion* ψ, by which we mean the game where each agent reports preferences, truthfully or not, and some outcome in $\psi(e)$, where e represents the "announced" economy, is then chosen. Consider the Nash equilibria of this game. Thomson shows that for most of the criteria we have discussed the equilibrium allocations of the associated manipulation game will be equal-income Walrasian allocations with respect to the reported preferences.

Thomson also shows that the equal-income Walrasian allocations with respect to the true preferences will always be among the equilibrium allocations, a result indicating that efficiency is not necessarily incompatible with manipulative behavior. In general there will be many other equilibrium allocations. In the manipulation games associated with monotonic correspondences, these equilibrium allocations can be completely characterized as essentially coinciding with the equilibrium allocations of the manipulation game associated with the Walrasian correspondence from equal division. Also, for most of the nonmonotonic correspondences studied, it turns out that equal division is efficient according to any equilibrium list of strategies. If property P is satisfied, then equal division will therefore appear to be efficient and it will seem that there is no problem of fair division to study.

6   **Applications of symmetry theories**

There have been several attempts to apply the concepts described to practical policy issues. For example Baumol [1980, 1982] investigated how considerations of symmetry might influence policy choices involving natural resources, choice of rationing schemes, and peak-load pricing. (Many of these issues will be discussed in his forthcoming book.) Crawford [1977, 1979, 1980] and Crawford and Heller [1979] considered a number of fair-division schemes that can be used as arbitration devices. (These schemes were described briefly in the last section along with other work on the classical problem of "fair division.") It has often seemed to us that there would be many opportunities in the legal profession for applying such schemes.

Brock and Scheinkman [1976] analyzed the implications of the no-envy criterion for analyzing questions of intergenerational equity, while Sobel [1979] considered the equitable division of a good whose supply is random. Svensson [1980] examined some related concepts concerning fair wage structures. Austen-Smith [1979] and Gaertner [1982] studied issues concerning the fair allocation of rights.

Several authors considered related symmetry notions in the evaluation of income distributions. Kolm [1976], Allingham [1977], Ulph [1978], and Archibald and Donaldson [1979] are representative pieces.

Yaari and Bar-Hillel [1984] examined the empirical basis for various theories of justice by conducting a small survey to determine the preferred divisions in some hypothetical problems. This sort of work could be very useful in delineating more precisely the moral intuitions held by the man in the street that economists and philosophers might hope to formalize in theoretical studies.

One difficulty of the equity concept reviewed here for the study of policy questions such as optimal taxation or optimal growth is that they are inherently utopian criteria meant to be used to evaluate the overall equity of an allocation. On the other hand many applications are concerned with the second best problem of locally improving upon a given situation. The no-envy criterion can tell you whether one allocation is equitable and another is not but it cannot ascertain whether one allocation is *more equitable* than another, which makes it difficult to use in second best problems where allocation must be compared with respect to some criterion such as a welfare function. Varian [1976] has proposed using an equal-income allocation to "normalize" a parametric welfare function in order to make such comparisons. He suggests that one choose the parameters of some given welfare function so that the function reaches its maximum at an equal-income allocation. The resulting welfare function can then be used to examine "second best" problems such as those described above.

7   Summary

We have examined several concepts of distributional justice based on considerations of symmetric treatment. In our opinion these concepts throw considerable light on important problems of distributional justice, but none can be said to be entirely satisfactory. Indeed, with a concept so complex and multifaceted as that of "justice," we can hardly expect that a single definition will be appropriate in all situations. However, we hope that the family of definitions described here can be used to examine the equity of distributional mechanisms and outcomes in a variety of frameworks.

In compiling this catalog of concepts of equity it has struck us how often equal-income Walrasian allocations have arisen. Such allocations are known to be efficient under standard assumptions and to

1. be envy free;
2. be coalitional envy-free;
3. be opportunity-fair;
4. be the only envy-free and efficient allocations when preferences vary continuously across a large population;
5. involve minimal informational requirements;
6. be central to the study of the vulnerability to manipulation of other criteria we have described.

Even in cases involving production, the two generalizations of equal-income Walrasian allocations, full-income-fair allocations and wealth-fair allocations, seem to have desirable normative properties. Certainly the fact that the concept of equal incomes arises in such a wide variety of contexts suggests that this idea is central to any discussion of economic justice.

BIBLIOGRAPHY

This bibliography contains several items that were not directly referenced in the text.

Allingham, M. [1977]. "Fairness and Utility." *Economie Appliquée*, 29(2):257–266.
Archibald, P., and D. Donaldson [1979]. "Notes on Economic Inequality." *Journal of Public Economics*, 12(2):205–214.
Austen-Smith, D. [1979]. "Fair Rights." *Economics Letters*, 4(1):29–32.
Baumol, W. [1980]. "Theory of Equity in Pricing for Resource Conservation." *Journal of Environmental Economics*, 7(4):308–320.
Baumol, W. [1982]. "Applied Fairness Theory and Rationing Policy." *American Economic Review*, 72(4):639–651.
Baumol, W. [1983]. "Applied Fairness Theory: Reply." *American Economic Review*, 73(5):1161–1162.
Brock, W., and J. Scheinkman [1976]. "On Just Savings Rules." Mimeo. University of Chicago.
Campbell, D. [1975]. "Income Distribution under Majority Rule and Alternative Taxation Criteria." *Public Choice*, 22(Summer):23–35.
Champsaur, P., and G. Laroque [1981]. "Fair Allocations in Large Economies." *Journal of Economic Theory*, 25:269–282.
Crawford, V. [1977]. "A Game of Fair Division." *Review of Economic Studies*, 44(2):235–247.
Crawford, V. [1979]. "A Procedure for Generating Pareto Efficient Egalitarian Equivalent Allocations." *Econometrica*, 47:49–60.
Crawford, V. [1980]. "A Self Administered Solution to the Bargaining Problem." *Review of Economic Studies*, 47(2):385–392.
Crawford, V. and W. Heller [1979]. "Fair Division with Indivisible Commodities." *Journal of Economic Theory*, 21(1):10–27.
Daniel, T. [1975]. "A Revised Concept of Distributional Equity." *Journal of Economic Theory*, 11(1):94–100.

Daniel, T. [1978]. "Pitfalls in the Theory of Fairness − Comment." *Journal of Economic Theory*, *19*(2):561−564.

Demange, G. [1982]. "Implementing Efficient Egalitarian Equivalent Allocations." Ecole Polytechnique Discussion Paper A244.

Dubins, L. E., and E. H. Spanier [1961]. "How To Cut a Cake Fairly." *American Mathematical Monthly*, *68*:1−17.

Feldman, A., and A. Kirman [1974]. "Fairness and Envy." *American Economic Review*, *64*(6):995−1005.

Feldman, A., and Weiman, D. [1979]. "Envy, Wealth and Class Hierarchies." *Journal of Public Economics*, *11*(1):81−91.

Foley, D. [1967]. "Resource Allocation and the Public Sector." *Yale Economic Essays*, *7*:45−98.

Gaertner, W. [1982]. Envy-Free Rights Assignments and Self-oriented Preferences. *Mathematical Social Sciences*, *2*:199−208.

Gardenfors, P. [1978]. "Fairness without Interpersonal Comparisons." *Theoria*, *44*(10):57−74.

Goldman, S., and C. Sussangkarn [1978]. "On the Concept of Fairness." *Journal of Economic Theory*, *19*(1):210−216.

Goldman, S., and C. Sussangkarn [1980]. "On Equity and Efficiency." *Economics Letters*, *5*:29−31.

Graff, J. [1978]. "Equity and Efficiency as Components of General Welfare." *South African Journal of Economics*, *19*(2):561−564.

Hammond, P. [1976]. "Equity, Arrow's Conditions and Rawls Difference Principle." *Econometrica*, *44*(4):793−804.

Hammond, P. [1979]. "Straightforward Individual Incentive Compatibility in Large Economies." *Review of Economic Studies*, *46*:263−282.

Hayashi, T. [1979]. "On a Positive Theory of Fair Allocation." Mimeo. Kobe University.

Henry, J. [1977]. "Efficiency, Equality, Equity, and Personal Income Distribution." *Actualité Economique*, *53*(2):154−192.

Hurwicz, L. [1979a]. "On Allocations Attainable through Nash Equilibria," in *Aggregation and Revelation of Preferences*, edited by J.-J. Laffont. pp. 397−419. Amsterdam: North Holland.

Hurwicz, L. [1979b]. "Outcome Functions Yielding Walrasian and Lindahl Allocations at Nash Equilibrium Points for Two or More Agents." *Review of Economic Studies*, *46*:217−225.

Jaskold-Gabszewicz, J. [1975]. "Coalitional Fairness of Allocations in Pure Exchange." *Econometrica*, *43*(4):661−668.

Kleinberg, N. [1978]. "Three Essays in Mathematical Economics." Ph.D. Thesis, Massachusetts Institute of Technology, Cambridge, Mass.

Kleinberg, N. [1980]. "Fair Allocations and Equal Incomes." *Journal of Economic Theory*, *23*(2):189−200.

Kolm, S. [1972]. *Justice et Equité*. Paris: Editions du Centre National de la Recherche Scientifique.

Kuhn, H. [1967]. "On Games of Fair Division," in *Essays in Honor of Oskar Morgenstern*, edited by M. Shubik, pp. 29−37. Princeton, N.J.: Princeton University Press.

Leffler, K., J. Long, and T. Russell [1979]. "Signaling − Efficiency and Equilibrium." *Economics Letters*, *4*:215−220.

Luce, D., and H. Raiffa [1957]. *Games and Decisions*. New York: Wiley.

McLennan, A. [1980]. "Fair Allocations." Ph.D. Thesis, Princeton University, Princeton, N.J.

Mas-Colell, A. [1982]. "On the Second Welfare Theorem for Anonymous Net Trades in Exchange Economies with Many Agents." Harvard University.

Maskin, E. [Forthcoming]. "Nash Equilibrium and Welfare Optimality," in *Mathematics of Operations Research*.

Moulin, H. [1980]. "Implementing Efficient, Anonymous and Neutral Social Choice Functions." *Journal of Mathematical Economics*, 7:249−269.

Moulin, H. [1981]. "Implementing Just and Efficient Decision Making." *Journal of Public Economics*, 16:193−213.

Musgrave, R. [1959]. *The Theory of Public Finance*. New York: McGraw-Hill.

Nozick, R. [1974]. *Anarchy, State, and Utopia*. New York: Basic Books.

Otsuki, M. [1980]. "On Distribution According to Labor − A Concept of Fairness in Production." *Review of Economic Studies*, 47(5):945−58.

Pazner, E. [1977]. "Pitfalls in the Theory of Fairness." *Journal of Economic Theory*, 14(2):458−466. [Chapter 13 in this book.]

Pazner, E. [1979]. "Individual Rationality and the Concept of Social Welfare." *Theory and Decision*, 10(1−4):281−292.

Pazner, E., and D. Schmeidler [1974]. "A Difficulty in the Concept of Fairness." *Review of Economic Studies*, 41:441−443. [Chapter 10 in this book.]

Pazner, E., and D. Schmeidler [1976]. "Social Contract Theory and Ordinal Distributive Equity." *Journal of Public Economics*, 5:261−268. [Chapter 12 in this book.]

Pazner, E., and D. Schmeidler [1978a]. "Egalitarian Equivalent Allocations: A New Concept of Economic Equity." *Quarterly Journal of Economics*, 92(4): 671−687. [Chapter 15 in this book.]

Pazner, E., and D. Schmeidler [1978b]. "Decentralization and Income Distribution in Socialist Economies." *Economic Inquiry*, pp. 257−264.

Rae, D. [1979]. "Egalitarian State − Notes on a System of Contradictory Ideals." *Daedalus*, 108(4):37−54.

Rawls, J. [1971]. *A Theory of Justice*. Cambridge, Mass.: Harvard University Press.

Roberts, K. [1980]. "Possibility Theorems with Interpersonally Comparable Welfare Levels." *Review of Economic Studies*, 47(2):409−420.

Samuelson, W. [1980]. "The Object Distribution Problem Revisited." *Quarterly Journal of Economics*, pp. 85−98.

Schick, F. [1980]. "Towards a Logic of Liberalism." *Journal of Philosophy*, 77(2):80−98.

Schmeidler, D. [1980]. "Walrasian Analysis via Strategic Outcome Functions." *Econometrica*, 48:1585−1593.

Schmeidler, D., and K. Vind [1972]. "Fair Net Trades." *Econometrica*, 40(4): 637−642.

Schmeidler, D., and M. Yaari [1971]. "Fair Allocations." unpublished.

Sen, A. [1977]. "Social Choice Theory − Re-Examination." *Econometrica*, 45(1):53−77.

Sen, A. [1979]. "Welfare Basis of Real Income Comparisons." *Journal of Economic Literature*, 17(1):1−45.

Singer, E. [1962]. "Extension of the Classical Rule of 'Divide and Choose'." *Southern Economic Journal*, 38:391−394.

Sobel, J. [1979]. "Fair Allocations of a Renewable Resource." *Journal of Economic Theory*, 21(2):235−248.

Steinhaus, H. [1948]. "The Problem of Fair Division." *Econometrica*, pp. 101–104.

Suppes, P. [1966]. "Some Formal Models of Grading Principles." *Synthése*, 6:284–306.

Sussangkarn, C., and S. Goldman [1980]. "Dealing with Envy." University of California, Berkeley.

Suzumura, K. [1980]. "On the Possibility of "Fair" Collective Choice Rules." Mimeo. Kyoto Institute of Economic Research, Kyoto, Japan.

Suzumura, K. [1981a]. "On Pareto-Efficiency and the No-Envy Concept of Equity." *Journal of Economic Theory*, 25:267–379.

Suzumura, K. [1981b]. "Equity, Efficiency and Rights in Social Choice." Kyoto Institute of Economic Research, Kyoto, Japan.

Svensson, L. [1980]. "Some Views on a Fair Wage Structure." *Ekonomiska Samfunddets Tidskrift*, 33(3):385–392.

Tamaklowe, E. [1980]. "Spatial Equity in Regional Transportation Investment Policies." *Traffic Quarterly*, 34(4):605–626.

Thomson, W. [1979]. "On Allocations Attainable through Nash-Equilibria, a Comment," in *Aggregation and Revelation of Preferences*, edited by J.-J. Laffont, pp. 420–431. Amsterdam: North Holland.

Thomson, W. [1982a]. "An Informationally Efficient Equity Criterion." *Journal of Public Economics*, 18:243–263.

Thomson, W. [1982b]. "The Manipulation of Mechanisms Designed to Select Equitable and Efficient Allocations." Harvard Institute of Economic Research Discussion Paper no. 909, Cambridge, Mass.

Thomson, W. [1983]. "Equity in Exchange Economies." *Journal of Economic Theory*, 29(2):217–244.

Ulph, D. [1978]. "Labor Supply and the Measurement of Inequality." *Journal of Economic Theory*, 19(2):492–512.

Varian, H. [1974]. "Equity, Envy, and Efficiency." *Journal of Economic Theory*, 9:63–91.

Varian, H. [1975]. "Distributive Justice, Welfare Economics, and the Theory of Fairness." *Philosophy and Public Affairs*, 4:223–247.

Varian, H. [1976]. "Two Problems in the Theory of Fairness." *Journal of Public Economics*, 5:249–260.

Vind, K. [1972]. "Lecture Notes in Mathematical Economics." Mimeo. Stanford University, Stanford, Calif.

Wittmean, D. [1979]. "Diagrammatic Exposition of Justice." *Theory and Decision*, 11(2):207–239.

Yannelis, N. [1981]. "Approximate Coalitionally Fair Allocations in Large "Mixed" Economies." Discussion Paper no. 130, Wayne State University, Detroit, Mich.

Yannelis, N. [1982]. "Nondiscriminatory Allocations in Finite Mixed Markets." Mimeo. Wayne State University, Detroit, Mich.

Yaari, M. [1982]. "A Remark on Competitive Equilibrium with Equal Incomes." Research Memorandum no. 49, Center for Research in Mathematical Economics, The Hebrew University, Jerusalem.

Yaari, M., and M. Bar-Hillel [1984]. "On Dividing Justly." *Social Choice and Welfare*, 1:1–24.

CHAPTER 5

Strategy-proofness: the existence of dominant-strategy mechanisms

Eitan Muller and Mark A. Satterthwaite

1   Introduction

Economic theory takes as axiomatic that individuals have preferences over possible allocations and that they seek their most preferred allocation. Except in unusual and happy circumstances the result is conflict: the several agents disagree over which outcomes are preferable and they resolve their conflict within the rules of whatever allocation mechanism under which they happen to be operating. Since the outcome is important, each agent devises a strategy that he believes will be effective in securing, as nearly as possible, an outcome that is highly preferred by his own lights.

This penchant that individuals have for strategizing causes economic theorists trouble because the essence of an individual's strategic choice is to guess correctly the actions of other individuals and then to choose the action that results in the best attainable outcome. This means that the properties of a particular allocation mechanism cannot be determined in any simple way. Specifically, an allocation mechanism might be thought to operate by asking agents to state their preferences and then calculating from this information an outcome that meets an appropriate optimality criterion. Strategic behavior confounds this process because one may calculate, given the probable strategies of other agents, that misrepresenting one's preferences may result in a more preferred outcome than stating them truthfully. Therefore in studying the properties of a particular allocation mechanism, theorists must not only understand how the mechanism aggregates the information individuals put into it, they must also model the information each agent has about every other agent and how each agent uses this information to decide what information to put into the mechanism. This is difficult.

Strategy-proof mechanisms represent the most direct and elegant

131

means conceivable for cutting through the problems that strategic behavior poses for our understanding of allocation mechanisms' performance. An allocation mechanism is defined to be strategy-proof if and only if telling the truth is always a dominant strategy for every agent. A strategy is dominant for an agent if, irrespective of what strategies the other agents play, no other strategy results in an outcome that the agent prefers. An agent who has a dominant strategy need not guess what other agents are likely to do, because that guessing has no utility; the agent's dominant strategy is best no matter what other agents do. Therefore for strategy-proof mechanisms the question of strategy never arises, because every agent has no reason not to follow the dominant strategy of truth telling. This makes the analysis of strategy-proof mechanisms trivial in comparison to the analysis of mechanisms that are not strategy-proof, because questions of the information that agents possess about other agents can be ignored.

This essay's purpose is to explore the current state of our knowledge concerning the possibilities for constructing strategy-proof mechanisms. We focus on strategy-proof mechanisms rather than dominant-strategy mechanisms because every dominant-strategy mechanism is equivalent to some strategy-proof mechanism. Consequently no generality is lost by our focus on strategy-proofness rather than dominant strategies. Section 2 presents an important, baseline result: the Gibbard–Satterthwaite theorem. It states that reasonable strategy-proof allocation mechanisms, while exceedingly attractive in the abstract, simply do not exist when agents' admissible preferences over the set of feasible alternatives are not a priori restricted to some subset of the set of all possible transitive orderings of the feasible alternatives. Thus, in the most general case, strategizing cannot be taken out of economic behavior by cleverly designing the allocation mechanism.

The remainder of the essay explores the degree to which the general case must be specialized in order to make the construction of a reasonable strategy-proof mechanism feasible. We pursue two approaches to this problem. In Section 3 we specify with increasing precision what we mean by a reasonable strategy-proof mechanism and then investigate how tightly the set of admissible preference orderings must be restricted in order to make construction of the specified mechanism possible. In Section 4 we reverse the procedure. There we specify restrictions on the set of a priori admissible preference orderings in ways that have economic relevance and then ask what reasonable strategy-proof mechanisms can be constructed given those particular restrictions on domains. Conceptually these two approaches are dual to each other; in practice, however, no one has succeeded in making an adequate formal connection between them. Therefore we present them separately.

No completely unambiguous conclusion can be drawn from the work discussed in this essay. As reported in Section 4, for several specific domains of admissible preferences the results are negative in that no reasonable strategy-proof mechanism can be constructed. In Section 3 we report results that show the existence of domains that (i) are large relative to the size of the unrestricted domain and (ii) do permit construction of reasonable strategy-proof mechanisms. Nevertheless no examples have as yet been constructed that succeed in showing that these relatively large restricted domains have relevance to the types of restrictions on admissible preferences that naturally occur in economics.

This essay is not a survey. We only report on a small fraction of the interesting work that has been done in the existence of strategy-proof mechanisms. We have tried to present some essential ideas from this body of research in a manner that contributes to the reader's intuition and understanding.

2   Problem formulation and a basic theorem

Basic model

Most of the work on strategy-proof mechanisms has been conducted in a very simple framework that focuses on agents' preferences and the incentive they may have to follow dominant strategies in revealing those preferences.[1] A group $I = \{1, 2, \ldots, n\}$ is a fixed set of n individuals who must select an alternative from a feasible set of alternatives. The set $A = \{x, y, z, \ldots, w\}$ is the set of all conceivable resource allocations; it has cardinality of $|A|$. Each individual $i \in I$ has a transitive binary preference relation P_i over the set A. Thus, for all pairs of alternatives $x, y \in A$ and for every individual $i \in I$, one of three cases is true: xP_iy denoting strict preference for x over y, yP_ix denoting strict preference for y over x, or neither xP_iy nor yP_ix denoting indifference between x and y. Indifference between x and y is alternatively denoted by $x\bar{P}_iy$.

Not every preference ordering is necessarily admissible. Let Ω be the set of all complete and transitive preference orderings P_i that any individual i might rationally hold. In other words, if $P_i \notin \Omega$, then P_i is a preference ordering that, while being transitive, violates some principle of

---

[1] An exception is Postlewaite [1979], who wrote about the incentives individuals may have to misrepresent their initial endowments.

rationality that clearly applies to the situation in question. For example, in economic contexts if the two-dimensional vector x represents a commodity bundle and that bundle dominates both components of a second bundle y, then the principle of nonsatiation implies that an ordering P_i for which xP_iy may be admissible (and thus be an element of Ω) while an ordering P_i for which yP_ix cannot be admissible. The set Ω^n is the n-fold Cartesian product of Ω. The group's preference profile is the n-tuple, $(P_1, \ldots, P_n) \in \Omega^n$, of the individual orderings.

The set of feasible allocations, B, may be either A in its entirety or a subset of it. The group's task is to select a single allocation from B. They do this, in effect, by voting. Each individual i reports a preference ordering $Q_i \in \Omega$ for input into the allocation mechanism F that aggregates the profile of reported preferences down to a single element of B. Formally, let $\mathcal{P}(A)$ be the set of subsets of A. An allocation mechanism is a function F: $\Omega^N \times \mathcal{P}(A) \to A$. Thus $F(Q, B)$ is the group's choice when the profile of reported preferences is Q and the feasible set is B. The preference ordering Q_i an individual reports may or may not be identical to his preferences P_i; the choice of what to report is his since preferences are private and impossible for outsiders to ascertain.

That individuals cannot be forced to report their preferences P_i sincerely for input into the allocation mechanism is the crux of the problem this essay considers. Each individual agent may calculate whether it is in his or her interest to report honestly. An agent i with preferences P_i has an incentive to *manipulate* the mechanism F at profile $P/P_i \in \Omega^n$ and feasible set $B \in \mathcal{P}(A)$ if

$$F(P/Q_i, B) \; P_i \; F(P/P_i, B), \tag{2.01}$$

where $Q_i \in \Omega$, $(P/Q_i) = (P_1, \ldots, Q_i, \ldots, P_n) \in \Omega^n$, and $(P/P_i) = P = (P_1, \ldots, P_i, \ldots, P_n)$. The content of (2.01) is that if agent i is to be able to manipulate the outcome at profile $P = P/P_i$, then he must have available an admissible ordering Q_i that, when played as a substitute for his true preferences P_i, results in an outcome he strictly prefers.

Dominance and strategy-proofness

A mechanism F is *strategy-proof* if no admissible profile $P \in \Omega^n$, no feasible set $B \in \mathcal{P}(A)$, and no agent i exists such that at profile P agent i can manipulate mechanism F. Individuals never have an interest in not reporting their preferences accurately when the mechanism is strategy-proof. An implication is that if a mechanism is strategy-proof, then every agent always has a dominant strategy. Formally, a strategy $Q_i \in \Omega$ is *dominant* at feasible set $B \in \mathcal{P}(A)$ for agent i with preferences P_i if no profile $P/Q_i' \in \Omega^n$ exists such that

$$F(P/Q_i', B) \ P_i \ F(P/Q_i, B). \qquad (2.02)$$

In other words, the ordering Q_i is dominant for agent i if and only if no profile exists for which playing another ordering Q_i' would result in the realization of a strictly preferred outcome for agent i. A mechanism, F, is a *dominant-strategy mechanism* if, at every $P \in \Omega^n$ and $B \in \mathcal{P}(A)$, every agent has a dominant strategy.

The great attraction of dominant-strategy mechanisms is that agents need no information about other agents' preferences in order to play optimally. Suppose F is not a mechanism for which agents have dominant strategies. Inspection of (2.02) shows that if agent i is to manipulate successfully mechanism F at profile P, then he or she must know that profile P/Q_i is being realized rather than, for example, profile P'/Q_i. To know this requires good information on i's part about other agents' preferences and strategizing. None of this information is needed if F always gives individual i a dominant strategy. No matter what profile is realized, he plays that ordering Q_i that is dominant for his true preference ordering P_i.

The set of all possible strategy-proof mechanisms is clearly a subset of the set of mechanisms that always give every agent a dominant strategy. We restrict ourselves to considering only strategy-proof mechanisms, because, as Gibbard [1973] showed, every dominant-strategy mechanism that is not strategy-proof is equivalent to a strategy-proof mechanism. No generality is gained by looking at the broader class. This equivalence is seen as follows. Suppose F is a dominant-strategy mechanism. Therefore for each agent i a function $\sigma_i\colon \Omega \to \Omega$ exists that associates his true preference ordering P_i with his dominant strategy Q_i for that particular ordering; that is, $\sigma_i(P_i) = Q_i$. Define a new mechanism, F^σ, as the composition of the F and σ functions:

$$F^\sigma(P_1, \ldots, P_n, B) = F[\sigma_1(P_1), \ldots, \sigma_n(P_n), B]. \qquad (2.03)$$

The mechanism F^σ is strategy-proof. If, contrary to the assertion, it were not strategy-proof, then an agent i, a profile $P \in \Omega^n$, a feasible set $B \in \mathcal{P}(A)$, and an ordering $Q_i' \in \Omega$ would exist such that i would have an incentive to manipulate F^σ:

$$F^\sigma(P/Q_i, B) \ P_i \ F^\sigma(P/P_i, B). \qquad (2.04)$$

Relation (2.04) may be rewritten in terms of the original mechanism F:

$$F(Q/Q_i'', B) \ P_i \ F(Q/Q_i, B) \qquad (2.05)$$

where $Q = [\sigma_1(P_1), \ldots, \sigma_n(P_n)]$ is the vector of the agents' dominant strategies, $Q_i = \sigma_i(P_i)$ is agent i's dominant strategy when his preferences are P_i, and $Q_i'' = \sigma_i(Q_i')$ is agent i's dominant strategy when his preferences are Q_i'. But (2.05) contradicts the hypothesis that $Q_i = \sigma_i(P_i)$ is a dominant strategy for agent i because he does better playing Q_i''. Therefore F^σ is a strategy-proof mechanism because if it were not, then F would not be a dominant strategy mechanism as initially assumed. Finally, in addition to being strategy-proof, F^σ is equivalent to F for agent i because if, in utilizing each mechanism, every agent always plays his dominant strategy, then, for any preference profile, F and F^σ give identical payoffs.[2]

Impossibility theorem

Can strategy-proof mechanisms be constructed? Certainly, inasmuch as we can easily identify four general types:

1. Let, for all admissible profiles $P \in \Omega^n$, $F(P, B) = x$, where x is a fixed element of A. This is an imposed mechanism. It is strategy-proof because the agents' preferences do not influence the outcome and therefore each agent has nothing to gain from misrepresenting his preferences.
2. Let, for some i, all admissible sets $B \in \mathcal{P}(A)$, and all admissible profiles $P \in \Omega^n$, $F(P, B) = \max_B(P_i)$ where $\max_B(\cdot)$ picks the element of B that is maximal according to the ordering P_i.[3] This is a dictatorial mechanism where agent i is the dictator. It is strategy-proof because agent i gets his most preferred alternative if he reports his preferences truthfully and no other agent has any influence on the decision.
3. Let A consist of only two elements, $\{x, y\}$, and define F to be majority rule: select y if the number of agents i for whom yP_ix exceeds the number for whom xP_iy and x otherwise (including ties). This is strategy-proof because, with only two alternatives, voting against one's preferred alternative can lead to its losing and cannot lead to its winning.
4. Let $A = \{x, y, z\}$ and let the set of admissible preference orderings consist of two orderings: $\Omega = \{(xzy), (yzx)\}$. The notation (xyz) stands for the ordering xP_iz, xP_iy, and zP_iy. If the

---

[2] This is the revelation principle in its original and simplest form.
[3] If more than one element of B is maximal, then the max operator uses an arbitrary rule to pick one element from among the set of maximal elements.

feasible set is the full set A, define F to be majority rule as before except that z is selected in the case of a tie between x and y. If the feasible set is just two elements, define F to be majority rule as in the previous example. This, too, is a strategy-proof mechanism because, with Ω restricted to two elements, the addition of the third alternative z changes nothing essential.

The first two of these mechanisms are unsatisfactory because they do not give sufficient scope for each agent's preferences to affect the choice. The second two mechanisms are unsatisfactory because they only apply to restricted situations: two alternatives in the case of (3) and a severely restricted set of admissible preferences in the case of (4).

Therefore the real question is: Do strategy-proof mechanisms exist that can accommodate any size feasible set, give agents' preferences an opportunity to affect the group's choice, and apply to a broad class of preference profiles? These three requirements are easily formalized. The first is simple: feasible sets of three or more elements should be admissible. Second, a mechanism should give agents influence over the outcome at least to the extent of satisfying the unanimity requirement of the Pareto principle and being nondictatorial. A mechanism F satisfies the *Pareto criterion* if, for any set $B \in \mathcal{P}(A)$, for any profile $P \in \Omega^n$, and for any $x, y \in B$, xP_iy for all $i \in I$ implies $F(P, B) \neq y$. It is *strongly nondictatorial* if no agent i exists such that, for at least one feasible set $B \in \mathcal{P}(A)$ $(|B| \geq 2)$, $F(P, B) = \max_B(P_i)$ for all $P \in \Omega^n$. Finally, let Σ_- be the set of all possible complete and transitive orderings that are defined on the conceivable set A. A somewhat narrower, but still very broad set is the set of all possible complete and transitive orderings that are strict; that is, indifference is excluded. We denote this set by Σ. Therefore, for a mechanism F to be maximally flexible and applicable, setting Ω equal to either Σ_- or Σ is desirable.

This set of requirements is impossible to meet. Gibbard [1973] and Satterthwaite [1973, 1975] showed this basic impossibility result.

Theorem 2.1 (Gibbard–Satterthwaite theorem): *If $|A| \geq 3$ and preferences are unrestricted ($\Omega = \Sigma_-$ or Σ), then an allocation mechanism F can not simultaneously be strategy-proof and satisfy both the Pareto criterion and strong nondictatorship.*

Feldman [1979] has devised a simple proof of the theorem for the special case of three alternatives, two agents, and domain Σ^2. We present his proof here because its construction yields insight into how the conditions of Theorem 2.1 may be modified in order to obtain possibility results.

Table 1. *Restrictions on $F(\cdot, A)$ imposed by the Pareto criterion*

Agent 1	Agent 2					
	1 (xyz)	2 (xzy)	3 (yxz)	4 (yzx)	5 (zxy)	6 (zyx)
1 (xyz)	x	x	$\neq z$[6]	$\neq z$[5]	$\neq y$[2]	?[4]
2 (xzy)	x	x	$\neq z$[7]	?[8]	$\neq y$[1]	$\neq y$[3]
3 (yxz)	$\neq z$	$\neq z$	y	y	?[12]	$\neq x$[9]
4 (yzx)	$\neq z$	?	y	y	$\neq x$[11]	$\neq x$[10]
5 (zxy)	$\neq y$	$\neq y$	?	$\neq x$	z	z
6 (zyx)	?	$\neq y$	$\neq x$	$\neq x$	z	z

The proof is this. The mechanism F is defined for the set $A = \{x, y, z\}$ and on the domain Σ^2. Table 1 shows the restrictions that the the Pareto criterion imposes on F when the feasible set is A. For example, if agent 1 has preferences (xyz) and agent 2 has preferences (zxy), then F cannot select y, because to do so would violate the Pareto criterion. Note that, because F is strategy-proof and thus induces truthful revelation, we need not make a distinction between reported preferences and true preferences. If both report (xyz), then the Pareto criterion requires selection of x. An entry that is a "?" indicates that the Pareto criterion places no restrictions on which alternative is selected.

The mechanism F is single-valued. Therefore a single element of A must be assigned to each cell that does not have a determinate element. Suppose element x is assigned to the cell labeled 1 (as indicated by the superscript 1). This violates neither the proposition nor the Pareto criterion. This assignment, however, implies that agent 1 is a dictator when the feasible set is A. We see this as follows.

Assigning x to cell 1 implies that x must be assigned to cell 2. Suppose to the contrary that the only other possibility, z, were assigned to cell 2. Agent 1 would then have an incentive to manipulate profile $[(xyz), (zxy)]$ by reporting (xzy) instead of (xyz). That would give him the preferred outcome of x rather than z. Therefore x must be assigned to cell 1, because to assign z to it would be to violate strategy-proofness. This same logic can be used to fill every indeterminate cell on Table 1.

Table 2 reports this logic for all cells above the diagonal. Consider as an example the assignment of y to cell 11. Since the proposition rules x out as a possibility for cell 11, the only alternative outcome that could have been assigned to it is z. If, however, z were assigned, then agent 2 could

Table 2. *Details of Feldman's proof*

Cell	Assigned outcome	Alternative outcome	Manip. situation	Manip. agent	Manip. strategy	Manip. outcome
2	x	z	$F(1, 5) = z$	one	$F(2, 5) =$	x
3	x	z	$F(2, 5) = x$	two	$F(2, 6) =$	z
4	x	y or z	$F(1, 6) = y$ or z	one	$F(2, 6) =$	x
5	x	y	$F(1, 6) = x$	two	$F(1, 4) =$	y
6	x	y	$F(1, 6) = x$	two	$F(1, 3) =$	y
7	x	y	$F(2, 3) = y$	one	$F(1, 3) =$	x
8	x	y or z	$F(2, 4) = y$ or z	one	$F(1, 4) =$	x
9	y	z	$F(3, 6) = z$	one	$F(2, 6) =$	x
10	y	z	$F(4, 6) = z$	one	$F(3, 6) =$	y
11	y	z	$F(4, 6) = y$	two	$F(4, 5) =$	z
12	y	x or z	$F(3, 5) = x$ or z	one	$F(4, 5) =$	y

manipulate F at the profile $[(yzx), (zyx)] \equiv (4, 6)$ by playing the manipulative strategy (zxy):

$$\{F[(yzx), (zxy), A] = z\} \, P_2 \, \{F[(yzx), (zyx), A] = y\}. \quad (2.06)$$

In the notation of Table 2, where each of the six orderings of A are assigned an integer label, (2.06) becomes

$$\{F(4, 5) = z\} \, P_2 \, \{F(4, 6) = y\}. \quad (2.07)$$

The assignment of outcome y to $F[(yzx), (zyx), A]$ was made on the previous line of Table 2. Therefore z cannot be assigned to cell 11, which leaves y as the sole possibility.

Filling in each indeterminate cell in this manner, both above and below the diagonal, results in agent 1 being a dictator for $F(\cdot, A)$ and therefore completes Feldman's proof. If, at the beginning, for cell 1 we had assigned alternative z instead of alternative x, then agent 2 would have ended up as F's dictator.

Comment: Theorem 2.1 is a negative result. The remainder of this chapter is concerned almost exclusively with how Theorem 2.1's conditions can be relaxed in order to obtain existence of a strategy-proof mechanism rather than nonexistence. Examination of the theorem's conditions shows immediately that only one condition − the assumption of unrestricted preferences − can sensibly be relaxed. Nondictatorship and the Pareto criterion are minimal conditions on how power should be distributed among the agents. If anything, they should be strengthened, not weakened. The definition of a voting mechanism cannot be relaxed in any obvious way.[4] The number of alternatives that the mechanism can handle certainly must be maintained at three or more.

Theorem 2.1 applies only when preferences are unrestricted; that is, $\Omega = \Sigma$. Within Feldman's proof if admissible preferences are restricted by, for example, excluding the ordering (zyx) from Ω, then the rightmost column and the bottom row are struck from Table 1 because the mechanism would not have to be defined for profiles that involve the ordering (zyx). But striking column 6 affects the construction of Table 2. Our demonstration that cell 11 must be filled with alternative y depended on cell 10, which is in column 6, being filled with alternative y in the proof's previous step. Column 6's presence is essential for this argument. If enough rows and columns are struck, then the chain of inference that we constructed in Table 2 may break causing existence rather than nonexistence.

Relationship with Arrow's impossibility theorem

Strategy-proof allocation mechanisms are intimately related to the social welfare functions about which Arrow [1963] proved his famous impossibility theorem. In order to understand the conditions under which reasonable strategy-proof mechanisms exist, one must understand the basics of this relationship. A social welfare function for A is a single-valued function f that maps the set Ω^n of admissible preference profiles into the set Σ (or Σ_{-}) of transitive orderings of A. Thus $f: \Omega^n \rightarrow \Sigma$. In other words, a social welfare function orders the set A, presumably from best to worst. Associated with every social welfare function f is an allocation mechanism: $F_f(P, B) = \max_B(f(P))$. If an allocation mechanism F has

---

[4] We have defined an allocation mechanism to be a single-valued function. This definition may appear to be a candidate for relaxation. For example, an allocation mechanism could be permitted to select as its output probability mixtures of two or more allocations that are contained in B, the set of feasible allocations. This relaxation is an illusion, however, because A, the set of conceivable outcomes, should be defined for such an allocation mechanism as all possible probability mixtures of the conceivable allocations, not simply as the set of conceivable allocations. Once this is done, then the allocation mechanism is again single valued and, unless preferences over this set of probability distributions are restricted, Theorem 2.1 continues to apply. For example, the assumption that each agent evaluates probability mixtures in accordance with a von Neumann–Morgenstern utility function is a strong restriction on agents' preferences. Two examples of papers that explore the consequences of permitting probability mixtures to be outcomes are Barbera [1977] and Gibbard [1978].

associated with it a social welfare function, then F is a *rational* allocation mechanism. Such a mechanism F_f earns this title because it selects that element of B that the social welfare function f ranks highest. Clearly not every allocation mechanism is rational.

Arrow investigated the existence of social welfare functions f whose associated rational allocation mechanisms F_f satisfy the Pareto criterion, weak nondictatorship, and two additional conditions, independence of irrelevant alternatives and monotonicity. A mechanism F satisfies *weak nondictatorship* if no agent $i \in I$ exists such that, for all feasible sets $B \in \mathcal{P}(A)$, $F(P, B) = \max_B(P_i)$ for all $P \in \Omega^n$. Contrast this with strong dictatorship, where an individual is classified a dictator if he is dictator over even a single feasible set B ($|B| \geqslant 2$) while here he is classified a dictator only if he is dictator over every feasible set.

A mechanism satisfies *independence of irrelevant alternatives* (IIA) if whenever any two profiles, P, $Q \in \Omega^n$, agree on the feasible set $B \in \mathcal{P}(A)$, then $F_f(P, B) = F_f(Q, B)$. Profiles P and Q agree on B if, for all agents i and for all pairs of allocations $(x, y) \in B \times B$, xP_iy if and only if xQ_iy. Independence means that agents' preferences over the feasible set should be the only determinant of the group's choice; preferences over the feasible set's complement should be irrelevent.

To define monotonicity, let $B \in \mathcal{P}(A)$ be a feasible set, let $x \in B$ be an allocation within the feasible set, and let $C = B - x$ be the feasible set less the element x. The mechanism satisfies *monotonicity* if whenever (i) two profiles P, $Q \in \Omega^n$ agree on C and (ii) xP_iy implies xQ_iy for all $y \in C$, then $F_f(P, B) = x$ implies $F_f(Q, B) = x$. Monotonicity means that if one or more agents move a feasible allocation x up in their preference orderings relative to other feasible allocations, then that cannot cause x to be dropped as the group's choice. Rational choice on the part of individuals obeys both of these conditions and as such they are reasonable requirements to place on group choice.[5]

Exactly as in Theorem 2.1, Arrow's conditions are impossible to meet when A contains at least three elements and preferences are unrestricted.

Theorem 2.2 (Arrow's theorem): *If* $|A| \geqslant 3$ *and preferences are unrestricted* ($\Omega = \Sigma_-$ *or* Σ), *then a social welfare function f and its associated allocation mechanism F_f cannot simultaneously satisfy the Pareto criterion, weak nondictatorship, independence of irrelevant alternatives, and monotonicity.*

---

[5] Blin and Satterthwaite [1978] discuss the parallels that exist between an individual's choices and a group's choices.

Social welfare functions that satisfy Arrow's requirements are inextricably intertwined with strategy-proof allocation mechanisms. If preferences are unrestricted and a social welfare function with its associated allocation mechanism satisfy IIA and monotonicity, then the mechanism is strategy-proof.[6] This permits Theorem 2.2 (Arrow) to be proved directly from Theorem 2.1 (Gibbard–Satterthwaite). Specifically, for the case of $|A| \geqslant 3$ and unrestricted preferences, suppose that − contrary to Arrow's theorem − a social welfare function exists that satisfies the Pareto criterion, nondictatorship, independence of irrelevant alternatives, and monotonicity. Then the associated rational allocation mechanism is strategy-proof. This is impossible, however, because no strategy-proof allocation mechanism (whether rational or not) exists that satisfies the Pareto criterion and nondictatorship for the case of $|A| \geqslant 3$ and unrestricted preferences. Therefore Arrow's theorem is true.

In the opposite direction, if preferences are unrestricted and an allocation mechanism is rational and strategy-proof, then it also satisfies independence of irrelevant alternatives and monotonicity.[7] This result together with Arrow's theorem can be used to show directly that, for the case of $|A| \geqslant 3$ and unrestricted preferences, no rational, strategy-proof allocation mechanism exists that satisfies the Pareto criterion and weak nondictatorship. This nonexistence result concerning rational, weakly nondictatorial, strategy-proof allocation mechanisms generalizes with some effort to Theorem 2.1, which applies to both rational and non-rational mechanisms and to strong nondictatorship as well as weak nondictatorship.[8]

3   Sufficiently restricted domains and strategy-proofness

Within the general theme of restricting the domain of admissible preferences, three approaches have been followed in trying to resolve the

---

[6] Blin and Satterthwaite [1978], Th. 2, stated this result for the case of unrestricted preferences.

[7] This result is stated in exactly this form in Blin and Satterthwaite [1978], Th. 4. Its forebears include Satterthwaite [1975], Lemma 8, an intermediate result of Gibbard [1973], and Pattanaik [1973], Th. 2.

[8] See Blin and Satterthwaite [1978] Th. 5. That particular proof was based on a proof of Schmeidler and Sonnenschein [1978], which in turn had been based on Gibbard's [1973] original proof of Theorem 1.1. All three of these proofs of Theorem 2.1 have the common feature of using Arrow's theorem to create a contradiction. Satterthwaite's [1973, 1975] original proof of Theorem 2.1 and a second proof of Schmeidler and Sonnenschein [1978] are constructive and do not use Arrow's theorem. Thus the discussion of using Theorem 2.1 to prove Arrow's theorem is not empty.

fundamental problem that Theorem 2.1 poses for the construction of strategy-proof mechanisms. The first approach begins with a specific allocation mechanism (e.g., majority rule) and searches for domain restrictions that are sufficient to make the mechanism strategy-proof.[9] We do not explore this approach in this chapter, because it is the least general of the three approaches. The second approach begins with a fixed restricted domain, expressed in terms of economic restrictions such as convexity, continuity, and the like, and then looks for nondictatorial strategy-proof mechanisms. We discuss this approach in Section 4. The third approach, which is the most general, fixes neither the domain nor the aggregation rule. It looks for necessary and sufficient conditions on preferences such that the resulting domain, Ω, permits construction of a strategy-proof mechanism that satisfies the Pareto criterion and nondictatorship plus, in some cases, additional criteria on the distribution of power. This is the approach we explore in this section.

In the previous section we discussed the relationship between rational, strategy-proof allocation mechanisms and social welfare functions that satisfy the conditions of monotonicity and IIA. This relationship is intensively exploited in this section; with one exception all the results presented apply exclusively to rational allocation mechanisms. Thus the typical result for this section is this: if Ω satisfies the following conditions, then Ω admits the construction of a weakly nondictatorial and rational strategy-proof allocation mechanism. This technique, however, is not costless. We discuss the rationality condition in greater depth at the end of this section and show an example of a domain that (i) permits construction of a nonrational, strongly nondictatorial, strategy-proof allocation mechanism and (ii) does not permit construction of a rational, weakly nondictatorial social welfare function. Thus, requiring rationality, as this section does, creates a binding constraint. To what extent the results of this section can be generalized if the rationality constraint were dropped is an open question.

Characterization of the domains that admit rational strategy-proof mechanisms requires some notation whose purpose is to allow the structure of a given domain, Ω, to be examined. The set of *ordered triples* within a domain Ω is defined as $t(\Omega) = \{(xyz)|\ P \in \Omega$ exists such that $xPyPz\}$. Two domains Ω_1 and Ω_2 are *equivalent* if they share the same set of ordered triples; that is, $t(\Omega_1) = t(\Omega_2)$. Two domains may be disjoint

---

[9] See, for example, Sen and Pattanaik [1969]. Their paper does not deal explicitly with strategy-proofness; rather it deals with the transitivity of majority rule. But, as the results of Section 3 show, if a mechanism is transitive and satisfies IIA as majority rule does over appropriately restricted domains, then it is also strategy-proof.

and equivalent. For example, if $\Omega_1 = \{(xyzw),(yxwz)\}$, $\Omega_2 = \{(xywz), (yxzw)\}$, the $t(\Omega_1) = t(\Omega_2) = \{(xyz), (yxz), (xyw), (yxw), (xzw), (xwz), (yzw), (ywz)\}$. The importance of the equivalence relation that $t(\Omega)$ defines on the set of possible domains is that if two domains are equivalent, then the first domain permits construction of a strategy-proof, nondictatorial, rational mechanism if and only if the second domain permits construction of such a mechanism.

The set of *ordered pairs* within Ω is $T(\Omega) = \{(xy) \in A \times A \mid x \neq y\}$. The set of *trivial ordered pairs* within Ω is $TR(\Omega) = \{(xy) \mid a P \in \Omega$ exists such that xPy and no $Q \in \Omega$ exists such that $yQx\}$. A trivial pair is a pair of alternatives over which no controversy exists because every agent, no matter what element of Ω describes his preferences, agrees on how those two alternatives should be ranked.

Decisiveness implications

The concept of decisiveness implications is of great importance because it constitutes the technology that has made the statements and proofs of the theorems presented in this section possible. This technology is inextricably bound up with the rationality requirement that we imposed for this entire section; decisiveness implications do not work for nonrational mechanisms. The thrust behind this technology may be summarized as follows.

Given a rational mechanism F, the members of J are said to be decisive for a over b if a is selected when the feasible set is $\{a, b\}$ and the members of J report preferences that rank a over b. Formally, J is *decisive* over the ordered pair (ab) if $F(P, \{a, b\}) = a$ for all $P \in \Omega^n$ such that, for all $i \in J$, aP_ib. In terms of social welfare functions, decisiveness means that coalition J can force a social preference for a over b. A dictator is decisive over all pairs in A because, no matter what other agents vote, he secures the outcome he desires.

Suppose a rational, strategy-proof mechanism F that satisfies the Pareto criterion is defined on a domain Ω^n. Because F is rational, a social welfare function f_F that satisfies the Pareto criterion underlies F. Because the mechanism is strategy-proof, both F and f_F satisfy monotonicity and IIA.[10] Now suppose that a coalition $J \subset I$ is decisive for an alternative

---

[10] For a rational mechanism F defined on some Ω, strategy-proofness is equivalent to monotonicity and IIA. This may be seen in two steps. For the first step, suppose voter i can manipulate F at profile P and feasible set B by playing Q_i. There then exists a pair of alternatives, x and y, such that $x = F(P, B)$, $y = F(P/Q_i, B)$, and yP_ix. This means, because F is rational and has a social welfare function f_F underlying it, $xf_F(P)y$ and

$a \in A$ against another alternative $b \in A$. Suppose additionally that an alternative $c \in A$ exists such that the ordered triples (abc) and (bca) are in $t(\Omega)$; that is, (abc), $(bca) \in t(\Omega)$. Let the coalition J vote (abc) while its complement votes (bca). In other words, the reported profile P has the property that aP_ibP_ic for all $i \in J$ and bP_icP_ia for all $i \notin J$. Since J is decisive over (ab), a is socially preferred to b. Application of the Pareto criterion implies that b is socially preferred to c and, as a consequence of transitivity, a is socially preferred to c. Coalition J is therefore decisive for a over c because (i) $a = \max_{\{a,c\}} f_F(P) = F(P, \{a, c\})$ and (ii) f_F's monotonicity and IIA together imply that no matter how members of J's complement change their votes, the outcome is fixed at a. Therefore, we can conclude, if (abc) and (bca) are in $t(\Omega)$, then any individual or coalition that is decisive over (ab) is necessarily decisive over (ac) as well. This is decisiveness implication number 1. Note the central role that transitivity (i.e., rationality) played in its derivation. Our use of the labels a, b, and c here for the elements of A is to emphasize that the implication applies to any ordered triple; for example, in a particular application a may be assigned the value y, b the value z, and c the value x.

Parallel arguments lead to decisiveness implications numbers (ii) through (iv): (ii) if (abc), $(bca) \in t(\Omega)$ and a coalition J is decisive over (ca), then J is necessarily decisive over (ba); (iii) if $(abc) \in t(\Omega)$, $(bca) \notin t(\Omega)$, and a coalition J is decisive over (ab) and (bc), then J is also decisive over (ac); (iv) if $(abc) \in t(\Omega)$, $(bca) \notin t(\Omega)$, and a coalition J is decisive over (ca), then J is decisive over either (ba) or (cb). Table 3 summarizes these.

Consider a domain Ω of admissible preferences and a set of ordered pairs $R \subset T$. The question is this: Does a rational, strategy-proof mechanism, F, satisfying the Pareto criterion exist such that some coalition J is decisive over exactly the set of pairs contained in R? The answer is that, for such a mechanism, the set R can be the collection of pairs over which coalition J is decisive only if R is closed with respect to the four decisiveness implications. The set R is *closed with respect to the decisiveness implications* if for every $(ab) \notin R$, then, given Ω and R, none of the decisiveness implications implies that J must be decisive over (ab). The

$yf_F(P/Q_i)x$. If yQ_ix then f_F violates IIA. If xQ_iy then f is nonmonotonic since, when agent i changes his reported preference from yP_ix to xQ_iy, the social ordering changes perversely for $xf(P)y$ to $yf(P/Q_i)x$. This proves that strategy-proofness implies monotonicity and IIA. For the second step, study the violation of IIA and the violation of monotonicity that are set up in the first step. Inspection shows that if either occurs, then agent i can manipulate F. Therefore, for rational mechanisms, monotonicity and IIA imply strategy-proofness. Blin and Satterthwaite [1978], Th. 2, and Blair and Muller [1983] stated this result for unrestricted preferences and restricted preferences, respectively.

Table 3. *Decisiveness implications*

	Domain conditions		Implication		Name
i	$(abc) \in t(\Omega)$	$(bca) \in t(\Omega)$	(ca)	(ba)	Direct branch
ii	$(abc) \in t(\Omega)$	$(bca) \in t(\Omega)$	(ab)	(ac)	Direct branch
iii	$(abc) \in t(\Omega)$	$(bca) \notin t(\Omega)$	(ab) (bc)	(ac)	Joining branch
iv	$(abc) \in t(\Omega)$	$(bca) \notin t(\Omega)$	(ca)	(ba) (cb)	Splitting branch

idea underlying the definition is that if J can be shown to be decisive over the pair (ab), then by definition (ab) belongs to R already. The domain Ω is *decomposable* if such a closed set R exists that is a strict subset of the set of all pairs and is a strict superset of the set of trivial pairs. Thus if Ω is decomposable, then $TR(\Omega) \subsetneq R \subsetneq T$.

Nondictatorial strategy-proof mechanisms

Kalai and Muller [1977] used the concept of decomposability to characterize the domains on which nondictatorial strategy-proof mechanisms can be constructed.

Theorem 3.1: *For $n \geq 2$ an n-person, weakly nondictatorial, rational, strategy-proof mechanism on $\Omega \subset \Sigma$ exists if and only if a two-person, weakly nondictatorial, rational, strategy-proof mechanism on Ω exists.*

Theorem 3.2: *For $n \geq 2$, the following three statements are equivalent for every Ω.*

    a.   *$\Omega \in \Sigma$ is decomposable.*
    b.   *The equivalence class of Ω permits construction of an n-person weakly nondictatorial, rational, strategy-proof mechanism that satisfies the Pareto criterion.*
    c.   *The equivalence class of Ω permits construction of an n-person weakly nondictatorial social welfare function that satisfies the Pareto criterion and IIA.*

Consider, for simplicity, the two-agent case ($n = 2$). The necessity that Ω be decomposable for construction of a nondictatorial strategy-proof mechanism follows directly from the observation that if the only set of pairs R that is closed and nontrivial is the set, T, of all ordered pairs, then one agent must be a dictator. Suppose, contrary to the observation, neither agent is a dictator and their orderings in the profile P disagree on the nontrivial pair $\{x, y\}$. Since $F(P, \{x, y\})$ is single valued, one agent or the other must get his way and is thus decisive on the pair. But if he is decisive over one pair, he is decisive on all pairs because the only closed nontrivial R is identical to T. Therefore the agent is a dictator.

As for the sufficiency of decomposability, if a closed set of ordered pairs $R_1 \subsetneq T$ exists, define R_2 as the set of ordered pairs whose inverses are not in R_1. With this we eliminate the risk of an agent being decisive over a pair (ab) while another agent is decisive over the inverse pair (ba). Define the following social welfare function. Let agent 1 be decisive over the pairs in R_1. Let agent 2 be decisive over the pairs in R_2. Let the coalition of agents 1 and 2 be decisive over all pairs. If there are more agents, let them be dummies who have no effect on the outcome. It can be shown that this function is a weakly nondictatorial social welfare function satisfying the Pareto criterion and IIA and that it underlies a nondictatorial, strategy-proof mechanism. That this mechanism may be only weakly nondictatorial follows from the fact that — in the sense of strong dictatorship — agent 1 is a dictator whenever the feasible set is a pair of alternatives, $\{a, b\}, \in \mathcal{P}(A)$, for which $(ab), (ba) \in R_1$. Agent 1 is then decisive over both (ab) and (ba); consequently $F(P, \{a, b\}) = \max_{\{a,b\}} P_1$.

The statement of parts (b) and (c) of the equivalence in Theorem 3.2 has a surprising feature. It would have been more intuitive, simpler to prove, and more consistent with the other theorems reported in this section to state in (c) that the social welfare function, f, satisfies the Pareto criterion, IIA, and monotonicity. In the theorem, however, monotonicity is not assumed and thus cannot be used. Instead when existence of a strategy-proof mechanism is to be established given that a nondictatorial n-person social welfare function exists, Theorem 3.1 implies the existence of a two-person nondictatorial social welfare function. Observe that a two-person social welfare function satisfying the Pareto criterion is necessarily monotonic and thus the two-person allocation mechanism that it underlies is strategy-proof. To construct the n-agent, nondictatorial, strategy-proof mechanism, which is the goal of the exercise, add the remaining $n - 2$ agents as dummies.

The generalization of Theorem 3.1 for allocation mechanisms that are not rational has been proven by Kim and Roush [1981]. To our knowledge this is the only result of this section that has been generalized from the rational case to the nonrational case.

$$
\begin{array}{ccccc}
(xy) & \rightleftarrows & (zy) & \rightleftarrows & (zx) \\
\Updownarrow & & & & \Updownarrow \\
(xz) & \rightleftarrows & (yz) & \rightleftarrows & (yx)
\end{array}
$$

Figure 1. $\Omega_1 = \Sigma \{xyz, yzx, zxy, zyx, yxz, xzy\}$.

Graphic representation

The graph[11] that the decisiveness implications create among the elements of the set of all pairs helps understand the decomposability condition. As a first step, consider Feldman's proof of Theorem 2.1, which we presented in Section 2, for the special case of two agents and three alternatives. Here we use decisiveness implications to create an analogous proof for a somewhat weaker result: for three alternatives and two agents every strategy-proof, rational mechanism that satisfies the Pareto criterion is dictatorial. The result is weaker because this section's technique only applies to rational mechanisms; Feldman's technique applies to both rational and nonrational mechanisms.

The domain, $\Omega_1 \equiv \Sigma$, consists of all six strict orderings that are possible when the number of alternatives is three. In Figure 1 the nodes of the graph consist of all the ordered pairs T. The *directed branches* represent application of decisiveness implications (i) and (ii) to each of the six orderings. For example, if agent 1 is decisive over a pair (xy) and, as is the case, (xyz), $(yzx) \in \Omega_1$, then decisiveness implication (ii) implies that he has to be decisive over (xz) as well. Thus a directed branch connects (xy) to (xz) because (xyz), $(yzx) \in \Omega_1$. This follows from the first decisiveness implication if x is assigned to a, y to b, and z to c. Similarly, decisiveness implication (i) implies that a directed branch connects (xy) to (zy) because (yzx), $(zxy) \in \Omega_1$. If all branches are filled in, the graph in Figure 1 results. It is evident that the direct branches generated by decisiveness implications (i) and (ii) span the whole set of pairs. No sinks (i.e., closed sets of ordered pairs that are strict subsets of T) exist there. A set R is identified graphically to be a sink if branches only go into it while none come out of it. Agent 1 is therefore necessarily decisive over all six pairs and is a dictator.

A slightly different way to see that one agent must be a dictator is to replicate for rational mechanisms the several steps of Feldman's proof (see Section 2) that led to the conclusion that if alternative x is assigned to cell 1, then agent 1 is necessarily a dictator. Assignment of x to cell 1 means that we resolve in favor of agent 1 the conflict over the pair $\{x, z\}$

---

[11] Muller [1982] developed this graphic analysis.

$$(xy) \quad \rightleftharpoons \quad (zy) \quad \leftarrow \quad (zx)$$
$$\downarrow \qquad\qquad\qquad\qquad\qquad\qquad \downarrow$$
$$(xz) \quad \leftarrow \quad (yz) \quad \rightleftharpoons \quad (yx)$$

Figure 2. $\Omega_2 = \Sigma - \{zyx\} = \{xyz, yzx, zxy, yxz, xzy\}$.

that occurs when agent 1 votes (xzy) and agent 2 votes (zxy). The Pareto criterion eliminates alternative y as a possible outcome. Thus that assignment makes voter 1 decisive over (xz). It also implies that x must be assigned to cells 2 and 3 because agent 1 is decisive over (xz) and the Pareto criterion eliminates y from consideration. In cell 4 agent 1's decisiveness over (xz) eliminates z as a possible outcome. If x is assigned to a, z to b, and y to c, then decisiveness implication (ii) states that agent 1 is decisive over (xy) because he is decisive over (xz). This process may be continued until all cells are assigned agent 1's preferred choice.

It we delete one ordering out of Σ, then a number of sinks result, which means that the resulting Ω is decomposable and, according to Theorem 3.2, a rational, nondictatorial, strategy-proof allocation mechanism can be constructed on Ω. To be specific, let (zyx) be deleted from Σ and call the resulting domain Ω_2. Figure 2 shows its graph. It differs from Figure 1 as follows. The two direct branches from (yx) to (zx) and from (xz) to (xy) that decisiveness implications (i) and (ii) respectively would generate if (zyx) were an element of Ω_2 are deleted. But because $(xzy) \in \Omega_2$ and $(zyx) \notin \Omega_2$ both a joining branch and a splitting branch are eligible to be added. Decisiveness implication (iii) generates the *joining branch*; it connects both (xz) and (zy) to (xy) and means that if R contains both (xz) and (zy), then it must also contain (xy). It is not drawn because the decisiveness implication $(zy) \rightarrow (xy)$ makes this joining branch redundant. Decisiveness implication (iv) generates the *splitting branch*; it connects (yx) to both (zx) and (yz) and means that if R contains (yx), then it must also contain either (zx) or (yz). It, too, is not shown because it is redundant. Note, however, that if in addition (yzx) were dropped as an element of Ω_2, then neither the joining nor the splitting branch would be redundant.

These changes cause Figure 2 to have four sinks: $R_1 = \{(xz)\}$, $R_2 = \{(zy), (xz), (xy)\}$, $R_3 = \{(xz), (yz), (yx)\}$, and $R_4 = R_2 \cup R_3 = T - (zx)$. Associated with each sink is a distinct, weakly nondictatorial, strategy-proof mechanism. Therefore four distinct, strategy-proof, nondictatorial, rational mechanisms can be constructed on the domain Ω_2. Note that R_4 includes (xy) and its inverse (yx) and (yz) and its inverse

(zy); this means the mechanism that is associated with it is not strongly nondictatorial because whenever $B = \{x, y\}$ or $\{z, y\}$ the agent who is decisive over the elements of R_4 dictates the choice. A similar argument applies for R_1, but not for R_2 or R_3. Thus if $|A| = 3$, the deletion of a single ordering form Σ is sufficient to reverse the Theorem 2.1's impossibility result.

Essentiality and symmetry

In the discussion that followed Theorems 3.1 and 3.2 we described how to construct a nondictatorial, strategy-proof mechanism when Ω is decomposable. That mechanism, however, distributes power with unacceptable unevenness: $n - 2$ of the individuals are dummies. As this particular mechanism illustrates, requiring that a mechanism satisfy nondictatorship is a toothless requirement that comes nowhere near describing the criteria by which we judge a distribution of power acceptable or not acceptable. Nondictatorship (strong or weak) is a necessary, but not sufficient, condition for a mechanism to be acceptable and as such is useful within the context of impossibility theorems. Possibility theorems need additional conditions that capture what we mean when we judge a particular power distribution acceptable.

Two such conditions are essentiality and symmetry. For a mechanism F an agent i is essential if a preference profile $P \in \Omega^n$ and ordering $Q_i \in \Omega$ exist such that if agent i changes his ordering from P_i to Q_i, then the outcome changes from $F(P, B)$ to $F(P/Q_i, B) \neq F(P, B)$. A mechanism is *essential* if all agents are essential. In essential mechanisms each individual has some, though not necessarily equal, power. Symmetry, on the other hand, mandates equal power without specifying the magnitude of the power. A mechanism F is *symmetric* (sometimes called anonymous) if any permutation of the individuals leaves the outcome unchanged: for all $P \in \Omega^n$, $B \in \mathcal{P}(A)$, and permutations $\rho: \{1, \ldots, n\} \to \{1, \ldots, n\}$, $F(\ldots, P_i, \ldots, B) = F(\ldots, P_{\rho(i)}, \ldots, B)$. Neither of these conditions completely supplants the strong nondictatorship conditions or the Pareto criterion. For example, an imposed mechanism is symmetric because under such a mechanism every individual is identical in having no influence over the outcome.

For the case of essential mechanisms Blair and Muller [1983] have generalized the concept of decisiveness implications and proved the natural extension of Theorem 3.2. The example, which follows, of an essential mechanism and the domain on which it is constructed shows that essential mechanisms, while an improvement over weakly nondictatorial mechanisms, only incompletely capture the considerations that enter our evaluations of whether a particular distribution of power is acceptable. Let $A = [X^1, \ldots, X^K]$ where each x^i is a vector of three alternatives. The domain Ω consists of all orderings in which the elements of X^k appear always above X^l for all $k < l$ and, within X^k, the three alternatives form a free triple; that is, all six orderings of the three elements of X^k are permissible. Let each voter be a dictator on at least one of the free triples. The result is an essential monotonic social welfare function for K or fewer voters. Any additional voters must be dummies and are therefore not essential.

Symmetry is a more stringent condition than that of essentiality. It too can be approached using the technology of decisiveness implications. A domain Ω is *transitively decomposable* if a nontrivial set R exists that is (i) closed under decisiveness implications (i) through (iv) and (ii) transitive. Transitivity in this context means that R must satisfy: (i) if (xy), $(yz) \in R$, then $(xz) \in R$ and (ii) $(xy) \in R$ if and only if $(yx) \in R$. The following two theorems summarize the symmetric case, and are adapted from Muller [1982]. The equivalence between the second and third parts of Theorem 3.4 are extensions that are not proven in the original paper, but can straightforwardly be shown by means similar to those used in Blair and Muller (1983).

Theorem 3.3: *A symmetric, n-person, rational strategy-proof mechanism on Ω exists for all $n \geq 3$ if and only if a symmetric, three-person rational strategy-proof mechanism on Ω exists.*

Theorem 3.4: *The following three statements are equivalent for every $\Omega \in \Sigma$:*

   a.   *Ω is transitively decomposable.*
   b.   *For all $n \geq 3$ the equivalence class of Ω permits construction of a symmetric, monotonic, social welfare function that satisfies the Pareto criterion and IIA.*
   c.   *For all $n \geq 3$ the equivalence class of Ω permits construction of a symmetric, rational, strategy-proof mechanism that satisfies the Pareto criterion.*

The social welfare function in part (b) is required to be monotonic because, unlike in the case of Theorems 3.1 and 3.2, no theorem exists that reduces the n-person case to the two-person case. Indeed, with respect to Theorem 3.3, an Ω exists for which a symmetric two-person social welfare function may be constructed, but not a symmetric three-person social welfare function. In parts (b) and (c) no reference is made to nondictatorship, because any symmetric mechanism that satisfies the Pareto criterion also satisfies strong nondictatorship.

Group strategy-proofness

A mechanism is strategy-proof if no single individual ever has an incentive to misrepresent his preferences. Blair and Muller (1983) have shown the surprising result that, for rational mechanisms, strategy-proofness for individuals is equivalent to strategy-proofness for coalitions of individuals. A coalition J, $|J| = k < n$, has an incentive to manipulate the mechanism F at profile P and feasible set $B \in \mathcal{P}(A)$ if orderings $Q_i \in \Omega$ exist such that, for all $i \in J$,

$$F[P/Q, B] \; P_i F(P, B) \tag{3.01}$$

where $Q = \{Q_i\}_{i \in J}$. A mechanism F is *group strategy-proof* if no admissible profile $P \in \Omega^n$, no set B, and no coalition J exists such that at profile P coalition J can manipulate mechanism F.

The driving force behind this equivalence of group strategy-proofness and individual strategy-proofness is the rationality condition. To show this we first observe that if a mechanism is group strategy-proof, then by definition it is individually strategy-proof. We then show that a rational mechanism that is individually strategy-proof is also group strategy-proof by demonstrating that if a mechanism is manipulable by some coalition, then it is also manipulable by some individual within the coalition. Therefore an individually strategy-proof mechanism must also be group strategy-proof.

Suppose, in order to see that group manipulability implies individual manipulability, that a group $J = \{1, \ldots, k\}$, $k < n$, can manipulate F at profile P and feasible set B:

$$F(Q_1, \ldots, Q_k, P_{k+1}, \ldots, P_n, B) \; P_i F(P, B). \tag{3.02}$$

Let $F(Q_1, \ldots, Q_k, P_{k+1}, \ldots, P_n, B) = x$ and $F(P, B) = y$. Note that xP_iy for all $i \in J$. The rationality of F implies that $F(Q_1, \ldots, Q_k, P_{k+1}, \ldots, P_n, \{x, y\}) = x$ and $F(P, \{x, y\}) = y$. Therefore (3.02) continues to be true when B is replaced as the feasible set by $\{x, y\}$. Moreover, because $F(P, \{x, y\}) \in \{x, y\}$ for all $P \in \Omega^n$, a $j \in J$ must exist such that $F(Q_1, \ldots, Q_{j-1}, P_j, P_{j+1}, \ldots, P_n, (x, y \}) = x$ and $F(Q_1, \ldots, Q_{j-1}, Q_j, P_{j+1}, \ldots, P_n, \{x, y\}) = y$; that is, $j \in J$ is the critical voter who switches the outcome. Voter j, as a member of J, has preferences xP_iy; therefore, he can individually manipulate F at feasible set $\{x, y\}$ and profile $(Q_1, \ldots, Q_{j-1}, P_j, P_{j+1}, \ldots, P_n)$. Note that the rationality requirement was what allowed us to reduce the problem to that of selection between two alternatives.

The private goods case

The discussion to this point has considered only a perfectly general conceivable set, A, that has no a priori structure imposed on it. Suppose, however, that each alternative within A is a vector of n distinct private goods' bundles, each one of which is to be allocated to one of the n agents. To accommodate this change, let A represent each individual's consumption set, $x_i \in A$ be the bundle of private goods agent i consumes, P_i be his preferences over A, and let $\Omega \subset \Sigma_-$ be the set of orderings over A to which P_i is a priori restricted. Note that indifference is permitted as indicated by Ω being contained in Σ_- rather than Σ. Also, note that every individual i is selfish in that he is concerned only with his own component of the alternative $x = (x_1, \ldots, x_n)$.

An allocation $x = (x_1, \ldots, x_n) \in A^n$ is the n-vector of the agents' private goods' bundles. Redefine, for this subsection, an allocation mechanism to be a function $F: \Omega^n \times \mathcal{P}(A) \to A^n$. Thus $F(P, B) = [F_1(P, B), \ldots, F_i(P, B), \ldots, F_n(P, B)]$ is a vector of n functions where the ith function, $F_i(P, B) \in B$, specifies the allocation of private goods agent i receives.

Two new definitions must be introduced in order to characterize the domains on which weakly nondictatorial, strategy-proof mechanisms can be constructed. First is a strengthening of the Pareto criterion. A mechanism F satisfies the *strong Pareto criterion* if, for any pair $x, y \in B$, xP_iy for at least one agent and yP_ix for no agent, then $F(P, B) \neq y$. This strong version differs from the weak version in that the strong version does not require unanimity and permits some agents to be indifferent between x and y; that is, it may apply even if $x\bar{P}_iy$ for some agents.

The second new condition is Ritz's [1981, 1983] noncorruptibility condition. A mechanism is *noncorruptible* if for all sets $B \in \mathcal{P}(A)$, all profiles $P \in \Omega^n$, all agents $i \in I$, and all orderings $Q_i \in \Omega$, $F_i(P, B) \bar{P}_i F_i(P/Q_i, B)$ implies $F_j(P, B) = F_j(P/Q_i, B)$ for all $j(j \neq i)$. Recall that $\bar{P}_i$ signifies indifference. Thus, for a noncorruptible mechanism, an agent must change the utility value of the outcome to himself in order to affect the physical outcome of other agents. Informally, if a mechanism is corruptible, then agent i, who may be thought of as a potential corruptor or boss, does not directly improve his own outcome as is the case in manipulation. Rather, he changes the value of the outcome to others. He thus creates a possibility of indirectly improving his position by threatening other agents and demanding side payments. Thus corruptibility sets the stage for indirect manipulation as opposed to the direct manipulation with which strategy-proofness is concerned.

Kalai and Ritz [1980] and Ritz [1981, 1983] have used the technology of decisiveness implications and decomposability to make substantial progress on the private goods case. The private goods decisiveness implications to which the following theorem of Ritz [1981, 1983] makes references are not reproduced here in the interests of brevity. They may be found in Ritz's original papers.[12]

Theorem 3.5: *For the private goods case, when $n \geq 2$, the following three statements are equivalent for every Ω:*

    a.   *Ω is decomposable over private alternatives.*

    b.   *Ω permits construction of an n-person, weakly nondictatorial social welfare function that satisfies the strong Pareto criterion and IIA.*

    c.   *Ω permits construction of an n-person, weakly nondictatorial, rational, noncorruptible strategy-proof mechanism that satisfies the strong Pareto criterion.*

This theorem parallels Theorem 3.2 in not requiring the social welfare function in part (b) of the theorem to be monotonic. The reason is that Ritz, like Kalai and Muller, exploited the permissiveness of the nondictatorship condition to construct, through the use of dummies, n-person mechanisms from two-person mechanisms.

Restrictiveness of the decomposability conditions

The results presented in this section succeed in characterizing for several contexts the domains on which construction of strategy-proof mechanisms is possible. The question that remains is: How restrictive are these conditions? The ideal way to answer this question would be to determine, for a variety of different economic environments, if the a priori restrictions on agents' preferences that those environments naturally induce satisfy the characterizations for strategy-proof domains that have been presented. This approach has not been successfully carried out. A second approach, which has met with some success, is to calculate how close to unity the ratio $|\Omega| / |\Sigma|$ can be made to come when Ω is restricted to admit the construction of a nondictatorial, strategy-proof mechanism. If exam-

---

[12] Ritz's theorem is true as stated here only if Ω permits an agent to have the strict preference ordering (abc) over some three alternatives a, b, and c contained in A. This is a very weak condition that is satisfied by any interesting Ω.

ples exist in which, even with a large number of alternatives, the size of the restricted domain is still "respectable" relative to the size of the full domain, then that is an indication that these characterizations are not very restrictive.

Kim and Roush [1981] have shown that if $|A| = m$, then

$$\frac{m!/2 + (m - 1)!}{m!} = \frac{1}{2} + \frac{1}{m} \tag{3.03}$$

is the upper bound on $|\Omega| / |\Sigma|$ for weakly nondictatorial, rational, strategy-proof mechanisms satisfying the Pareto criterion. Because essential and symmetric mechanisms are also weakly nondictatorial, (3.03) is also the upper bound for domains that permit construction of essential (or symmetric) *rational* strategy-proof mechanisms. Blair and Muller [1983], based on the work of Kalai and Ritz [1979], have constructed an example of an essential mechanism that achieves this bound. Expression (3.03) is thus a least lower bound for essential and weakly nondictatorial mechanisms.

The domain, $\Omega \subset \Sigma$, for Blair and Muller's example is defined by a single restriction: it contains an ordered pair, $(xy) \in T(\Omega)$, with the property that no alternative $z \in A$ and ordering $P_i \in \Omega$ exist such that xP_izP_iy; that is, no $z \in A$ exists such that $(xzy) \in t(\Omega)$. The pair (xy) is thus inseparable in the sense that an admissible ordering can rank x immediately above y or someplace below y. Given this domain, an essential rational mechanism is this. Let voter 1 be decisive over all ordered pairs $(ab) \in T(\Omega)$ except (xy) and let each other individual have veto power over (xy). Thus $x = F(P, \{x, y\})$ if and only if xP_iy for all $i \in \{2, 3, \ldots, n\}$. This defines a social welfare function that, with one exception, makes agent 1 the dictator in the sense that his ordering becomes the social ordering. The exception occurs when agent 1 ranks x just above y and some other agent (the vetoer) objects by ranking y above x. In that event the social ordering is modified by placing y immediately above x. It is straightforward to check that this defines an essential, monotonic, weakly nondictatorial social welfare function that satisfies the Pareto criterion and IIA. It thus also defines an essential, weakly nondictatorial, strategy-proof, rational allocation mechanism that satisfies the Pareto criterion.

The size of this domain is $m!/2 + (m - 1)!$. This formula is easily derived by considering that subset of Ω for which xP_iy separately from that subset for which yP_ix. Since m alternatives may be strongly ordered in $m!$ different ways, the $|\Omega| / |\Sigma|$ ratio equals the value of (3.03). The weakness of this example is the already emphasized fact that essential

Table 4. *Nonrational, strategy-proof mechanism*

	Agent 1					
Agent 2	1 (*xzyw*)	1 (*yzwx*)	3 (*yxwz*)	4 (*wxzy*)	5 (*zwxy*)	6 (*wzyx*)
1 (*xzyw*)	*x*	*y*	*y*	*x*	*z*	*z*
2 (*yzwx*)	*y*	*y*	*y*	*y*	*y*	*y*
3 (*yxwz*)	*y*	*y*	*y*	*y*	*y*	*y*
4 (*wxzy*)	*x*	*y*	*y*	*w*	*z*	*w*
5 (*zwxy*)	*z*	*y*	*y*	*z*	*z*	*z*
6 (*wzyx*)	*z*	*y*	*y*	*w*	*z*	*w*

mechanisms may incorporate an unacceptable distribution of power among the participating individuals. In this particular example that is surely the case, because agent 1 is nearly a dictator. Therefore this particular example is not convincing as evidence that the decomposability conditions are relatively unrestrictive.

Examples for the symmetric case, which might be more convincing, have not been constructed yet. Kim and Roush (1981) showed that if mechanisms that give agents veto power are excluded from consideration, then the $|\Omega| / |\Sigma|$ ratio goes to zero as m goes to infinity. This is not convincing evidence in the opposite direction, however, because, since symmetric mechanisms with veto power may be constructed, no compelling reason to prohibit the use of the veto is apparent.

The rationality requirement

Throughout this section we have only considered rational allocation mechanisms. This is not a benign requirement. If the rationality condition is dropped, then the opportunities for constructing strategy-proof mechanisms increase. This point is made most concretely by an example due to Maskin [1976]. His example identifies a domain, Ω, that has two important properties: (i) a strategy-proof, strongly nondictatorial mechanism satisfying the Pareto criterion exists on it and (ii) no weakly nondictatorial social welfare function satisfying the Pareto criterion and IIA exists on it.

We present in this subsection a corrected and much simplified version of Maskin's example. Let $\Omega = \{(xzyw), (yzwx), (yxwz), (wxzy), (zwxy), (wzyx)\}$. Denote these six admissible orderings by P_i, $i = 1, \ldots, 6$, according to the order they appear in Ω. It is straightforward to check that the mechanism defined in Table 4 is strategy-proof when the feasible set consists of all four alternatives in $A = \{w, x, y, z\}$.

The nonrationality of F means that, for each of the four feasible sets B containing three of the four alternatives in A ($\{x, y, z\}$, $\{w, x, y\}$, etc.), the mechanism $F(\cdot, B)$ may be defined without reference to the way Table 4 defines it for the case where A is the feasible set. Inspection of the orderings contained within Ω shows that if one alternative is eliminated from each of its constituent orderings, then five (out of the six possible) distinct orderings of the three remaining alternatives are left. For example, if $B = \{x, y, z\}$, then the domain that results by striking w from each ordering in Ω is

$$\Omega_{\{x,y,z\}} = \{(xzy), (yxz), (yzx), (zxy), (zyx)\} = \Sigma - (xyz). \tag{3.04}$$

Earlier in this section we showed that, when $|A| = 3$, elimination of one ordering from Σ is sufficient to permit construction of a strongly non-dictatorial, rational mechanism on that feasible set. Define $F(\cdot, B)$ to be one of those mechanisms whenever $|B| = 3$ or $|B| = 2$. The result is a nonrational, strongly nondictatorial strategy-proof mechanism that satisfies the Pareto criterion.

To complete the example, we have to show that this domain does not permit construction of a weakly nondictatorial social welfare function that satisfies the Pareto criterion and IIA. This is easily done by constructing the graph of Ω to arrive at Figure 3. Since that graph does not contain any sink, Theorem 3.2 implies that a weakly nondictatorial social welfare function does not exist on Ω.

This example shows that the upper bounds on the $|\Omega| / |\Sigma|$ ratio that Kim and Roush [1981] derived for rational mechanisms do not necessarily hold for nonrational mechanisms. This emphasizes that our knowledge is quite imperfect concerning the degree to which the admissible domain must be restricted in order to permit construction of a reasonable strategy-proof mechanism.

4   Strategy-proofness on specific restricted domains

The last section reported on work that has been done to characterize those domains of preferences that are restrictive enough to permit the construction of strategy-proof allocation mechanisms that share power among a group's members in some acceptably democratic way. Considerable progress has been made on this approach, but as yet no researcher has succeeded in relating those characterizations to the domains of admissible preferences that occur in economic situations. This section reports on work that has taken the less general approach of beginning with a domain where preferences are restricted to belong to a class that naturally arise in economic environments and then characterizing the strategy-

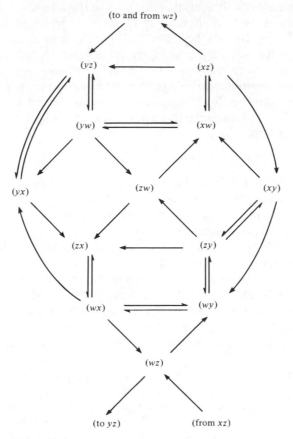

Figure 3

proof allocation mechanisms that can be constructed on that domain. In other words, the methodology of the last section is turned on its head here. Instead of beginning with properties that a strategy-proof mechanism should possess and deriving those domains that are consistent with those properties, we begin with a domain and derive the properties of the mechanisms that are consistent with that domain.

Economists often represent bundles of commodities as points in Euclidean space. Therefore, in this section where we are concerned exclusively with economic environments, A is no longer a set of discrete points without structure. Instead an alternative $x = (x_1, \ldots, x_l)$ is a point within a consumption set A that is itself a subset of l-dimensional Euclidean space. The interpretation of x_k, the kth component of x, is that the bundle x contains x_k units of good k. Imposition of this Euclidean structure on A enables us to utilize the concepts of continuity and differentiability. Specifically, given this structure on A, a natural restriction to place on the admissible preferences of agents is that they be representable by twice differentiable, strictly concave utility functions, $u_i(x)$, that are increasing with respect to each of their arguments.

Clearly such a restriction on Ω, the set of admissible preferences, is strong. Its strength can be seen by letting $l = 2$ and considering a sequence of ten points $\{x^1, \ldots, x^{10}\}$ that are randomly selected from a convex consumption set A that has a nonempty interior. The probability that the ordering $(x^1, x^2, \cdots x^{10})$ is consistent with Ω is miniscule – certainly less than 0.5. It therefore is in some sense a stronger restriction than some of the restrictions on preferences identified in Section 3. Recall, in particular, Blair and Muller's [1983] example of a domain Ω that (i) contains more than half the possible orderings that can be defined on A and (ii) admits the construction of a rational, weakly nondictatorial, strategy-proof mechanism satisfying both essentiality and the Pareto criterion.

In addition to restricting ourselves in this discussion to preferences that are sufficiently smooth, we also restrict ourselves to mechanisms that have continuous derivatives. A sensible allocation mechanism in an economic environment cannot be everywhere nondifferentiable. To be nondifferentiable everywhere would mean that whenever an individual agent perturbed his preferences, then the outcome would jump in a new direction. Clearly, however, an allocation mechanism need not be smooth everywhere; it is quite acceptable for the allocation to jump at some points. This means that the results reported in this section should be considered to be local characterizations of the possible strategy-proof mechanisms. As a consequence we do not discuss the results, for example, of Border and Jordan [1983], who for a very restrictive domain of admissible preferences consider strategy-proof mechanisms that are nondifferentiable at isolated points.

These ideas are easily formalized provided that we change the manner in which the agent i reports his preferences from being P_i, a binary relation on A, to u_i, a real-valued utility function on A. A utility function $u_i(\cdot)$ represents the preference ordering P_i if: xP_iy if and only if $u_i(x) \geqslant u_i(y)$.[13] Let A, the set of admissible alternatives, be a compact, convex subset of $\mathbb{R}^l$ with nonempty interior. Redefine Ω to be the set of admissible

---

[13] For a given P_i many utility representations u_i exist. This indeterminacy has no effect on the results that we present in this section, because the results are impossibility theorems.

utility functions on A. We assume that every $u_i \in \Omega$ is twice continuously differentiable and that Ω itself is a convex subset of a linear function space that is endowed with the C^2 topology.[14]

Rationality plays no role in this section. Therefore the feasible set, $B \in \mathcal{P}(\Lambda)$, can be fixed equal to Λ because, with rationality no longer an issue, permitting B to vary serves no function. An allocation mechanism within economic environments is therefore a function $F: \Omega^n \to A$. Note that, since the feasible set is fixed, B is dropped as an argument. A mechanism F is *strategy-proof* if, for all profiles $u \in \Omega^n$, all utility functions $u_i' \in \Omega$, and all agents i, $u_i[F(u)] \geq u_i[F(u/u_i')]$.

Let $C^2(A)$ be the set of all twice continuously differentiable functions on A. The mechanism F is continuously differentiable at $u \in \Omega^n$ if for all $v \in [C^2(A)]^n$,

$$D_v F(u) = \lim_{\lambda \to 0} \frac{F(u + \lambda v) - F(u)}{\lambda} \tag{4.01}$$

exists, is continuous in both u and v, and has the standard property that $D_{cv+dw}F(u) = cD_v F(u) + dD_w F(u)$ for all scalars c, $d \in \mathbb{R}$ and all functions v, $w \in [C^2(A)]^n$. Note that v and w are vectors of n distinct C^2 functions. This means that D_v is defined in terms of all n of the agents' utility functions being perturbed simultaneously. To represent the more restrictive case where only one agent's utility function is perturbed, let (v/i) be the element of $[C^2(A)]^n$ that has as its ith component the function $v_i \in C^2(A)$ and has as its other $n - 1$ components the constant function with value zero. The derivative $D_{(v/i)}F$ is therefore the direction within A in which the allocation $F(u)$ moves as the function v_i perturbs agent i's utility function u_i. Agent i *affects* the allocation $F(u)$ at $u \in \Omega^n$ if a $v_i \in C^2(A)$ exists such that $D_{(v/i)}F(u) \neq 0$. Agent i *affects agent j's utility* at $u \in \Omega^n$ if a $v_i \in C^2(A)$ exists such that $D_{(v/i)}u_j[F(u)] \neq 0$ where $D_{(v/i)}u_j[F(u)]$ represents the derivative of agent j's utility when i's utility function is perturbed by v_i.

The simplest case

The constraints that strategy-proofness places on the design of allocation mechanisms within economic environments are most easily seen within the simple one-agent, two-good implementation problem (i.e., $n = 1$

---

[14] Under the C^2 topology two utility functions, u and u', are close to each other if at every point within A their values are close, their vectors of first derivatives are close, and their matrices of second derivatives are close.

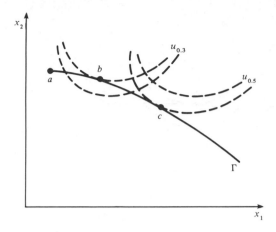

Figure 4

and $l = 2$) that Guesnerie and Laffont [1982] have analyzed. Let the function to be implemented be $G: \Omega \rightarrow A$ where A is convex subset of $\mathbb{R}^2$. Thus if $u \in \Omega$ represents the agent's true preferences, then the outcome should be $G(u) = x \in A$. The goal, as it always is in dominant strategy implementation problems, is to devise a mechanism F such that (i) the agent has an incentive to report u accurately and (ii) the outcome that reporting u accurately generates is $G(u)$. The second requirement means that F must be identical to G; otherwise F would not select $G(u)$ when it induces accurate revelation. Consequently G is implementable in dominant strategies if and only if G is a strategy-proof mechanism.

Let $u, u' \in \Omega$ be smooth and strictly concave utility functions defined on A and let, for all $x \in A$ and all $\theta \in [0, 1]$, $u_\theta(x) = \theta u(x) + (1 - \theta)u(x)$ be a linear combination of u and u'. Define the single agent's admissible preferences to be $\Omega = \{u_\theta \mid \theta \in [0, 1]\}$; that is, Ω is the family of smooth and strictly concave functions u and u' generate. The agent reports his preferences to the mechanism by reporting an $\eta \in [0, 1]$. He then receives allocation $G(u_\eta) \in A$. Therefore as θ (or η) varies between zero and one the image of $G(u_\theta)$ traces out a curve in A. This curve is the choice set for the agent. Depending on his true value of θ he reports the η that maximizes his true preferences.

The solid curves Γ and Γ' that appear in Figures 4 and 5, respectively, represent two possible images of G. In both figures point a corresponds to $G(u_\theta)$ when $\theta = 0.0$, point b to $G(u_\theta)$ when $\theta = 0.3$, and point c to $G(u_\theta)$ when $\theta = 0.5$. The dotted curves represent the indifference curves that u_θ generates: the left pair of dotted curves in each diagram are for $u_{0.3}$

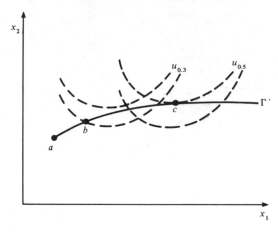

Figure 5

and the right pair are for $u_{0.5}$. Figure 4 is consistent with G being strategy-proof because at points b and c, respectively, the indifference curves of $u_{0.3}$ and $u_{0.5}$ are tangent with Γ. Therefore, subject to the constraint that he must pick a point on Γ, the agent maximizes his utility by reporting his preferences truthfully: $\eta = \theta$. Figure 5 is inconsistent with strategy-proofness because the indifference curves of $u_{0.3}$ are not tangent to Γ' at point b, though the indifference curves of $u_{0.5}$ are tangent at point c.

Figure 5 is the generic case while Figure 4 is the exceptional case. Given a family of utility functions such as u_θ and an arbitrary function G, then typically a not strategy-proof situation like Figure 5 occurs. It, in an informal sense, is an exceptional event (occurring with zero probability) that Figure 4 with its very special, carefully drawn tangencies occurs. More formally, Guesnerie and Laffont's [1982] result is that generically in the single-agent case an arbitrary function G cannot be implemented in dominant strategies.

An impossibility theorem for many agents

Satterthwaite and Sonnenschein [1981] have shown that the Gibbard–Satterthwaite Theorem carries over to economic environments whenever public goods only are being allocated and the mechanism F is broadly applicable. Public goods only means that agents care about and have preferences over all l dimensions of the consumption set. A mechanism is *broadly applicable* if Ω, the set of admissible utility functions, is open.

The openness of Ω, coupled with its linearity and C^2 topology, has an important implication: if Ω is open, $u_i \in \Omega$, and $v \in C^2$, then a $\delta > 0$ exists such that $(u_i + \lambda v) \in \Omega$ for all $\lambda \in [0, \delta)$. In other words, if a mechanism is broadly applicable, then any admissible utility function remains an admissible utility function when it is perturbed slightly through the addition of another C^2 function, λv. The logic behind the broad applicability requirement is that a perturbed admissible utility function should itself be admissible because "while preferences within an economic environment may have considerable a priori structure such as strict convexity, preferences are not naturally limited to any particular parametric form."[15]

Let $\Gamma_i(u_{-i}) = \{x \in A \mid x = F(u/u_i'), \text{ where } u_i' \in \Omega\}$, be the choice set of agent i. Note that Γ_i only varies with $u_{-i} = (u_1, \ldots, u_{i-1}, u_{i+1}, \ldots, u_n)$. A profile $u \in \Omega^n$ is a *regular point* of a strategy-proof mechanism F if

    a.   The mechanism, F, is continuously differentiable in u.

    b.   For all i and all u'_{-i} in some neighborhood of u, $\Gamma_i(u_{-i})$ is continuously differentiable in u_{-i} and is a k_i-dimensional, $0 \leq k_i \leq l - 1$, smooth manifold in a neighborhood of the allocation $F(u)$.

    c.   For all i, $F(u)$ is the unique and well-behaved maximizer of u_i on $\Gamma_i(u_{-i})$.

A regular point therefore is a point where each agent faces a smooth choice set that changes position smoothly as the other agents' preferences change.

These definitions and notation allow us to state Satterthwaite and Sonnenschein's [1981] public-goods-only result.

Theorem 4.1: *If an allocation mechanism F allocates public goods only, is strategy-proof, and is broadly applicable, then at every regular point u $\in \Omega^n$ an agent i exists who is a dictator at u.*

A dictator within this context is an agent who selects his most preferred point from an exogenously given set of achievable points. In other words, an agent i is a *dictator* if $\Gamma_i(u_{-1})$ is a constant as u_{-i} varies.

Several comments should be made about this result. First, the result is true only for public goods. The private goods analogue is discussed subsequently. Second, the result is local. If agent i is a dictator in some neighborhood of u, then a second regular point u', which is separated

---

[15] Satterthwaite and Sonnenschein [1981], p. 591.

from u, may exist at which some different agent is the dictator. Satterthwaite and Sonnenschein observe, however, that if the set of regular points is a connected set and the mechanism, for all regular points, is total, then a single agent i is the dictator at all the regular points. In the public-goods-only context, a mechanism is total if at every regular point u at least one agent affects the allocation $F(u)$.

Third, the theorem is stated without the Pareto criterion. Therefore imposed mechanisms are consistent with the theorem. An imposed mechanism permits no individual to influence the choice of outcome; that is, $F(u)$ is a constant function as u varies. Thus if a mechanism is imposed at u, then, for all agents i, the manifold $\Gamma_i(u_{-i})$ is a zero-dimensional, nonvarying point within A, which means formally that every agent is an (inconsequential) dictator. Fourth, if a mechanism is not imposed and agent i is dictator at u, then for all agents j $(j \neq i)$, $\Gamma_j(u_{-j})$ is the point within A that agent i, the dictator, selects from his exogenously given choice set Γ_i.

The most interesting step in the proof of Satterthwaite and Sonnenschein's proof of Theorem 4.1 is contained in their Lemma 2. That lemma in the public-goods-only case is this: If at a regular point u of a broadly applicable and strategy-proof mechanism an agent i exists who affects the utility of some other agent j, then agent j cannot affect the utility of agent i. To begin a simple proof by contradiction, suppose that each of the two agents can affect the other's utility, the mechanism F is both broadly applicable and strategy-proof, and that (without loss of generality) $n = 2$ and $l = 2$.

Figure 6 shows what this supposition means. Point a is the base point for the proof and is the allocation $F(u) = F(u_1, u_2)$ where $(u_1, u_2) \in \Omega^2$ is a regular point. At u agent 1's choice set is $\Gamma_1(u_2)$ and agent 2's is $\Gamma_2(u_1)$. The indifference curves of agents 1 and 2 that pass through point a are the dotted lines labeled, respectively, u_1 and u_2; in conformance with the requirements of strategy-proofness and regularity, they are tangent to their respective choice sets. If agent 1 perturbs his preferences u_1 slightly to become u_1', which is admissible because the mechanism is broadly applicable, then his most preferred point on his choice set, $\Gamma_1(u_2)$, becomes $F(u_1', u_2)$, which is labeled as point b. His indifference curve through point b is labeled u_1'. This changes agent 2's achievable set to become $\Gamma_2(u_1')$. Note that agent 2 prefers point b to point a; therefore the hypothesis that agent 1 can affect agent 2's utility is met.

Figure 7 develops the contradiction from the basic situation of Figure 6. Because F is broadly applicable, agent 2 can construct a small perturbation of his preferences from u_2 to u_2' so that the following three specifications hold simultaneously:

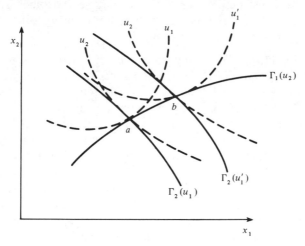

Figure 6

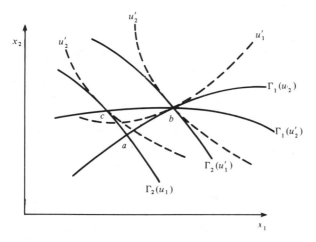

Figure 7

a. Point c is $F(u_1, u_2')$. The indifference curve for u_2' is tangent to $\Gamma_2(u_1)$ at point c. Agent 1, when his utility function is u_1, prefers point c to point a, which means that agent 2 affects agent 1's utility as the proof's initial hypothesis requires.

b. Point b, by construction, is $F(u_1', u_2')$ as well as $F(u_1', u_2)$.

    c.   Again by construction, agent 1's choice set becomes $\Gamma_1(u_2')$ when agent 2 perturbs his utility function from u_2 to u_2'. Note that $\Gamma_1(u_2')$ crosses $\Gamma_1(u_2)$ at point b.

Because point b is $F(u_1', u_2')$, strategy-proofness and regularity require that point b be that point on $\Gamma_1(u_2')$ where agent 1's utility is maximized when his preferences are u_1'; that is, u_1' indifference curve must be tangent to $\Gamma_1(u_2')$ at point b. But this is a contradiction because the u_1' indifference curve through point b is necessarily tangent to $\Gamma_1(u_2)$ and, at b, $\Gamma_1(u_2')$ crosses $\Gamma_1(u_2)$. Therefore the proof is complete: at a regular point of a broadly applicable and strategy-proof mechanism agents 1 and 2 cannot each affect the other's utility.

Theorem 4.1 generalizes from the public-goods-only case to settings that include private as well as public goods. To accommodate this change from public to public and private goods, let A be each agent's consumption set and redefine an allocation mechanism to be a function $F: \Omega^n \rightarrow A^n$. Thus $F(u) = [F_1(u), \ldots, F_i(u), \ldots, F_n(u)]$ is a vector of n functions where the ith function, $F_i: \Omega^n \rightarrow A$, specifies the allocation agent i receives. The function F_i itself has l components: $F_i = [F_{i1}, \ldots, F_{il}]$ where F_{ik} is the amount agent i receives of good k. If some components of each agent's allocation is a public good, then all the functions F_i are constrained to give each agent the same amount of the public good. Thus if good 1 is a public good, then $F_{11} = F_{21} = \cdots = F_{n1}$. Agents are assumed to have preferences over only their own consumption set, for example, agent i's utility is $u_i[F_i(u)]$.

Satterthwaite and Sonnenschein call a mechanism *nonbossy* if, for all $u \in \Omega^n$, all agents i, and all $u_i' \in \Omega$, $F_i(u) = F_i(u/u_i')$ implies $F_j(u) = F_j(u/u_i')$ for all agents j. The idea of nonbossiness is that if an agent i changes his preferences in a manner that leaves his own allocation unchanged, then the allocations that all other agents receive should also remain unchanged. This condition, which has intuitive appeal, is satisfied at most points by the competitive allocation mechanism.[16] It is closely related to Ritz's noncorruptibility condition; in fact, noncorruptibility implies nonbossiness. Within the private goods setting agent i *affects* agent j at a regular point $u \in \Omega^n$ if a $(v/i) \in [C^2(A)]^n$ exists such that $D_{(v/i)}F_j(u) \neq 0$. At each regular point the "affects" relation defines a

---

[16] Note that nonbossiness is trivially satisfied in the public-goods-only case because every agent receives the same allocation. In the private-goods-only case the competitive mechanism satisfies nonbossiness except, as Mark Walker has privately pointed out, in special circumstances where a continuum of equilibria exist. Satterthwaite and Sonnenschein [1981] incorrectly assert that the competitive mechanism is nonbossy at all regular points.

binary relation among the agents; we write $iH(u)j$ if agent i affects agent j at u.

The private – public goods version of Theorem 4.1 is this. If an allocation mechanism is broadly applicable, nonbossy, and strategy-proof, then at each regular point $u \in \Omega^n$ the affects relation H is acyclic. This means if agent i affects agent j, then no agent k (or sequence of agents) can exist who is affected by agent j and who in turn affects agent i. Thus the theorem states that agents cannot mutually accommodate each other's preferences; all accommodation must consist of agents who rank lower on an exogenously given hierarchy adjusting to the preferences of those agents who rank higher on the hierarchy.

Serial dictatorship is an example of a strategy-proof mechanism that is nonbossy, broadly applicable, and – as the result requires – acyclic in the affects relation. The canonical serial dictatorship is the mechanism where agent 1 selects from an exogenously fixed feasible set Γ_1, agent 2 selects from a feasible set $\Gamma_2(u_1)$ that depends on agent 1's choice (or, equivalently, his utility function provided nonbossiness is respected), and so on. Serial dictatorship is unattractive because the distribution of power is lopsided and, as Satterthwaite and Sonnenschein showed, the outcome generally violates Pareto optimality whenever the production possibility frontier is not linear.

5   Conclusions

This essay has used two approaches to examine the possibility of constructing strategy-proof (i.e., dominant-strategy implementable) mechanisms. The first approach begins with the environment within which the mechanism is to be applied and then characterizes the strategy-proof mechanisms that are possible within it. In Section 2 we applied this approach to the most unstructured of environments: discrete alternatives and all preference orderings admissible. The main result for this environment is negative: if there are at least three alternatives, then all strategy-proof mechanisms that satisfy the Pareto criterion are dictatorial. In Section 4 we applied this approach to the structured environments found in economic models: the alternative set is a subset of Euclidean space and preferences are a priori restricted, for example, to be representable by a twice differentiable utility function. There we reported additional negative results.[17]

---

[17] Sections 2 and 4 neglected two well-known cases of preference restrictions: single-peaked profiles and transferable utility. For the case of single-peaked profiles majority rule is strategy-proof. See Blin and Satterthwaite [1976]. For the case of public goods in

The second approach, which we employed in Section 3, is exactly the opposite of the first approach. In it we first specify the properties the mechanism should possess in addition to strategy-proofness and then characterize the environments in which that mechanism can exist. Substantial progress has been made in this area, though it is difficult to characterize this progress as either positive or negative. The positive aspect is that nondictatorial, strategy-proof mechanisms do exist for particular environments in which preferences are restricted only slightly. The negative aspect is that the environments for which these reasonable mechanisms do exist have, as of yet, no known relation to environments of the sort that naturally arise in economic models.

From the results that are presented and developed in this essay, we believe there are three main lessons that can be drawn. First, the theory of strategy-proof mechanisms is not a neatly finished body of knowledge. Numbers of interesting questions are still open. For example, on the technical side, the two approaches we have used in this essay need to be drawn together; that is, how do the results of Section 3 relate to the results in Section 4? A tantalizing, but unexploited, connection is the parallel that exists between Ritz's noncorruptibility condition and Satterthwaite and Sonnenschein's nonbossiness condition. On the substantive side, very little work has been done on strategy-proofness in repetitive situations. Our intuition is that an important reason why individuals often choose not to misrepresent their desires in group decision situations is that they do not find it in their interest to acquire the reputation of a manipulator.

Second, with only one important exception, economic life is by and large not straightforward in the sense of always giving each agent a dominant strategy. Even though the theory as it currently stands is not absolutely conclusive concerning the impossibility of constructing strategy-proof mechanisms for economic environments, it has clearly established that strategy-proofness can be achieved only in certain environments and then only by using carefully designed mechanisms. Thus an economic agent in his individual optimizing behavior does generally find it in his interest to worry about other agents' intentions and to play the game of trying to anticipate their actions correctly in planning his own actions even as they try to anticipate his actions in planning their actions.

Footnote 17 (*contd.*)

the presence of transferable utility, Groves schemes are strategy-proof. A large literature exists on Groves schemes; see, for example, Groves [1970], Clarke [1971], Groves and Loeb [1975], Green and Laffont [1979], and Holmstrom [1979]. We have not included these two cases in this chapter for reasons of space and because our judgment is that they are special cases that do not generalize.

The exception to this generalization is the large-number-of-agents case. For example, in an exchange economy that has a continuum of competitors, every agent is unable to influence prices, becomes a price taker, and finds it a dominant strategy to report his demand function accurately and without consideration of the demands that other agents are reporting. If the number of agents is small, however, then each agent can affect the price and no longer has a dominant strategy. The demand function an agent wants to report then depends importantly on the demands other agents are expected to report.[18]

Finally, the theory of strategy-proof mechanisms has philosophic implications. Bok [1978], Ch. 1, in her book that reviews and expands the ethical arguments extant against lying defines a lie to be an intentionally misleading statement. By this definition, in those situations where a group's decision process can usefully be represented by an allocation mechanism, an agent who misrepresents his preferences may sometimes legitimately be said to be lying. The impossibility results concerning strategy-proof mechanisms suggest that, no matter how well we redesign the social system, agents from time to time have an incentive to lie. This incentive is intrinsic to social mechanisms. It is as much a reflection of the imperfectability of society generally as it is of the imperfectness of society specifically. Therefore an individual's decision to be honest and not to lie is truly an ethical decision, because, even in principle, society cannot be designed so that honesty is self-enforcing. The excuse that a lie is society's fault since its structure gave the liar the incentive to perpetrate his deception is empty because a society that gives no incentive to lie is logically impossible.

REFERENCES

Arrow, K. J. [1963]. *Social Choice and Individual Values*. 2nd ed. New Haven, Conn.: Yale University Press.

Barbera, S. [1977]. "The Manipulability of Social Choice Mechanisms That Do Not Leave Too Much up to Chance." *Econometrica*, 45:1573–1589.

Blair, D. H., and E. Muller. [1983]. "Essential Aggregation Procedures on Restricted Domains of Preferences." *Journal of Economic Theory*, 30: 34–53.

Blin, J.-M., and M. A. Satterthwaite [1976]. "Strategy-Proofness and Single-Peakedness." *Public Choice*, 26:51–58.

---

[18] Pazner and Wesley [1977, 1978 (Chapter 14, this book)] analyzed the properties of voting procedures for the large-number-of-agents case. Roberts and Postlewaite [1976] investigated the incentive to become a price taker in an exchange economy as the number of agents increases.

Blin, J.-M., and M. A. Satterthwaite [1978]. "Individual Decisions and Group Decisions: The Fundamental Differences." *Journal of Public Economics*, 10:247–267.
Border, K. C., and J. S. Jordan [1983]. "Straightforward Elections, Unanimity and Phantom Voters." *Review of Economic Studies*, 50(January):153–70.
Clarke, E. [1971]. "Multipart Pricing of Public Goods." *Public Choice*, 11:17–33.
Feldman, A. [1979]. "Manipulating Voting Procedures." *Economic Inquiry*, 17(July):452–474.
Gibbard, A. [1973]. "Manipulation of Voting Schemes: A General Result." *Econometrica*, 41:587–602.
Gibbard, A. [1978]. "Straightforwardness of Game Forms with Lotteries as Outcomes." *Econometrica*, 46:595–614.
Green, J. R., and J.-J. Laffont [1979]. *Incentives in Public Decision-making.* Studies in Public Economics, vol. 1. Amsterdam: North Holland.
Groves, T. [1970]. The Allocation of Resources under Uncertainty. Unpublished Ph.D. dissertation, University of California, Berkeley.
Groves, T., and M. Loeb [1975]. "Incentives and Public Inputs." *Journal of Public Economics*, 4:211–226.
Guesnerie, R., and J.-J. Laffont [1982]. "On the Robustness of Strategy Proof Mechanisms." *Journal of Mathematical Economics*, 10:5–15.
Holmström, B. [1979]. "Groves' Scheme on Restricted Domains." *Econometrica*, 47(September):1137–1144.
Kalai, E., and E. Muller [1977]. "Characterization of Domains Admitting Nondictatorial Social Welfare Functions and Nonmanipulable Voting Procedures." *Journal of Economic Theory*, 16:457–469.
Kalai, E., and Z. Ritz [1980]. "Characterization of the Private Domains admitting Arrow Social Welfare Functions." *Journal of Economic Theory*, 22:22–36.
Kim, K., and F. Roush [1981]. "Effective Nondictatorial Domains." *Journal of Economic Theory*, 24:40–47.
Maskin, E. [1976]. "Social Choice on Restricted Domains." Unpublished Ph.D. dissertation, Harvard University, Cambridge, Mass.
Muller, E. [1982]. "Graphs and Anonymous Social Welfare Functions." *International Economic Review*, 23:609–622.
Pattanaik, P. [1973]. "On the Stability of Sincere Voting Situations." *Journal of Economic Theory*, 6:558–574.
Pazner, E. A., and E. Wesley [1977]. "Stability of Social Choice in Infinitely Large Societies." *Journal of Economic Theory*, 14:252–262.
Pazner, E. A., and E. Wesley [1978]. "Cheatproofness Properties of the Plurality Rule in Large Societies." *Review of Economic Studies*, 45:85–92. [Chapter 14 in this book.]
Postlewaite, A. [1979]. "Manipulation via Endowments." *Review of Economic Studies*, 46:255–262.
Ritz, Z. [1981]. "On Arrow Social Welfare Functions and on Nonmanipulable and Noncorruptible Social Choice Functions." Unpublished Ph.D. dissertation, Northwestern University, Evanston, Ill.
Ritz, Z. [1983]. "Restricted Domains, Arrow Social Welfare Functions and Noncorruptible and Nonmanipulable Social Choice Correspondence: The Case of Private Alternatives." *Mathematical Social Sciences*, 2:155–180.

Roberts, D. J., and A. Postlewaite [1976]. "The Incentive for Price-Taking Behavior in Large Exchange Economies." *Econometrica*, *44*:115−28.

Satterthwaite, M. A. [1973]. "The Existence of a Strategy Proof Voting Procedure: A Topic in Social Choice Theory." Unpublished Ph.D. Dissertation, University of Wisconsin, Madison.

Satterthwaite, M. A. [1975]. "Strategy-proofness and Arrow's Conditions: Existence and Correspondence Theorems for Voting Procedures and Social Welfare Functions." *Journal of Economic Theory*, *10*(April):187−217.

Satterthwaite, M. A., and H. Sonnenschein [1981]. "Strategy-proof Allocation Mechanisms at Differentiable Points." *Review of Economic Studies*, *48*: 587−597.

Schmeidler, D., and H. Sonnenschein [1978]. "Two Proofs of the Gibbard−Satterthwaite Theorem on the Possibility of a Strategy-proof Social Choice Function," in *Proceedings of a Conference on Decision Theory and Social Ethics at Schloss Reisenberg*, edited by H. Gottinger and W. Ensler. Dordrecht, Holland: Reidel.

Sen, A., and P. Pattanaik [1969]. "Necessary and Sufficient Conditions for Rational Choice under Majority Decision." *Journal of Economic Theory*, *1*:178−202.

CHAPTER 6

The theory of implementation in Nash equilibrium: a survey

Eric S. Maskin

The theory of implementation concerns the problem of designing game forms (sometimes called "mechanisms" or "outcome functions") the equilibria of which have properties that are desirable according to a specified criterion of social welfare called a *social choice rule*. A game form, in effect, decentralizes decision making. The social alternative is selected by the joint actions of all individuals in society rather than by a central planner.

Formally, a social choice rule assigns a set of alternatives to each profile of preferences (or other characteristics) that individuals in society might have; the set consists of the "welfare optima" relative to the preference profile. A *game form* is a rule that specifies an alternative (or *outcome*) for each configuration of actions that individuals take. A game form *implements* (technically, fully implements) a social choice rule if, for each possible profile of preferences, the equilibrium outcomes of the game form coincide with the welfare optima of the social choice rule. Of course, the equilibrium set depends on the particular solution concept being used. Implementation theory has considered a variety of solution concepts, including equilibrium in dominant strategies, Bayesian equilibrium, and Nash equilibrium. Other chapters of this book treat the first two equilibrium concepts. In the main, this chapter is confined to implementation in Nash equilibrium, although it relates this theory to those of other solution concepts, dominant strategies in particular.

Nash equilibrium is the noncooperative solution concept par excellence, and so it is not surprising that implementation theory should have employed it extensively. Nonetheless, one reason often advanced for the

Financial support from the NSF and the A. P. Sloan Foundation is gratefully acknowledged. I wish to thank Bhaskar Dutta, David Schmeidler, and Hugo Sonnenschein for helpful comments.

desirability of decentralization is that information is incomplete, and so it may seem strange to use a solution concept of complete information. (I am distinguishing here between Nash equilibrium in its original sense (Nash [1950]) and the incomplete information extension due to Harsanyi [1967], commonly called Bayesian equilibrium.) There are at least three alternative justifications for so doing.

First, as the work of Hurwicz [1972] and Groves and Ledyard [1977] at least implicitly assumes, a Nash equilibrium can be viewed as a stationary point of an iterative adjustment process. In such a process, players may have incomplete information but continually revise their actions until a point is reached where unilateral deviation no longer pays. Such a point is a Nash equilibrium.

There are several difficulties with this interpretation. If an individual believes that others play "naively" in the sense of always adjusting their actions optimally, assuming that the distribution of current actions will continue to prevail, then it will, in general, pay him to act as a Stackelberg leader and allow others to adapt to an action that he does *not* adjust. But if one or more players attempt to behave as Stackelberg leaders, there is no longer any reason to suppose that a stationary point of the process is a Nash equilibrium.

There are two cases where we might be able to rule out such Stackelberg behavior. One is where society is sufficiently large so that one individual's effect on others is slight enough as to have no appreciable effect on their actions. In that case, the individual would best play in "Nash-like" fashion (see, for example, Roberts and Postlewaite [1976]). The other is where the individual believes that any given iteration is the last (at least with very high probability), in which event, from his perspective, there is no opportunity for influencing future behavior.

Clearly, though, these cases are highly restrictive. When they do not apply, we cannot expect naive behavior. But if all individuals are "sophisticated," then each must realize that, when adjusting his action, he may affect others' (probabilistic) beliefs about his preferences. Because these beliefs, in turn, may affect *their* behavior, individuals may, again, be induced to behave in a non-Nash-like way.

The second reason for using Nash equilibrium is more satisfactory game theoretically. There are many circumstances where the planner (game form designer) can be thought of as having highly incomplete information, whereas individuals themselves are well informed. For example, the individuals may be firms that are experts in research and development and know a great deal about each other, whereas the planner may be the government, who knows next to nothing about R&D but wants to influence firms' behavior. Alternatively, the planner might be a "constitution designer," who must devise the procedural rules (the game form) by which committee members make decisions long in advance of any particular application. Indeed, the planner may not literally exist as a physical entity; rather he may simply stand for the committee as a whole. But, by the time, any particular decision has to be made, committee members may be well aware of one another's preferences.

In either of these two examples, Nash equilibrium is the appropriate solution concept. It is important in the examples that individuals have good information about each other; otherwise, Bayesian rather than Nash equilibrium pertains. It is necessary as well that the planner have poor information; otherwise, he could simply impose a welfare optimal social alternative by fiat.

Finally, implementation in Nash equilibrium may be thought of as a *positive* theory. To the extent that the theory can characterize the set of implementable social choice rules, it can predict the kinds of outcomes that can rise as equilibria of already existing (complete-information) games.

This chapter is divided into ten sections. The first introduces notation and the basic concepts. The second presents the fundamental theorem characterizing the set of implementable social choice rules. This theorem is cast in terms of two properties, monotonicity and weak no-veto power. Section 3 discusses the so-called "revelation principle" with respect to implementation in Nash equilibrium and several other equilibrium concepts. I clarify the relevance for Nash implementation of the principle, as usually stated, and propose an alternative formulation. Section 4 discusses the connection between implementability and several common properties of social choice rules, namely, weak no-veto power, neutrality, and individual rationality. Section 5 introduces the concept of effectivity and explores its connection with implementability. Section 6 exposits the relation between Nash and dominant-strategy implementation. Section 7 treats implementation in a much-studied special case, where preferences are of a "quasilinear" form.

Through Section 7, all analysis assumes noncooperative behavior on the part of individuals. Section 8, however, allows for collusion and studies implementation in strong equilibrium. Section 9 considers an implementation concept, double implementation, that accommodates both noncooperative and cooperative behavior simultaneously. Finally, Section 10 briefly discusses two concepts related to Nash implementation.

1   Notation and basic concepts

Let A be a set of social alternatives (A can be either finite or infinite). A utility function, u, on A is a real-valued function

$$u: A \rightarrow R,$$

where R denotes the real numbers. Let U_A be the set of all utility functions. For each $i = 1, \ldots, n$, let U_i be a subset of U_A. Then, an n-person *social choice rule* (SCR) on $(U_1, \ldots, U_n)$ is a correspondence[1]

$$f: U_1 \times \cdots \times U_n \rightarrow A.$$

For any profile $(u_1, \ldots, u_n)$ of utility function, one interprets $f(u_1, \ldots, u_n)$ (sometimes called the choice set and which we assume to be nonempty) as the set of welfare optimal alternatives. Common examples of social choice rules include the Pareto correspondence, which selects all Pareto optima corresponding to a given profile, and the Condorcet correspondence, which selects all alternatives for which a majority does not prefer some other alternative. Notice that, in principle, we allow the SCR to select two different choice sets for two utility profiles that correspond to the *same* preference orderings. That is, the choice set may depend on *cardinal* properties of utility functions. This flexibility will be eliminated subsequently, in the discussion of implementation. However, the present formulation enables the ordinal nature of an implementable SCR to be proved (albeit trivially) rather than postulated.

Given action spaces $S_1, \ldots, S_n$ for each individual, an n-person game form g is a mapping

$$g: S_1 \times \cdots \times S_n \rightarrow A.$$

If individuals 1 through n play the action configuration $(s_1, \ldots, s_n)$, the outcome is alternative $g(s_1, \ldots, s_n)$.

For a game form g, let $NE_g(u_1, \ldots, u_n)$ be the set of Nash-equilibrium outcomes corresponding to the profile $(u_1, \ldots, u_n)$. Slightly diverging from the terminology of Dasgupta, Hammond, and Maskin [1979], we shall say that the game form g *weakly implements* the SCR f in Nash equilibrium if, for every $(u_1, \ldots, u_n) \in U_1 \times \cdots \times U_n$

$$NE_g(u_1, \ldots, u_n) \text{ is nonempty} \tag{1}$$

$$NE_g(u_1, \ldots, u_n) \subseteq f(u_1, \ldots, u_n). \tag{2}$$

Thus, if g weakly implements f, an equilibrium always exists, and all equilibria lie in the social choice set.

Requirements (1) and (2) are, by now, the standard requirements in

---

In this chapter we shall suppose throughout that preferences alone constitute the relevant data about individuals. See the chapter by Postlewaite in this book for a treatment that allows for other information (e.g., endowments) as well.

Nash-implementation theory. We shall see below, however, that the analogue of (2) is not always imposed in the corresponding theories for other solution concepts.

If for all $(u_1, \ldots, u_n) \in U_1 \times \cdots \times U_n$ and all $a \in f(u_1, \ldots, u_n)$ there exists a game form g that weakly implements f and for which $a \in NE_g(u_1, \ldots, u_n)$, then we say that f is *implementable* (in Nash equilibrium). The difference between weak and ordinary implementability is that the latter requires every element of every choice set to arise as a Nash equilibrium of *some* implementing game form. An ostensibly still stronger requirement is that a single game form yield all these equilibria. We shall say that the game form g *fully implements* the SCR f if for all $(u_1, \ldots, u_n) \in U_1 \times \cdots \times U_n$,

$$NE(u_1, \ldots, u_n) = f(u_1, \ldots, u_n). \tag{3}$$

It will be shown in Section 4 that, in fact, implementability and full implementability are equivalent.

2 The fundamental characterization theorem

To characterize those SCRs that are implementable, we must first define two properties of SCRs. I shall argue that the first of these is in many circumstances extremely weak.

Weak no-veto power: An SCR f satisfies weak no-veto power if, for all $(u_1, \ldots, u_n) \in U_1 \times \cdots \times U_n$ and $a \in A$, $a \in f(u_1, \ldots, u_n)$ whenever there exists i such that for all $j \neq i$ and all $b \in A$ $u_j(a) \geq u_j(b)$.

In words, an SCR satisfies weak no-veto power if, whenever all individuals except possibly one agree that an alternative is *top ranked* (i.e., no other alternative is higher in their preference orderings), then that alternative is in the social choice set; the remaining individual cannot veto it. The hypothesis that the alternative be top ranked is what distinguishes this property from other no-veto conditions and what makes it so weak. Indeed, in many circumstances the hypothesis cannot be satisfied at all. Suppose, for example, that we equate a social alternative with an allocation of goods across consumers. Assume also that at least one of these goods is a divisible private good that all individuals find desirable. Then no two individuals will agree that any given alternative is top ranked, since each would like all the private good to himself. Thus if there are at least three individuals, our weak no-veto power condition is satisfied vacuously.

Our other condition is considerably stronger, although quite standard.

It sometimes goes under the name "strong positive association" (see Muller and Satterthwaite [1977] and Moulin and Peleg [1982]).

Monotonicity: An SCR f is monotonic if, for all $(u_1, \ldots, u_n)$, $(\bar{u}_1, \ldots, \bar{u}_n) \in U_1 \times \cdots \times U_n$ and $a \in A$, $a \in f(\bar{u}_1, \ldots, \bar{u}_n)$ whenever (i) $a \in f(u_1, \ldots, u_n)$ and, (ii) for all $b \in A$ and i, $u_i(a) \geq u_i(b)$ implies $\bar{u}_i(a) \geq \bar{u}_i(b)$.

In words, an SCR is monotonic if, whenever an alternative a is in the choice set for a profile of preferences, and then those preferences are altered in a way such that a does no fall in anyone's preference ordering relative to any other alternative, it remains in the choice set.

Clearly, monotonicity is a purely ordinal property, and an SCR that satisfies it will reflect only ordinal properties of utility functions. That is, if, for all i, $\bar{u}_i = h_i \circ u_i$, where $h_i: R \to R$ is strictly increasing, then a monotonic f satisfies $f(u_1, \ldots, u_n) = f(\bar{u}, \ldots, \bar{u}_n)$. Thus monotonicity rules out the interpersonal comparisons inherent in, say, utilitarianism or the Rawlsian difference principle. Moreover, as we shall see below (see Section 6), it amounts to something very close to independence of irrelevant alternatives in the sense of Arrow [1951]. Nonetheless it is satisfied by such common SCRs as the Pareto and Condorcet correspondences and, in economic contexts, by the correspondence that selects core allocations.

Monotonicity does not require that all Pareto-optimal alternatives be in the choice set (the Condorcet correspondence is a counterexample), but, if f is onto A, it does imply that a *subset* of Pareto-optimal alternatives is in the choice set, namely, those that are top ranked by all individuals.

Lemma 1: *Suppose that f is monotonic and onto A. For any $(\bar{u}_1, \ldots, \bar{u}_n) \in U_1 \times \cdots \times U_n$ and $a \in A$ if, for all b and i, $\bar{u}_i(a) \geq \bar{u}_i(b)$, then $a \in f(\bar{u}_1, \ldots, \bar{u}_n)$.*

Proof: Because, by assumption, f is onto A, there exists $(u_1, \ldots, u_n) \in U_1 \times \cdots \times U_n$ such that $a \in f(u_1, \ldots, u_n)$. If, for all i and b, $\bar{u}_i(a) \geq \bar{u}_i(b)$, then, from monotonicity, $a \in f(\bar{u}_1, \ldots, \bar{u}_n)$.

Q.E.D.

We can now state the fundamental characterization result.

Theorem 1 (Maskin [forthcoming]): *Suppose that f is an n-person SCR. If f is implementable in Nash equilibrium, then it is monotonic. Furthermore,* *if $n \geqslant 3$ and f satisfies weak no-veto power and monotonicity, then it is fully implementable.*

Proof: To see that implementability implies monotonicity, suppose that f is not monotonic. Then there exist $(u_1, \ldots, u_n)$ and $(\bar{u}_1, \ldots, \bar{u}_n)$ $\in U_1 \times \cdots \times U_n$ and $a \in A$ such that $a \in f(u_1, \ldots, u_n)$ and, for all $b \in A$ and all i,

$$u_i(a) \geqslant u_i(b) \text{ implies } \bar{u}_i(a) \geqslant \bar{u}_i(b) \tag{4}$$

but

$$a \notin f(\bar{u}_1, \ldots, \bar{u}_n). \tag{5}$$

Now, if f is implementable, there exists a game form $g: S_1 \times \cdots \times S_n \to A$ and a configuration of strategies $(s_1^*, \ldots, s_n^*)$ such that $g(s_1^*, \ldots, s_n^*) = a$ and $(s_1^*, \ldots, s_n^*)$ is a Nash equilibrium for profile $(u_1, \ldots, u_n)$. But from (4), $(s_1^*, \ldots, s_n^*)$ is also a Nash equilibrium for $(\bar{u}_1, \ldots, \bar{u}_n)$, which, in view of (5), contradicts (2). Hence, f is not implementable.

We only sketch the proof that weak no-veto power and monotonicity imply that f is fully implementable. For the omitted details see Maskin [forthcoming]. For any $a \in A$ and $u_i \in U_i$, let

$$L(a, u_i) = \{b \in A | u_i(a) \geqslant u_i(b)\}.$$

$L(a, u_i)$ is the lower contour set of u_i at a (that is, the set of alternatives that someone with utility function u_i does not prefer to a). For each i, let

$$S_i = \{(u_1, \ldots, u_n, a) | (u_1, \ldots, u_n) \in U_1 \times \cdots \times U_n \text{ and } a \in A\}. \tag{6}$$

That is, each player's action consists of announcing a profile of utility functions and an alternative. Define $g: S_1 \times \cdots \times S_n \to A$ so that

$$\begin{aligned} &\text{if } \bar{s}_1 = \cdots \bar{s}_n = (u_1, \ldots, u_n, a) \text{ and } a \in f(u_1, \ldots, u_n), \\ &\quad \text{then } g(\bar{s}_1, \ldots, \bar{s}_n) = a; \end{aligned} \tag{7}$$

$$\begin{aligned} &\text{if } \bar{s}_j = (u_1, \ldots, u_n, a) \text{ and } a \in f(u_1, \ldots, u_n) \text{ for all } j \neq i, \\ &\quad \text{then } \{b \in A | b = g(s_i, \bar{s}_{-i}), s_i \in S_i\} = L(a, u_i) \end{aligned} \tag{8}$$

and

if, for given i, there exist j and k, with $j \neq i \neq k$, such that either $\bar{s}_j \neq \bar{s}_k$, or $\bar{s}_j = (u_1, \ldots, u_n, a)$ with $a \notin f(u_1, \ldots, u_n)$ then $\{b \in A | b = g(s_i, \bar{s}_{-i}), s_i \in S_i\} = A.$ \tag{9}

The notation "$g(s_i, \bar{s}_{-i})$" is shorthand for $g(\bar{s}_1, \ldots, \bar{s}_{i-1}, s_i, \bar{s}_{i+1}, \ldots, \bar{s}_n)$. That there exist game forms satisfying conditions (6)–(9) is

demonstrated in Maskin [forthcoming]. I claim that any such game form
fully implements f.

To see this, first choose $(u_1, \ldots, u_n) \in U_1 \times \cdots \times U_n$ and $a \in f(u_1, \ldots, u_n)$. From (7), if all individuals take the action $(u_1, \ldots, u_n, a)$, the outcome is a. Furthermore if $(u_1, \ldots, u_n)$, in fact, *are* individuals' utility functions, then, from (8), each individual cannot obtain an alternative he prefers to a by varying his action unilaterally. Hence, all individuals' taking the action $(u_1, \ldots, u_n, a)$ is a Nash equilibrium for the profile $(u_1, \ldots, u_n)$. This establishes that for all $(u_1, \ldots, u_n)$, $f(u_1, \ldots, u_n) \subseteq NE_g(u_1, \ldots, u_n)$.

To establish the opposite inclusion, suppose that $(\bar{s}_1, \ldots, \bar{s}_n)$ is a Nash equilibrium of g for the profile $(\bar{u}_1, \ldots, \bar{u}_n)$ and that $a = g(\bar{s}_1, \ldots, \bar{s}_n)$. We must establish that $a \in f(\bar{u}_1, \ldots, \bar{u}_n)$. There are three cases to consider: (α) $\bar{s}_1 = \cdots = \bar{s}_n = (u_1, \ldots, u_n, a)$ and $a \in f(u_1, \ldots, u_n)$; ($\beta$) there exist i and action $s = (u_1, \ldots, u_n, a)$ with $a \in f(u_1, \ldots, u_n)$ such that for all $j \neq i$ $\bar{s}_j = s$ but $\bar{s}_i \neq s$; and (γ) all other configurations.

Consider case (α) first. Suppose that $\bar{s}_i = (u_1, \ldots, u_n, a)$ for all i and $a \in f(u_1, \ldots, u_n)$. We have already observed that, from (7) and (8), $g(\bar{s}_1, \ldots, \bar{s}_n) = a$ and that $(\bar{s}_1, \ldots, \bar{s}_n)$ is a Nash equilibrium for the profile $(u_1, \ldots, u_n)$. For any i consider b such that $u_i(a) \geq u_i(b)$, in other words such that $b \in L(a, u_i)$. From (8) there exists $s_i \in S_i$ such that $g(s_i, \bar{s}_{-i}) = b$. Hence $\bar{u}_i(a) \geq \bar{u}_i(b)$; otherwise, $\bar{s}_i$ could not be an equilibrium action for utility function $\bar{u}_i$, contrary to our assumption. Therefore, the hypotheses of the monotonicity condition are satisfied, and we conclude that $a \in f(\bar{u}_1, \ldots, \bar{u}_n)$, as required.

Next, consider case (β). Suppose that, for all $j \neq i$, $\bar{s}_j = (u_1, \ldots, u_n, a)$ with $a \in f(u_1, \ldots, u_n)$ and that $\bar{s}_i \neq (u_i, \ldots, u_n, a)$. Since, for each $k \neq i$, $\bar{s}_k \neq \bar{s}_i$ and $n \geq 3$, (9) implies that, for all $j \neq i$ and all $b \in A$, there exists $s_j \in S_j$ such that $g(s_j, \bar{s}_{-j}) = b$. Hence, because $(\bar{s}_1, \ldots, \bar{s}_n)$ was assumed to be a Nash equilibrium for $(\bar{u}_1, \ldots, \bar{u}_n)$, we can conclude that $\bar{u}_j(a) \geq \bar{u}_j(b)$ for all $j \neq i$ and all $b \in A$. Our weak no-veto power condition then implies that $a \in f(\bar{u}_1, \ldots, \bar{u}_n)$, as required.

Finally, in case (γ), for all i, there exist j and k, with $j \neq i \neq k$, such that either $\bar{s}_j = (u_1, \ldots, u_n, a)$ with $a \notin f(u_1, \ldots, u_n)$ or $\bar{s}_j \neq \bar{s}_k$. Hence, as in case (β), weak no-veto power implies that $a \in f(\bar{u}_1, \ldots, \bar{u}_n)$, completing the proof.   Q.E.D.

The proof of Theorem 1 is constructive. Given an SCR satisfying weak no-veto power and monotonicity, we produce a game form that fully implements it. It may be helpful to summarize the construction in words. An action consists of announcing a profile of utility functions and an alternative. Condition (7) says that if all individuals announce the same profile $(u_1, \ldots, u_n)$ and alternative a, then a is the outcome if a is optimal for $(u_1, \ldots, u_n)$. Condition (8) says that if all individuals but one play the same action $(u_1, \ldots, u_n, a)$ and a is optimal for $(u_1, \ldots, u_n)$, then, by varying his action, the remaining individual can "trace out" the entire lower contour set (and only that set) corresponding to the utility function the others announce for him and to the alternative that they announce. Condition (9) stipulates that if, in a configuration of actions, two individuals' actions differ or one entails an alternative that is not optimal with respect to the announced preferences, then any third individual can trace out the entire set A by varying his action.

As we have noted, the Pareto correspondence is monotonic. Also, it obviously satisfies weak no-veto power. Theorem 1 implies, therefore, that the Pareto correspondence is implementable for $n > 3$, even when the U_i's are unrestricted (i.e., equal to U_A). This result, however, does not obtain when $n = 2$, as Theorem 2 demonstrates.

Pareto optimality: An SCR $f: U_1 \times \cdots \times U_n \rightarrow A$ is Pareto optimal if for all $(u_1, \ldots, u_n) \in U_1 \times \cdots \times U_n$ and all $a \in f(u_1, \ldots, u_n)$, a is weakly Pareto optimal with respect to $(u_1, \ldots, u_n)$; that is, there does not exist $b \in A$ such that, for all i, $u_i(b) > u_i(a)$.

Dictatorship: An SCR $f: U_1 \times \cdots \times U_n \rightarrow A$ is dictatorial if there exists an individual i such that, for all $(u_1, \ldots, u_n) \in U_1 \times \cdots \times U_n$ and all $a \in A$, $u_i(a) \geq u_i(b)$ for all $b \in A$ if $a \in f(u_1, \ldots, u_n)$. That is, an SCR is dictatorial if there exists an individual (the dictator) who always gets his way.

Theorem 2: *Let $f: U_A \times U_A \rightarrow A$ be a two-person, Pareto-optimal SCR. Then f is implementable in Nash equilibrium if and only if f is dictatorial.*

Proof: See Maskin [1977] and Hurwicz and Schmeidler [1978].

The hypothesis that the U_i's are equal to U_A is crucial to the validity of Theorem 2. As we shall see in Section 7, many two-person, Pareto-optimal, and nondictatorial SCRs on restricted domains are implementable.

Given a set of SCRs satisfying the hypotheses of Theorem 1, we can generate new implementable SCRs:

Corollary to Theorem 1: *For $n \geq 3$, suppose that $\{f_1, f_2, \ldots\}$ is a sequence of n-person monotonic SCRs. Then, if one of the f_i's satisfies no-veto power $\cup_{i=1}^{\infty} f_i$ is fully implementable in Nash equilibrium, and if each of f_i's satisfies weak no-veto power $\cap_{i=1}^{\infty} f_i$ is fully implementable (assuming $\cap_{i=1}^{\infty} f_i(u_1, \ldots, u_n)$ is nonempty for all profiles).*

Proof: The proof simply consists of verifying that $\cup_{i=1}^{\infty} f_i$ and $\cap_{i=1}^{\infty} f_i$ both satisfy monotonicity, that $\cup_{i=1}^{\infty} f_i$ satisfies weak no-veto power if one of f_i's does, and that $\cap_{i=1}^{\infty} f_i$ satisfies weak no-veto power if all the f_i's do.

3   The revelation principle

Let us temporarily broaden the idea of an SCR. Rather than limiting its domain to sets of utility functions, we shall define it to be a correspondence on $\Theta_1 \times \cdots \times \Theta_n$, where Θ_i is individual i's space of possible "characteristics." A characteristic θ_i not only describes i's preferences, but perhaps also his endowment, information about others, and whatever else might be relevant.

Suppose that the SCR $f: \Theta_1 \times \cdots \times \Theta_n \to A$ is weakly implemented by a game form $g: S_1 \times \cdots \times S_n \to A$ according to some noncooperative solution concept. Thus we require the analogues of (1) and (2) to hold for the solution concept under consideration. Because the solution concept is noncooperative, we can write each individual's equilibrium action as a function $s_i^*(\theta_i)$ of his characteristic. Hence, for all profiles $(\theta_1, \ldots, \theta_n)$, $(s_1^*(\theta_1), \ldots, s_n^*(\theta_n))$ is an equilibrium. Now, define the induced game form

$$g^*: \Theta_1 \times \cdots \times \Theta_n \to A$$

so that, for all $(\theta_1, \ldots, \theta_n)$,

$$g^*(\theta_1, \ldots, \theta_n) = g(s_1^*(\theta_1), \ldots, s_n^*(\theta_n)).$$

Notice that for all $(\theta_1, \ldots, \theta_n)$, the *actions* $(\theta_1, \ldots, \theta_n)$ constitute an equilibrium[2] for the profile $(\theta_1, \ldots, \theta_n)$ and that, furthermore, $g^*(\theta_1, \ldots, \theta_n) \in f(\theta_1, \ldots, \theta_n)$. This is the *revelation principle* (see

---

Actually this assertion is a bit too strong. It is true only for solution concepts that have the property that an individual's best action does not change when one deletes from the action spaces of other individuals all actions that are never equilibrium actions for any possible characteristic they might have. This property holds for dominant strategy, Bayesian, and Nash equilibrium, but not for, say, maximin equilibrium. However it does hold for a modified version of maximin equilibrium (see Dasgupta, Hammond, and Maskin [1979]).

Gibbard [1973], Dasgupta, Hammond, and Maskin [1979], Myerson [1979, 1982, Chapter 14, this book] and the references cited in Myerson's chapter. The revelation principle is the observation that if a game form implements an SCR, then there exists a "direct revelation" game form whose action spaces coincide with the characteristic spaces and which has the properties that (1) playing one's true characteristic is always an equilibrium action and (2) such a "truth-telling" equilibrium is in the choice set.

Although the revelation principle is a useful technical device, I must stress that g^* does *not* necessarily implement f. That is because, although $g^*(\theta, \ldots, \theta_n)$ is in the choice set for $(\theta_1, \ldots, \theta_n)$, there may be other equilibrium outcomes that are not, even if g (the original game form) *does* implement f.

Thus, we cannot conclude from the revelation principle that all one ever need consider are direct-revelation game forms. Unfortunately, one may draw that incorrect conclusion from reading much of the literature on implementation in dominant and Bayesian equilibria. For the most part, this literature has implicitly used an implementation concept different from (the analogue of) (1) and (2), namely "truthful implementation," which requires only that the truthful equilibrium of a direct revelation game form be in the choice set (See Dasgupta, Hammond, and Maskin [1979], Laffont and Maskin [1982a], and Sections 5 and 6 of this chapter). Although the connection between truthful and ordinary implementation has been (partially) elucidated for the case of dominant-strategy equilibrium, almost nothing is known about it for Bayesian equilibrium. In any case, the Nash-implementation theory is the sole implementation literature where much attention has been given to the issue of *multiple* equilibria. Indeed that is the aspect that lends the literature interest, since for any SCR, it is extremely easy to construct a direct-revelation game form for which, for each profile, the truthful equilibrium is in the choice set. All we have to do is satisfy (7), which is possible for *any* SCR.

There *is*, nonetheless, a version of the revelation principle that is consistent with our definition of Nash implementation. When Nash equilibrium is the solution concept, an individual needs to know not just his *own* preferences but the preferences of everyone else in order to determine his equilibrium action. Therefore, in the framework of Sections 1 and 2, a characteristic of an individual is an entire profile of utility functions. Indeed, if instead we interpreted individual i's characteristic to be u_i alone, we would, in effect, be requiring dominant strategies (see Theorem 7.1.1 of Dasgupta, Hammond, and Maskin [1979]).

Notice that having individuals announce utility profiles is, essentially, what the game forms in the proof of Theorem 1 do (individuals also announce alternatives, but that is only because f may be multivalued; if f were single-valued, the strategy spaces could be taken to be $U_1 \times \cdots \times U_n$). Thus these game forms may be thought of as ones of direct revelation. Now, as we shall see in Section 4, not all implementable SCRs satisfy weak no-veto power. Therefore, Theorem 1 does not quite completely characterize the set of implementable SCRs. Nevertheless, the kind of game form constructed in the proof, only slightly modified, is capable of fully implementing any SCR that can be implemented at all. Thus, in this sense, we need consider only a "canonical" class of SCRs.

Suppose that f is an implementable SCR. For each i and $\bar{u}_i \in U_i$ let $N_i(\bar{u}_i) = \{a \in A|$ there exists $\bar{u}_{-i}$ such that, for all $j \neq i$ and all $b \in A$, $\bar{u}_j(a) \geq \bar{u}_j(b)$ but $a \notin f(\bar{u}_1, \ldots, \bar{u}_n)\}$. That is, the set $N_i(\bar{u}_i)$ consists of all the alternatives a that individual i can veto if he has utility function $\bar{u}_i$ even if a is a top-ranked alternative for everyone else. Clearly, $N_i(\bar{u}_i)$ is empty if f satisfies weak no-veto power. As in the proof of Theorem 1, let

$$S_i = \{(u_1, \ldots, u_n, a)|(u_1, \ldots, u_n) \in U_1 \times \cdots \times U_n \text{ and } a \in A\}. \quad (6)$$

Define $g: S_1 \times \cdots \times S_n \to A$ to satisfy (7),

if $\bar{s}_j = (u_1, \ldots, u_n, a)$ and $a \in f(u_1, \ldots, u_n)$ for all $j \neq i$, then
$$\{b \in A|b = g(s_i, \bar{s}_{-i}), s_i \in S_i\} = L(a, u_i) - M_i(a, u_i), \quad (8^*)$$

where $M_i(a, u_i) = \{b \in A|$ there exists $\bar{u}_i \in U_i$ such that $b \in N_i(\bar{u}_i)$ and $\bar{u}_i(b) \geq \bar{u}_i(c)$ for all $c \in L(a, u_i)\}$, and

if, for given i, there exist j and k, with $j \neq i \neq k$, such that either
$$\bar{s}_j \neq \bar{s}_k \text{ or } \bar{s}_j = (u_1, \ldots, u_n, a) \text{ with } a \notin f(u_1, \ldots, u_n),$$
$$\text{then } \{b \in A| b = g(s_i, \bar{s}_{-i}), s_i \in S_i\} = A - P, \quad (9^*)$$

where $P = \{a \in A|$ there exists $(u_1, \ldots, u_n)$ such that $u_t(a) \geq u_t(b)$ for all t and b but $a \notin f(u_1, \ldots, u_n)\}$. From Lemma 1, if $a \in P$, then a is not in the range of f. Therefore P is empty if f is onto A. To see that such a construction is possible, see Maskin [forthcoming].

Condition (8^*) says that if all individuals but i take the same action $(u_1, \ldots, u_n, a)$, then, by varying his action, i can trace out the lower contour set corresponding to u_i and a, except for those alternatives b for which there exists a profile $(\bar{u}_1, \ldots, \bar{u}_n)$ such that (α) b is top ranked by all individuals other than i, (β) individual i (with utility function $\bar{u}_i$) prefers b to all alternatives in the lower contour set corresponding to $L(a, u_i)$, and (λ) b is not in the choice set corresponding to $(\bar{u}_1, \ldots, \bar{u}_n)$. Condition (9^*) requires that if, in a configuration of actions, two individuals' actions differ or entail an alternative that is not optimal with respect to the announced preferences, then any third individual, by varying *his* action, can trace out the entire set A except for those alternatives a for which there exists a profile in which a is top ranked by everyone but not in the choice set.

Theorem 3 (The revelation principle): *Suppose that, for $n \geqslant 3$, f is an n-person SCR that is implementable in Nash equilibrium. Then a game form satisfying (6), (7), (8*), and (9*) exists. Furthermore, f is fully implementable by any such game form.*

For the details of the proof, see Maskin [forthcoming]. Here we give only an indication of the idea behind the proof by way of an example.

The construction in Theorem 1 will not serve to implement all implementable SCRs. This is because an implementable SCR may fail to satisfy weak no-veto power (however, some implementable SCRs that violate weak no-veto power *can* be implemented by the Theorem 1 construction, e.g., the individual rationality correspondence of Section 4 below). For example, consider the three-person SCR f that chooses alternative a if and only if all three individuals top rank a, and also chooses b or c according to whichever commands a majority over the other. Defined on the domain of strong orderings, this SCR is clearly monotonic,[3] but it does not satisfy weak no-veto power because if individuals 2 and 3 both prefer a to b and b to c, and individual 1 prefers b to a and a to c, then a is not chosen, even though two of three individuals top rank it. Moreover, the construction of Theorem 1 does not implement the SCR.

To see this, suppose, for instance, that individuals' preferences are as just described. However, suppose, in the Theorem 1 construction, that individuals 2 and 3 both play the strategy consisting of announcing the profile

1	2	3
b	c	c
c	a	a
a	b	b

(*)

and the alternative c. If individual 1 does the same, then the outcome is c, since this is an f-optimal alternative. By playing some alternative strategy s', furthermore, individual 1 can obtain alternative a, since a lies in the lower contour set of 1's preference ordering as specified by (*). Individual 1 cannot, however, obtain alternative b. Therefore, a strategy triple where individual 1 plays s' and individuals 2 and 3 each play (*) is a Nash

---

[3] I am grateful to B. Dutta, who pointed out that an example used in a previous version was not monotonic.

equilibrium with respect to individuals' (true) preferences. Because the corresponding outcome, a, is not optimal for those preferences, we conclude that the game form does not implement f.

However, f *is* implementable by a game form satisfying (6), (7), (8*), and (9*). Specifically, (8*) guarantees that a nonoptimal equilibrium as in the preceding cannot arise because, starting from a configuration where all individuals play the same strategy, an individual *cannot* trace out the whole lower contour set and, in particular, cannot obtain, for any profile of preferences, any alterantive that is top ranked by all others and, within his lower contour set, top ranked for him. Thus, in the example, if individuals 2 and 3 play (*), individual 1 cannot obtain a (in this example, we did not have to invoke (9*), which applies only to SCRs that permit non-Pareto-optimal outcomes).

Notice that Theorem 3 establishes that implementability implies full implementability, as I claimed earlier. The theorem can be used to extend the corollary to Theorem 1 to the case of SCRs that do no necessarily satisfy weak no-veto power.

Corollary 1: *Suppose that, for $n \geq 3$, $f_1, f_2, \ldots$ is a sequence of monotonic SCRs. Suppose one of the f_i's is implementable in Nash equilibrium. Then $\bigcup_{i=1}^{\infty} f_i$ is implementable also.*

It remains an open question whether $\bigcap_{i=1}^{\infty} f_i$ is necessarily implementable. However, a case in which the intersection of two implementable SCRs *is* implementable is where one of the f_i's is the Pareto correspondence.

Corollary 2: *For $n \geq 3$, if f_1 is an implementable SCR and f_2 is the Pareto correspondence, then $f_1 \cap f_2$ is implementable if it is nonempty for all profiles.*

Closely related to Corollary 2 is the observation that the "Pareto frontier" of an implementable SCR is implementable.

Pareto frontier of an SCR: The Pareto frontier of an SCR f is the SCR $PF(f)(u_1, \ldots, u_n) = \{a \in f(u_1, \ldots, u_n) | \text{for all } b \in f(u_1, \ldots, u_n), u_i(a) \geq u_i(b) \text{ for some } i\}$.

Corollary 3: *For $n \geq 3$, if f is an implementable SCR, then the Pareto frontier $PF(f)$ is also implementable.*

The proofs of Corollaries $1-3$ are straightforward applications of Theorem 3 (see Maskin [forthcoming]).

4   No-veto power, individual rationality, and neutrality

I have already mentioned that weak no-veto power is not necessary for implementability. One prominent example of an implementable SCR that violates this property is the individual rationality correspondence. Let a_0 be an element of A. We interpret a_0 to be the status quo. The individual rationality correspondence, f_{IR}, selects all alternatives that weakly Pareto dominate a_0, i.e.

$$f_{IR}(u_1, \ldots, u_n) = \{a \in A \,|\, u_i(a) \geq u_i(a_0) \text{ for all } i\}.$$

Clearly, f_{IR} does not satisfy weak no-veto power on all domains of utility functions, because every individual must be guaranteed at least the utility he derives from a_0. Nonetheless it is a simple matter to fully implement f_{IR}. For instance, the construction of Theorem 1 will do the trick. For a simpler example, let $S_i = A$ for all i. Define the game form $g\colon S_1 \times \cdots \times S_n \to A$ so that

$$g(s_1, \ldots, s_n) = \begin{cases} s, & \text{if } s_1 = \cdots = s_n \\ a_0, & \text{otherwise.} \end{cases} \tag{10}$$

That is, each individual chooses an alternative as an action. If the alternatives agree, the common alternative is the outcome; otherwise, a_0 is the outcome. It is immediate that g fully implements f_{IR}. Notice that this is true even for $n = 2$.

The SCR f_{IR} is implementable not only by itself but in conjunction with other implementable SCRs.

Corollary 4 to Theorem 3: *Suppose that, for $n \geq 3$, f is an n-person SCR that is implementable. Then $f \cap f_{IR}$ is implementable too.*

The individual rationality correspondence is highly "nonneutral"; it treats the alternative a_0 very differently from all others. But, just as it is implementable, so is any neutral and monotonic SCR.

Neutrality: An SCR $f\colon U_A \times \cdots \times U_A \to A$ is neutral if for any permutation $\pi\colon A \to A$ and any profile $(u_1, \ldots, u_n)$

$$f(u_1 \circ \pi, \ldots, u_n \circ \pi) = \pi \circ f(u_1, \ldots, u_n).$$

Neutrality simply says that an alternative's labeling is irrelevant. Notice that in the formal statement, we have defined f on the unrestricted domain. This is to ensure that f is defined on the permutation profile $(u_1 \circ \pi, \cdots u_n \circ \pi)$. The following result is another simple application of Theorem 3.

Theorem 4 (Maskin [1977]): *For $n \geq 3$, an n-person SCR that is monotonic and neutral is implementable in Nash equilibrium.*

Theorem 4 and Corollary 4 raise the question of whether weak no-veto power is a redundant condition for implementability when $n \geq 3$. In fact, the following example demonstrates that it is not, by exhibiting a three-person monotonic SCR that is not implementable.

Example 1: (Maskin [1977], A nonimplementable, monotonic SCR): Let $n = 3$ and $A = \{a, b, c\}$. For each i, let U_i consist of all utility functions corresponding to strict preference orderings (i.e., $u_i(a) = u_i(b)$ implies $a = b$). Define the SCR $f: U_1 \times U_2 \times U_3 \to A$ so that for all $(u_1, u_2, u_3) \in U_1 \times U_2 \times U_3$ and all $x, y \in A$, $x \in f(u_1, u_1, u_3)$ if and only if

$$x \text{ is Pareto optimal;} \tag{11}$$

$$\text{if } x \in \{a, b\} \; u_1(x) > u_1(y) \text{ for all } y \neq x; \tag{12}$$

$$\text{if } x = c, \text{ there exists } y \in A \text{ such that } u_1(x) > u_1(y). \tag{13}$$

Thus, a or b is optimal if it is top ranked by individual 1, and c is optimal if it is Pareto optimal and not bottom ranked by individual 1.

It is easy to see that f is monotonic. Choose (u_1^*, u_2^*, u_3^*), $(u_1^{**}, u_2^{**}, u_3^{**})$, and $(u_1^{***}, u_2^{***}, u_3^{***}) \in U_1 \times U_2 \times U_3$ so that

$$u_1^*(b) > u_1^*(c) > u_1^*(a)$$

$$u_2^*(c) > u_2^*(a) > u_2^*(b)$$

$$u_3^*(c) > u_3^*(a) > u_3^*(b)$$

$$u_1^{**}(a) > u_1^{**}(b) > u_1^{**}(c)$$

$$u_2^{**}(c) > u_2^{**}(b) > u_2^{**}(a)$$

$$u_3^{**}(c) > u_3^{**}(a) > u_3^{**}(b)$$

$$u_1^{***}(b) > u_1^{***}(a) > u_1^{***}(c)$$

$$u_2^{***}(a) > u_2^{***}(b) > u_2^{***}(c)$$

$$u_3^{***}(a) > u_3^{***}(b) > u_3^{***}(c).$$

Then

$$f(u_1^*, u_2^*, u_3^*) = \{b, c\}; \tag{14}$$

$$f(u_1^{**}, u_2^{**}, u_3^{**}) = \{a\}; \tag{15}$$

$$f(u_1^{***}, u_2^{***}, u_3^{***}) = \{b\}. \tag{16}$$

If f is implementable, there exists a weakly implementing game form $g: S_1 \times S_2 \times S_3 \to A$ and a vector of actions (s_1, s_2, s_3) such that $g(s_1, s_2, s_3) = c$ and (s_1, s_2, s_3) is a Nash equilibrium for the profile (u_1^*, u_2^*, u_3^*). Because $u_1^*(b) > u_1^*(c)$, there does not exist $s_1'' \in S_1$ such that $g(s_1'', s_2, s_3) = b$. If there exists $s_1' \in S_1$ such that $g(s_1', s_2, s_3) = a$, then (s_1', s_2, s_3) is a Nash equilibrium for $(u_1^{***}, u_2^{***}, u_3^{***})$,* contradicting (16). If there does not exist $s_1^{*'} \in S_1$ with $g(s_1', s_2, s_3) = a$, then (s_1, s_2, s_3) is an equilibrium for $(u_1^{**}, u_2^{**}, u_3^{**})$, contradicting (15). Hence f is not implementable.

*Since there does not exist s_1'' such that $g(s_1'', s_2, s_3) = b$

5   Effectivity functions

So far, monotonicity has been the crucial concept by which we have characterized implementable SCRs. As Moulin [1981] and Moulin and Peleg [1982] have shown, however, we can also relate implementability to effectivity.[4]

For an n-person ($n \geqslant 3$) SCR $f: U_A \times \cdots \times U_A \to A$ we say that a coalition of individuals $C \subseteq \{1, \ldots, n\}$ is α-effective with respect to f for the subset $B \subseteq A$ of alternatives if there exists u_C such that, for all u_{-C}, $f(u_C, u_{-C}) \subseteq B$.[5] That is, the coalition C is α-effective for B if there exist preferences for the members of C such that regardless of the preferences of individuals outside C the welfare optimal set is contained in B. Similarly, the coalition C is α-effective with respect to the game form $g: S_1 \times \cdots \times S_n \to A$ for subset B if there exists $s_C \in \Pi_{i \in C} S_i$ such that, for all $s_{-C} \in \Pi_{i \notin C} S_i$, $g(s_C, s_{-C}) \in B$.

A weaker concept than α-effectivity is β-effectivity. The coalition C is β-effective with respect to f for the subset B if for all u_{-C} there exists u_C such that $f(u_C, u_{-C}) \subseteq B$. The concept of β-effectivity with respect to a game form is analogous.

Although β-effectivity is weaker than α-effectivity, for some SCR it may happen that, for all C and B, if C is β-effective for B then it is α-effective for B. In this case we say that the SCR is *tight*.

[4] This section is based on Moulin [1981].
[5] The notation "u_C" stands for a vector of preferences for members of C.

Given a coalition C, preferences u_C, and subset B, we say that B is *on top of* u_C if and only if

$$\forall i \in C \quad \forall b \in B \quad \forall a \notin B \quad u_i(b) > u_i(a).$$

We shall say the SCR f satisfies property (***) if, for nonempty C and B, C is α-effective for B if and only if

$$\forall u_C \ \forall u_{-C} \ B \text{ is on top of } u_C \text{ implies } f(u_C, u_{-C}) \subseteq B.$$

We can now state

Theorem 5 (Moulin [1981]): *If an n-person ($n \geq 3$) SCR f $U_A \times \cdots \times U_A \to A$ is monotonic and tight and satisfies property (***), then it is fully implementable.*

A monotonic SCR f is *inclusion-minimal* if for all $f' \subseteq f$ such that f' is monotonic, $f' = f$. One reason Theorem 5 is of interest is that inclusion-minimal monotonic SCRs are tight and satisfy property (***) (see Moulin [1981]). Hence we have the following:

Corollary: *If an n-person ($n \geq 3$) SCR f: $U_A \times \cdots \times U_A \to A$ is inclusion-minimal monotonic, then it is fully implementable.*

The unrestricted domain hypothesis is essential to the validity of both Theorem 5 and its corollary. It is not difficult, for instance, to give examples of monotonic, single-valued SCRs that are not implementable because they are defined on restricted U_i's.

6   Nash versus dominant-strategy implementation

A dominant strategy is an action that an individual is willing to take regardless of the actions of others. Formally, we have

Dominant strategy: In a game form g: $S_1 \times \cdots \times S_n \to A$, an action $\bar{s}_i$ is a dominant strategy for individual i with utility function u_i if for all $s_i \in S_i$ and $s_{-i} \in \Pi_{j \neq i} S_j$

$$u_i(g(\bar{s}_i, s_{-i})) \geq u_i(g(s_i, s_{-i})).$$

The definition of implementability in dominant strategies is analogous to that for Nash equilibrium. The game form g: $S_1 \times \cdots \times S_n \to A$ weakly implements the SCR f if for all profiles $(u_1, \ldots, u_n)$

$$\text{DSE}_g(u_1, \ldots, u_n) \text{ is nonempty.} \tag{17}$$

and

$$\text{DSE}_g(u_1, \ldots, u_n) \subseteq f(u_1, \ldots, u_n), \tag{18}$$

where $\text{DSE}_g(u_1, \ldots, u_n)$ consists of all dominant-strategy equilibrium outcomes corresponding to $(u_1, \ldots, u_n)$. If (18) is an equality, g fully implements f.

As we suggested in Section 3, however, the literature on dominant strategies has emphasized not *this* definition but rather the concept of *truthful* implementation. For dominant strategies, a direct-revelation game form is a mapping

$$g: U_1 \times \cdots \times U_n \to A.$$

The game form g truthfully implements f in dominant strategies if, for all $(u_1, \ldots, u_n)$, the actions $(u_1, \ldots, u_n)$ constitute a dominant-strategy equilibrium with respect to the utility functions $(u_1, \ldots, u_n)$ and

$$g(u_1, \ldots, u_n) \in f(u_1, \ldots, u_n).$$

Clearly, if f is weakly implementable in dominant strategies, it is truthfully implementable. However, it is easy to give examples where the converse does not hold (e.g., Example 4.1.2 in Dasgupta, Hammond, and Maskin [1979]). Nonetheless, there is an important case in which we *can* deduce the converse; viz., where the U_i's contain only strict preferences.

Lemma 2: *Suppose the U_i's contain only strict preferences. If the SCR $f: U_1 \times \cdots \times U_n \to A$ is truthfully implementable, then it is weakly implementable in dominant strategies.*

Proof: See Dasgupta, Hammond, and Maskin [1979].

For much of the rest of this section, we will concentrate on SCRs that are single valued, SCRs whose choice sets contain only a single element. For such SCRs (denoted "SSCRs" for *single-valued* social choice rules) we can characterize truthful implementability in terms of independent person-by-person monotonicity.

Independent person-by-person monotonicity (IPM): An SSCR f satisfies IPM if for all $(u_1, \ldots, u_n) \in U_1 \times \cdots \times U_n$, all i, all $\bar{u}_i \in U_i$ and all $a, b \in A$ such that $a \in f(u_1, \ldots, u_n)$ and $\bar{u}_i(a) > \bar{u}_i(b)$, it must be the case that $b \notin f(\bar{u}_i, u_{-i})$.

[handwritten note: → Apparently, this should read as indicated]

Lemma 3: *An SSCR f*: $U_1 \times \cdots \times U_n \to A$ *is truthfully implementable if and only if it satisfies IPM.*

Proof: See Dasgupta, Hammond, and Maskin [1979].

We should point out that IPM does not, in general, imply monotonicity. That is, truthful implementability (even full implementability) in dominant strategies does not imply Nash implementability.

Example 2: Let $A = \{a, b, c, d\}$ and $n = 3$. Suppose that each U_i consists of four utility functions: u^a, u^{ab}, u^b, u^c, where

$$u^a(a) > u^a(b) > u^a(d) > u^a(c)$$

$$u^{ab}(a) = u^{ab}(b) > u^{ab}(c) > u^{ab}(d)$$

$$u^b(b) > u^b(a) > u^b(d) > u^b(c)$$

$$u^c(c) > u^c(d) > u^c(a) > u^c(b).$$

Define the SSCR f: $U_1 \times U_2 \times U_3 \to A$ so that

$$f(u_1, u_2, u_3) = \begin{cases} \{c\} & \text{if } u_i = u^c \text{ for some } i \text{ and a majority} \\ & \text{prefers } c \text{ to } d. \\ \{d\} & \text{if } u_i = u^c \text{ for some } i \text{ and a majority} \\ & \text{prefers } d \text{ to } c. \\ \{b\} & \text{if at least two individuals have utility} \\ & \text{function } u^b \text{ and no one has } u^c. \\ \{a\} & \text{otherwise.} \end{cases} \quad (19)$$

One can verify straightforwardly that f is truthfully implementable in dominant strategies. In fact, the direct-revelation game form corresponding to f *fully* implements f (and has the strong property that truth telling is dominant even for coalitions). However, f is not monotonic because, for example, $f(u^b, u^b, u^a) = \{b\}$ but $f(u^{ab}, u^b, u^a) = \{a\}$ even though, for all $x \in A$, $u^b(b) \geq u^b(x)$ implies $u^{ab}(b) \geq u^{ab}(x)$. Thus f is not implementable in Nash equilibrium. This may seem odd, because the concept of dominant strategy equilibrium is much more demanding than that of Nash equilibrium. The apparent paradox is resolved by remembering that, to implement an SCR, one not only has to ensure that the elements of the choice set can arise as equilibrium outcomes, one has to *prevent* the existence of equilibrium outcomes *outside* the choice set. It is easier to meet this second requirement when dominant strategies are the solution concept, since by the very stringency of a dominant-strategy equilibrium, a nonoptimal equilibrium is less likely to arise.

Nonetheless, when preferences are strict, dominant-strategy implementability *does* imply monotonicity:

Theorem 6 (Dasgupta, Hammond, and Maskin [1979]): *If the U_i's contain only strict preferences, then an SSCR f that is truthfully implementable in dominant strategies is also monotonic.*

Proof: From Lemma 3, an SSCR that is truthfully implementable satisfies IPM. Consider $(u_1, \ldots, u_n)$, $(\bar{u}_1, \ldots, \bar{u}_n)$, and $a \in A$ such that $a \in f(u_1, \ldots, u_n)$ and, for all $b \in A$ and i, $u_i(a) > u_i(b)$ implies $\bar{u}_i(a) > \bar{u}_i(b)$. Suppose that $c \in f(\bar{u}_1, u_2, \ldots, u_n)$ for some $c \in A$. If $c \neq a$, then IPM implies that $\bar{u}_1(c) > \bar{u}_1(a)$ and $u_1(a) > u_1(c)$. But $u_1(a) > u_1(c)$ implies $\bar{u}_1(a) > \bar{u}_1(c)$, by hypothesis. Therefore $a = c$, and so $a \in f(\bar{u}_1, u_2, \ldots, u_n)$. Continuing iteratively, we have $a \in f(\bar{u}_1, \ldots, \bar{u}_n)$.
Q.E.D.

Not surprisingly, monotonicity does not in general imply IPM. Still, there is a large class of cases where the implication holds. To discuss this class, we need the following definition.

Monotonically closed domain:[6] A class U of utility functions is a monotonically closed domain if, for all pairs $\{u, u'\} \subseteq U$ and $\{a, b\} \subseteq A$ such that (i) $u(a) \geq u(b)$ implies $u'(a) \geq u'(b)$ and (ii) $u(a) > u(b)$ implies $u'(a) > u'(b)$, there exists $u'' \in U$ such that for all $c \in A$ (iii) $u(a) \geq u(c)$ implies $u''(a) \geq u''(c)$, and (iv) $u'(b) \geq u'(c)$ implies $u''(b) \geq u''(c)$.

One way of generating a u'' satisfying the requirements of the definition is by taking minimums: if $u(a) = u'(a)$ and $u(b) = u'(b)$, then $u'' = \min(u, u')$ will suffice.

Clearly, the unrestricted domain U_A and the domain $\bar{U}_A$ of all strict preferences are monotonically closed. Trivially, any domain consisting of a single utility function is also monotonically closed. Suppose that A is the set of allocations across individuals of fixed stocks of m divisible commodities. If U consists of all utility functions corresponding to continuous, strictly monotone, strictly convex, selfish (i.e., no externalities) preferences over A, then, as shown by Dasgupta, Hammond, and Maskin [1979], U is monotonically closed as well.

---

[6] A monotonically closed domain is called a "rich domain" in Dasgupta, Hammond, and Maskin [1979].

Theorem 7: (Dasgupta, Hammond, and Maskin [1979]): *If U_i is monotonically closed for all i, then if the SSCR f is implementable in Nash equilibrium, it is truthfully implementable in dominant strategies.*

Proof: If f is implementable in Nash equilibrium, then it is monotonic. If f violated IPM, there would exist $(u_1, \ldots, u_n)$, $\bar{u}_i$, a, and b such that $a \in f(u_1, \ldots, u_n)$ and $\bar{u}_i(a) > \bar{u}_i(b)$ but $b \in f(\bar{u}_i, u_{-i})$. From the monotonic closure of U_i, however, there exists $\bar{\bar{u}}_i \in U_i$ such that for all c

$$u_i(a) \geqslant u_i(c) \text{ implies } \bar{\bar{u}}_i(a) \geqslant \bar{\bar{u}}_i(c)$$

and

$$\bar{u}_i(b) \geqslant \bar{u}_i(c) \text{ implies } \bar{\bar{u}}_i(b) \geqslant \bar{\bar{u}}_i(c).$$

From monotonicity applied to (u_i, u_{-i}) and $(\bar{\bar{u}}_i, u_{-i})$, we have $a \in f(\bar{\bar{u}}_i, u_{-i})$. But from monotonicity applied to $(\bar{u}_i, u_{-i})$ and $(\bar{\bar{u}}_i, u_{-i})$, $b \in f(\bar{\bar{u}}_i, u_{-i})$, a contradiction of f's single-valuedness. Therefore, f satisfies IPM and so is truthfully implementable in dominant strategies.
    Q.E.D.

Theorem 7 implies that if a planner wishes to implement a single-valued SCR, he will get no extra mileage from using the ostensibly weaker concept of Nash implementation if the domain of utility functions is monotonically closed. In particular, we have the following negative result.

Corollary 1 (Dasgupta, Hammond, and Maskin [1979], Roberts [1979]): *Suppose that A contains at least three elements and that $f: \bar{U}^n_A \to A$ is an n-person SSCR that is onto A. If f is implementable in Nash equilibrium, it is dictatorial.*

Proof: Because $\bar{U}_A$ is monotonically closed, Theorem 7 implies that f is truthfully implementable in dominant strategies. But then, from the Gibbard [1973]/Satterthwaite [1975] theorem on dominant strategies, f is dictatorial.   Q.E.D.

Roberts (1979) extends Corollary 1 to the case of "conjectural" equilibria, where, rather than taking other players' strategies as given, an individual conjectures that others will respond to his strategy choice. This result is, in turn, closely related to one of Pattanaik [1976].
    Another implication we can draw from Theorem 7 is a set of conditions under which an implementable f can be thought of as maximizing a social aggregation function.

Social aggregation function: Let B_A be the class of all complete, reflexive, binary relations on A. A social aggregation function (SAF) is a mapping

$$F: U_1 \times \cdots \times U_n \to B_A.$$

If the range of F consists of acyclic relations, F is called a social decision function, and if these relations are also transitive, F is a social welfare function. F satisfies the *Pareto property* if whenever all individuals strictly prefer a to b (that is, $u_i(a) > u_i(b)$ for all i) then $F(u_1, \ldots, u_n)$ ranks a above b. F satisfies *nonnegative response* if, for all $\{a, b\}$ and $\{(u_1, \ldots, u_n), (\bar{u}_1, \ldots, \bar{u}_n)\}$, if, for all i, $u_i(a) \geqslant u_i(b)$ implies $\bar{u}_i(a) \geqslant \bar{u}_i(b)$ and $u_i(a) > u_i(b)$ implies $\bar{u}_i(a) > \bar{u}_i(b)$, then that a is ranked weakly (strictly) above b by $F(u_1, \ldots, u_n)$ implies that a is ranked weakly (strictly) above b by $F(\bar{u}_1, \ldots, \bar{u}_n)$.

The SSCR f maximizes F if, for all $(u_1, \ldots, u_n)$, $a \in f(u_1, \ldots, u_n)$ implies that, for all $b \neq a$, a is strictly preferred to b by $F(u_1, \ldots, u_n)$.

Corollary 2: *Suppose that the U_i's are monotonically closed and consist only of strict preferences. The SSCR f is implementable in Nash equilibrium if and only if there exists an SAF F satisfying nonnegative response such that f maximizes F. Furthermore, if f is onto A, F satisfies the Pareto property.*

Proof: See Dasgupta, Hammond, and Maskin [1979].

Nonnegative response implies independence of irrelevant alternatives (IIA) in the sense of Arrow [1951]. Corollary 2, therefore, illustrates the close relationship among monotonicity, IPM, and IIA.

7   Quasilinear preferences

So far, the only particular domain of utility functions that we have discussed in any detail is the unrestricted domain U_A. We next consider an important restricted domain: the class of quasilinear preferences. Here we shall assume that there are at least two individuals, that is, $n \geqslant 2$.

Suppose that a social alternative consists of a public decision d (which is an element of some set D) and a vector $(t_1, \ldots, t_n)$ of transfers of some private good (the t_i's are real numbers). Individual i's preferences are *quasilinear* if his utility function u takes the form

$$v(d) + t_i. \tag{20}$$

Let U_i^{QL} be the class of all preferences of form (20). This class has been the object of much study in the dominant-strategy−implementation literature (see, for example, Clarke [1971], Groves [1973], Green and Laffont [1979]). Rather less has been done with it in the Nash-implementation literature (see, however, Laffont and Maskin [1982a] and Roberts [1979]).

It is readily verified that the domain U_i^{QL} is not monotonically closed. Therefore, Theorem 10 does not apply, and we cannot conclude that the sets of Nash- and dominant-strategy−implementable SSCRs are the same. Nevertheless, as Roberts (1979) shows, the *public decision* parts of the SSCRs are identical.

In view of (20) we can express an SSCR as a function of the public parts of individuals' utility functions. Write

$$f(v_1, \ldots, v_n) = (d(v_1, \ldots, v_n), \quad t_1(v_1, \ldots, v_n), \ldots,$$
$$t_n(v_1, \ldots, v_n)),$$

where $u_i = v_i + t_i$.

Theorem 8: *Suppose that D, the public decision space, is finite. Let $f: U_1^{QL} \times \cdots \times U_n^{QL} \to A$ be an SSCR such that d( ) is onto D. Then if f is either Nash-implementable or truthfully implementable in dominant strategies, there exist $v_0: D \to R$ and numbers $\alpha_1, \ldots, \alpha_n$ such that $\alpha_i \geqslant 0$ for all i and $\Sigma_{i=1}^n \alpha_i = 1$ such that $d(v_1, \ldots, v_n) =$ arg $\max_d(v_0(d) + \Sigma_{i=1}^n \alpha_i v_i(d))$.*

Proof: See Roberts [1979].

Laffont and Maskin [1982a] place more structure on the problem by assuming that

$$D = [0, 1]$$

and that the individuals' v_i functions are concave and differentiable and take their maxima in the interior of D. Let V be the class of such functions. They also assume that the public decision function d( ) is *weakly efficient* [if $v_1 = \cdots v_n$, then $d(v_1, \ldots, v_n) = $ arg max v_i], and *neutral* $(d(\bar{v}_1, \ldots, \bar{v}_n) = d(v_1, \ldots, v_n) + c$, where for all i, $\bar{v}_i(d) = v_i(d - c))$.

Theorem 9: *Let f be an SSCR on $V \times \cdots \times V$ that is either Nash implementable or truthfully implementable in dominant strategies. If d is weakly efficient and neutral, then*

(i)   there exists a continuous and semistrictly increasing[7] function $h: R^n \to R$ such that $h(0, \ldots, 0) = 0$ and $d(v_1, \ldots, v_n)$ solves $h(v_1'(d), \ldots, v_n'(d)) = 0$, where primes denote derivatives;

(ii) if f is Nash implementable, then t_i is a function of the numbers $d(v_1, \ldots, v_n)$ and $v_1'(d(v_1, \ldots, v_n)), \ldots, v_n'(d(v_1, \ldots, v_n))$;

(iii) if f is truthfully implementable in dominant strategies, then

$$t_i = - \int_0^{d(v_1, \ldots, v_n)} h_i(v_{-i}'(t)) \, dt + H_i(v_{-i}),$$

where $h_i: R^{n-1} \to R$ satisfies

$h(h_i(a_{-i}), a_{-i}) = 0,$ if there exists a_i with $h(a_i, a_{-i}) = 0$

$h_i(a_{-i}) = 0,$ otherwise.

Proof: See Laffont and Maskin [1982a].

Notice that the set of implementable public decisions is defined by varying h, whether it be Nash or dominant-strategy implementation. When, for example, $h = \Sigma_{i=1}^n \lambda_i v_i'$, the public decision becomes

$$d(v_1, \ldots, v_n) = \arg \max_d \sum_{i=1}^n \lambda_i v_i(d).$$

The form of the transfers, however, depends on the type of implementation. Nash implementation demands that the transfers be a function of the optimal public decision and the derivatives of individuals' utility functions evaluated at the optimum. Dominant-strategy implementation requires that an individual's transfer be the sum of two terms: a term depending on the derivatives of the utility functions and the public decision, and a term depending only on the utility functions of the other individuals.

8   Strong equilibrium

Nash equilibrium is a noncooperative concept; it implicitly assumes that individuals do not act in concert. When individuals can collude, strong equilibrium may be a more appropriate solution concept.

---

[7] By "semistrictly increasing" we mean that if x is bigger in every component than y, then $h(x) > h(y)$.

Strong Equilibrium: A strong equilibrium for the game form $g\colon S_1 \times \cdots \times S_n \to A$ with respect to the profile $(u_1, \ldots, u_n)$ is a configuration $(\bar{s}_1, \ldots, \bar{s}_n)$ such that for all coalitions $C \subseteq \{1, \ldots, n\}$ and all $s_C \in \Pi_{j \epsilon C} S_j$ there exists $i \epsilon C$ such that $u_i(g(\bar{s})) \geqslant u_i(g(s_C, \bar{s}_{-C}))$.

By analogy with Nash equilibrium, a game form g fully implements the f in strong equilibrium if for all profiles $(u_1, \ldots, u_n)$

$$SE_g(u_1, \ldots, u_n) = f(u_1, \ldots, u_n),$$

where $SE_g(u_1, \ldots, u_n)$ consists of the strong equilibrium outcomes of g for the profile $(u_1, \ldots, u_n)$.

We should note that if g fully implements f in strong equilibrium, it does *not* necessarily implement f in Nash equilibrium. The reason for this apparent anomaly is that g may possess Nash equilibria that are not strong and which, furthermore, do not lead to outcomes in the choice set. For example, consider the following two-person game form, where individual 1 chooses rows as actions, and individual 2, columns:

	s_2	s_2'
s_1	a	a
s_1'	a	b

This game form fully implements the SSCR $f^*\colon U_1 \times U_2 \to \{a, b\}$ in strong equilibria, where the U_i's contain the strict preferences on $\{a, b\}$ and

$$f^*(u_1, u_2) = \begin{cases} b & \text{if both individuals prefer } b \text{ to } a \\ a & \text{otherwise.} \end{cases}$$

However, the game form does *not* implement f^* in Nash equilibrium, because (s_1, s_2) is a non-f^*-optimal Nash equilibrium when both individuals prefer b to a. Moreover, from Theorem 2, *no* game form can implement f^* in Nash equilibrium.

We have seen that monotonicity is a necessary condition for implementability in Nash equilibrium. The same is true for strong equilibrium.

Theorem 10: (Maskin [1979b]): If an SCR f is implementable in strong equilibrium, it is monotonic.

On the other hand, weak no-veto power, which played an important role in establishing positive results for Nash implementation, *prevents* implementation in strong equilibrium when the number of individuals does not exceed the number of alternatives and the domain is unrestricted.

Theorem 11: *If the n-person SCR* $f: U_A \times \cdots \times U_A \to A$ *is onto A, where n is less than or equal the cardinality of A but greater than or equal to 3, and f is implementable in strong equilibrium, f does not satisfy weak no-veto power.*

Proof: The proof consists of considering a "cyclic" profile of preferences $(u_1, \ldots, u_n)$, where

$$u_1(a_1) > u_1(a_2) > \cdots > u_1(a_n)$$
$$u_2(a_2) > u_2(a_3) > \cdots > u_2(a_1)$$

$$\vdots$$

$$u_n(a_n) > u_n(a_1) > \cdots > u_n(a_{n-1}).$$

Such a profile exists because there are at least as many alternatives as individuals. But then it is straightforward to show that *no* alternative can be a strong equilibrium, since no single individual has veto power. For the details, see Maskin [1979b]. Q.E.D.

Theorem 11 is false if the number of individuals exceeds the number of alternatives, as the following example shows.

Example 3: Let $n = 3$, $A = \{a, b\}$, and U_i consist of the strict preferences on A. Let f be majority rule, that is, an alternative is in the choice set if and only if it is top ranked by two or more individuals. The following game form implements f:

where individual 1 chooses rows, 2 columns, and 3 matrices. A large class of other examples has been constructed by Moulin and Peleg [1982].

Clearly, if an SCR f is onto its range and fully implementable in strong equilibrium, it must be Pareto optimal. In Section 4 we demonstrated that the SCR that selects all Pareto-optimal and individually rational alternatives is implementable in Nash equilibrium. In fact, this is the *only* individually rational SCR on the unrestricted domain that is fully implementable in strong equilibrium.

Individually rational SCR: If $a_0 \in A$ is the status quo, an SCR f: $U_1 \times \cdots \times U_n \rightarrow A$ is individually rational if for all $(u_1, \ldots, u_n)$ and all $a \in f(u_1, \ldots, u_n)$ $u_i(a) \geq u_i(a_0)$ for all i.

Theorem 12: (Maskin [1979b]): *Let* f_Q: $U_A \times \cdots \times U_A \rightarrow A$ *be the SCC such that for all* $(u_1, \ldots, u_n)$

$$f_Q(u_1, \ldots, u_n) = \{a \in A | \textit{for all } j \; u_j(a) \geq u_j(a_0)$$
$$\textit{and for all } i, \textit{ and for all } b \in A, \textit{ there exists } i \textit{ such that}$$
$$u_i(a) \geq u_i(b)\}.$$

Then f_Q *is the unique individually rational SCC on* $U_A \times \cdots \times U_A$ *that is onto A and implementable in strong equilibrium.*

Proof: It is easy to verify that f_Q is fully implemented by the game form (10) (which, interestingly, also implements the individual rationality correspondence in Nash equilibrium). That f_Q is the *only* implementable individually rational SCR on the unrestricted domain follows from an argument in Maskin [1979b].

Besides being an important concept for Nash implementability, effectivity bears significantly on strong implementability.

Theorem 13: (Moulin and Peleg [1982]): *If an n-person* $(n \geq 3)$ *SCR* f: $U_A \times \cdots \times U_A \rightarrow A$ *is implementable in strong equilibrium, then it is tight and satisfies property* (***) *(see Section 5).*

In view of Theorems 5 and 13, we can conclude that, for $n \geq 3$, an n-person SCR on the unrestricted domain that is implementable in strong equilibrium is also implementable in Nash equilibrium. (That this is false for $n = 2$ is illustrated by the example from the beginning of this section.) One interesting conjecture is that all inclusion-minimal monotonic SCRs on the unrestricted domain are implementable in strong equilibrium.

9 Double implementation

Whereas implementation in Nash equilibrium ignores the possibility of collusion, implementation in strong equilibrium may, in effect, *require* coalitions to form. To see this, consider the game form (10). In order to obtain any alternative other than a_0, all individuals have to take the same action. Clearly, there are many (nonstrong) Nash equilibria in which different individuals take different actions, and to avoid ending up in one of these presumably involves some coordination – that is, collusion is necessary.

Because the game form designer may not know the extent to which collusion can or will take place, it is desirable to have an implementation concept that does not posit any particular degree of collusion. One possibility is to require a game form to fully implement simultaneously in both strong and Nash equilibrium. This game form would yield optimal outcomes regardless of collusion. We shall say that such a game form (fully) *doubly* implements the SCR.

Of course, double implementation is a very demanding requirement. Not surprisingly, when the number of alternatives is at least three and the domain of utility functions is unrestricted, the only SCRs that are onto A and doubly implementable are dictatorial.

Theorem 14 (Maskin [1979a]): *Suppose A contains at least three elements and f: $U_A \times \cdots \times U_A \to A$ is an n-person SCR that is onto A. If f is doubly implementable, then it is dictatorial.*

The results are more encouraging, however, when preferences are restricted. Suppose, in particular, that there exists (at least) one divisible and transferable private good that all individuals find desirable and that does not create externalities (i.e., one individual's allotment of this good does not affect any other's utility). Let us express a social alternative a as $(b, t_1, \ldots, t_n)$, where t_i is the transfer of this private good to individual i, and b represents all other social decisions inherent in a. We shall call b the "public decision," although it may itself entail the allocation of private goods. Denote the status quo, a_0, by $(b_0, 0, \ldots, 0)$. Suppose that the private good is sufficiently desirable (and that consumers have enough of it in the status quo so that, for all i and all public decisions b, there exist $(\bar{t}_1, \ldots, \bar{t}_n)$ such that

$$(b, \bar{t}_1, \ldots, \bar{t}_n) \in A \text{ and, for all } t_i < \bar{t}_i \text{ and all } u_i, u_i(a_0) > $$
$$u_i(b, t_i, \bar{t}_{-i}). \tag{21}$$

Condition (21) provides for the existence of "punishments." It says that regardless of the public decision, it is always possible to take away enough of the private good from individual i to make him worse off than under the status quo. We have the following result.

Theorem 15: *Assume the existence of a desirable and divisible private good. If (21) is satisfied, then any monotonic, individually rational and Pareto-optimal SCR is fully doubly implementable.*

Proof: See Maskin [1979a].

10   Related concepts

This chapter has discussed Nash, strong Nash, and "double" implementation. We should, however, mention two related lines of work.

Farquharson [1969] proposed the concept of a "sophisticated" equilibrium. This is a refinement of Nash equilibrium in which weakly dominated strategies are successively eliminated. For example, consider the following two-player game:

	d	e	f
a	2, 2	1, 1	1, 1
b	0, 0	1, 1	2, 1
c	0, 0	1, 2	0, 0

The strategy configurations (a, d), (b, e), (c, e), and (b, f) are all Nash equilibria. However, strategies c and f are weakly dominated for players I and II. If we delete them, the game becomes

	d	e
a	2, 2	1, 1
b	0, 0	1, 1

Notice that here strategies *b* and *e* are weakly dominated. Once these are deleted, the players have one strategy each. Hence (*a*, *d*) forms a *sophisticated* or *dominance-solvable* equilibrium.

The theory of implementation in dominance-solvable equilibrium has been developed largely by Moulin [1979, 1980, 1981, forthcoming -a,b]. Although a full characterization of the implementable SCRs is not available, there are by now many examples of Pareto-optimal, neutral, and anonymous SCRs that can be implemented, including many that are not Nash implementable.

An SSCR can itself be thought of as a game form; a player's strategy is the announcement of a utility function (not necessarily his true one) and the outcome is the alternative optimal with respect to the announced preferences. An SSCR is said to be consistent if for any profile of (true) preferences there exists a strong equilibrium of the SSCR (when viewed as a game form) whose outcome is optimal with respect to those (true) preferences. Notice that the qualification about optimality is not super-fluous, because the strategies played in equilibrium may themselves be untruthful. The concept of consistency is due to Peleg [1977]. Besides Peleg, contributors to the subject include Dutta and Pattanaik [1978].

REFERENCES

Arrow, K. [1951]. *Social Choice and Individual Values*. New York: John Wiley.
Clarke, E. [1971]. "Multipart Pricing of Public Goods." *Public Choice*, 8:19–33.
Dasgupta, P., P. Hammond, and E. Maskin [1979]. "The Implementation of Social Choice Rules." *Review of Economic Studies*, 46:185–216.
Dutta, B., and P. Pattanaik [1978]. "On Nicely Consistent Voting Systems." *Econometrica*, 46:163–170.
Farquharson, R. [1969]. *The Theory of Voting*. New Haven, Conn.: Yale University Press.
Gibbard, A. [1973]. "Manipulation of Voting Schemes: A General Result." *Econometrica*, 41:587–602.
Green, J., and J.-J. Laffont [1979]. *Incentives in Public Decision-Making*. Amsterdam: North-Holland.
Groves, T. [1973]. "Incentives in Teams." *Econometrica*, 41:617–631.
Groves, T., and J. Ledyard [1977]. "Optimal Allocation of Public Goods: A Solution to the Free Rider Problem." *Econometrica*, 45:783–810.
Harsanyi, J. [1967]. "Games with Incomplete Information Played by 'Bayesian' Players." *Management Science*, 14:159–182, 320–334, 486–502.
Hurwicz, L. [1972]. "On Informationally Decentralized Systems," in *Decision and Organization*, edited by C.B. McGuire and R. Radner. Amsterdam: North-Holland.
Hurwicz, L., and D. Schmeidler [1978]. "Outcome Functions Which Guarantee the Existence and Pareto Optimality of Nash Equilibria." *Econometrica*, 46:144–174.

Laffont, J.-J., and E. Maskin [1982a]. "Nash and Dominant Strategy Implementation in Economic Environments." *Journal of Mathematical Economics*, *10*:17–47.

Laffont, J.-J. and E. Maskin [1982b]. "The Theory of Incentives: An Overview," in *Advances in Economic Theory*, edited by W. Hildenbrand, Cambridge: Cambridge University Press.

Maskin, E. [1979a]. "Incentive Schemes Immune to Group Manipulation." Mimeo.

Maskin, E. [1979b]. "Implementation and Strong Nash Equilibrium," in *Aggregate and Revelation of Preferences*, edited by J.-J. Laffont, Amsterdam: North-Holland.

Maskin, E. [Forthcoming]. "Nash Equilibrium and Welfare Optimality." *Mathematics of Operations Research*.

Moulin, H. [1979]. "Dominance-Solvable Voting Schemes," *Econometrica*, *47*: 1337–1351.

Moulin, H. [1980]. "Implementing Efficient, Anonymous, and Neutral Social Choice Functions." *Journal of Mathematical Economics*, 7:249–269.

Moulin, H. [1981]. *The Strategy of Social Choice*. Paris: Laboratoire d'Econometrie de l'Ecole Polytechnique.

Moulin, H. [Forthcoming-a]. "Implementing Just and Efficient Decision Making." *Journal of Public Economics*.

Moulin, H. [Forthcoming-b]. "Prudence versus Sophistication in Voting Strategy." *Journal of Economic Theory*.

Moulin, H., and B. Peleg [1982]. "Cores of Effectivity Functions and Implementation Theory." *Journal of Mathematical Economics*, *10*:115–145.

Muller, E., and M. Satterthwaite [1977]. "The Equivalence of Strong Positive Association and Strategy-Proofness." *Journal of Economic Theory*. *14*: 412–418.

Myerson, R. [1979]. "Incentive Compatibility and the Bargaining Problem." *Econometrica*, *47*:61–73.

Myerson, R. [1982]. "Optimal Coordination Mechanisms in Principal-Agent Problems." *Journal of Mathematical Economics*, *10*.

Nash, J. [1950]. "Equilibrium Points in *n*-Person Games." *Proceedings of the National Academy of Sciences*, *36*:48–50.

Pattanaik, P. [1976]. "Counter-threats and Strategic Manipulation under Voting Schemes." *Review of Economic Studies*, *43*:11–18.

Peleg, B. [1977], "Consistent Voting Systems." *Econometrica*, *46*:153–162.

Roberts, J., and A. Postlewaite [1976]. "The Incentive for Price-taking Behavior in Large Exchange Economies." *Econometrica*, *44*:115–128.

Roberts, K. [1979]. "The Characterization of Implementable Choice Rules," in *Aggregation and Revelation of Preferences*, edited by J.-J. Laffont. Amsterdam: North Holland.

Satterthwaite, M. [1975]. "Strategy-Proofness and Arrow's Conditions: Existence and Correspondence Theorems for Voting Procedures and Social Welfare Functions." *Journal of Economic Theory*, *10*:187–217.

CHAPTER 7

Implementation via Nash equilibria in economic environments

Andrew Postlewaite

1 Introduction

The Walrasian general-equilibrium model of an economy is a basic foundation of economic theory. It is a simple, elegant model capable of many interpretations. Further, the first welfare theorem, which states that Walrasian allocations are Pareto efficient, is the basis for the efficiency properties of a free market or competitive system. There are, however, several explicit assumptions in the hypothesis of this theorem.

Typically, these assumptions include an assumption that preferences must be "private"; that is, another person's consumption does not enter my utility. This assumption rules out, among other things, externalities. Thus, for example, this theorem cannot be the basis for claims that a "free market" system will be efficient in problems involving pollution. In fact, many (but not all) economists believe that the free market system produces *inefficient* outcomes in the face of such externalities.

Besides the explicit assumptions in the first welfare theorem there is often an implicit assumption made in its application or interpretation. The welfare properties of a competitive allocation are independent of the plausibility of the competitive allocation in a particular circumstance. However, to use the first welfare theorem to deduce the efficiency of an outcome of real institutions, one is assuming that the outcome is a Walrasian or competitive allocation. One often hears a heuristic description of the circumstances under which agents are "price takers" and hence the circumstances in which we expect a competitive allocation to arise. The circumstances typically involve the idea that there are many

This research was partially supported by NSF Grant no. SES-8026086. I would like to thank Jenny Wissink for careful proofreading and editing and R. McLean for helpful comments.

agents, each relatively small. There are, however, many economic problems of interest that fail this heuristic test, namely much of international trade, analysis of monopoly or oligopoly problems, public goods problems, and so forth. In these cases the truth or falsity of the efficiency of a competitive allocation is not the question; rather, it is the relevancy of the relationship.

The preceding comments suggest that the efficiency of market outcomes for problems involving externalities does not follow from the first welfare theorem because the assumptions of the theorem are violated. The efficiency of market outcomes in monopoly or international trade will not follow from the first welfare theorem if we do not believe that the agents in these problems are price takers. Thus for one reason or another we have no a priori reason to believe in the efficiency of free market outcomes for a broad class of problems.

If there is doubt about the efficiency of existing market outcomes, a natural question to ask is whether there exist alternative market institutions or structures that yield Pareto-efficient outcomes, or at least outcomes that are Pareto superior to those of existing institutions. We want to analyze alternatives to existing institutions. We can think of the problem as that faced by a group of agents setting out to prescribe the institutions that will govern production and exchange. To examine the range of performance possibilities they must think of the universe of potential institutions and predict the outcome of each institution in each environment or set of circumstances in which it might operate. This essay describes a body of research that addresses this problem: Specify the set of all possible institutions and compare the performance of these institutions in diverse settings.

In the next section I describe the problem of mechanism design in detail. I present a largely verbal survey of implementation via Nash equilibria in economic environments, both normative and descriptive lines of research. In Section 3 research involving equity and implementation is discussed. Section 4 deals with the plausibility of the Nash equilibrium solution concept for these problems. Formal definitions of the concepts and precise statements of some of the results can be found in the appendix.

2   The problem of mechanism design

2.1   *Revelation mechanisms*

At the outset we assume that whatever the specific problem the social planner is facing, there is some relevant economic information that the planner does not have at the time the mechanism must be specified. If the planner *did* have all the relevant information, his problem would be a relatively simple maximization problem: Decide which of the alternatives is best and "impose" it. The definition of "best" is the traditional social choice problem of aggregating preferences with all the attendant problems. There is no incentive problem, however; the interesting incentive problems involve some relevant information (generally the agents' preferences but possibly their endowments or production possibilities) being unknown to the planner. Further it cannot be costlessly learned. Here the planner faces significant problems. The set of possible alternatives may not be known, so that imposition of some alternative may not be feasible. Even if the set of feasible alternatives is known, the outcome the planner would desire may well depend on the individual's preferences, which may not be known.

Thus at least some individual agents possess information that is relevant to the choice of outcome but not known to the planner. The planner's problem is to design a mechanism that will extract the necessary information in the process of choosing an alternative. A naive approach to mechanism design might be to ask agents to reveal any information they have that is pertinent to the choice of an alternative and then choose an alternative on the basis of this information. This approach will generally be unsatisfactory. We assume that agents will act in their own best (selfish) interests. There may be a number of things that an agent can report as representing his private information, many of which are false but undetectably so. It is possible that for some mechanisms the planner may consider, some agent may find that lies result in better outcomes from his personal point of view than had he told the truth. Thus one constraint that a planner always faces is that he cannot ignore the incentive effects his mechanism induces.

One of the first uses of this framework was by Hurwicz [1972]. He considered the set of pure exchange economies with an arbitrary finite number of agents, each of whom was characterized by an initial endowment of commodities and preferences (or a utility function) over commodity bundles. The endowments are assumed to be known by the planner, but an agent's preferences are assumed to be known only to the agent. To capture the strategic aspect of truthful or nontruthful revelation of agents' preferences, Hurwicz modeled a mechanism as a game in strategic form. Each agent was assumed to have as a strategy set the set of neoclassical convex, continuous, and monotonic preferences. Different mechanisms were completely characterized by different outcome functions mapping vectors of announced preferences into vectors of feasible net trades. For a mechanism, every vector of announced preferences, truthful or false, is associated with the vector of net trades the planner would like to be effected for the economy with those preferences (and the fixed known initial endowments).

As pointed out before, we expect individual agents to be the only ones to know their own preferences. We do not expect agents to truthfully report their respective preferences if it is not in their best interests to do so. Hurwicz formalized this incentive compatibility problem by asking that truthful revelation of preferences be a Nash equilibrium for every economy. Formally, for every n-tuple of preferences the outcome associated with the true profile of preferences should be as good for agent i as any outcome that is associated with a profile in which all agents except i announce their preferences truthfully and agent i announces an arbitrary preference ordering.

If truthful revelation of preferences was not a Nash equilibrium for some profile, then some agent in that profile could do better than reveal truthfully, thus thwarting the desired outcome. There is a question about the information necessary for an agent to be sure that deviation from truthful revelation is to his advantage; I will say more about this subsequently.

There are trivial mechanisms that are incentive compatible in the sense described earlier. Consider a mechanism in which the outcome for any announced preferences is no trade; that is, the vector of initial endowments is the final allocation for every economy. Clearly, truthful revelation is a Nash equilibrium, because any agent who deviates from truthful revelation does not alter the outcome. This mechanism is not very interesting; we would hope to do better. In particular, we can ask that the mechanism associate to every preference profile an allocation that is Pareto efficient (PE) for that profile. This clearly rules out the trivial mechanism mentioned before.

We can still write down trivial mechanisms that satisfy both incentive compatibility and Pareto efficiency. Let a mechanism associate with any profile the outcome in which all goods are given to a specific agent − say, agent 1. Again truthful revelation is a Nash equilibrium since no agent can alter the outcome by announcing other than his true preferences. Further, given our assumptions on preferences, the outcome is Pareto efficient for any preference profile.

This mechanism is not very interesting because of the extreme asymmetry among agents. There are a number of restrictions we could place on the mechanism to rule out such asymmetry. For example, we could ask that for every profile a mechanism always give each agent an outcome at least as desirable as his initial endowment with respect to his preferences. A mechanism that satisfied this form of individual rationality (IR) would

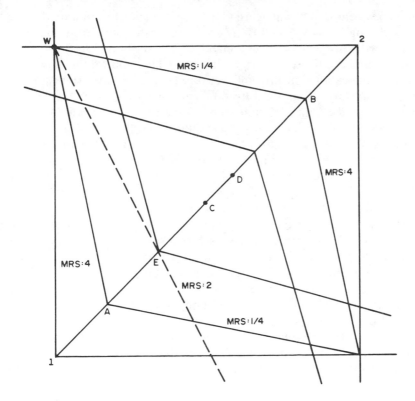

Figure 1

be voluntary: no agent would have to be coerced into a group using such a mechanism.

By adding individual rationality to Pareto efficiency, we rule out the trivial incentive-compatible mechanisms described before, as long as preferences are monotonic. What remains? Hurwicz's result was that there is no mechanism with strategies of this form that is incentive compatible, Pareto efficient, and individually rational.

I will sketch a proof of this result. To be incentive compatible, truthful revelation must be a Nash equilibrium for every profile. To show that there does not exist an incentive compatible mechanism that is PE and IR we need only construct one economy (profile) for which this is impossible. Such an economy is described as follows.

Consider an economy with two agents with endowments (0, 1) and (1, 0) and with indifference curves as shown in Figure 1. Each agent has the same preferences, which are piecewise linear with a kink on the line going through points A and B. The marginal rates of substitution are 4 and $\frac{1}{4}$ on the two segments, respectively. Thus, the line going through the points A and B is the set of Pareto-efficient allocations for this economy. Further, allocations on this line between A and B (inclusive) are the individually rational and Pareto-efficient allocations. Any mechanism that is PE and IR must pick an allocation from the segment AB. The allocation must be on one side or the other of the midpoint, C, of the box (possibly on C). Without loss of generality suppose the allocation associated with this economy is D. Suppose now that agent 2 announces his preferences to be linear with marginal rate of substitution 2. The Pareto efficient set is unchanged; the allocations that are PE and IR are now represented by the segment AE. If the mechanism is to choose an allocation that is PE and IR with respect to the *announced* preferences, an allocation on the segment AE must be chosen. Every allocation in this segment is preferred by Mr. 2 to the allocation D, however. Thus, truthful revelation is not a Nash equilibrium. If the chosen allocation had been "below" C on the segment AB, Mr. 1 would have had an incentive to misrepresent his preferences. It is impossible to choose an allocation that is PE and IR without one of the two agents (possibly both) having an incentive to misrepresent his preferences. Thus there can be no mechanism that is incentive compatible, PE, and IR for this economy, a fortiori there cannot be one for all economies.   Q.E.D.

A few comments are in order. First, the piecewise linear and kinked indifference curves are used for expository purposes. In Hurwicz's proof smooth preferences are used. Second, the particular misrepresentation used in the proof is not an optimal lie. For any point on AE chosen after misrepresentation, an indifference curve with a steeper slope for Mr. 2 that lies between the chosen point and point A would yield Mr. 2 an even better outcome. This is irrelevant, of course, since we are only trying to show that *truth* is not optimal. Third, it may be that *both* agents can do better than truthfully reporting their preferences, assuming that the other is truthful. Again this means that truth is not an equilibrium, which is all that is at issue here. Finally, the result does not depend in any way on there being two agents in the economy. Similar examples exist with an arbitrary finite number of agents.

A question arises as to why we care whether preferences are misrepresented. After all, the outcome is still individually rational and Pareto efficient with respect to the true preferences *after* the misrepresentation indicated. It should be noted that the fact that the outcome is Pareto efficient with respect to the true preferences after the misrepresentation is a happenstance, arising primarily because of the simple form of the preferences we have used. In general, one would not expect the contract curve with the false preferences to coincide with the contract curve associated with the true preferences. The outcome after misrepresentation would not be efficient with respect to the true preferences. Further, the distribution of the gains from trade will probably be altered after misrepresentation. Finally, we cannot be certain *what* the outcome will be when truth is not a Nash equilibrium. We would presumably have to determine what the Nash equilibria of this game actually were. Though I will not pursue this question, I note that is has been studied by Hurwicz [1979] and Otani and Sicilian [1978].

Bibliographic notes: Roberts and Postlewaite [1976] show (under appropriate assumptions) that the incentive to misrepresent preferences (as measured by utility gain) goes to zero as the number of agents gets large. Ledyard and Roberts [1974] prove the analog to Hurwicz's theorem in the case of public goods. Roberts [1976] shows that for public goods the analog of Roberts and Postlewaite is false: the incentive to misrepresent preferences increases as the number of agents increases. Green, Kohlberg, and Laffont [1976] investigate asymptotic incentive compatibility in a partial equilibrium setting with public goods. Postlewaite [1979] proves the analog of Hurwicz's theorem in the case of known preferences and possible misrepresentation of endowments.

2.2   *General mechanisms*

Hurwicz's result pointed to a basic problem: If a planner designs a mechanism that is Pareto efficient and individually rational when people reveal their preferences correctly, then in some economies some agents will find it in their own best interest to misrepresent their preferences. The outlook is not so dismal for the planner though. He can ask what the outcome would be if agents *did* misrepresent their preferences. The initial concern was that this would destroy any efficiency properties that the planner might have incorporated in the mechanism, but this is only if the planner ignored possible misrepresentation. It is at least conceivable that the planner may be able to "undo" this manipulation by designing a mechanism to take it into account. No longer should he be concerned that the outcome be efficient with respect to the reported preferences. Rather he should care only that the outcome be efficient with respect to the true preferences.

When we begin to look at the problem in this light, there is no reason to insist that the message or strategy spaces be agents' preferences or other characteristics. It makes sense for agents to announce their characteristics if we can design a mechanism that gives them an incentive to do so truthfully. If, as we have seen, this is impossible and the equilibrium statements have only an indirect relationship to the truth, why restrict attention to mechanisms for which the acts, or strategies, that agents choose are their possible characteristics? By choosing some quite abstract set of available strategies for agents, the planner might be able to avoid the problems pointed to by Hurwicz's theorem.

So we leave the realm of strategies in which an agent necessarily has a correct or truthful strategy. Instead agents are faced with some arbitrary sets of acts or strategies from which they are to choose whichever they wish; an outcome will arise depending upon their selections.

Groves and Ledyard [1977] suggested a mechanism, or *strategic outcome function* (SOF), for the class of economies with both public and private goods. For their mechanism, agents' strategies were not simply their possible characteristics. The Nash equilibria for their mechanism were always efficient, but not necessarily individually rational. The equilibria did, however, possess a symmetry property that differentiated it from the trivial mechanism described previously. Their mechanism had a deficiency, however; some vectors of strategies lead to nonfeasible outcomes. Equilibria were efficient, but for some economies there may not exist an equilibrium.

Schmeidler [1980] described a mechanism for which all agents have the same strategy set, independent of their preferences and endowments. A strategy for an agent consists of a pair, a price and compatible net trade — that is, a net trade with value 0 at the associated price. Agents who have announced the same price trade, and to the extent that their aggregate net trade is not 0 they are rationed equally. Given the strategies chosen by the other agents, an agent has a strategy that will give him as an outcome his Walrasian demand for any price announced by other agents. The Nash equilibrium outcomes of this game (when there are at least three agents) are precisely the Walrasian allocations. Thus, for this mechanism, under the same assumptions that guarantee the existence of Walrasian equilibria, we are guaranteed the existence of Nash equilibria. The mechanism has the drawback that for some (nonequilibrium) strategy vectors, the net trades some agents are to carry out are not feasible given their initial endowments.

Hurwicz [1979b] also constructed a mechanism with the property that the Nash outcomes are precisely the Walrasian outcomes for each economy. The strategy sets are the same as in Schmeidler but the (strategic) outcome function associating outcomes to each vector of strategies is different from that used by Schmeidler. Here an agent trades at the average of the prices announced by the other agents. The price he announces does not affect the price he pays, but affects the prices the others face. More important, Hurwicz constructed a similar mechanism with these properties for public goods. In this case the Nash outcomes coincide with the Lindahl outcomes. Both examples have the same characteristic as Schmeidler's: nonequilibrium strategies may lead to nonfeasible outcomes. Walker [1981] presents an alternative mechanism for which the Nash outcomes coincide with the Lindahl outcomes.

The mechanisms described show that efficient Nash equilibria can be obtained. The Nash equilibria were precisely the same allocations as the Walrasian allocations (Lindahl in the case of public goods). Thus, despite Hurwicz's initial negative result on the possibility of an incentive-compatible mechanism that generated individually rational and Pareto-efficient allocations, we see that altering the strategy spaces has allowed the design of mechanisms whose performance satisfies the two criteria, Pareto efficiency and individual rationality.

What performance other than Walrasian or Lindahl is possible as Nash equilibria of mechanisms? Hurwicz [1979a] explored the individually rational and Pareto-efficient performance correspondences that can be implemented by Nash equilibria of strategic outcome functions. These are performance correspondences for which there would be a strategic outcome function whose Nash equilibria were precisely the same as the values of the correspondence for each economy. He showed that if the Nash-equilibrium correspondence is upper semicontinuous and the set of economies has a sufficiently rich set of preferences, then for any economy the Walrasian allocations must be in the performance correspondence: Walrasian allocations must be Nash allocations. Hurwicz also showed that with somewhat strong assumptions on the strategic outcome function the "converse" was true: all interior Nash allocations must be Walrasian. To get this result Hurwicz assumes that for any strategies chosen by the other agents, the set of outcomes available to the particular agent is convex (assuming free disposal).

The assumptions for the two parts of the theorem are somewhat different in nature. The upper semicontinuity required for the first half of the theorem can be justified on the grounds that small changes in the parameters of an economy should cause at most a small change in the equilibrium. Further, the assumption is on the performance function, an "exogenous" variable. The convexity assumption, on the other hand, is an assumption on the strategic outcome function – the object being investigated. This assumption seems less compelling than upper semicontinuity to us. Thus, in general, for mechanisms which have individually rational Pareto efficient Nash equilibria we expect that Walrasian allocations (Lindahl in the public goods case) will be Nash. We may, in general, have other Nash equilibria besides Walrasian (Lindahl) allocations if we consider outcome functions other than those satisfying the convexity assumption.

Bibliographic notes: Wilson [1978] provided an example of a noncooperative game of exchange for which the Nash equilibria were in the core, a fortiori efficient. His model does not fit into the structure we have adopted here since in his model a central agent who did not behave strategically was introduced. Green and Laffont [1979] provide an excellent analysis of models in the Groves–Ledyard framework and precursors of their work. Schmeidler [1982] showed that the convexity condition used by Hurwicz [1979a] to show that interior Nash equilibria were Walrasian could be replaced by the assumption that the attainable sets were star shaped with respect to the origin.

2.3   *Feasible mechanisms*

As I have pointed out, the mechanisms of Schmeidler [1980], Hurwicz [1979b], and Walker [1981] that implemented the Walrasian and Lindahl performance correspondences were not always feasible. For any economy equilibria exist and the equilibria are Walrasian or Lindahl as the case may be, but nonequilibrium strategies may give rise to net trades not compatible with agents' initial endowments for each of the mechanisms. That this drawback cannot be corrected by altering the strategic outcome function is shown in Hurwicz, Maskin, and Postlewaite [1980]. It is shown there that it is impossible to implement the Walrasian performance correspondence if one adds the requirement that the outcome be feasible for every vector of strategies. If one desires feasibility out of equilibrium then wherever the Walrasian allocations are Nash, so will be the "constrained Walrasian" allocations. The notion of a constrained excess demand function for an agent is explained below. Consider an agent who is constrained from demanding more of a good than exists; that is, he cannot ask for more than the total endowment of any good. We will call the excess demand function generated by this behavior a *constrained excess demand function*. A constrained Walrasian allocation is the allocation associated with a price for which the aggregate constrained excess demand is zero. Hurwicz, Maskin, and Postlewaite show that, if the Walrasian allocations are to be Nash-equilibrium allocations, then so must these constrained Walrasian allocations. We can combine this with the theorem of Hurwicz [1979a], which states that any individually rational, Pareto-efficient, upper semicontinuous performance correspondence that is implementable via Nash equilibria must contain Walrasian allocations to get the following corollary: Any *feasible*, individually rational, Pareto-efficient, upper semicontinuous performance correspondence that is implementable via Nash equilibria must contain the constrained Walrasian allocations. Further, Hurwicz, Maskin, and Postlewaite give an example of a strategic outcome function that implements the constrained Walrasian equilibria.

The preceding result still leaves open what other performance correspondences can be implemented. There exist implementable performance correspondences that do not satisfy individual rationality and Pareto efficiency. Such correspondences may or may not contain the constrained Walrasian allocations. There are also many performance correspondences that contain the constrained Walrasian correspondences; there can be a great diversity of allocations in addition. We would like a characterization of performance correspondences that are implementable.

Maskin [1977] addressed this question of implementation in the social choice framework. Maskin introduced the concept of monotonicity of a performance correspondence. To illustrate monotonicity, consider two profiles, or n-tuples of preferences, 1 and 2. Suppose there is an outcome x such that for any agent, the set of outcomes he prefers given his preferences in profile 1 is a subset of the outcomes preferred to x given his preferences in profile 2. Monotonicity of a performance correspondence dictates that if x is in the performance correspondence for profile 2, then it is in the performance correspondence for profile 1. Monotonicity is a necessary condition for the performance correspondence to be implementable. This is a straightforward consequence of the definitions: If x is to be a Nash-equilibrium outcome for profile 2, there must be an n-tuple of strategies that yields x and no agent who has a strategy that yields an outcome preferred to x. If the preferred outcomes "shrink" for each agent when we move to profile 1, x will of necessity be an equilibrium outcome here as well.

Maskin showed that if a performance correspondence was veto-proof, (that is, if for a profile all agents, except possibly one, have an identical first choice, then that outcome must be in the performance correspondence for this profile) and monotonic then the performance correspondence was implementable via Nash equilibria.

Hurwicz, Maskin, and Postlewaite [1980] deal with these questions in an economic framework with at least three agents. If there are only private goods, the veto-proof property is vacuously satisfied since it is impossible that any two agents have the same first choice (see next section). Thus monotonicity of a performance correspondence is necessary and sufficient for implementation. This essentially characterizes implementable performance correspondences.

Bibliographic notes: Hurwicz, Maskin, and Postlewaite [1980] study the question of implementation of social choice correspondences in the case where endowments and production possibility sets are unknown. In this case the set of feasible alternatives is not the same across economic environments. They exhibit SOFs that implement the constrained Walrasian performance correspondence in these cases. Further, they deal with the public goods cases as well. Postlewaite and Wettstein [1983] exhibit a continuous SOF that implements the constrained Walrasian correspondence.

2.4   *Descriptive mechanisms*

The aforementioned literature deals with the formal question of implementability. The analysis involves determining the qualitative properties of performance correspondences. The aim of this research is not to describe existing institutions accurately. Rather, as we pointed out in the introduction, much of the motivation for the work stems from a dissatisfaction with the performance of existing institutions for at least some types of problems. Each agent's most preferred allocation is the one in which he consumes everything. The research is meant to determine in formal models what alternative performance a planner might strive for while taking into account the incentive problems arising from the design of mechanisms.

There has been another line of research involving the Nash equilibria of general equilibrium economies. This line of research has been essentially descriptive; that is, the goal was not to examine alternatives to a competitive market, but rather to model a competitive market accurately. The belief was that while the Walrasian model was one of the most useful models in economics, it was inadequate in describing the *process* by which Walrasian prices and allocations arose in a competitive market. Without the process of price formation being specified, one can only make ad hoc assumptions as to when agents are sufficiently small so as to be "price takers" and when they are sufficiently large so as to affect prices. To make an agent's ability to affect prices endogenous, it is necessary to describe precisely what agents *do* and how their actions are transformed into production and trade outcomes. What is needed is to model the economy as a game in strategic form.

Shubik [1973] introduced a model of a general equilibrium economy that addressed this problem. In this model one good is used as a commodity money. Each agent offers a quantity of any (nonmoney) commodity for sale and simultaneously bids an amount of money for the purchase of any (nonmoney) commodity. Each seller of a good will receive a proportion of the money bid for that good equal to the proportion of the good he offered to sell. Similarly, each buyer of a good will receive a proportion of the good equal to the proportion of his bid for the good to the total bid. If each agent is constrained to bidding no more for any good than his initial endowment of the commodity money, the preceding defines a game in strategic form for which Nash equilibria exist.

It is straightforward to show that for any n-tuple of strategies, all agents pay identical prices for the same good. It is also straightforward to show that in any finite economy agents affect prices: as an agent bids more for a good, the price per unit increases. Similarly, the price per unit decreases as an agent increases his supply of a good. The amount by which prices change when the bid or supply of a good changes by a fixed amount depends on the total quantity bid or supplied. When the total bid (supply) is large relative to the fixed increment, prices change by only a small amount. Shubik's model thus has many attractive features. It defines a process in which agents' actions are described and the manner in which those actions are translated into prices and outcomes. Further, the process accords with what one might intuitively think happens in actual markets: agents affect the prices they face, but less so the larger the market, ceteris paribus.

A Nash equilibrium of this model is not Walrasian, nor is it even efficient. But this should not be surprising. If there is a small number of agents, each may have a large impact on price, and when taken into account is reflected in equilibrium bids and supplies that give rise to Pareto-inefficient outcomes. In fact, we might have been disappointed if the outcome had been efficient regardless of the number of agents, because the point here is descriptive realism. Nevertheless, we would want to know whether the equilibria were efficient, or nearly efficient, when there was a large number of agents. Jaynes, Okuno, and Schmeidler [1978] showed, however, that inefficiency can arise from a fixed initial distribution of money even in nonatomic economies.

Pazner and Schmeidler [1975 (Chapter 10, this book)] formulated a version of the model that eliminates the need for commodity money by introducing "units of account" and a bankruptcy rule for agents who spend more than they receive from sales.

In this model there may be equilibria in which some markets are inactive in the sense that there are no bids or supplies for a particular good. No agent in isolation would want to enter a bid or supply, because there is nothing on the other side of the market to be exchanged.

Alternatively, an equilibrium may have the property that for each agent, the equilibrium outcome is contained in a neighborhood of the range of the outcome function that is homeomorphic to the Euclidean space of dimension one less than the number of commodities. We call the equilibrium "full" in this case. Postlewaite and Schmeidler [1978] showed that as the number of agents increased, full Nash equilibrium allocations were asymptotically efficient (where efficiency was measured by Debreu's coefficient of resource utilization). Thus for this model, the proportion of resources that are "wasted" in any full Nash equilibrium allocation will be arbitrarily small if the number of agents is sufficiently large.

It is straightforward to show that with a continuum of agents a full Nash equilibrium allocation is Walrasian in this model. There are many variants of this model that involve somewhat different trading rules, bankruptcy rules, and so forth. These alternative rules capture the differing aspects of institutions or of various ways a particular institution might be modeled. A natural question that arises is how sensitive the efficiency, or approximate efficiency results are to these alternative rules. As we pointed out, these formulations of strategic market games are meant to be descriptive. Efficiency results are meant to have positive meaning in these models and if the efficiency or inefficiency of equilibrium allocations is highly sensitive to what seem to be minor changes in the model's specification, we obviously must be more cautious in the conclusions we draw. Dubey, Mas-Colell, and Shubik [1980] provide an elegant answer to this question. They provide an axiomatization of strategic market games that guarantee that full Nash equilibrium allocations are Walrasian for continuum economies. Roughly, the axioms state that

(i)   Agents have identical convex strategy sets.
(ii) The outcome function is anonymous or symmetric in that if in any n-tuple of strategies two agents choose the same strategy, their net trades are identical.
(iii) The outcome function is continuous with respect to strategies.
(iv) The strategy sets lie in a vector space and for any agent and any n-tuple of strategies, an agent's net trade depends only on his strategy and the average of the others' strategies.

Many variants of strategic market games satisfy these axioms and have full Nash equilibria; thus, they have Walrasian allocations as Nash equilibria when there is a continuum of agents.

Bibliographic notes: Shapley [1976] examined one of the early many-commodity strategic market games. Dubey, Mas-Colell, and Shubik [1980] and Dubey [1980] examine the question of *inefficiency* of strategic

market games in the case of a finite number of agents. These references
and Shubik [1981] are also a source of variants of strategic market games.

3   Equity and Nash implementation

In Section 2.3, Walrasian and constrained Walrasian allocations played a
central role in the analysis. Indeed one of the main conclusions of the
work described there is that while other allocations may be included in a
performance correspondence that is to be implemented, the Walrasian
allocations cannot be excluded. The requirement that outcomes be individually rational with respect to the initial endowment is in a large sense
responsible for this. That this is true can be easily seen in the proof of the
theorem that Walrasian allocations must be Nash allocations, in Hurwicz
[1979a].

There are several reasons why one might require individual rationality
of a proposed outcome correspondence. As mentioned previously, if one
asks nothing more than Pareto-efficient outcomes, trivial mechanisms
such as dictatorial mechanisms exist. Since these are generally unin-
teresting, one is led to make some assumption that rules them out;
individual rationality does precisely this.

There are other reasons to impose individual rationality besides this
purely formal reason. Competitive markets are essentially voluntary in
that each agent has an option not to participate if he chooses. For a
number of reasons this voluntary property is desirable and one would
quite possibly want to preserve the property in investigating alternatives
to competitive markets. In addition, there may be applications for which
an agent's endowment is completely within his control, possibly not even
known to other agents. Various human capital endowments come to
mind in this regard. If the existence of endowments is not even known, it
may be technologically impossible to force agents to participate in particular markets. Requiring individual rationality avoids these problems;
agents presumably will freely participate in institutions in which they will
be made better off, or at least not disadvantaged vis-à-vis the status quo.

Having argued the interest in individually rational performance correspondences, we suggest that there is also interest in performance correspondences that do *not* satisfy individual rationality. We motivated the
normative interest in mechanism design on the grounds that competitive
markets might not be entirely satisfactory in all situations. The existence
of large agents or monopolies, public goods, or differential information
are circumstances in which the efficiency of competitive markets is
questionable. Even if markets pass an efficiency test, though, we might
be interested in the distribution of welfare. If the distribution of initial

endowments was highly inequal, competitive allocations will probably give rise to highly unequal distributions of goods as well. We can ask what performance functions can be implemented that are efficient but generate more equitable outcomes. In this case we may not care about the "voluntariness" of the procedure: we may be willing to force agents to participate, assuming this is technologically possible. Presumably requiring some equity property of the performance correspondence would rule out dictatorial mechanisms as did individual rationality.

In general then, we are interested in what performance correspondences can be implemented that are Pareto efficient and equitable. We need to define our notion of equity before proceeding. Everything we have done until now has been ordinal; only agents' preference orderings mattered, not the particular utility representation of them. We would like to continue to avoid problems raised by cardinal orderings if possible.

Foley [1967] introduced the ordinal equity notion of an envy-free allocation: no agent would prefer another agent's bundle to his own. Thomson [1979] proved an analog of the theorem in Hurwicz [1979a]. This analog is as follows: Suppose for a performance correspondence we replace the individual rationality requirement with the requirement that any allocation for an economy be envy free while maintaining the efficiency, continuity, and richness assumptions. Then if the correspondence is implementable, it contains the equal-income Walrasian allocations, those allocations that are Walrasian with respect to the endowment vector in which the aggregate endowment is divided equally among the agents. Thomson also considered a weaker notion of equity called mean envy free. An allocation is mean envy free if no agent prefers the average bundle of the other agents to his own. The same conclusion as described above holds when envy free is replaced by mean envy free.

Envy free is a compelling notion of equity. It has a disadvantage that there may exist no allocation that is Pareto efficient and envy free in the case of production and nontransferable commodities such as labor (see Pazner and Schmeidler [1974 (Chapter 10, this book)], Varian [1976], and Pazner [1977 (Chapter 13, this book)]). For these circumstances at least, we are forced to consider alternative notions of equity if we insist on efficiency.

Pazner and Schmeidler [1978 (Chapter 15, this book)] proposed an alternative concept of equity that is consistent with Pareto efficiency in a broader set of circumstances than is envy free. They called an allocation *egalitarian equivalent* if there exists a reference commodity bundle such that each agent is indifferent between this reference bundle and his part of the given allocation. It is straightforward to show that in general the sets of envy-free allocations and the set of egalitarian-equivalent allocations are not identical; they may in fact be disjoint.

As stated previously Thomson's result was that an implementable performance correspondence that satisfies the efficiency, continuity, and richness conditions and whose allocations are envy free or mean envy free contains the equal-income Walrasian allocations. Thomson also showed the same conclusion holds if we substitute egalitarian equivalent for envy free or mean envy free.

Using a different approach, Crawford [1977] examined a model of *divide and choose*. The divide-and-choose process is a scheme for allocating a bundle of (divisible) goods between two people. It is assumed that both agents know the other's preferences. One person divides the bundle into two parts from which the second chooses. The resulting allocation will be envy free. The chooser clearly cannot envy the other and, if the divider envied the chooser's bundle, the divider should have divided differently.

There is some inequity in this process at a higher level. Although neither agent envies the other's bundle, in general the chooser envies the divider's *role*. That is, if one had a choice between being a divider and a chooser in this model, one would always do at least as well being the divider, generally strictly better. (See Crawford [1977] on this point.)

Crawford [1979] presented an alternative scheme for the many-person version of this problem. In this scheme each agent bids for the right to be divider, where the bid is in the form of a "guarantee level." This guarantee level takes the form of a proportion of the goods all choosers can take if they wish. The highest bidder becomes the divider in the problem. It is shown that the equilibrium of the game is such that each agent is indifferent between being divider or chooser, and further, the equilibrium allocation is egalitarian equivalent and Pareto efficient.

Neither of Crawford's models is exactly consistent with the framework of this chapter. In each model Crawford looks at Nash equilibria of a single (but arbitrary) economy. Implicitly the preferences of the agents are used in the rules of the game. This is somewhat stronger than assuming that the agents' preferences are common knowledge.

One can write down variants of Crawford's models in which the agents' preferences are not used in the definition of the games, but rather are announced by the agents as part of a larger strategy. Such strategic outcome functions could be applied to a large class of economies in a manner similar to many of the models described in the previous sections. For some such variants, the Nash equilibria include the envy-free, or egalitarian-equivalent allocations as the case may be. They also contain other Nash equilibria as well, however.

The results of Maskin [1977] show that for a social choice correspondence to be implementable, it must satisfy a monotonicity condition. To illustrate the monotonicity condition, consider a given allocation for a given economy and consider a second economy in which the preferences for the agents have been altered in a specific way: for each agent the allocations that are preferred to the given allocation with respect to the altered preferences are a subset of the preferred set with respect to the original preferences. A social choice correspondence is monotonic if whenever an allocation is associated with an economy, it is also associated with any economy that arises by altering the preferences in the manner described previously. But this implies that among the equilibria for a particular economy must be included any equilibrium for an economy with "flattened" indifference curves. Thus it is not surprising that when egalitarian-equivalent allocations are Nash, there are generally others as well.

Bibliographic note: Schmeidler and Vind [1972] investigated envy-free and Pareto-efficient net trades.

4   The plausibility of Nash equilibria in mechanism design

In the previous sections of this chapter we have dealt with the form of Nash equilibria for economic mechanisms. (Some of the material in the present section draws upon Postlewaite and Schmeidler [1979].) Nash equilibrium is only one of several solution concepts (or equilibrium concepts) one could consider in such an investigation. Dominant-strategy equilibria, or Nash equilibria in which each agent's optimal strategy is independent of the strategies chosen by others, is one such alternative. Indeed, this is actually the solution concept used in Hurwicz's [1972] seminal paper, which motivated much of the research I have described. In some sense it was the impossibility result of Hurwicz which shifted attention to the concept of Nash equilibrium; it is with this solution concept that the positive results described in the previous sections were derived.

There is an essential difference between the two solution concepts, however. If there is a dominant-strategy equilibrium, an agent does not need any information on what strategies are chosen by other agents to calculate his optimal behavior; regardless of their choice, optimal or otherwise, *his* optimal choice is his part of the dominant-strategy equilibrium. Because of this, it is quite plausible that if there is a dominant-strategy equilibrium, the agents in the economy will arrive at it, at least if they know the strategic outcome function.

The switch to Nash equilibrium complicates the problem for an agent. Now an agent trying to choose his "best" strategy finds that, in general, this best strategy will depend on the other agents' strategy choices. Thus in addition to knowing the strategic outcome function, an agent also needs to "predict" the other agents' strategy choices in order to determine his optimal strategy.

One justification of Nash equilibrium as a solution concept is based on the notion of self-enforcing agreements. We can think of the players of the game gathering before the play of the game and deciding upon the strategies they will play. If the n-tuple of strategies they decide upon is a Nash equilibrium, no agent has an incentive to deviate from the agreement; it is self-enforcing. Conversely, an agreement that is *not* a Nash equilibrium is not plausible, since at least one agent will have an incentive to deviate if the other agents follow their agreed upon strategies.

If there are multiple Nash equilibria of the game, there is some sort of bargaining game to be analyzed before we can predict the outcome of the process, but if *some* outcome occurs it is plausible to believe it will be in the set of Nash equilibria. Thus if the set of Nash equilibria are uniformly "nice" in some respect, we might believe the outcome of this two-stage procedure to have this nice property without being able to pinpoint the precise outcome.

This pregame meeting at which communication and agreement takes place violates the spirit of the problems we are analyzing here, however. Our goal was to analyze the problem of institutional design in a decentralized manner. Part of the goal was to prescribe rules and institutions that have the property that they elicit the information necessary to determine the outcome. For at least some problems, we want the institutions to be able to operate without pregame meetings.

If all aspects of the game that arise for a given strategic outcome function and a particular set of agents' characteristics are common knowledge, the agents can in principle calculate the Nash equilibria without any meeting. If there is a unique Nash equilibrium, each agent *might* predict that other agents' choices will be their equilibrium strategies, and, thus, his optimal strategy is his own equilibrium strategy. We could extend this argument to the case where there are multiple Nash equilibria, one of which was "salient" in some respect. For example, if some Nash equilibrium Pareto dominated all others, it is plausible to postulate that agents would focus on this equilibrium in forming their "predictions" of other agents' actions. If all agents behaved in this manner, their expectations would be fulfilled.

The preceding argument hinges on agents being able to calculate the (salient or unique) Nash equilibrium. Leaving aside questions of computational complexity, there is still the problem of an agent's ability to compute the Nash equilibrium; this presupposes having a large amount of information about the other agents' characteristics. It may be possible that an agent does *not* need to have such information to compute his part of a Nash equilibrium. If there is a dominant-strategy equilibrium, *no* information other than the outcome function and one's own characteristics are necessary; this is one reason dominant-strategy equilibria would be desirable.

For many of the mechanisms described in previous sections, the information needed is disturbing. Some of the mechanisms have discontinuous outcome functions (see, e.g., Maskin [1977], Schmeidler [1980] and Hurwicz, Maskin, and Postlewaite [1980]). In this case, *precise* knowledge of other agents' strategies is needed to compute an optimal strategy, and thus precise knowledge of their characteristics. Many of the descriptive models of Section 2.4 have continuous outcome functions. An agent still needs the other agents' strategies to compute his optimal choice; however, the continuity (and a convexity property) of the outcome function means that a small error in an agent's prediction of other agents' strategies will result in a small error in his choice of strategy and hence in the outcome. While the actual outcome would not be precisely a Nash equilibrium, it seems obvious that the information requirements of an agent are less bothersome in the case of continuous outcome functions. The mechanisms of Hurwicz [1979b] and Postlewaite and Wettstein [1982] are examples of continuous mechanisms with efficient outcomes.

There is a second issue regarding the information requirements of Nash equilibrium besides the exactness problem due to discontinuities in outcome functions. Even to know "approximately" other agents' strategies is a heroic assumption in some environments, say large economies. If an agent is supposed to know (predict) the strategies of all other agents, he obviously has to be in possession of "arbitrarily large" amounts of information if we consider economies with arbitrarily many agents.

Nash equilibrium is a more plausible equilibrium concept for a mechanism if an agent needs only an aggregate "summary" of other agents' strategies to compute his optimal strategy. An aggregate summarization would be a function from the strategy spaces of the other agents into a Euclidean space of the same dimension as the individual strategy spaces. Summations and averages of agents' strategies are examples of summarizations. The existence of such a summarization sufficient for calculation of optimal strategies would ensure that the information requirements of a mechanisms did not grow as we consider large economies.

Many of the descriptive mechanisms of Section 2.4 have summarizations; that is, the summation of others agents' strategies is sufficient for any agent's calculation of his optimal strategy. That such a summarization exists is, in fact, one of the axioms of the theorem of Dubey, Mas-Colell, and Shubik [1980]. Most of the normative models of Section 2.3 do not have summarization functions in this sense.

The issues raised above concerning the plausibility of Nash equilibrium as a solution concept based on information requirements are somewhat odd in that Nash equilibrium is meant to be a solution concept for games of complete information — that is, for games in which agents know the utility valuations of all outcomes and can in principle, therefore, calculate equilibria. If some agents do *not* know all relevant aspects of a game, the Bayesian extension of Nash equilibria for incomplete information games as introduced by Harsanyi [1967−68] is a more "accepted" solution concept. Myerson (Chapter 8, this book) surveys the literature involving Bayesian implementation. That literature is typically somewhat different in that it generally does not deal with general equilibrium economies as we have treated them here. Two papers using the Bayesian extension of Nash equilibrium for general equilibrium economies are the following: Dubey, Geanokopolis, and Shubik [1983] investigate a descriptive model similar to those of Section 2.4 explicitly introducing incomplete information, and Postlewaite and Schmeidler [1983] investigate the question of implementation via Bayesian equilibria in incomplete information economies in a spirit similar to that of Section 2.2 of this essay.

Appendix: Formal definitions and results

Let T, the set of traders, be a finite nonempty set. R^l_+ will denote the nonnegative orthant of the l-dimension Euclidean space where l denotes the number of commodities. We denote by $w_t \in R^l_+$ the initial endowment of agent t. The set of alternatives A is assumed to be the set of feasible allocations, $A \equiv \{\mathbf{x} = (x_t)_{t\in T} \in (R^l)^T | \Sigma_{t\in T} x_t = \Sigma_{t\in T} w_t\}$. Each agent is assumed to have a reflexive ordering P_t on R^l_+ induced by a convex, continuous, and monotonic utility function. P^T will denote the set of all such orderings. A *performance correspondence* is a correspondence $h\colon P^T \to A$. S_t will denote the (nonempty) strategy set for agent t and $S \equiv X_{t\in T} S_t$. A function $f\colon S \to A$ is called a *strategic outcome function* (SOF). In the event that $S_t = P^T$ for all $t \in T$, f is called a *revelation outcome function*. An element $\mathbf{P} = (P_t)_{t\in T} \in P^T$ is called a *preference profile* and an element $\mathbf{s} = (s_t)_{t\in T} \in S$ is called a *strategy selection*. Given a SOF f and $\mathbf{P} \in P^T$, a strategy selection $\mathbf{s}^* \in S$ is said to be a *Nash equilibrium* (NE) if for all $h \in T$ and all $s_h \in S_h$: $f(\mathbf{s})^* P_h f(\mathbf{s}^*|s_h)$ where $(\mathbf{s}^*|s_h)$ denotes the strategy selection obtained by substituting s_h for s_h^*. Given a SOF $f\colon S \to A$, its *Nash performance correspondence* NEf is the correspondence from P^T to A that assigns to each $\mathbf{P} \in P^T$ the set

$NEf(\mathbf{P}) \equiv \{f(\mathbf{s}) \in A \,|\, \mathbf{s}$ is a NE for $\mathbf{P}$ (and f) in $A\}$. We say that a correspondence g: $P^T \to A$ is *implemented via Nash equilibrium* by a SOF f if g is the Nash performance correspondence for f. We say that g is *implementable via Nash equilibrium* if there is a SOF f such that g is implemented via Nash equilibrium by f. We now define several performance correspondences with which we will be concerned. The first is the Walrasian correspondence (WE). Given $\mathbf{P} \in P^T$, $WE(\mathbf{P}) = \{x = (x_t)_{t \in T}$ $\in A \,|\, p \in R^l_+,\ p \neq 0$ such that for all $t \in T$, $y \in R^l$: $p \cdot x_t = p \cdot w_t$ and $p \cdot y \leqslant p \cdot w_t => x_t P_t y\}$. The second performance correspondence we will be concerned with is the *constrained Walrasian correspondence* (CWE). Given $\mathbf{P} \in P^T$, $CWE(\mathbf{P}) = \{x = (x_t)_{t \in T} \in A \,|\, \exists\ p \in R^l_+,\ p \neq 0$ such that for all $t \in T$, $y \in R^l$: $p \cdot x_t = p \cdot w_t$, $p \cdot y \leqslant p \cdot w_t$ and $x \leqq \Sigma_{t \in T}\ w_t => x_t P_t y\}$. The last performance correspondence we will define is the Pareto efficient and individually rational correspondence (PEIR). Given $\mathbf{P} \in P^T$, PEIR $(\mathbf{P}) \equiv \{x = (x_t)_{t \in T} \in A \,|\,$ for all $t \in T$, $x_t P_t w_t\} \cap \{x = (x_t)_{t \in T} \in A \,|\,$ for all $(y_t)_{t \in T} \in A$: [for all $t \in T\ y_t P_t x_t] => $ [for all $t \in T\ x_t P_t y_t]\}$.

Theorem (Schmeidler [1980]; Hurwicz [1979b]): *If $\#T \geqslant 3$ then there is a SOF f such that $WE(\cdot) = NEf(\cdot)$ on P^T.*

Theorem (Hurwicz [1979a]): *Let a SOF f be given such that on P^T $NEf(\cdot) \subset PEIR(\cdot)$ and $NEf(\cdot)$ is upper semicontinuous. Then on P^T $WE(\cdot) \subset NEf(\cdot)$.*

Theorem (Hurwicz, Maskin, and Postlewaite [1980]): *If $\#T \geqslant 3$ then there is a feasible SOF such that $CWE(\cdot) = NEf(\cdot)$ on P^T. A performance correspondence h: $P^T \to A$ is monotonic if $[\mathbf{P}, \mathbf{P}' \in P^T,\ x \in h\mathbf{P}$ and $\forall t \in T\ yP'_t x => yP_t x] => [x \in h(\mathbf{P}')]$.*

REFERENCES

Crawford, V. [1977]. "A Game of Fair Division." *Review of Economic Studies*, 44:235–247.
Crawford, V. [1979]. "A Procedure for Generating Pareto-Efficient Egalitarian-Equivalent Allocations." *Econometrica*, 47:49–60.
Debreu, G. [1951]. "The Coefficient of Resource Utilization." *Econometrica*, 19:273–292.
Dubey P. [1980]. "Nash Equilibria of Market Games: Finiteness and Inefficiency." *Journal of Economic Theory*, 22:363–376.
Dubey, P., J. Geanokopolis, and M. Shubik [1983]. "Revelation of Information in Strategic Market Games: A Critique of Rational Expectations." Mimeo. Cowles Foundation Discussion Paper.

Dubey, P., A. Mas-Colell, and M. Shubik [1980]. "Efficiency Properties of Strategic Market Games: An Axiomatic Approach." *Journal of Economic Theory*, 22:339–362.

Foley, D. [1967]. "Resource Allocation and the Public Sector." *Yale Economic Essays*, 7.

Green, J., E. Kohlberg, and J.-J. Laffont [1976]. "Partial Equilibrium Approach to the Free-Rider Problem." *Journal of Public Economics*, 6:375–394.

Green, J., and J.-J. Laffont [1979]. *Incentives in Public Decision-Making*. Amsterdam: North-Holland.

Groves, T., and J. Ledyard [1977]. "Optimal Allocation of Public Goods: A Solution to the Free Rider Problem." *Econometrica*, 45:783–810.

Harsanyi, J. [1967, 1968]. "Games with Incomplete Information Played by Bayesian Players." *Management Science*, 14:159–182, 320–334, 486–502.

Hurwicz, L. [1972]. "On Informationally Decentralized Systems." in *Decision and Organization*, edited by T. McGuire and R. Radner. Amsterdam: North Holland.

Hurwicz, L. [1979]. "On the Interaction between Information Transfer and Incentives in Organizations," in *Communication and Control in Society*, edited by Klaus Krippendorff. New York: Gordon and Breach.

Hurwicz, L. [1979a]. "On Allocations Attainable through Nash Equilibria." *Journal of Economic Theory*, 21:140–165.

Hurwicz, L. [1979b]. "Outcome Functions Yielding Walrasian and Lindahl Allocations at Nash Equilibrium Points." *Review of Economic Studies*, 46: 217–225.

Hurwicz, L., E. Maskin, and A. Postlewaite [1980]. "Feasible Implementation of Social Choice Correspondences by Nash Equilibria." Mimeo.

Jaynes, G., M. Okuno, and D. Schmeidler [1978]. "Efficiency in an Atomless Economy with Fiat Money." *International Economic Review*, 19:149–157.

Ledyard, J., and D. J. Roberts [1974]. "On the Incentive Problem with Public Goods." Discussion Paper no. 116, the Center for Mathematical Studies in Economics and Management Science, Northwestern University, Evanston, Ill.

Maskin, E. [1977]. "Nash Equilibrium and Welfare Optimality." Mimeo.

Myerson, R. [1979]. "Incentive Compatibility and the Bargaining Problem." *Econometrica*, 47:61–74.

Otani, Y., and J. Sicilian [1982]. "Equilibrium of Walras Preference Games." *Journal of Economic Theory*, 27:47–68.

Pazner, E. [1977]. "Pitfalls in the Theory of Fairness." *Journal of Economic Theory*, 14:458–466. [Chapter 13 in this book.]

Pazner, E., and D. Schmeidler [1974]. "A Difficulty in the Concept of Fairness." *Review of Economic Studies*, 41(3):441–443. [Chapter 10 in this book.]

Pazner, E., and D. Schmeidler [1975]. "Non-Walrasian Nash Equilibrium in Arrow–Debreu Economics." University of Illinois, Urbana. Mimeo.

Pazner, E., and D. Schmeidler [1978]. "Egalitarian-Equivalent Allocations: A New Concept of Economic Equity," *Quarterly Journal of Economics*, 92, 671–87. [Chapter 15 in this book.]

Postlewaite, A. [1979]. "Manipulation via Endowments." *Review of Economic Studies*, 46:255–62.

Postlewaite, A., and D. Schmeidler [1978]. "Approximate Efficiency of Non-Walrasian Nash Equilibria." *Econometrica*, 46:127–135.

Postlewaite, A., and D. Schmeidler [1979]. "Notes on Optimality and Feasibility of Informationally Decentralized Allocation Mechanisms," in *Game Theory and Related Topics*, edited by O. Moeschlin and D. Pallaschke. Amsterdam: North Holland.

Postlewaite, A., and D. Schmeidler [1983]. "Revelation and Implementation under Differential Information." CARESS Working Paper #83-14, University of Pennsylvania, Philadelphia.

Postlewaite, A., and D. Wettstein [1983]. "Implementing Constrained Walrasian Equilibria Continuously." CARESS Working Paper #83-24, University of Pennsylvania, Philadelphia.

Roberts, J. [1976]. "The Incentives for Correct Revelation of Preferences and the Number of Consumers." *Journal of Public Economic*, 6:359−374.

Roberts, J., and A. Postlewaite [1976]. "The Incentives for Price-taking Behavior in Large Exchange Economies." *Econometrica*, 44:115−28.

Schmeidler, D. [1980]. "Walrasian Analysis via Strategic Outcome Functions." *Econometrica*, 48:1585−1594.

Schmeidler, D. [1982]. "A Condition Guaranteeing That the Nash Allocation Is Walrasian." *Journal of Economic Theory*, 28:376−378.

Schmeidler, D., and K. Vind, [1972]. "Fair Net Trades." *Econometrica*, 40: 637−642.

Shapley, L. S. [1976]. "Non-Cooperative General Exchange," in *Theory and Measurement Externalities*, edited by A. Y. Lin. New York: Academic Press.

Shubik, M. [1973]. "A Theory of Money and Financial Institutions: Commodity Money, Oligopoly Credit and Bankruptcy in a General Equilibrium Model." *Western Economic Journal*, 11:24−38.

Shubik, M. [1981]. "Game Theory Models and Methods in Political Economy," in *Handbook of Mathematical Economics*, vol. 2, edited by K. Arrow and M. Intriligator. New York: North Holland.

Thomson, W. [1979]. "Comment on L. Hurwicz: On Allocations Attainable through Nash Equilibria," in *Aggregation and Revelation of Preferences*, edited by J.-J. Laffont. Amsterdam: North Holland, pp. 420−431.

Varian, H. [1974]. "Equity, Envy, and Efficiency." *Journal of Economic Theory*, 9:63−91.

Varian, H. [1976]. "Two Problems in the Theory of Fairness." *Journal of Public Economics*, 5:249−260.

Walker, M. [1981]. "A Simple Incentive Compatible Scheme for Attaining Lindahl Allocations." *Econometrica*, 49:65−73.

Wilson, R. [1978]. "Competitive Exchange," *Econometrica*, 46:577−585.

CHAPTER 8

Bayesian equilibrium and incentive-compatibility: an introduction

Roger B. Myerson

1 Introduction

Two kinds of incentive constraints limit people's ability to reach mutually beneficial agreements in social and economic affairs. First, when one person has unverifiable private information that is not available to the others, then he cannot be compelled to reveal that information honestly unless he is given the correct incentives. Second, when a person controls some private decision variable that others cannot control or monitor, then he cannot be directed to choose any particular decision or action unless he is given the incentive to do so. That is, a social contract or coordination system may not be feasible if it gives people incentives to lie about their information or to cheat in their actions. An organization must give its members the correct incentives to share information and act appropriately. An individual cannot be relied upon to testify against himself or to exert efforts for which he will not be rewarded.

It is widely recognized by economists and other social scientists that this need to give correct incentives may be quite costly for society. In the insurance industry, for example, the inability to get individuals to reveal unfavorable information about their chances of loss is known as *adverse selection*, and the difficulty of getting fully insured individuals to exert efforts against their insured losses is known as *moral hazard*. These factors generally prevent the insurance industry from offering risk-averse individuals the full insurance that they would like to buy. Arrow [1970] has written a seminal analysis of these issues and their impact on markets for riskbearing.

Research for this chapter was supported by the Kellogg Center for Advanced Study in Managerial Economics and Decisions Sciences, and by a research fellowship from IBM. The author is grateful to Hugo Sonnenschein for detailed comments and discussion.

A theory of incentives must go beyond simply telling us that certain ideal forms of social organization are infeasible because they violate incentive constraints, and that incentive constraints cause losses in social welfare. We also need to know how to minimize these losses. That is, given a social welfare function, we may want to find the best contract or social system that maximizes social welfare subject to these incentive constraints. This essay shows how the theory of Bayesian equilibrium and incentive-compatibility can be used to actually find such optimal contracts.

The basic object of analysis in this essay is a Bayesian game with incomplete information, as defined by Harsanyi [1967−68]. In the notation used here, we suppose that there are n players in the game, and that they are numbered $1, 2, \ldots, n$. For each player i in $\{1, 2, \ldots, n\}$, we let D_i denote the set of possible *actions* or *strategic decisions* available to player i in the game. We let T_i denote the set of possible *types* for player i. Each type t_i in T_i is a complete description of one possible state of player i's private information and beliefs about any uncertain factors relevant to the game (for example, about the preferences and abilities of various players). That is, a player's type is supposed to be a random variable summarizing all information that he may have that is not available to the other players.

Let D denote the set of possible combinations of decisions available to the n players, and let T denote the set of possible types of the n players, so that

$$D = D_1 \times \cdots \times D_n, \tag{1.1}$$

$$T = T_1 \times \cdots \times T_n. \tag{1.2}$$

Let T_{-i} denote the set of possible combinations of types for all players other than i, so

$$T_{-i} = T_1 \times \cdots \times T_{i-1} \times T_{i+1} \times \cdots \times T_n. \tag{1.3}$$

Except in Section 2, we will usually assume that D and T are finite sets.

Let $p_i(t_{-i}|t_i)$ denote the subjective probability that player i would assign to the event that t_{-i} in T_{-i} is the combination of other players' types, if i's actual type were t_i. We let $u_i(d, t)$ denote utility payoff (measured in some von Neumann−Morgenstern utility scale) that player i would get if $d = (d_1, \ldots, d_n)$ were the combination of decisions chosen by the n players and $t = (t_1, \ldots, t_n)$ were the combination of the players' types.

Thus, in general, we say that Γ is a *Bayesian game* iff it is of the form

$$\Gamma = (D_1, \ldots, D_n, T_1, \ldots, T_n, p_1, \ldots, p_n, u_1, \ldots, u_n) \tag{1.4}$$

where, for each i, D_i and T_i are nonempty sets, p_i is a function specifying a probability distribution $(p_i(\cdot|t_i))$ over T_{-i} for each t_i in T_i, and u_i is a function mapping $D \times T$ into the real numbers $\mathbb{R}$. In a Bayesian game, we assume that the structure of Γ in (1.4) is common knowledge among all the players; we also assume each player i knows his own actual type in T_i. (Following Aumann [1976], we say that a fact is *common knowledge* iff everyone knows it, everyone knows that everyone knows it, and so on, including every statement of the form "Everyone knows that everyone knows that . . . everyone knows it".)

Bayesian games are important for economic theory because they give us a general model for situations involving moral hazard and adverse selection. The goal of this essay is to provide a general introduction to the analysis of Bayesian games. In Section 2, I try to show why the Bayesian game model is (in principle) the appropriate model for any game with incomplete information, following the work of Harsanyi [1967−68] and Mertens and Zámir [1985]. In Section 3, I discuss equivalence relations between Bayesian games. In Section 4, I argue that Bayesian equilibrium is the appropriate solution concept for Bayesian games, if the players cannot communicate. For games in which the players can communicate, I define Bayesian incentive compatibility in Section 5, to characterize the set of feasible coordination mechanisms for the players. An *incentive-efficient* mechanism is one that is Pareto undominated within the set of incentive-compatible mechanisms. In Sections 6−8 I develop necessary and sufficient conditions that can be used to actually compute incentive-efficient mechanisms. Section 6 is devoted to the special case in which there are only informational incentive constraints (the case of pure adverse selection); Section 7 is devoted to the case in which there are only strategic incentive constraints (pure moral hazard); and Section 8 covers the general case.

2   Modeling games with incomplete information

We say that there is *incomplete information* in a game if, at the time when the players choose their strategies for playing the game, they have different private information about their preferences and abilities. This term was introduced by von Neumann and Morgenstern [1944]. (They also used the term *imperfect information*, to describe games in which the players may get different private information during the course of the game, but all players begin the game with the same information. The distinction between the two terms seems to depend on whether the players actually could have planned their strategies in the game before learning their private information.) The real understanding and analysis of games with incomplete information began with the work of Harsanyi [1967–68], who introduced the basic definition of a Bayesian game and argued that it is the appropriate model for games with incomplete information. Mertens and Zamir [1985] developed a rigorous mathematical formulation of Harsanyi's argument. In this section, we review the ideas of these two important papers, using a formulation based on (but slightly different from) that of Mertens and Zamir. Armbruster and Böge [1979] have also considered a related formulation.

A model of a game with incomplete information must include variables that describe what private information each player might have that is unavailable to other players. In Harsanyi's Bayesian games, these variables are the players' types. Thus, player i's type must specify everything that player i knows that is not common knowledge among all players. For example, if player i's only private information is his reservation wage rate, then we can let his set of possible types T_i be a subset of the real numbers, where each t_i in T_i is a possible value of player i's reservation wage. On the other hand, if some players do not know what are i's beliefs about other players' reservation wages, then player i's type must be expanded to include as well parameters that specify player i's beliefs about other players' reservation wages. In this case, T_i might have to be a set of vectors, rather than a set of numbers.

The basic question to be considered in this section is the following. When we are trying to model some real-world situation in which players have incomplete information, can we always find type sets $(T_1, \ldots, T_n)$ that are large enough to characterize all of the possible private information and beliefs that a player might have relevant to the game? To answer this question, we must consider what are the uncertainties that may arise in the structure of a game, and we must show that the players' beliefs about all these uncertainties can be specified within the type sets of some Bayesian game.

There are several basic issues in a game about which players might have different information: how many players are actually in the game; what actions or strategic decisions are available to each player; how the outcome of the game depends on the actions chosen; and what are the players' preferences over the set of possible outcomes. Harsanyi showed that all of these issues can be modeled in a unified way. Uncertainty about whether a particular player is "in the game" can be converted into uncertainty about the set of feasible decisions, by always including the player in the game but then giving him only one decision (= "nonparticipation") when he is supposed to be "out of the game." Uncertainty about whether a particular decision is feasible for player i can in turn be converted into uncertainty about the outcome, by saying that player i will get a very bad (negative) payoff if he uses a decision that is supposed to be infeasible. Uncertainty about outcomes and uncertainty about preferences can be unified by modeling each player's utility function directly from the space of decision combinations into utility payoffs (representing the composition of an outcome function, that maps decision combinations into outcomes, and a utility function, that maps outcomes into a von Neumann–Morgenstern utility scale for the player).

So let $\{1, 2, \ldots, n\}$ be the set of players, let D_i be the set of possible actions or strategic decisions for player i, and let D be the set of possible combinations of decisions, as in (1.1). To be consistent with the preceding discussion, we might say that n is the maximal number of players, and D_i is the maximal set of feasible decisions for player i.

To model the uncertainty in the game, we must put some unknown parameter $\bar{\theta}$ into the utility functions. Thus, we let $w_i(d, \bar{\theta})$ denote the utility payoff to player i if $d = (d_1, \ldots, d_n)$ is the combination of actions chosen by the n players and if $\bar{\theta}$ is the value of this unknown parameter. We let H denote the set of possible values of $\bar{\theta}$, and we refer to H as the domain of basic uncertainty in the game. If D is finite, we can assume without loss of generality that H is a subset of $\mathbb{R}^{n|D|}$, because the only role of $\bar{\theta}$ is to specify the n utility functions from D into the real numbers $\mathbb{R}$. Furthermore, if the players' utility functions are bounded, then we can assume that H is a subset of the $n|D|$-dimensional unit cube.

These structures $(D_1, \ldots, D_n, H, w_1, \ldots, w_n)$ are not sufficient to describe the game with incomplete information, because they do not tell us what are the players' beliefs or information about the unknown parameter $\bar{\theta}$. The subjectivist theory of Bayesian decision making, as developed by Savage [1954], Raiffa [1968], and others, emphasizes that any individual must have a subjective probability distribution over the possible values of any parameter that he does not know. That is, if player i does not know $\bar{\theta}$, then he must at least have some subjective probability distribution over H that summarizes his beliefs about this unknown parameter $\bar{\theta}$. His subjective probability distribution for $\bar{\theta}$ can be measured by asking him questions about which gambles depending on $\bar{\theta}$ he would prefer. (For example, to assess a player's subjective probability of the event that $\bar{\theta}$ is in a set Ψ, where $\Psi \subseteq H$, we would ask him, for what objective probability of getting an increase of one utility unit independently of $\bar{\theta}$ would he be just barely willing to give up a prospect of gaining one extra utility unit if $\bar{\theta}$ is in Ψ.) Our description of a player as a rational decision maker will be incomplete until we specify these subjective probabilities.

We let $\bar{q}_i^1$ represent player i's subjective probability distribution over H. That is, for any $\Psi \subseteq H$, $\bar{q}_i^1(\Psi)$ is i's subjective probability for the event that $\bar{\theta} \in \Psi$. We refer to $\bar{q}_i^1$ as the *first-order beliefs* of player i.

In a game, a player's optimal decision will generally depend on what he expects the other players to do. And what he expects the other players to do will depend on what he thinks they believe. Thus we must now ask, what does player i think are the other $n - 1$ players' first-order beliefs? Subjectivist decision theory implies that each player i must have a subjective probability distribution for these unknown first-order beliefs ($\bar{q}_1^1$, ..., $\bar{q}_{i-1}^1$, $\bar{q}_{i+1}^1$, ..., $\bar{q}_n^1$) as well as for $\bar{\theta}$ denote this subjective probability distribution. We refer to $\bar{q}_i^2$ as the *second-order beliefs* of player i. But now there are third-order beliefs (beliefs about the other players' second-order beliefs) to be assessed, and so on. We seem to be getting into an infinite regress.

Mertens and Zamir [1985] have shown that it is possible to keep track of this infinite hierarchy of beliefs within a consistent mathematical model, so that there does exist a Bayesian game with type sets that are sufficiently large to include all of a player's possible beliefs of all orders. To see how this is done, we must use some relatively sophisticated mathematics. Readers with less mathematics are encouraged to skim or even omit the rest of this section, as nothing in Sections 3 through 8 will depend on it.

Given any metric space X, we let $\Delta(X)$ denote the set of all probability distributions on X that are defined on the set of Borel-measurable subsets of X. We give $\Delta(X)$ the weak topology, which is defined so that $\int f(x)p(dx)$ is a continuous function of p in $\Delta(X)$ for every bounded continuous $f: X \to \mathbb{R}$. If X is compact, then $\Delta(X)$ is also compact and metrizable. Billingsley [1968] gives a full development of this result.

Now, let Q_i^1 denote the set of i's possible first-order beliefs (probability distributions over H); that is,

$$Q_i^1 = \Delta(H). \tag{2.1}$$

We can inductively define Q_i^k, the set of possible k-order beliefs of player i, for $k = 2, 3, 4, \ldots$, by

$$Q_i^k = \Delta(H \times Q_{-i}^{k-1}) \tag{2.2}$$

where

$$Q_{-i}^{k-1} = Q_1^{k-1} \times \cdots \times Q_{i-1}^{k-1} \times Q_{i+1}^{k-1} \times \cdots (\times) Q_n^{k-1}.$$

That is, a k-order belief for player i is a probability distribution over the possible values of $\bar{\theta}$ and the other players' $(k - 1)$-order beliefs. By induction, if H is compact, then every Q_i^k is also a compact set (with the weak topology). We let $\bar{q}_i^k$ denote the actual k-order beliefs of player i, in Q_i^k.

A player's k-order beliefs determine his beliefs of all orders lower than k, through a series of functions $\phi_i^{k-1}: Q_i^k \to Q_i^{k-1}$, which can be defined inductively. The function ϕ_i^1 is defined by

$$[\phi_i^1(q_i^2)](\Psi) = q_i^2(\Psi \times Q_{-i}^1), \qquad \forall q_i^2 \in Q_i^2, \forall \Psi \subseteq H. \tag{2.3}$$

That is, the first-order beliefs $\phi_i^1(q_i^2)$ that correspond to second-order beliefs q_i^2 are just the marginal distribution of q_i^2 on H. We inductively define $\phi_i^{k-1}(q_i^k)$, for every $k \geqslant 3$ and every q_i^k in Q_i^k, by

$$(\phi_i^{k-1}(q_i^k))(\Psi) = q_i^k(\{(\theta, [q_j^{k-1}]_{j \neq i}) \mid ((\theta, [\phi_j^{k-2}(q_j^{k-1})]_{j \neq i}) \in \Psi\}),$$

$$\forall \Psi \subseteq H \times Q_{-i}^{k-2}. \tag{2.4}$$

That is, the probability under $\phi_i^{k-1}(q_i^k)$ of a set of $(k-2)$-order beliefs is the probability under q_i^k of the $(k-1)$-order beliefs that are mapped into the set by the functions ϕ_j^{k-2}. By the laws of probability, each player's first-order beliefs must be the marginal distribution of his second-order beliefs on H, so $\bar{q}_i^1 = \phi_i^1(\bar{q}_i^2)$ for each player i. Each player i also knows that $\bar{q}_j^1 = \phi_j^1(\bar{q}_j^2)$ for every other player j (since i knows that j's beliefs satisfy the laws of probability), and this fact implies that $\bar{q}_i^2 = \phi_i^2(\bar{q}_i^3)$ for player i. Continuing inductively, we conclude that

$$\bar{q}_i^{k-1} = \phi_k^{k-1}(\bar{q}_i^k) \ \forall i, \forall k \geqslant 2,$$

because it is common knowledge that every player's beliefs satisfy the laws of probability.

We let Q_i^∞ denote the set of all possible beliefs of all orders for player i, that is

$$Q_i^\infty = \left\{ q_i = (q_i^1, q_i^2, \ldots) \in \bigtimes_{k=1}^{\infty} Q_i^k \mid q_i^{k-1} = \phi_i^{k-1}(q_i^k), \ \forall k \right\}. \tag{2.5}$$

In the terminology of Mertens and Zamir [1985], Q_i^∞ is the *universal belief space* for player i generated by H, the domain of basic uncertainty. Mertens and Zamir have shown that, if H is compact, then the universal belief space generated by H is also a compact topological space (with the product topology).

Any q_i in Q_i^∞ induces a probability distribution on $H \times Q_{-i}^\infty$, where

$$Q_{-i}^\infty = Q_1^\infty \times \cdots \times Q_{i-1}^\infty \times Q_{i+1}^\infty \times \cdots \times Q_n^\infty,$$

and we let $P_i(\cdot \mid q_i)$ denote this probability distribution. If Ψ is any closed subset of $H \times Q_{-i}^\infty$, then the induced probability of Ψ is

$$P_i(\Psi|q_i) = \lim_{k \to \infty} q_i^k(\{\theta, (q_j^{k-1})_{j\neq i})|(\theta, (q_j)_{j\neq i}) \in \Psi\}). \qquad (2.6)$$

(Here q_i^k denotes the k-order component of q_i, and q_j^{k-1} denotes the $(k-1)$-order component of q_j.) In fact, Mertens and Zamir have shown that $P_i(|\cdot)$ is a homeomorphism between Q_i^∞ and $\Delta(H \times Q_{-i}^\infty)$. That is, player i's universal belief space Q_i^∞ includes all possible (Borel-measurable) beliefs about the basic uncertainty in H and the other players' infinite hierarchies of beliefs in Q_{-i}^∞.

Notice now that the random variable $\tilde\theta$ cannot directly influence any player's behavior in the game, except to the extent that players have information about $\tilde\theta$ that is expressed in their beliefs $(\tilde q_1, \ldots, \tilde q_n)$. So we can integrate the basic uncertainty variable out of the probability and utility functions without losing any structures relevant to predicting players' behavior. For any q_i in Q_i^∞, we let $p_i(\cdot|q_i)$ be the marginal probability distribution of $P_i(\cdot|q_i)$ on Q_{-i}^∞. For any $q = (q_1, \ldots, q_n)$ in $\times_{j=1}^n Q_j^\infty$, we let $u_i(d, q)$ denote the conditional expectation of $w_i(d, \tilde\theta)$, under the conditional probability distribution for $\tilde\theta$ induced by q_i, given that $\tilde q_{-i}$ (the vector of *actual* beliefs of players other than i) is equal to the vector $q_{-i} = ((q_1, \ldots, q_{i-1}, q_{i+1}, \ldots, q_n)$. That is, we may write:

$$p_i(\Psi|q_i) = P_i(H \times \Psi|q_i), \qquad \forall i, \quad \forall q_i \in Q_i^\infty, \quad \forall\Psi \subseteq Q_{-i}^\infty; \qquad (2.7)$$

$$u_i(d, q) = \mathbf{E}_{q_i}(w_i(d, \tilde\theta)|\tilde q_{-i} = q_{-i}), \qquad \forall i, \quad \forall d \in D, \quad \forall q \in \overset{n}{\underset{j=1}{\times}} Q_j^\infty. \qquad (2.8)$$

Thus at last we get the universal Bayesian game,

$$\Gamma^\infty = (D_1, \ldots, D_n, Q_1^\infty, \ldots, Q_n^\infty, p_1, \ldots, p_n, u_1, \ldots, u_n).$$

For each i and each q_i in Q_i^∞, $p_i(\cdot|q_i)$ is a probability distribution over Q_{-i}^∞, and u_i is a function from $D \times (\times_{j=1}^n Q_j^\infty)$ into $\mathbb{R}$; so Γ is indeed a Bayesian game. By construction, Q_i^∞ is large enough to include all possible private information or beliefs that player i might have about the preferences and beliefs of all players in the game.

At this point, however, we must admit that our model seems to have gotten out of hand. Compact or not, Q_i^∞ is an extremely complex mathematical object, by any standards of intuition. We started out to describe games in which players have some uncertainty about each others' preferences and beliefs. We found that, in such games, the beliefs of each player consist of an infinite sequence of subjective probability distributions over sets of probability distributions. The higher-order beliefs of a player could be critical to determining how he plays the game, so game-theoretic analysis requires that, for each player, this whole sequence of subjective probability distributions must be specified by a variable in our model. But the set of all such sequences of probability distributions is too large for practical analysis, either by game theorists or by the players in the game! Thus, for a tractable and relevant model, the players' beliefs must be restricted to some smaller subsets of universal belief space.

The way to limit the explosion of uncertainty about beliefs about beliefs is to assume that it is common knowledge that the beliefs of each player i are in some set T_i that is a small subset of Q_i^∞. This idea is the key insight of Harsanyi's classic paper. If each set T_i is tractably small (finite, or parameterized by a single variable in $\mathbb{R}$, for example) the result will be a manageable model which can give useful insights.

For it to be common knowledge that the actual type of each player i is in T_i, the set $T_1 \times \cdots \times T_n$ must be a *belief-closed* subset of $Q_1^\infty \times \cdots \times Q_n^\infty$, in the sense that

$$p_i(T_{-i}|t_i) = 1, \qquad \forall i, \ \forall t_i \in T_i, \tag{2.9}$$

where T_{-i} is as in (1.3). That is, (2.9) asserts that every type in T_i puts probability 1 on the event that every other player j has beliefs corresponding to some type in T_j.

Mertens and Zamir have shown that finite belief-closed subsets are dense among the belief-closed subsets of $Q_1^\infty \times \cdots \times Q_n^\infty$, in a topology that seems natural (the Hausdorff topology for closed sets). This result suggests that there may be "almost" no loss of generality in assuming that the players' beliefs are in such a finite belief-closed subset. (However, it remains to be shown whether any solution concepts are continuous in this particular topology.)

Thus, let us assume that there is such a finite belief-closed set $T = T_1 \times \cdots \times T_n$ such that it is common knowledge that every player i has beliefs that correspond to some point in T_i. Then we can refer to T_i as the set of possible types for player i; and by restricting the functions p_i and u_i to the domain $T \subseteq Q_1^\infty \times \cdots \times Q_n^\infty$, we get a finite Bayesian game Γ as in (1.4).

In general, of course, the type sets $(T_1, \ldots, T_n)$ in a Bayesian game Γ do not actually need to be specified as subsets of universal belief space. For example, as remarked above, if a player's only private information is his reservation wage rate, then we can simply let T_i be a set of the real numbers, where each t_i in T_i is a possible value of i's reservation wage. Given any Bayesian game Γ as in (1.4), for every type t_i in T_i, the corresponding infinite hierarchy of beliefs (i's beliefs about the other players' types, his beliefs about their beliefs, and so on) can be computed from the probability functions $(p_1, \ldots, p_n)$; so T_i is isomorphic to a subset of a universal belief space, even if it is not identified as such. The purpose here of developing the concept of universal belief space was only to verify that any game situation with incomplete information can in principle be modeled as a Bayesian game, by letting each T_i equal Q_i^∞ if no smaller sets will do. On the other hand, we must recognize that the complexity of universal belief space implies that the Bayesian-game model will in practice be applicable only to those game situations where there is enough common-knowledge structure so that each player's private information can be described within a small and tractable set of types.

3   Consistent beliefs and equivalent Bayesian games

Harsanyi defined the beliefs $(p_1, \ldots, p_n)$ to be *consistent* iff there exists a probability distribution p^* on the set T such that each players' conditional distribution, given his own type, is identical to that which would have been computed from p^* by Bayes theorem; that is,

$$p_i(t_{-i} | t_i) = p^*(t)/p_i^*(t_i), \qquad \forall t_i \in T_i, \forall t_{-i} \in T_{-i}, \tag{3.1}$$

where

$$p_i^*(t_i) = \sum_{t_{-i} \in T_{-i}} p^*(t), \qquad \forall t_i \in T_i. \tag{3.2}$$

(We use here the convention that, whenever t, t_{-i}, and t_i appear in the same formula, then t is the vector of types with i^{th} component t_i and all other components as in t_{-i}.) Harsanyi has argued that we might expect that most Bayesian games that describe real situations ought to be consistent, because the players' types may have been jointly determined before the game by some chance event governed by the distribution p^*.

We have been careful not to speak of "i's subjective probability distribution over T_i" at any point in this discussion. This is because player i already knows his type when the game begins. Even if there had been a time before the game when he did not know his type (and there might not have been any such time, for example if the type is his or her gender), the subjective probability distribution that he would have assessed for his own type cannot have any decision-theoretic significance in the play of the game. However, if there had been a time before the game when no player knew his type and if all players had the same prior beliefs p^*, then the type-conditional beliefs $(p_1, \ldots, p_n)$ should be consistent with p^*.

Interpersonal comparisons of utility cannot be given decision-theoretic significance. That is, there is no decision-theoretic meaning for a statement such as "a movie gives me more utility than an opera gives you," because neither of us could ever be forced to choose between being me at a movie or being you at an opera. Now, for games with incomplete information, we assume that each player already knows his own type before he makes any decisions relevant to the game. Thus, when the game is played, intertype comparisons of utility are also decision theoretically meaningless. When a player already knows his type, he cannot be asked to choose it. We cannot ask a player, "Would you prefer to be an opera fan at the opera or be a non-opera-fan at the movies?", when he already knows whether he is an opera fan or not.

Thus, the utility scales of different types can be specified separately. From basic decision theory, it is well known that von Neumann–Morgenstern utility scales can only be defined up to increasing linear transformations. Thus we say that two Bayesian games with the same decision sets and type sets

$$\Gamma = (D_1, \ldots, D_n, T_1, \ldots, T_n, p_1, \ldots, p_n, u_1, \ldots, u_n)$$

and

$$\hat{\Gamma} = (D_1, \ldots, D_n, T_1, \ldots, T_n, \hat{p}_1, \ldots, \hat{p}_n, \hat{u}_1, \ldots, \hat{u}_n)$$

are *utility equivalent* iff they have the same conditional probability distributions (so $\hat{p}_i = p_i$ for all i) and there exist numbers $a_i(t_i)$ and $b_i(t_i)$, for each i and each t_i in T_i, such that

$$a_i(t_i) > 0 \quad \text{and} \quad \hat{u}_i(d, t) = a_i(t_i) \, u_i(d, t) + b_i(t_i), \qquad \forall d \in D, \forall t \in T.$$

That is, utility-equivalent Bayesian games differ only in that the utility functions of some types of some players may be linearly rescaled. The Bayesian equilibria and incentive-compatible mechanisms (to be defined later) of two utility-equivalent games will be the same.

Whenever a player chooses an action or decision in a Bayesian game, his criterion for the best decision is that it should give him the highest conditionally expected utility, given his actual type. Expected utility is computed by multiplying utilities times probabilities and then summing over all possible values of the unknowns. For example, if some function $\sigma\colon T \to D$ determined how the players' decisions depend on their types, then the conditionally expected utility for type t_i of player i would be

$$\sum_{t_{-i} \in T_{-i}} p_i(t_{-i} | t_i) \, u_i(\sigma(t), t).$$

We define $z_i\colon D \times T \to \mathbb{R}$ by

$$z_i(d, t) = p_i(t_{-i} | t_i) \, u_i(d, t), \qquad \forall d \in D, \quad \forall t \in T,$$

and we call z_i the *evaluation function* for player i. (See Wilson [1968] and Myerson [1979b] for the origins of this term.) Because only this product of probability times utility matters in computing expected utilities, we say that two Bayesian games are *probability equivalent* iff they have the same decision sets D_i and type sets T_i and evaluation functions z_i for all players; that is,

$$\hat{p}_i(t_{-i}|t_i)\, \hat{u}_i(d, t) = p_i(t_{-i}|t_i)\, u_i(d, t), \qquad \forall i, \quad \forall d \in D, \quad \forall t \in T.$$

Probability equivalence is important because it assures us that consistency of beliefs is not an issue of basic importance in studying general Bayesian games. In particular, if the type sets are all finite, then any Bayesian game is probability equivalent to another Bayesian game with consistent beliefs, and even with stochastically independent types for the n players. Simply let

$$\hat{p}_i(t_{-i}|t_i) = \frac{1}{|T_{-i}|} \text{ and } \hat{u}_i(d, t) = |T_{-i}|\, p_i(t_{-i}|t_i)\, u_i(d, t).$$

Consistency of beliefs can be important only when we also want to make some restrictions on the form of the utility functions, such as when we assume that there is transferable utility, or that one player's utility depends only on his own type, or that utility funtions are continuous in strategies and types. (This last condition would only be relevant when infinite type sets are considered. See Milgrom and Weber [1985] for a comprehensive analysis of this issue.)

In fact, a more general equivalence relation can be defined among Bayesian games. We say that two Bayesian games Γ and $\hat{\Gamma}$ with the same decision sets and type sets are *evaluation equivalent* iff, for every player i, there exist functions $a_i\colon T_i \to \mathbb{R}$ and $b_i\colon T \to \mathbb{R}$ such that $a_i(t_i) > 0$ for every t_i and

$$\hat{p}_i(t_{-i}|t_i)\, \hat{u}_i(d, t) = a_i(t_i)\, p_i(t_{-i}|t_i)\, u_i(d, t) + b_i(t), \qquad \forall d \in D, \forall t \in T.$$

Notice that the additive constant can depend on all players' types, while the multiplicative constant can only depend on i's type. All our solution concepts (Bayesian equilibrium and Bayesian incentive compatibility) will be invariant under any evaluation-equivalent transformation of the game. It can be shown that evaluation equivalence is the most general equivalence relation that preserves each type's preference ordering over coordination mechanisms (which will be defined in Section 5).

4   Bayesian equilibrium

The decision or action chosen by a player in a Bayesian game will generally depend on his type. However, other players do not know player i's actual type, so in choosing their actions they must be concerned with what actions would be chosen by each of player i's possible types. An equilibrium of a Bayesian game is a set of conjectures about how each player would choose his action as a function of his type, such that each type of each player is maximizing his conditionally expected utility given his own type and the functional conjectures about the other players. Formally, $(\sigma_1, \ldots, \sigma_n)$ is a *Bayesian equilibrium* of the Bayesian game Γ iff, for every player i, σ_i is a function from T_i to D_i such that, for every t_i in T_i,

$$\sum_{t_{-i} \epsilon T_{-i}} p_i(t_{-i}|t_i) \, u_i(\sigma(t), t)$$

$$= \max_{d_i \epsilon D_i} \sum_{t_{-i} \epsilon T_{-i}} p_i(t_{-i}|t_i) \, u_i((\sigma_{-i}(t_{-i}), d_i), t).$$

(4.1)

(Here $\sigma(t) = (\sigma_1(t_1), \ldots, \sigma_n(t_n))$, and

$(\sigma_{-i}(t_{-i}), d_i) = (\sigma_1(t_1), \ldots, \sigma_{i-1}(t_{i-1}), d_i, \sigma_{i+1}(t_{i+1}), \ldots, \sigma_n(t_n)).)$

Equation (4.1) asserts if player i were of type t_i and he expected the other players to select their actions according to their $\sigma_j(\cdot)$ rules, then the action $\sigma_i(t_i)$ would be optimal for him, in that it maximizes his conditionally expected utility.

Bayesian equilibrium is the fundamental solution concept for Bayesian games with incomplete information. Our goal, as theorists analyzing a Bayesian game, must be to predict how each player will choose his decision as a function of his type. Without knowing his type, we cannot hope to predict his actual decision; we can only predict how his decision functionally depends on his type in T_i. If the players themselves also understand these predictions, then, unless the predictions constitute a Bayesian equilibrium, at least one type of one player would expect to do better by using some unpredicted decision. Thus, a prediction of the players' behavior can be rationally self-fulfilling if and only if it is a Bayesian equilibrium.

For a simple two-player example, suppose that $D_1 = \{x_1, y_1\}$, $D_2 = \{x_2, y_2\}$, $T_1 = \{1\}$ (so player 1 has only one possible type and no private information), $T_2 = \{2a, 2b\}$, $p_1(2a|1) = 0.6$, $p_1(2b|1) = 0.4$, and the payoffs (u_1, u_2) depend on the actions and player 2's type through the following two bimatrices:

$t_2 = 2a$	x_2	y_2
x_1	1, 2	0, 1
y_1	0, 4	1, 3

$t_2 = 2b$	x_2	y_2
x_1	1, 3	0,4
y_1	0, 1	1,2

In this game, x_2 is a dominant strategy for type $2a$, and y_2 is a dominant strategy for type $2b$. Player 1 wants to get either (x_1, x_2) or (y_1, y_2), and he thinks that type $2a$ is more likely than $2b$. Thus, the unique Bayesian equilibrium of this game is

$$\sigma_1(1) = x_1, \quad \sigma_2(2a) = x_2, \quad \sigma_2(2b) = y_2.$$

This example is of interest because it illustrates the danger of analyzing each bimatrix separately, as if it were a game with complete information, when the game is really one of incomplete information. If it were common knowledge that player 2's type was $2a$, then the players would be in the left bimatrix, where the unique equilibrium is (x_1, x_2). If it were common knowledge that 2's type was $2b$, then the players would be in the right bimatrix, where the unique equilibrium is (y_1, y_2). Thus, if we looked only at the full-information Nash equilibria of the two bimatrices, then we might make the prediction "the outcome of this game will be (x_1, x_2) if player 2's type is $2a$ and will be (y_1, y_2) if player 2's type is $2b$."

This prediction would be absurd, however, for the actual game with incomplete information, in which player 1 does not initially know player 2's type. Notice first that this prediction ascribes two different actions to player 1, depending on 2's type (x_1 if $2a$, and y_1 if $2b$). So player 1 could not behave as predicted unless he got some information from player 2. But player 2 prefers (y_1, y_2) over (x_1, x_2) if he is $2a$, and he prefers (x_1, x_2) over (y_1, y_2) if he is $2b$. Thus, even if we revised the game to allow communication between the players before player 1 chooses among x_1 and x_2, player 2 would never communicate the information needed to fulfill this prediction, because it always gives him his less-preferred outcome. Instead, he would rather manipulate his communications to get the outcomes (y_1, y_2) if $2a$, and (x_1, x_2) if $2b$.

5   Bayesian games with communication

When we defined Bayesian equilibrium as the solution concept for Bayesian games, we assumed that each player's decision in a Bayesian game could depend only on his own type. Let us now consider what can happen if the players are allowed to communicate in a given Bayesian game Γ, as in (1.4). To simplify our analysis, we will henceforth assume that the decision sets D_i, as well as the type sets T_i, are all finite sets.

Let us suppose first that the players communicate with the help of a mediator, who first asks each player to report his type, and who then recommends a strategic action to each player. The mediator's recommendations may depend on the players' reports in a deterministic or random fashion. We let $\mu(d_1, \ldots, d_n | t_1, \ldots, t_n)$ denote the conditional probability that the mediator would recommend to each player i that he should use action d_i, if each player j reported his type to be t_j. Obviously, these numbers $\mu(d|t)$ must satisfy the following probability constraints:

$$\sum_{c \in D} \mu(c|t) = 1 \quad \text{and} \quad \mu(d|t) \geq 0, \qquad \forall d \in D, \quad \forall t \in T. \tag{5.1}$$

In general, any function $\mu: D \times T \to \mathbb{R}$ that satisfies (5.1) will be called a *mechanism* (or *coordination mechanism*) for the Bayesian game Γ.

If every player reports his type honestly and obeys the recommendations of the mediator, then the expected utility for type t_i of player i from mechanism μ would be

$$U_i(\mu|t_i) = \sum_{t_{-i} \in T_{-i}} \sum_{d \in D} p_i(t_{-i}|t_i) \, \mu(d|t) \, u_i(d, t). \tag{5.2}$$

We must allow, however, that each player could choose to lie about his type or disobey the mediator's recommendation. That is, we assume that the players' types cannot be verified by the mediator, and each selection of an action d_i in D_i can ultimately be controlled only by player i. Thus, the coordination mechanism μ induces a *communication game* $\hat{\Gamma}_\mu$ in which each player must select his type report and his plan for choosing an action in D_i as a function of the mediator's recommendation. Formally, $\hat{\Gamma}_\mu$ is itself a Bayesian game, of the form

$$\hat{\Gamma}_\mu = (\hat{D}_1, \ldots, \hat{D}_n, \quad T_1, \ldots, T_n, \quad p_1, \ldots, p_n, \quad \hat{u}_1, \ldots, \hat{u}_n)$$

where

$$\hat{D}_i = \{(s_i, \delta_i) \mid s_i \in T_i \text{ and } \delta_i: D_i \to D_i\}, \text{ and}$$

$$\hat{u}_i(((s_1, \delta_1), \ldots, (s_n, \delta_n)), t)$$

$$= \sum_{t_{-i} \in T_{-i}} \sum_{d \in D} p_i(t_{-i}|t_i) \, \mu(d|s_1, \ldots, s_n) \, u_i((\delta_1(d_1),$$

$$\ldots, \delta_n(d_n)), t).$$

A strategy (s_i, δ_i) in D_i represents a plan by player i to report s_i to the mediator, and to then choose his action in D_i as a function of the mediator's recommendation according to δ_i, so that he would do $\delta_i(d_i)$ if the mediator recommended d_i. We assume that each player communicates with the mediator separately and confidentially, so that player i's action cannot depend on the recommendations to the other players.

Suppose, for example, that the true type of player i were t_i, but that he chose to use the strategy (s_i, δ_i) in the communication game $\hat{\Gamma}_\mu$. If all other players were expected to report their types honestly and choose their actions obediently to the mediator, then i's expected utility would be

$$U_i^*(\mu, \delta_i, s_i|t_i) = \sum_{t_{-i}\epsilon T_{-i}} \sum_{d\epsilon D} p_i(t_{-i}|t_i) \, \mu(d|t_{-i}, s_i) \, u_i((d_{-i}, \delta_i(d_i)), t).$$
(5.3)

[Here $(d_{-i}, \delta_i(d_i)) = (d_1, \ldots, d_{i-1}, \delta_i(d_i), d_{i+1}, \ldots, d_n)$ and (t_{-i}, s_i) = $(t_1, \ldots, t_{i-1}, s_i, t_{i+1}, \ldots, t_n)$.]

Bayesian equilibrium is still the appropriate solution concept for a Bayesian game with communication, except that we must now consider the Bayesian equilibria of the induced communication game $\hat{\Gamma}_\mu$, rather than just the Bayesian equilibria of Γ. We say that a mechanism μ is *(Bayesian) incentive compatible* iff it is a Bayesian equilibrium for all players to report their types honestly and to obey the mediator's recommendations when he uses the mechanism μ. (Hurwicz [1972] introduced the phrase *incentive compatible* in a non-Bayesian context, with a somewhat different meaning. Bayesian incentive compatibility was first defined by d'Aspremont and Gérard-Varet [1979]. In this essay, this term is always used in the Bayesian sense.) Thus, μ is incentive compatible iff

$$U_i(\mu|t_i) \geq U_i^*(\mu, \delta_i, s_i|t_i), \qquad \forall i, \quad \forall t_i \epsilon T_i, \quad \forall s_i \epsilon T_i, \forall \delta_i: D_i \to D_i.$$
(5.4)

If the mediator uses an incentive-compatible mechanism and each player communicates independently and confidentially with the mediator, then no player could ever gain by being the first one to lie to the mediator or disobey his recommendations. Conversely, we cannot expect all the players to participate honestly and obediently in a coordination mechanism unless it is incentive compatible.

In general, there may be many different Bayesian equilibria of a communication game $\hat{\Gamma}_\mu$, even if μ is incentive compatible. Furthermore, we could consider more general classes of coordination mechanisms, in which the messages sent and received by each player i are not necessarily in the sets T_i and D_i. However, for any given coordination mechanism and for any given Bayesian equilibrium of the induced communication game, there exists an equivalent incentive-compatible mechanism, in which every type of every player gets the same expected utility (when all players are honest and obedient) as in the given Bayesian equilibrium of the given mechanism. In this sense, there is no loss of generality in assuming that the players communicate with one another through a mediator who first asks each player to reveal all of his private information (his "type"), and who then gives each player only the minimal information needed to guide his action, in such a way that no player has any incentive to lie or cheat. This result has been observed by many writers independently and it is known as the *revelation principle*. (See Dasgupta, Hammond, and Maskin [1979], Holmström [1977], Myerson [1979a,

1982], Rosenthal [1978], Harris and Townsend [1981], Forges [1982] and, in a non-Bayesian context, Gibbard [1973].)

For any given equilibrium of any given mechanism, the mediator can construct such an equivalent incentive-compatible mechanism as follows. First, he asks each player to (simultaneously and confidentially) reveal his type. Next, the mediator computes what reports would have been sent by the players, with these revealed types, in the given equilibrium. Then, he computes what recommendations or messages would have been received by the players, as a function of these reports, in the given mechanism. Then, he computes what actions would have been carried out by the players, as a function of these recommendations (and the revealed types) in the given equilibrium. Finally, the mediator tells each player to do the action computed for him in this last step. Thus, the constructed mechanism simulates the given equilibrium of the given mechanism. To check that this constructed mechanism is incentive compatible, notice that any player who could gain by disobeying the mediator in the constructed mechanism could also gain by similarly disobeying his equilibrium strategy in the given mechanism, which is impossible (by definition of equilibrium).

The set of all incentive-compatible mechanisms is a closed convex set, characterized by a system of inequalities (5.1) and (5.4), which are linear in μ. On the other hand, it is generally a difficult problem to characterize the set of all Bayesian equilibria of any given Bayesian game. Thus, by the revelation principle, it may be easier to characterize the set of all Bayesian equilibria of all communication games induced from Γ, than it is to compute the set of Bayesian equilibria of Γ, or of any one communication game $\hat{\Gamma}_\mu$. This observation explains why the revelation principle can be so useful.

For example, let us reconsider the two-player game shown in the preceding section. Suppose now that the players can communicate, either directly or through a mediator or through some tatonnement process, before they choose their actions in D_1 and D_2. In the induced communication game, could there ever be a Bayesian equilibrium giving the outcomes (x_1, x_2) if player 2 is type $2a$, and (y_1, y_2) if player 2 is type $2b$, as naive analysis of the two bimatrices separately might suggest? The answer is No, by the revelation principle. If there were such a communication game, then there would be an incentive-compatible mechanism achieving the same results. But this would be the mechanism satisfying

$$\mu(x_1, x_2 | 1, 2a) = 1, \quad \mu(y_1, y_2 | 1, 2b) = 1;$$

and it is not incentive compatible, since player 2 could gain by lying about his type. In fact, there is only one incentive-compatible mechanism for this example and this mechanism is μ^*, defined by

$$\mu^*(x_1, x_2 | 1, 2a) = 1, \quad \mu^*(x_1, y_2 | 1, 2b) = 1.$$

Of course, μ^* is equivalent to the unique Bayesian equilibrium of this game without communication.

In general, it may be possible for all players to increase their expected utility with effective communication. Suppose that there is some given social welfare function that we want to maximize. By the revelation principle, the maximum value that can be achieved by an incentive-compatible mechanism is also the maximum that can be achieved among all Bayesian equilibria of all communication games that can be induced from Γ.

We say that a mechanism μ *is incentive efficient* iff μ is incentive compatible and there does not exist any other incentive-compatible mechanism $\hat{\mu}$ such that

$$U_i(\hat{\mu} | t_i) \geq U_i(\mu | t_i), \qquad \forall i \in \{1, \ldots, n\}, \ \forall t_i \in T_i, \qquad (5.5)$$

with at least one strict inequality. That is, if μ is incentive efficient, then there is no Bayesian equilibrium of any communication game that gives higher expected utility to some types of some players without giving lower expected utility to at least one type of some player. Conversely, if μ is not incentive efficient then it is common knowledge that all players would prefer to use some incentive-compatible coordination mechanism. Incentive efficiency is thus the basic normative concept for welfare analysis of coordination mechanisms. See Holmström and Myerson [1983] for a more detailed discussion of this concept.

The main goal of the rest of this essay will be to develop more useful conditions for characterizing the incentive-efficient mechanisms. In the next two sections, we will do this for two special cases. First, we will consider Bayesian collective-choice problems, which are situations in which the incentive constraints are purely informational (pure adverse-selection problems). Then we will consider games with complete information, in which the incentive constraints are purely strategic (pure moral hazard problems).

6   Bayesian collective-choice problems

A Bayesian collective-choice problem differs from a Bayesian game in that we are given a set of possible outcomes that are jointly feasible for all the players together, rather than a set of strategic decisions or actions for each player separately. That is, a *Bayesian collective-choice problem* is any Γ^o such that

$$\Gamma^o = (C, T_1, \ldots, T_n, p_1, \ldots, p_n, u_1, \ldots, u_n) \qquad (6.1)$$

where C is the set of possible *outcomes* or *social choices*; each T_i is the set of possible types for player i; each p_i is a function specifying i's conditional probability distribution over T_{-i} for each t_i in T_i; and each u_i is a function specifying i's utility payoff $u_i(c, t)$ for every c in C and every t in $T = T_1 \times \cdots \times T_n$.

When we discussed Bayesian games with communication in the preceding section, we assumed that the choice of an action in D_i was inalienably controlled by player i. That is, we assumed that player i could not commit himself to choosing some particular d_i when some other $\hat{d}_i$ in D_i would give him higher expected utility. (For example, this assumption would be appropriate if D_i were a set of unobservable effort levels that i must choose among when he performs some task, as in a principal-agent problem.) Now, if we assume instead that the players can cooperatively determine their actions in $D_1 \times \cdots \times D_n$ with jointly binding agreements, then the Bayesian game Γ becomes a Bayesian collective-choice problem Γ^o with $C = D_1 \times \cdots \times D_n$.

For another example, to model an exchange economy as a Bayesian collective-choice problem, we could let C be the set of all possible net trades among the players.

In any Bayesian collective-choice problem as in (6.1), the problem is to find efficient or optimal mechanisms for determining the chosen outcome in C as a function of the players' types. We shall assume that C is a finite set, but that random mechanisms are allowed. Thus a *mechanism* for Γ^o can be defined as any function $\mu: C \times T \to \mathbb{R}$ such that

$$\sum_{e \in C} \mu(e|t) = 1, \quad \mu(c|t) \geqslant 0 \qquad \forall c \in C, \forall t \in T, \qquad (6.2)$$

where $\mu(c|t)$ is interpreted as the probability that c will be the chosen outcome if $t = (t_1, \ldots, t_n)$ is a vector of types reported by n players. As in (5.2) and (5.3), the expected utility for type t_i from mechanism μ if all players report their types honestly is

$$U_i(\mu|t_i) = \sum_{t_{-i} \in T_{-i}} \sum_{c \in C} p_i(t_{-i}|t_i) \, \mu(c|t) \, u_i(c, t); \qquad (6.3)$$

and the expected utility for t_i if he reports s_i while the other players are honest is

$$U_i^*(\mu, s_i|t_i) = \sum_{t_{-i} \in T_{-i}} \sum_{c \in C} p_i(t_{-i}|t_i) \, \mu(c|t_{-i}, s_i) \, u_i(c, t). \qquad (6.4)$$

The mechanism μ is *incentive compatible* iff honest reporting by all players is a Bayesian equilibrium of the game induced by μ; that is,

$$U_i(\mu|t_i) \geq U_i^*(\mu, s_i|t_i) \qquad \forall i \in \{1, \ldots, n\}, \, \forall t_i \in T_i, \, \forall s_i \in T_i. \qquad (6.5)$$

These definitions $(6.3)-(6.5)$ are the same as $(5.2)-(5.4)$ except that there is no longer any question of players disobeying recommended actions. In fact, one can easily construct a Bayesian game with $n + 1$ players that is equivalent to the collective choice problem Γ^o, in the sense of generating the same set of incentive-compatible mechanisms. (Let $D_i = \{0\}$ for every i in $\{1, \ldots, n\}$, $D_{n+1} = C$, $T_{n+1} = \{0\}$, and $u_{n+1}(d, t) = 0$ for every d and t.) The revelation principle holds for Bayesian collective-choice problems, just as for Bayesian games with communication. We say that μ is an *incentive-efficient* mechanism for Γ^o iff μ is incentive compatible and is not dominated by any other incentive-compatible mechanism, in the sense of (5.5).

To simplify our formulas, we will henceforth assume that the players' beliefs are consistent with a common prior p^*, as in (3.1). Furthermore, we will assume that the players' types are independent random variables in the common prior; that is,

$$p^*(t) = \prod_{i=1}^{n} p_i^*(t_i), \qquad \forall t \in T,$$

where $p_i^*(t_i)$ is the marginal probability that player i is type t_i. (As was remarked in Section 3, any Bayesian collective-choice problem is probability equivalent to another Bayesian collective-choice problem in which beliefs are consistent with such an independent common prior.)

Suppose now that λ and α are vectors of the form

$$\lambda = [[\lambda_i(t_i)]_{t_i \in T_i}]_{i=1}^{n}, \quad \alpha = [[\alpha_i(s_i|t_i)]_{s_i \in T_i, t_i \in T_i}]_{i=1}^{n}$$

(read "$|$" here as "given") such that

$$\lambda_i(t_i) > 0 \quad \text{and} \quad \alpha_i(s_i|t_i) \geq 0, \qquad \forall i \in \{1, \ldots, n\}, \, \forall t_i \in T_i. \qquad (6.6)$$

Then let us define $v_i(c, t, \lambda, \alpha)$ by the following formula:

$$v_i(c, t, \lambda, \alpha) = [[\lambda_i(t_i) + \sum_{s_i \in T_i} \alpha_i(s_i|t_i)] u_i(c, t)$$

$$- \sum_{s_i \in T_i} \alpha_i(t_i|s_i) u_i(c, (t_{-i}, s_i))]/p_i^*(t_i). \qquad (6.7)$$

We shall refer to $v_i(c, t, \lambda, \alpha)$ as player i's *virtual utility* for outcome c in state t, with respect to the parameters λ and α. This definition (6.7) may seem obscure at first, but it is important because it permits us to state the following characterization of incentive-efficient mechanisms.

Theorem 1: *Suppose that μ is an incentive-compatible mechanism for Γ^o. Then μ is incentive efficient if and only if there exist vectors λ and α satisfying (6.6), such that*

$$\alpha_i(s_i|t_i)[U_i(\mu|t_i) - U_i^*(\mu, s_i|t_i)] = 0, \qquad i, \; s_i \in T_i, \; t_i \in T_i, \tag{6.8}$$

and

$$\sum_{c\in C} \mu(c|t) \sum_{i=1}^{n} v_i(c, t, \lambda, \alpha) = \max \sum_{c\in C} \sum_{i=1}^{n} v_i(c, t, \lambda, \alpha), \qquad t \in T. \tag{6.9}$$

To prove this theorem, observe first that the set of all incentive-compatible mechanisms satisfying (6.2) and (6.5) is a compact convex polyhedron. Thus, by the supporting hyperplane theorem of convex analysis, a mechanism μ is incentive efficient if and only if there exists a positive vector λ such that μ is an optimal solution to the following problem

$$\underset{\mu}{\text{maximize}} \sum_{i=1}^{n} \sum_{t_i\in T_i} \lambda_i(t_i) \, U_i(\mu|t_i) \tag{6.10}$$

subject to (6.2) and (6.5).

We interpret $\alpha_i(s_i|t_i)$ as the dual variable or Lagrange multiplier for the incentive constraint (6.5) that asserts that player i should not expect to gain by reporting type s_i if his true type is t_i. Then the Lagrangian function for problem (6.10) is

$$\sum_{i=1}^{n} \sum_{t_i\in T_i} [\lambda_i(t_i)U_i(\mu|t_i) + \sum_{s_i\in T_i} \alpha_i(s_i|t_i)(U_i(\mu|t_i) - U_i^*(\mu, s_i|t_i))]$$

$$= \sum_{t\in T} p^*(t) \sum_{c\in C} \mu(c|t) \sum_{i=1}^{n} v_i(c, t, \lambda, \alpha). \tag{6.11}$$

That is, the Lagrangian for (6.10) equals the expected sum of the players' virtual utilities. The virtual utility functions were defined in (6.7) precisely so that this equation (6.11) would hold, as may be verified by straightforward algebra. (See Myerson [1984a,b] for an introduction to the role of virtual utility in the theory of bargaining under incomplete information.)

Condition (6.8) in Theorem 1 asserts that, if the dual variable $\alpha_i(s_i|t_i)$ is positive then the associated incentive constraint must be binding. Condition (6.9) asserts that $\mu(\cdot|t)$ maximizes the sum of the players' virtual utilities in each state t, subject only to the probability constraint (6.2). Thus, the conditions in Theorem 1 assert that μ and α form a saddlepoint of the Lagrangian function, and so μ must be an optimal solution to (6.10). This completes the proof of Theorem 1.

An incentive-efficient mechanism may be inefficient ex post (after the players have revealed their types) because of the cost of satisfying incentive constraints. However, an incentive-efficient mechanism must maximize ex post the sum of the players' virtual utilities (with respect to some λ and α), so the mechanism will be ex post efficient in terms of these *virtual* utility functions. Thus, the key to understanding ex post inefficiency in incentive-efficient mechanisms is to understand how virtual utility differs from real utility.

If λ and α satisfy the conditions of Theorem 1 for an incentive-efficient mechanism μ and if $\alpha_i(s_i|t_i) > 0$, then we say that type t_i *jeopardizes* type s_i in the mechanism μ. That is, t_i jeopardizes s_i if the constraint that t_i should not be tempted to claim to be s_i is binding and has a positive Lagrange multiplier. Notice that, in (6.7), a player's virtual utility is a positive multiple of his real utility minus a positive linear combination of the utilities of the types that jeopardize his actual type. That is, the virtual utility of a type t_i differs from the real utility in that it exaggerates the difference from the other types that jeopardize t_i. So to understand how the costs of incentive compatibility should be borne in an incentive-efficient mechanism, we need to recognize which types are jeopardized by which.

There are many situations in which a player's types can be naturally ranked in some order, say from "best" to "worst." In such situations, we can often guess that the better types are jeopardized by the worse types, but not vice versa, so that the worst type is not jeopardized by any other. In fact, it often happens that each type is jeopardized only by the next-worse type. Optimal auctions in Harris and Raviv [1981] have this structure, where the unjeopardized type of bidder is the one with the highest reservation price.

To illustrate these ideas, suppose that a firm is negotiating with a potential employee, who may either be a "good" type of worker or a "bad" type. We may expect that the bad type jeopardizes the good type; that is, the firm may have difficulty preventing a bad worker from claiming to be good. So the virtual utility of the good type will exaggerate the difference from the bad type. If there is some useless educational process that would be slightly unpleasant for a good worker, but would be intolerably painful for a bad worker, then the good worker may get positive virtual utility from this education, so as to exaggerate his difference from the bad type. As in Spence's [1973] labor-market equilibria, an incentive-efficient mechanism may force a good worker to go through this costly and unproductive educational process (as if he enjoyed it), before he is hired. On the other hand, it seems unlikely that a good worker would be tempted to claim that he is bad in such negotiations. So the bad type of worker is not jeopardized, and the bad type's virtual utility is just a positive multiple of his real utility. Thus, if the worker is bad, the incentive-efficient mechanism should be ex post efficient (in terms of both real and virtual utility), and the bad worker should not suffer through any unproductive educational process.

For another simple example, consider a bargaining problem between one seller of a commodity (player 1) and one buyer (player 2) in a bilateral monopoly situation. The seller has one unit available, and he knows whether it is good quality (type "1a") or bad quality (type "1b"). If it is good quality, then it is worth $40 per unit to the seller and $50 per unit to the buyer. If it is bad quality, then it is worth $20 per unit to the seller and $30 per unit to the buyer. The buyer thinks that the probability of good quality is .2.

To formulate this example, we let $T_1 = \{1a, 1b\}$, $T_2 = \{2\}$ (so that the variable t_2 can be ignored, since it has only one possible value), and

$$C = \{(x, y) \mid 0 \leqslant y \leqslant 1, x \in \mathbb{R}\}.$$

Here, for each (x, y) in C, we interpret x as the amount of money paid by the buyer to the seller, and y as the amount of the commodity delivered by the seller to the buyer. The probability and utility functions are

$$p_1^*(1a) = .2, \quad p_1^*(1b) = .8,$$
$$u_1((x, y), 1a) = x - 40y, \quad u_2((x, y), 1a) = 50y - x,$$
$$u_1((x, y), 1b) = x - 20y, \quad u_2((x, y), 1b) = 30y - x.$$

(C is an infinite set in this example, but all of our results will still apply.)

In this example, ex post efficiency would require that the seller should always sell his unit of the commodity, no matter what his type is, since the commodity is always worth $10 more to the buyer. However, it can be easily shown that there is no incentive-compatible mechanism that is ex post efficient and gives nonnegative expected utility to the buyer and to both types of the seller (i.e., such that $U_2(\mu) \geqslant 0$, $U_1(\mu \mid 1a) \geqslant 0$, $U_1(\mu \mid 1b) \geqslant 0$).

For this example, let λ and α be

$$\lambda_1(1a) = .3, \quad \lambda_1(1b) = .7, \quad \lambda_2 = 1, \quad \alpha_1(1a \mid 1b) = .1, \quad \alpha_1(1b \mid 1a) = 0.$$

By (6.7), the virtual utility functions for these parameters are

$$v_1((x, y), 1a, \lambda, \alpha) = [.3u_1((x, y), 1a) - .1\, u_1((x, y), 1b)]/.2 = x - 50y,$$
$$v_2((x, y), 1a, \lambda, \alpha) = u_2((x, y), 1a) = 50y - x,$$
$$v_1((x, y), 1b, \lambda, \alpha) = (.7 + .1)\, u_1((x, y), 1b)/.8 = x - 20y,$$
$$v_2((x, y), 1b, \lambda, \alpha) = u_2((x, y), 1b) = 30y - x.$$

That is, the bad type of seller (1b) jeopardizes the good type (1a), so the good type's virtual utility exaggerates the difference from the bad type and has a virtual reservation price of \$50 (instead of \$40) for the commodity. With this λ and α, virtual ex post efficiency would require only that all of the commodity must be sold to the buyer if it is of bad quality; there are no virtual gains from trade between the buyer and a good-type seller. Thus, this λ and α will satisfy the conditions of Theorem 1 for any mechanism μ such that all the commodity is sold to the buyer if the seller's type is 1b, and the constraint that the 1b-type seller should not claim to be "1a" is binding. For example, consider μ such that

$$\mu(30, 1 \mid 1b) = 1, \quad \mu(50/3, 1/3 \mid 1a) = 1$$

(that is, the bad type sells all of his commodity for \$30, and the good type sells one-third of his supply at a price of \$50 per unit). This mechanism satisfies both of the preceding conditions (check that $U_1(\mu \mid 1b) = U_1^*(\mu, 1a \mid 1b) = 10$), and so it is incentive efficient, even though the seller cannot sell two-thirds of his commodity if it is good.

7   Correlated equilibria of games with complete information

If the players have no private information (so that each has only one possible type) then the Bayesian game reduces a game in *strategic form* (or *normal form*) with complete information. That is, we get

$$\Gamma = (D_1, \ldots, D_n, u_1, \ldots, u_n), \tag{7.1}$$

where each $u_i(\cdot)$ is a function from $D = D_1 \times \cdots \times D_n$ into $\mathbb{R}$. For such games, we can derive a characterization of incentive-efficient mechanisms closely analogous to Theorem 1.

For a game with complete information, a coordination mechanism μ is just a probability distribution over D, satisfying

$$\sum_{e \in D} \mu(e) = 1 \quad \text{and} \quad \mu(d) \geqslant 0, \qquad \forall d \in D. \tag{7.2}$$

(There are no longer any alternative types for the mechanism to depend on.) The condition of incentive compatibility, (5.4), reduces to

$$\sum_{d_{-i} \in D_{-i}} \mu(d) \, u_i(d) \geqslant \sum_{d_{-i} \in D_{-i}} \mu(d) \, u_i(d_{-i}, e_i), \qquad \forall i, \forall d_i \in D_i, \forall e_i \in D_i. \tag{7.3}$$

(Here $D_{-i} = D_1 \times \cdots \times D_{i-1} \times D_{i+1} \times \cdots \times D_n$ and $d = (d_{-i}, d_i)$.) To interpret this condition, suppose that a mediator randomly selected a joint action in D, selecting d with probability $\mu(d)$, and each player i was then informed only as to which action d_i was his component of the mediator's selection. Then (7.3) asserts that each player's optimal action is to do what the mediator has told him, if all other players are also expected to obey the mediator's recommendation. (To see this, first divide both sides of (7.3) by the marginal probability of d_i being selected; that is,

$$\sum_{d_{-i} \epsilon D_{-i}} \mu(d).$$

Then the left-hand side and right-hand side are player i's conditionally expected utility from using d_i and e_i, respectively, given that the mediator recommended d_i.)

Conditions (7.2) and (7.3) are also the definition of a *correlated equilibrium*, due to Aumann [1974]. Thus, the concept of an incentive-compatible mechanism is just a generalization of Aumann's concept of correlated equilibrium, and the two concepts coincide for games with complete information.

In this context, a mechanism μ is incentive efficient if and only if there exists a vector $\lambda = (\lambda_1, \ldots, \lambda_n)$ such that every $\lambda_i > 0$ and μ is an optimal solution to the following problem.

$$\underset{\mu}{\text{maximize}} \sum_{i=1}^{n} \sum_{d \epsilon D} \lambda_i \, \mu(d) \, u_i(d) \tag{7.4}$$

subject to (7.2) and (7.3).

The following theorem, analogous to Theorem 1, is derived by a standard Lagrangian analysis of (7.4), letting $\beta_i(e_i|d_i)$ denote the Lagrange multiplier for the constraint (7.3) that says that player i should not be tempted to do e_i when told to do d_i.

Theorem 2: *Suppose that μ is a correlated equilibrium. Then μ is incentive efficient if and only if there exist vectors λ and β such that*

$$\lambda_i > 0 \text{ and } \beta_i(e_i|d_i) \geq 0, \qquad \forall i, \ \forall d_i \epsilon D_i, \ \forall e_i \epsilon D_i; \tag{7.5}$$

$$\beta_i(e_i|d_i) \left[\sum_{d_{-i} \epsilon D_{-i}} \mu(d)(u_i(d) - u_i(d_{-i}, e_i)) \right] = 0,$$

$$\forall i, \ \forall d_i \epsilon D_i, \ \forall e_i \epsilon D_i; \tag{7.6}$$

and

$$\sum_{d \epsilon D} \mu(d) \sum_{i=1}^{n} v_i(d, \lambda, \beta) = \max_{d \epsilon D} \sum_{i=1}^{n} v_i(d, \lambda, \beta); \tag{7.7}$$

where we define the virtual utility functions $v_i(\cdot)$ by

$$v_i(d, \lambda, \beta) = \lambda_i u_i(d) + \sum_{e_i \in D_i} \beta_i(e_i | d_i)(u_i(d) - u_i(d_{-i}, e_i)).$$
(7.8)

Here condition (7.6) asserts that if $\beta_i(e_i | d_i) > 0$ then the constraint that "*i* should not gain by doing e_i when told to do d_i" is binding. Condition (7.7) asserts that μ puts all probability weight on the joint actions that maximize the sum of the players' virtual utilities.

If $\beta_i(e_i | d_i) > 0$ then we may say that action e_i *jeopardizes* action d_i for player *i*. Then *i*'s virtual utility $v_i(d, \lambda, \beta)$ is a positive multiple of his real utility $u_i(d)$ minus a positive linear combination of what he would get if he changed to some other action that jeopardizes d_i. Thus, player *i*'s virtual utility when he does d_i differs from his real utility in that it exaggerates the difference from what he would get from other actions that jeopardize d_i.

To understand these results, let us consider an example based on one of Aumann [1974]. There are two players, $D_1 = \{x_1, y_1\}$, $D_2 = \{x_2, y_2\}$, and the utility payoffs (u_1, u_2) are as follows:

	x_2	y_2
x_1	5, 1	0, 0
y_1	4, 4	1, 5

There are three Nash equilibria of this game: (x_1, x_2), (y_1, y_2), and a randomized Nash equilibrium in which each player gives equal probability to his two strategies. In the randomized equilibrium, all four outcomes have equal probability, and each player gets expected utility 2.5.

The best symmetric payoff in this example is (4, 4), but the players cannot achieve this because (y_1, x_2) is not an equilibrium. Player 1 would choose x_1 if he expected player 2 to choose x_2. However, with communication, the players can make self-enforcing plans of action that give them both higher expected utility than 2.5. For example, they could agree to toss a coin and then choose (x_1, x_2) if it is heads and (y_1, y_2) if it is tails. This plan of action is self-enforcing, even though the coin toss has no binding impact on the players. (Player 1 could not gain by choosing x_1 after tails, since player 2 is then expected to choose y_2). Thus, this plan is a correlated equilibrium, and it gives each player an expected utility of 3.

With the help of a mediator, the players can achieve even higher expected utility in a correlated equilibrium. Suppose that the mediator randomizes among outcomes according to μ, where

$$\mu(x_1, x_2) = \mu(y_1, x_2) = \mu(y_1, y_2) = \tfrac{1}{3}, \quad \mu(x_1, y_2) = 0.$$

When the mediator tells each player separately which of his actions was in the randomly selected pair, then it is self-enforcing for both players to use the action designated by the mediator. For example, if player 1 is told "y_1", then he thinks that it is equally likely that player 2 has been told "x_2" or "y_2"; so y_1 would be as good as x_1 for player 1 (both give expected utility 2.5) if he expects that player 2 will also do as he is told. Thus, μ is a correlated equilibrium, and it gives each player an overall expected utility of 3.33.

In fact, this mechanism μ is incentive efficient, so that (3.33, 3.33) is the highest symmetric expected-utility allocation that the players can achieve in any correlated equilibrium. To check that μ is incentive efficient, let

$$\lambda_1 = \lambda_2 = 1, \quad \beta_1(x_1|y_1) = \beta_2(y_2|x_2) = \tfrac{2}{3}, \quad \beta_1(y_1|x_1) = \beta_2(x_2|y_2) = 0.$$

Then the virtual utility functions (v_1, v_2) are

	x_2	y_2
x_1	5.00, 1.66	0, 0
y_1	3.33, 3.33	1.66, 5.00

and μ puts all weight on the outcomes that maximize $v_1 + v_2$. Furthermore, as required by (7.6), μ satisfies without slack the two incentive constraints that have positive Lagrange multipliers.

8   General conditions for incentive efficiency

In Myerson [1982], a class of Bayesian incentive problems were defined in a way which includes strategic-form games, Bayesian collective-choice problems, and Bayesian games, all as special cases. Formally, a *Bayesian incentive problem* is any Γ of the form

$$\Gamma = (D_0, D_1, \ldots, D_n, T_1, \ldots, T_n, p_1, \ldots, p_n, u_1, \ldots, u_n)$$
$$(8.1)$$

where D_0 is a set of *enforceable* or *public* actions, and, for each i in

$\{1, \ldots, n\}$, D_i, T_i, p_i, and u_i are as in a Bayesian game, except that now the domain of the utility function u_i is

$$D \times T = (D_0 \times D_1 \times \cdots \times D_n) \times (T_1 \times \cdots \times T_n).$$

That is, a general Bayesian incentive problem differs from a Bayesian game in that there may be some publicly controllable actions, as well as the privately controlled actions in $D_1, D_2, \ldots, D_n$. For example, suppose that the players are managers of different divisions in a firm. For each player i, his type in T_i may represent his private information about the production function in his division, and his private action in D_i may be his level of effort in carrying out his management responsibilities. The public actions in D_0 may be specifications of how the firm's capital resources are to be allocated to the divisions, and how each manager is to be paid as a function of output.

In general, all decision variables that the players can control cooperatively, or about which they can make binding promises, should be components of the "public actions" in D_0. Any decision variables that player i controls inalienably, or about which he cannot make any promises that conflict with his own utility-maximizing behavior, must be components of the "private actions" in D_i.

Thus, a Bayesian collective-choice problem is just a Bayesian incentive problem in which each player i has only one possible private action ("doing nothing"), so that $|D_i| = 1$ and the variable d_i can be ignored. On the other hand, a Bayesian game is just a Bayesian incentive problem in which $|D_0| = 1$. (Actually, any Bayesian incentive problem could be reduced to a Bayesian game, by introducing an $(n + 1)$th player "0" who controls the action in D_0 as his private action, has no private information, and has $u_0(d, t) = 0$ for all d and t.)

The definitions of incentive-compatible and incentive-efficient mechanisms for a Bayesian incentive problem are the same as for a Bayesian game, except that now in equations (5.1)−(5.4) we let

$$D = D_0 \times D_1 \times \cdots \times D_n, \quad d = (d_0, d_1, \cdots, d_n), \quad \text{and}$$

$$(d_{-i}, \delta_i(d_i)) = (d_0, d_1, \ldots, d_{i-1}, \delta_i(d_i), d_{i+1}, \ldots, d_n).$$

The following theorem generalizes Theorems 1 and 2 to the general case of the Bayesian incentive problem. We assume that D and T are finite sets, and that the players' beliefs are consistent with an independent common prior p^*, as in Theorem 1.

Theorem 3: *Suppose that μ is an incentive-compatible mechanism for the Bayesian incentive problem Γ, as above. Then μ is incentive efficient if and only if there exist vectors λ, α, and γ such that*

$$\lambda_i(t_i) > 0, \quad \alpha_i(s_i|t_i) \geq 0, \quad \gamma_i(e_i|d_i, s_i, t_i) \geq 0 \qquad \forall i \in \{1, \ldots, n\},$$
$$\forall t_i \in T_i, \ \forall s_i \in T_i, \ \forall d_i \in D_i, \ \forall e_i \in D_i; \tag{8.2}$$

$$\sum_{e_i \in D_i} \gamma_i(e_i|d_i, s_i, t_i) = 1, \qquad \forall i, \ \forall d_i \in D_i, \ \forall s_i \in T_i, \ \forall t_i \in T_i; \tag{8.3}$$

$$\sum_{t_{-i}} \sum_{d} \sum_{e_i} p_i(t_{-i}|t_i) \ \mu(d|t_{-i}, s_i) \ \gamma_i(e_i|d_i, s_i, t_i) \ u_i((d_{-i}, e_i), t)$$

$$= \max_{\delta_i : D_i \to D_i} U_i^*(\mu, \delta_i, s_i|t_i), \qquad \forall i, \ \forall s_i \in T_i, \ \forall t_i \in T_i; \tag{8.4}$$

$$0 = \alpha_i(s_i|t_i) \ [U_i(\mu|t_i) - \max_{\delta_i} U_i^*(\mu, \delta_i, s_i|t_i)], \qquad \forall i, \ \forall s_i \in T_i,$$

$$\forall t_i \in T_i; \quad and \tag{8.5}$$

$$\sum_{d \in D} \mu(d|t) \sum_{i=1}^{n} v_i(d, t, \lambda, \alpha, \gamma) = \max \sum_{d \in D} \sum_{i=1}^{n} v_i(d, t, \lambda, \alpha, \gamma), \qquad \forall t \in T, \tag{8.6}$$

$$v_i(d, t, \lambda, \alpha, \gamma) = \left[\left[\lambda_i(t_i) + \sum_{s_i} \alpha_i(s_i|t_i) \right] u_i(d, t) \right.$$

$$\left. - \sum_{s_i} \alpha_i(t_i|s_i) \sum_{e_i} \gamma_i(e_i|d_i, t_i, s_i) \ u_i((d_{-i}, e_i), (t_{-i}, s_i)) \right] / p_i^*(t_i). \tag{8.7}$$

As before, these conditions are derived from the Lagrangian conditions for an optimization problem, to maximize

$$\sum_{i} \sum_{t_i \in T_i} \lambda_i(t_i) \ U_i(\mu|t_i)$$

subject to the probability constraints (5.1) and the incentive constraints (5.4). Let $\alpha_i^o(\delta_i, s_i|t_i)$ denote the Lagrange multiplier of the incentive constraint that type t_i of player i should not be tempted to claim that he is type s_i and then to disobey his recommended action according to $\delta_i(\cdot)$. Let us choose α and γ so that they satisfy (8.2), (8.3),

$$\alpha_i(s_i|t_i) = \sum_{\delta_i : D_i \to D_i} a_i^o(\delta_i, s_i|t_i), \qquad \forall i, \ \forall s_i \in T_i, \ \forall t_i \in T_i, \tag{8.8}$$

and

$$\gamma_i(e_i|d_i, s_i, t_i) \ \alpha_i(s_i|t_i) = \sum_{\{\delta_i|\delta_i(d_i) = e_i\}} \alpha_i^o(\delta_i, s_i|t_i), \qquad \forall i, \ \forall d_i \in D_i,$$
$$\forall e_i \in D_i, \ \forall t_i \in T_i, \ \forall s_i \in T_i. \tag{8.9}$$

(If $\alpha_i(s_i|t_i) = 0$ then we can choose $\gamma(\cdot|\cdot, s_i, r_i)$ so that it also satisfies (8.4).) Then the Lagrangian function of this optimization problem can be written

$$\sum_i \sum_{t_i} \lambda_i(t_i)\ U_i(\mu|t_i) + \sum_i \sum_{t_i} \sum_{s_i} \sum_{\delta_i} \alpha_i^0(\delta_i,\ s_i|t_i)[U_i(\mu|t_i)$$
$$- U_i^*(\mu,\ \delta_i,\ s_i|t_i)]$$

$$= \sum_t p^*(t) \sum_d \mu(d|t) \sum_{i=1}^n v_i(d,\ t,\ \lambda,\ \alpha,\ \gamma).$$

The conditions of Theorem 3 follow directly from this equation and the saddlepoint conditions of Lagrangian analysis.

To interpret the conditions in Theorem 3, think of $\gamma_i(e_i|d_i,\ s_i,\ t_i)$ as the probability that player i would choose action e_i if he were cheating when his type was t_i, he reported s_i, and he was told to do d_i. Condition (8.4) asserts that using $\gamma_i(\cdot|\cdot,\ s_i,\ t_i)$ should be an optimal plan for type t_i after reporting s_i. Condition (8.5) asserts that $\alpha_i(s_i|t_i)$ can be positive only if type t_i would be willing to report type s_i. (We may have $\alpha_i(t_i|t_i) > 0$, if type t_i would be willing to disobey the mediator's recommended actions after reporting honestly.) Formula (8.7) extends the virtual utility formula (6.7) for Bayesian collective-choice problems. The virtual utility of type t_i differs from the real utility in that it exaggerates the difference from the types that jeopardize t_i, when they use their optimal disobedience plans γ_i. By (8.6) an incentive-efficient mechanism must maximize the sum of the players' virtual utilities, in every state t. Thus, the conditions of Theorem 3 can give us some intuition as to the qualitative nature of incentive-efficient mechanisms, even though these conditions may be too complex to apply numerically in many problems.

REFERENCES

Armbruster, W., and W. Böge [1979]. "Bayesian Game Theory," in *Game Theory and Related Topics*, edited by O. Moeschlin and D. Pallaschke, pp. 17–28. Amsterdam: North Holland.

Arrow, K. J. [1970]. *Essays in the Theory of Risk-Bearing*. Amsterdam: North Holland.

Aumann, R. J. [1974]. "Subjectivity and Correlation in Randomized Strategies." *Journal of Mathematical Economics*, 1:67–96.

Aumann, R. J. [1976]. "Agreeing to Disagree." *Annals of Statistics*, 4:1236–1239.

Billingsley, P. [1968]. *Convergence of Probability Measures*. New York: Wiley.

Dasgupta, P. S., P. J. Hammond, and E. S. Maskin [1979]. "The Implementation of Social Choice Rules: Some Results on Incentive Compatibility." *Review of Economic Studies*, 46:185–216.

d'Aspremont, C., and L.-A. Gérard-Varet [1979]. "Incentives and Incomplete Information." *Journal of Public Economics*, 11:25–45.

Forges, F. [1982]. "A First Study of Correlated Equilibria in Repeated Games with Incomplete Information." CORE Discussion Paper No. 8218, Université Catholique de Louvain.

Gibbard, A. [1973]. "Manipulation of Voting Schemes: A General Result." *Econometrica*, 41:587–602.

Harris, M., and A. Raviv [1981]. "Allocation Mechanisms and the Design of Auctions." *Econometrica*, *49*:1477–1499.

Harris, M., and R. M. Townsend [1981]. "Resource Allocation under Asymmetric Information." *Econometrica*, *49*:231–259.

Harsanyi, J. C. [1967–68]. "Games with Incomplete Information Played by 'Bayesian' Players." *Management Science*, *14*:159–189, 320–334, 486–502.

Holmström, B. [1977]. "On Incentives and Control in Organizations. Unpublished Ph.D. dissertation, Stanford University, Stanford, Calif.

Holmström, B., and R. B. Myerson [1983]. "Efficient and Durable Decision Rules with Incomplete Information." *Econometrica*, *53*:1799–1819.

Hurwicz, L. [1972]. "On Informationally Decentralized Systems." in *Decision and Organization*, edited by R. Radner and B. McGuire, pp. 297–336. Amsterdam: North Holland.

Mertens, J.-F., and S. Zamir [1985]. "Formalization of Bayesian Analysis for Games with Incomplete Information." *International Journal of Game Theory*, *14*:1–29.

Milgrom, P. R., and R. J. Weber [1985]. "Distributional Strategies for Games with Incomplete Information." Center for Mathematical Studies Discussion Paper no. 427, Northwestern University, Evanston, Ill. (to appear in *Mathematics of Operations Research*).

Myerson, R. B. [1979a]. "Incentive Compatibility and the Bargaining Problem." *Econometrica*, *47*:61–73.

Myerson, R. B. [1979b]. "An Axiomatic Derivation of Subjective Probability, Utility and Evaluation Functions." *Theory and Decision*, *11*:339–352.

Myerson, R. B. [1982]. "Optimal Coordination Mechanisms in Generalized Principal-Agent Problems." *Journal of Mathematical Economics*, *10*:67–81.

Myerson, R. B. [1984a]. "Two-Person Bargaining Problems with Incomplete Information." *Econometrica*, *52*:461–487.

Myerson, R. B. [1984b]. "Cooperative Games with Incomplete Information." *International Journal of Game Theory*, *13*:69–96.

Raiffa, H. [1968]. *Decision Analysis*. Reading, Mass.: Addison-Wesley.

Rosenthal, R. W. [1978]. "Arbitration of Two-Party Disputes under Uncertainty." *Review of Economic Studies*, *45*:595–604.

Savage, L. J. [1954]. *The Foundations of Statistics*. New York: Wiley.

Spence, M. [1973]. "Job Market Signaling." *Quarterly Journal of Economics*, *87*:355–374.

von Neumann, J., and O. Morgenstern [1944]. *Theory of Games and Economic Behavior*. Princeton, N.J.: Princeton University Press.

Wilson, R. [1968]. "The Theory of Syndicates." *Econometrica*, *38*:119–132.

CHAPTER 9

The economics of competitive bidding:
a selective survey

Paul R. Milgrom

1   Introduction

In Western economies, a wide variety of institutions have emerged for determining prices and conducting trade. In retail stores, the price of each good is usually posted by the seller, and individual buyers can do little to influence that price. When costly inputs are sold to manufacturing firms, the price is often negotiated — so the buyer and seller both take an active part in setting the price. A third common institution for setting prices is the auction, in which the price of goods is determined by competition among potential buyers. Hybrid trading institutions can also be found; for example, on some securities exchanges, specialists bidding against one another determine the market bid and ask prices, while public customers act as price takers.

Each of these various arrangements for conducting trade has some unique merits.[1] Detailed negotiations provide a flexible way to determine prices, product features, financing terms, and so on. But negotiations are costly and time consuming. In contrast, posted prices are inexpensive to administer, but they are also relatively inflexible and unresponsive to the wants and needs of particular consumers and to short-run fluctuations in demand.

Auctions have properties that place them somewhere between negotiations and posted prices. Billions of dollars of U.S. Treasury bills are sold each week using a sealed-tender auction, and while that causes resources to be spent by potential buyers in preparing bids, it also allows T-bill

---

[1] Harris and Raviv [1981, 1982], Maskin, Riley [1981], and Riley and Zeckhauser [1983] all consider various arrangements for selling goods from the point of view of profit maximization in an attempt to explain why, out of all conceivable selling arrangements, posted prices and competitive bidding are so popular. Their analyses focus on production and selling costs, rather than such factors as shifting demand, buyer transactions costs, uniqueness of the goods, and the need to adapt to newly arriving information.

prices to reflect current demand conditions and to respond to new information about variables like the federal deficit or the money supply. Antiques are commonly sold at auction, and although bringing together the potential buyers at one place and time entails moderate costs, there are compensating benefits: the auction procedure leads to prices that reflect the unique features and appeal of each piece, rather than setting a single price for all "Early American Rockers."

There are many kinds of auctions, but we shall limit our attention primarily to the most popular forms: the Dutch, English, discriminatory, and Vickrey auctions. In the *Dutch auction*, the auctioneer begins by calling a relatively high price for the goods being sold, and then gradually reduces the price until some bidder claims the goods for the current price. The *English auction* is an increasing price auction; the auctioneer gradually raises the price until only one bidder is still active. That bidder is then awarded the goods for the specified price. (The early Roman auctions were probably also of this kind, for the word "auction" is derived from the Latin root "auctus," meaning "an increase" [Cassady, 1967].)

The discriminatory and Vickrey auctions are sealed-bid tender auctions that can be used to sell units of a homogeneous good. In the *discriminatory auction*, each bidder submits one or more sealed bids, and the available units are awarded to the highest bidders according to the terms of their bids. Thus, each unit may be sold at a different price. The discriminatory auction is currently used for the sale of U.S. Treasury bills to major buyers. (Individual customers are permitted to buy a small number of bills for the average price paid by the major buyers.)

The *Vickrey auction* is a sealed-bid tender auction that, like the discriminatory auction, awards the units to the highest bidders. The price paid by a bidder for the jth unit he acquires is equal to the jth highest rejected bid from among his competitors. Vickrey [1961] pointed out that the prices a bidder must pay under this procedure do not depend on his own bids; that is, each bidder is a price taker. Consequently (assuming there are no income effects), a bidder can maximize his expected payoff by submitting bids equal to his marginal willingness to pay for each unit. Notice that this bidding strategy is optimal regardless of the bids made by one's competitors; it is a dominant strategy. Vickrey argued that an advantage of this procedure is that it eliminates the bidders' incentives to gather strategic information about their competitors and so reduces bid preparation costs. Moreover, if every bidder adopts his dominant strategy, the allocation of goods resulting from the auction will be Pareto optimal, because each unit is assigned to the bidder for whom its marginal value is highest.

Closely related to the Vickrey auction is the *uniform-price* auction in which the units are all sold at a uniform price equal to the highest rejected bid. Most formal analyses of auctions focus on the case where each bidder desires only one unit, and in that case the uniform price auction and the Vickrey auction are identical. Moreover, in that case, the uniform price is a competitive price: it is the lowest price at which supply (the number of units being offered) equals demand.

A storm of controversy arose in the 1960s when it was suggested that a uniform-price auction be used in place of the discriminatory auction for selling U.S. Treasury bills (Carson [1959], Friedman [1960], Brimmer [1962], Goldstein [1962], Rieber [1964], Smith [1966]). Proponents of the move argued that the uniform-price auction would lead to more efficient allocations than the discriminatory auction. Moreover, because uniform-price auctions are strategically simpler, the change would reduce bid preparation costs and encourage more bidders to participate. Opponents retorted that efficiency is but one objective of government; getting favorable terms on financing is another. In a discriminatory auction, it was argued, the government captures substantial advantages from price discrimination; more anxious buyers will pay higher prices to raise the likelihood of acquiring a unit. Experiments conducted by Cox, Roberson, and Smith [in press] lend support to this view.

As the following simple example shows, both the increased efficiency argument made by the proponents of the uniform price procedure and the increased revenue argument made by its opponents are subject to important qualifications. Let there be four bidders named A, B, C, and D, each of whom wants only one unit. Let their reservation prices be 22, 20, 15, and 12, respectively. Suppose that two units are available for sale. We model the auction as a noncooperative game among these bidders. If bidder A is awarded an object and pays a price p, his payoff is $22 - p$. If he loses, his payoff is zero. The payoffs of the other bidders are similarly determined. Each bidder selects a nonnegative real number to be his bid, and the outcome is then determined according to the rules of the auction.

In the uniform price auction, each player has a dominant strategy: A bids 22, B bids 20, C bids 15, and D bids 12. The units are awarded to A and B for a price of 15, and the seller's revenue is 30.

In the discriminatory auction, no bidder has a dominant strategy, but the bidders do have dominated strategies: they should never bid higher than their respective reservation prices. Because there is no dominant-strategy equilibrium, we shall seek a Nash equilibrium in undominated strategies. At every such equilibrium, A and B both bid 15 and C adopts some randomized strategy. For example, at one equilibrium, C selects his bid at random from the interval (14,15), using a uniform distribution, and D makes some undominated bid. At each equilibrium, the winners are A and B. Both pay a price of 15, and the seller's revenue is 30, just as with the uniform-price auction.

In this example, then, there are neither differences in efficiency nor differences in revenues generated between these two auctions. It seems clear that to reach any general conclusions, a more careful analysis is needed.

2   Equilibrium models of competitive bidding

The theoretical literature on competitive bidding consists mostly of studies of noncooperative game models of auctions in which a single item is offered for sale. To specify a game model, one must identify (i) the players, (ii) the information known by the players, (iii) the actions available to them, and (iv) how payoffs are determined. In addition, one must specify a solution concept that predicts how players in a game will behave.

In a typical auction game, the players are the bidders. All of the bidders share certain common knowledge about their environment − the rules of auction, certain characteristics of the item being sold, and so on. In addition, each bidder may have private information concerning his own tastes or the characteristics of the item being sold. To capture the idea that this information is private (and therefore not known by the other bidders), each player's information is modeled by a random variable that he alone observes. The bidders' uncertainty about one another's information is then represented by a joint-probability distribution over all these random variables. This distribution is itself assumed to be common knowledge among the bidders. Thus, but for the differences in their information, the bidders would share identical beliefs about the item being offered and about their competitors.

The auctions available to individual bidders depend on the particular auction game being played. In a sealed-bid auction, each bidder selects a single number, representing his bid. The payoff to the winning bidder will most often be the excess of the value of the item to the bidder over the price he pays. In most bidding games, the losing bidders' payoffs is set equal to zero.

A *strategy* for a bidder specifies what action to take as a function of what he knows. For example, in a sealed-bid auction, a bidder who estimates the value of the item to himself at x might bid an amount $\beta(x)$. Then, the function β is his strategy.

All formal auction models developed to date have assumed that the bidders do not collude or cooperate with each other. The noncooperative solution most often used in game theory is the *Nash equilibrium* or one of its variants. A set of strategies (one for each player) is a Nash equilibrium if every player, believing that his competitors will use their equilibrium strategies, maximizes his own payoff by playing his equilibrium strategy. Thus, if it were common knowledge that all planned to use their equilibrium strategies, no bidder would have an incentive to alter his plan.

There have been many formal equilibrium models of competitive bidding. The assumptions of these models differ along many dimensions, but two of these dimensions are of preeminent importance for our analysis: the determinants of the bidders' payoffs (*value assumptions*) and the determinants of their beliefs about their competitors (*distributional assumptions*).

The original Vickrey [1961, 1962] studies of competitive bidding as well as many more recent studies (Griesmer, Levitan, and Shubik [1967], Ortega-Reichert [1968], Matthews [1979], Holt [1980], Riley and Samuelson [1981], Harris and Raviv [1982]) adopted the *private-values* assumption. According to this assumption, a bidder's payoffs can depend only on (i) what he knows, (ii) whether he wins, and (iii) how much he pays. Value is treated as a purely personal matter: each bidder knows what the goods are worth to himself, and no bidder cares what they are worth to others, except possibly as strategic information to be used in choosing a bid. Thus, the object being sold is not a painting that may eventually be resold for a price depending on the tastes of others; it is not the rights to minerals or timber on federal territory, whose value depends on the unknown amounts and composition of the recoverable minerals or timber; and it is not a financial security, whose value depends on future prices, dividends, interest rates, and the like.

In extreme contrast to the private-values assumption is the *common-value* assumption, used most often in analyzing auctions for mineral rights (Wilson [1967], Ortega-Reichert [1968], Rothkopf [1969], Reece [1978], Engelbrecht-Wiggans, Milgrom, and Weber [1981], Milgrom and Weber [1982b]). According to the common-value assumption, the actual value (V) of the mineral rights is the same to all bidders, but the value will not be known until the resource is extracted. Also, the bidders may presently differ in their estimates of V.

Let X_i be bidder i's estimate of V, and suppose that it is an unbiased estimate; that is, $E[X_i|V] = V$. Other things being equal, the winning bidder will be the one with the highest estimate. The estimate of the winning bidder is biased upward; that is, $E[\max X_i|V] > \max E[X_i|V] = V$ (because "max" is a convex function). Intuitively, a bidder wins often when he overestimates V but wins only rarely when he underestimates V. Consequently, even if his estimates are unbiased, his estimates will be systematically high in those cases where he wins. The phenomenon is called the *winner's curse*.

Oil companies bidding for tracts of land in unexplored territory are allegedly among those accursed (Capen, Clapp, and Campbell [1971]), and other examples of the curse are easy to find. The new entrant in a local construction industry who is inexperienced in making competitive cost estimates may find that his bid wins the job only when he has underestimated the construction cost – he suffers from the winner's curse (cf. Brown [1975]). The university that makes the highest salary offer to a young assistant professor and the first-time homebuyer who outbids all rivals may both suffer the curse.

The analysis of common-value models focuses on the winner's curse and related issues. How does one bid to alleviate the curse? (Cautiously!) What are the incentives to acquire information? (Private information alleviates the curse for the informed bidder and intensifies the curse for his competitors.) How efficiently do prices aggregate information? How should the seller manage any information to which he may be privy?

A few papers develop bidding models that accommodate both private-values and common-value models, as well as a range of intermediate models (Wilson [1977], Milgrom [1979a,b, 1981a], Milgrom and Weber [1982a,b]). The most general models allow the value of the goods to any one bidder to depend on his tastes, the tastes of other bidders, the preferences of nonparticipants, and various unobserved qualities of goods. All of the issues described can be treated in this framework.

The second important way in which bidding models differ is in their distributional assumptions. The value estimate that a bidder makes – or his reservation price in a private-values model – is represented by a real-valued random variable, called the bidder's *type*. One common assumption is that the types are statistically independent. In an auction for a painting, the independent types assumption rules out the possibility that a bidder, finding the painting to be quite beautiful, might expect others to admire it as well. In the sale of mineral rights, it rules out the possibility that a bidder, upon receiving a discouraging geological report, may expect his competitors to receive discouraging reports. In Section 4, we consider a model in which the bidders' types are positively correlated or, more precisely, *affiliated*. The concept of affiliation is defined in that section.

The *independent private-values* model combines the independent types and private-values assumptions. We begin the formal analysis of auctions by studying that model. Henceforth, we make the simplifying assumption that each bidder wants only one unit of the good.

3   The independent private-values model

To penetrate to the heart of a bidder's decision problem, it is useful to abstract from the particular rules of the auction and focus directly on

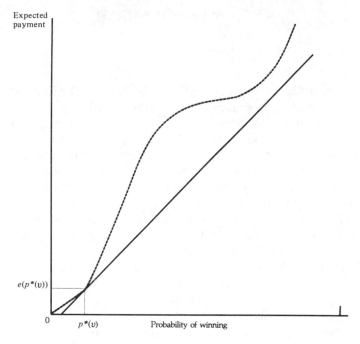

Expected
payment

$e(p^*(v))$

0          $p^*(v)$ Probability of winning

Figure 1

matters of concern to a bidder. Given the private-values assumption, if
the bidder is risk neutral, his choice of bids affects his payoff only to the
extent that it affects either his probability of winning a unit or the amount
he expects to pay. Figure 1 displays the bidder's abstract choice problem.

In the figure, the curve $(p, e(p))$ represents the menu of (probability,
expected payment) pairs available to the bidder. If the bidder values
a unit at v, his expected payoff u from the point $(p, e(p))$ is $u =
p \cdot v - e(p)$, so his indifference curves are lines with slope v. The inter-
cept of the indifference line with the vertical axis is $-u$, the negative
of the expected payoff.

Let $(p^*, e(p^*))$ denote the most preferred point for the bidder; then
we may write $p^* = p^*(v)$.[2] One can see from the figure that the p^*
function must be increasing and that if $e(\cdot)$ is differentiable at $p^*(v)$, then
$e'(p^*(v)) = v$. Even if e is not differentiable, one can establish the
following result.

---

[2] If there are several optimal points, p^* may be chosen arbitrarily from among them. Note
that p^* is essentially the dual functional of e.

Lemma 1 (Myerson [1981], Riley and Samuelson [1981]):

$$e(p^*(x)) = e(p^*(0)) + \int_0^x s \, dp^*(s).$$

In most treatments of the independent private-values model, it is assumed that the seller sets some minimum price r (the "reserve" price) and that bidders' types are drawn from some known distribution F with a positive density f. For the Vickrey and discriminatory auctions, a strategy is a function β that maps a bidder's type x into his nonnegative bid $\beta(x)$. Because the rules of the auctions treat bidders symmetrically and because we have made symmetric assumptions about the bidders, we shall look for a symmetric equilibrium point.

For the Vickrey auction, the analysis of equilibrium is relatively easy. Let there be n bidders ($n > k$) and let their types be $\mathbf{X}_1, \ldots, \mathbf{X}_n$. Let $\mathbf{Y}_1, \ldots, \mathbf{Y}_{n-1}$ denote the maximum, $\ldots$, minimum among $\mathbf{X}_2, \ldots, \mathbf{X}_n$. A typical bidder, say bidder 1, has a dominant strategy. If he observes $\mathbf{X}_1 = x$, he bids $\beta(x) = x$. If the others also adopt this strategy, bidder 1 of type x will be awarded a unit of the good if $x > \max(r, \mathbf{Y}_k)$, and the price charged will be $\mathbf{Y} = \max(r, \mathbf{Y}_k)$. Bidder 1's probability of winning at equilibrium with type x is zero if $x < r$ and is $P\{\mathbf{Y} < x\}$ otherwise. In summary, we have $p^*(x) = P\{\mathbf{Y} \leq x\}$ and $e(p^*(x)) = P\{\mathbf{Y} \leq x\} \cdot E[\mathbf{Y}|\mathbf{Y} \leq x]$.

In the discriminatory auction, the required monotonicity of p^* implies that the symmetric equilibrium strategy β must be nondecreasing, and it isn't hard to show that β must be increasing. Hence, for this auction, $p^*(x) = P\{\mathbf{Y} \leq x\}$, just as it was for the Vickrey auction. Also, as with the Vickrey auction, $e(p^*(0)) = e(0) = 0$. Hence, by Lemma 1, the bidders must have the same expected payment function as in the Vickrey auction. Then since $e(p^*(x)) = p^*(x) \cdot \beta(x)$, we have the following result.

Proposition 1 (Vickrey [1961], Ortega-Reichert [1968]): *The symmetric equilibrium strategy of the discriminatory auction game is given by*

$$\beta(x) = \begin{cases} E[\mathbf{Y}|\mathbf{Y} < x] & \text{if } x \geq r \\ 0 & \text{if } x < r. \end{cases}$$

The expected price, the expected number of sales, and the seller's expected revenue from the discriminatory auction are the same as from the Vickrey auction.

One can analyze a wide variety of auctions by the same technique and always reach the same conclusion: the equilibrium allocation of goods, the expected bidder profits, and the expected seller revenues are the same as in the Vickrey auction. A general statement of this equivalence principle, based on the lemma, goes as follows.

Proposition 2 (Revenue equivalence principle): *Consider the independent private-values symmetric auction model with risk-neutral bidders. If, at equilibrium, units of the good are awarded to just those bidders whose types exceed* $\mathbf{Y}$, *and if bidders whose types are less than r pay nothing, then the expected payment of a bidder of type x is equal to* $P\{\mathbf{Y} \leq x\} \cdot E[\mathbf{Y}|\mathbf{Y} < x]$.

Proposition 2 applies to a large number of auction games including both simultaneous auctions like the discriminatory and Vickrey auctions and some *sequential* auctions − auctions where units are sold in sequence, one at a time. The proposition can be used to derive the equilibrium strategies in some sequential auction games. For example, suppose k objects are to be sold by a sequence of k discriminatory auctions. Suppose that the winning bid is announced after each round, and let b_1, $b_2, \ldots, b_k$ denote these winning bids. A strategy is a collection of functions $\beta_1(\cdot)$, $\beta_2(\cdot; b_1), \ldots, \beta_k(\cdot; b_1, \ldots, b_{k-1})$ that specify how to bid at each round, as a function of the bidder's type and the winning bids at earlier rounds.

Let us hypothesize that each $\beta_j(\cdot; b_1, \ldots, b_{j-1})$ is increasing, so that the winner at the jth round will be the jth highest type. By Proposition 2, at equilibrium, the expected payment by a bidder of type x $(x \geq r)$ who has not yet won an object after the jth round is $P\{\mathbf{Y} \leq x|\mathbf{Y}_j > x\} \cdot E[\mathbf{Y}|\mathbf{Y} < x, \mathbf{Y}_j > x]$. Starting with $j = k$ and working backward, one can deduce that a bidder's expected payment at stage j is $P\{\mathbf{Y}_{j-1} > x > \mathbf{Y}_j\} \cdot E[\mathbf{Y}|\mathbf{Y}_{j-1} > x > \mathbf{Y}_j]$, and from that one can guess the equilibrium strategy.

Proposition 3: *The symmetric equilibrium strategy in the sequential discriminatory auction game is given by*

$$\beta_j(x; b_1, \ldots, b_{j-1}) = \begin{cases} E[\mathbf{Y}|\mathbf{Y}_{j-1} > x > \mathbf{Y}_j] & \text{if } x \geq r \\ 0 & \text{if } x < r \end{cases}$$

for $j = 1, \ldots, k$.

One can similarly analyze the sequential Vickrey auction. That auction has no dominant-strategy equilibrium, because at each round (except the last) the bidder must weigh the value of submitting a low bid at the current round and possibly acquiring a unit at a later round against the value of acquiring a unit immediately. It is clear that at the last round, the dominant strategy is $\beta_k(x; b_1, \ldots, b_{k-1}) = x$. At the next to last round, the expected payment of a player of type x who has not yet won is $P\{\mathbf{Y} \leqslant x | \mathbf{Y}_{k-2} < x\} \cdot E[\mathbf{Y} | \mathbf{Y}_k < x < \mathbf{Y}_{k-2}]$ by Proposition 2. If he wins at the last round, his expected payment is $E[\mathbf{Y} | \mathbf{Y}_k < x < \mathbf{Y}_{k-1}]$, so his conditional expected payment at the next to last round, conditional on winning then, must be $E[\mathbf{Y} | \mathbf{Y}_{k-1} < x < \mathbf{Y}_{k-2}]$. This must be equal to $E[\beta_{k-1}(\mathbf{Y}_{k-1}; b_1, \ldots, b_{k-2}) | \mathbf{Y}_{k-1} < x < \mathbf{Y}_{k-2}.]$ So, $\beta_{k-1}(x; b_1, \ldots, b_{k-2}) = E[\mathbf{Y} | \mathbf{Y} < x < \mathbf{Y}_{k-1}]$. Arguing inductively leads to the following result.

Proposition 4: *The symmetric equilibrium strategy in the sequential Vickrey auction game is given by*

$$\beta_j(x; b_1, \ldots, b_{j-1}) = \begin{cases} E[\mathbf{Y} | \mathbf{Y}_{j+1} < x < \mathbf{Y}_j] & \text{if } x \geqslant r \\ 0 & \text{if } x < r \end{cases}$$

for $j = 1, \ldots, k$.

Several authors have considered the problem of designing an auction for a single object that maximizes the seller's expected revenue (an "optimal auction"). The intent of this theory is both positive (to explain existing selling arrangements) and normative (to determine an appropriate auction design for the sale of T-bills or government-owned properties, or for purchasing supplies or services). The various papers in the "optimal auctions" literature vary in their distributional assumptions: Myerson [1981] and Riley and Samuelson [1981] assume that the bidders' types are continuously distributed on a convex set, while Harris and Raviv [1982] and Maskin and Riley [1981] work with discrete distributions. By adopting Vickrey's [1961, 1962] original approach to modeling uncertainty in auctions, one can unify these diverse results. Indeed, using this approach, we extend them to the case where more than one item is to be sold, and more generally to the case where the kth item can be produced and delivered at a cost c_k where the sequence $\{c_k\}$ is nondecreasing. However, we retain the independence and private-value assumptions along with the assumptions that bidders are risk neutral and that each bidder desires only one item.

Vickrey's approach was this: Let each bidder's type be distributed uniformly on the interval $(0,1)$. A bidder of type x has a reservation price $\bar{F}(x)$, where $\bar{F}$ is some nondecreasing function. Thus, a bidder of type x who acquires a unit for the price b has a payoff of $\bar{F}(x) - b$. Essentially,

$\bar{F}$ is the inverse of the distribution F of bidder reservation prices: for y in the support of F, $\bar{F}(F(y)) = y$. In general, for any given distribution of reservation prices F, $\bar{F}(x) = \inf\{t|F(t) > x\}$.

If, faced with a single buyer, the seller sets a price of $\bar{F}(t)$, he will sell the goods with probability $(1 - t)$, so his expected revenue is $(1 - t)\bar{F}(t)$. If this expected revenue function is not concave, then for some values of t there exist types $t' > t > t''$ and $s \in [0,1]$ such that

$$st' + (1 - s)t'' = t,$$

and

$$s(1 - t') \, \bar{F}(t') + (1 - s)(1 - t'') \, \bar{F}(t'') > (1 - t) \, \bar{F}(t).$$

In that case, the seller could randomize among the prices $\bar{F}(t')$ and $\bar{F}(t'')$ with probabilities s and $(1 - s)$, sell the object with probability $1 - t$, and gain more expected revenue than would be possible by fixing a price of $\bar{F}(t)$. Hence, the maximal expected revenue to a seller among all schemes that involve picking a price at random, and for which the probability of sale is exactly $1 - t$ is $H(t)$, where H is the minimum concave function such that for all t, $H(t) \geq (1 - t)\bar{F}(t)$.

As was noted earlier, in any auction game, the probability of acquiring a unit p^* must be a nondecreasing function of the bidder's type, and the seller's expected revenue depends only on that probability function p^* and $e(p^*(0))$. The seller can implement any nondecreasing p^* by randomizing over the price he demands. Then $-e(p^*(0))$ can be interpreted as a lump sum the seller chooses to pay buyers just for participating in the auction. In an expected-revenue maximizing auction, one must certainly have that $e(p^*(0)) = 0$. Therefore, $H(t)$ is the maximal expected revenue to a seller among all selling schemes that sell with a probability of precisely $1 - t$.[3] If the cost of supplying the item is c, then the seller's optimal selling scheme can be determined by maximizing $H(t) - (1 - t)c$. If the optimum value t^* is not zero or one, we must have $H'(t^*) = -c$. Generally, to allow that H' may not be differentiable at t^*, let $t^* = \inf\{t|H'(t) < -c\}$.

The general optimal selling problem for the independent private-values model with n risk-neutral buyers can be formulated by allowing the cost c_k of supplying the kth unit to vary with k. Consider the case where $c_1 \leq c_2 \leq \ldots$. By setting $c_1 = 0$ and $c_j = +\infty$ for all $j \geq 2$, one obtains the optimal selling strategy for a single costless object. Except for Harris and Raviv [1981], previous analysis have limited attention to this special case.

---

[3] Roger Myerson suggested this interpretation of H to me.

One particularly transparent case to analyze that suggests the general solution is the case of constant unit production costs c. In that case, the optimal selling problem decomposes into n individual problems. Applying the previous analysis leads to the conclusion that an optimal scheme is to sell to buyer i if $H'_i(x_i) \leq -c$, at a price determined as in the one-buyer problem. The generalizable attributes of this solution turn out to be the following ones: (i) the number of items sold is the largest k such that there are at least k buyers with $H'_i(x_i) \leq -c_k$ (by convention, $c_o = 0$), (ii) the buyers awarded items are the k buyers with the smallest values of $H'_i(x_i)$ (ties can be broken in any fashion), and (iii) the price is determined as in the one-buyer problem.

Combining this result with the revenue equivalence theorem leads to the following result, which generalizes several previous optimal auction results.

Proposition 5: *A symmetric auction game with production cost c_k for the kth item maximizes seller profits if at its equilibrium, (i) the number of items sold is the largest k such that at least k bidders have $H'(x_i) \leq -c_k$, (ii) the items are awarded to the k buyers for which $H'(x_i)$ is lowest, with ties broken at random, and (iii) the expected payment by each bidder not awarded an item is zero.*

A great deal of attention has been focused on the case where exactly k items are offered for sale and the seller's personal reservation price is c. One question that is sometimes asked is: How do the standard auction mechanisms perform in this setting?

The answer hinges on the concavity of the function $(1 - t)\bar{F}(t)$. When that function is not concave, the standard auctions do not maximize expected seller revenues; but when it is concave (as it is when F is the cumulative distribution function of a normal, exponential, or uniform distribution), then the discriminatory, Vickrey, sequential discriminatory, and sequential Vickrey auctions with a reserve price of $\bar{F}(t^*)$ (where $H'(t^*) = c$) are all expected-revenue-maximizing auctions. This result relies on the independent types, private values, symmetry, and risk-neutrality assumptions. It does not generalize to the case of risk-averse bidders.

When bidders are risk averse, it is still a dominant strategy in the Vickrey auction for a bidder of type x to bid x. In the discriminatory auction, however, risk-averse bidders will tend to bid higher than is required to maximize expected profits. To see why this is so, notice that a small increase Δb in the bid from the expected-profit-maximizing level reduces profits on the order of $(\Delta b)^2$ (that follows from the first-order maximality condition), but the increase Δb reduces the riskiness of the lottery a bidder faces by raising his chance of winning (on the order of Δb) and reducing his expected profit conditional on winning.

Implicitly, by raising their bids slightly, risk-averse bidders can buy "partial insurance," on actuarially fair terms, against losing, and this opportunity is seized in the equilibrium strategies of the discriminatory, sequential discriminatory, and sequential Vickrey auctions. That fact leads to this result.

Proposition 6 (Matthews [1979], Holt [1980], Maskin and Riley [1980], Harris and Raviv [1982], Milgrom and Weber [1982a]): *In the indepen-dent private-values model with risk-averse bidders, the expected pay-ment by a winning bidder of any type x (conditional on winning) is larger in the discriminatory auction than in the Vickrey auction. In particular, the expected revenue is larger in the discriminatory auction.*

Proposition 6 provides some formal justification for the argument that price discrimination in T-bill auctions raises the government's ex-pected revenue from the sale. However, we shall see in Section 4 that statistical dependence among the bidders' types favors Vickrey auctions over discriminatory auctions, so the matter remains ambiguous.

Two common auction forms that we have not yet discussed in this section are the English and the Dutch. These auctions are most com-monly used to sell one object at a time. In the English auction for a single object, each bidder has a dominant strategy: he should remain active until the price called by the auctioneer exceeds his reservation price. If this strategy is universally adopted, the object will be awarded to the bidder who values it most highly for a price equal to the second highest valuation. This outcome is identical to the outcome in the Vickrey auction, and for that reason Vickrey considered the two auctions equivalent. Actually, this equivalence hinges on the private-values assumption: when we drop that assumption, quite a different conclusion will emerge.

In the Dutch auction, a bidder of type x must decide as the price falls whether to stop the auction and claim the prize or whether to let the price continue to fall. Given any strategy that the bidder may adopt, there is a highest price $b = \beta(x)$ at which he will stop the auction. Thus, a strategy can be described as a function from types into nonnegative real numbers, which we may call "bids." The bidder choosing the highest "bid" wins and is awarded the object for a price equal to his "bid."

Notice that the Dutch auction game is identical to the discriminatory auction game. In both games, the bidder selects a "bid" as a function of his type, the high bid wins, and the winning bidder pays his bid. In short, the Dutch and discriminatory auctions are strategically equivalent, and this equivalence, unlike that of the Vickrey and English auctions, does not depend on any value or distributional assumption. However, experimental evidence obtained by Cox, Roberson, and Smith [in press] tends to refute this conclusion.

4   Affiliated types and monotone values

The model that we study in this section is more general in both its value assumptions and its distributional assumption than the independent private-values model. Specifically, let $X_1, \ldots, X_n$ be the types of the n bidders, and let $S_1, \ldots, S_m$ be any other variables that may influence the value of the goods to the bidders. The value of a unit to bidder i is designated by V_i where

$$V_i = V(X_i, \{X_j\}_{j \neq i}, S)$$

where $S = (S_1, \ldots, S_m)$. The expression $\{X_j\}_{j \neq i}$ is designed to emphasize the assumed symmetry of the valuation function; bidder, i's payoffs may depend on the preferences of the competing bidders, but only in a symmetric fashion. The *monotone values* assumption asserts that the valuation function V is nondecreasing and $E[V_i]$ is finite. The private-values assumption is the special case of the monotone-values assumption in which $V_i = X_i$. The common-value assumption is the special case in which $V_i = S_1$. Intermediate cases, in which the bidders' valuations are partly a matter of personal preference and partly dependent on observed qualities, can also be accommodated by the monotone-values assumption. Like the common-value model, these intermediate models include aspects of a winner's curse.

The equilibrium strategies in an auction game will implicitly reflect an adjustment for the winner's curse. Thus, consider bidder 1's problem in a first-price auction. Let W_1 denote the highest bid among the $n - 1$ opposing bidders; it is a random variable from bidder 1's point of view. The bidder's expected payoff from a bid of b is

$$E[(V_1 - b) \, 1_{\{W_1 < b\}} | X_1] = P\{W_1 < b \mid X_1\} \, E[V_1 - b | X_1, \{W_1 < b\}],$$

where $1_{\{W_1 < b\}}$ designates an indicator function that is one if $W_1 < b$ and zero otherwise. In words, the bidder computes his expected payoff as his probability of winning (given the information X_1) times his conditional expected winnings $V_1 - b$ *given both on his actual information* X_1 *and the hypothesis that* $W_1 < b$; the bidder anticipates the winner's curse in choosing his bid.

In addition to the monotone-values assumption, assume that all of the random elements of the model have positive partial correlations, and further that these positive correlations are preserved conditional on arbitrary restrictions on the ranges of the individual variables. Such restrictions arise in bidding models when one bidder learns or conjectures something about his competitors' bids.

The restriction on distributions just described is not vacuous. Indeed, it is identical to the assumption that the exogenous random elements of the bidding model are affiliated. A random vector $\mathbf{Z} = (\mathbf{Z}_1, \ldots, \mathbf{Z}_l)$ is *affiliated* if for every z and z' in R_l, (*) $f(z) f(z') \leq f(z \vee z') f(z \wedge z')$, where

$$z \vee z' = (\max(z_1, z_1'), \ldots, \max(z_l, z_l'))$$

$$z \wedge z' = (\min(z_1, z_1'), \ldots, \min(z_l, z_l')).$$

The inequality (*) is known as the *affiliation inequality* (and also as the "FKG inequality" and the "MTP$_2$ property"). The general theory of affiliation has been developed by Milgrom and Weber [1982a].[4]

Notice that if $\mathbf{Z}_1, \ldots, \mathbf{Z}_l$ are independent, then the affiliation inequality holds an equality. Also, in common-value models, it is usual to specify that the bidder's types $\mathbf{X}_1, \ldots, \mathbf{X}_n$ are independent estimates of S_1 drawn from some common distribution with density $f(\cdot|s_1)$, where the family of densities $\{f(\cdot|s_1)\}$ is lognormal with mean s_1, or exponential with mean s_1, or uniform on $(0, s_1)$, or some other family with the monotone likelihood ratio property. In all such cases, regardless of the prior distribution for S_1, the vector $(S_1, \mathbf{X}_1, \ldots, \mathbf{X}_n)$ is affiliated.

The key property of affiliation for our analysis is this:

Proposition 7 (Milgrom and Weber [1982a]): *If $(\mathbf{Z}_1, \ldots, \mathbf{Z}_l)$ is affiliated and g is a nondecreasing function, then the function*

$$h(a_1, \ldots, a_l; b_1, \ldots, b_l) = E[g(\mathbf{Z}) \mid a_1 \leq \mathbf{Z}_1 \leq b_1, \ldots,$$
$$a_l \leq \mathbf{Z}_l \leq b_l]$$

is nondecreasing.

To describe the equilibria of various auction games, it is useful to define the random variables $\mathbf{Y}_1, \ldots, \mathbf{Y}_{n-1}$ to be the maximum, $\ldots$, minimum from among $\mathbf{X}_2, \ldots, \mathbf{X}_n$. It has been shown (Milgrom and Weber [1982a]) that $S, \mathbf{X}_1, \mathbf{Y}_1, \ldots, \mathbf{Y}_{n-1}$ are affiliated.

Let $F_j(y|x) = P\{\mathbf{Y}_j \leq y|\mathbf{X}_1 = x\}$ and let $f_j(y|x)$ be the corresponding density. Let $v_j(x, y) = E[\mathbf{V}_1|\mathbf{X}_1 = x, \mathbf{Y}_j = y]$. In view of Proposition 7, v_j is nondecreasing.

---

[4] A survey of the theory of affiliated variables is also given by Karlin and Rinott [1980].

The model with monotone values and affiliated types is called the *general symmetrical model*. The equilibrium strategies for the Vickrey and discriminatory auctions for this model are given by the next two propositions, where $x^* = \inf\{x | E[V_k | X_1 = x, Y_k \leq x] \geq r\}$; x^* is called the *screening level* corresponding to r.

Proposition 8 (Milgrom [1981]): *The symmetric equilibrium strategy in the Vickrey auction game is given by*

$$\beta^V(x) = \begin{cases} v_k(x, x) & \text{if } x \geq x^* \\ 0 & \text{if } x < x^*. \end{cases}$$

Proposition 9 (Milgrom and Weber [1982a,b], Wilson [1977]): *The symmetric equilibrium strategy in the discriminatory auction game is given by*[5]

$$\beta^D(x) = \begin{cases} r \cdot L_k(x^*|x) + \int_{x^*}^{x} v_k(t, t) \, dL_k(t|x) & \text{if } x \geq x^* \\ 0 & \text{if } x < x^* \end{cases}$$

where

$$L_k(\alpha|x) = \exp\left[- \int_{\alpha}^{x} \frac{f_k(t|t)}{F_k(t|t)} \, dt \right].$$

Notice that with a private-values assumption, the equilibrium strategy in the Vickrey auction becomes $\beta^V(x) = x$. With independent types, $L_k(t|x) = F_k(t) / F_k(x)$, and the discriminatory auction equilibrium strategy becomes $\beta^D(x) = E[\max(r, v_k(Y_k, Y_k)) | Y_k < x]$, which further simplifies under private values to $\beta^D(x) = E[\max(r, Y_k) | Y_k < x]$, in accordance with Proposition 1.

Now, motivated by the Treasury bill controversy, we may ask which of the two auctions, Vickrey or discriminatory, leads to greater revenues for the seller in the general symmetric model.

Proposition 10 (Milgrom and Weber [1982a,b]): *The expected price paid by a winning bidder of type x in the Vickrey auction is as high as, or higher than, that paid in the discriminatory auction:*

$$\beta^D(x) \leq E[\max(r, \beta^V(Y_k)) | X_1 = x, Y_k < x].$$

Consequently, the expected revenue to the seller is higher for the Vickrey auction than for the discriminatory auction.

---

[5] For s not in the support of X_1, $f_k(s|s)/F_k(s|s)$ is taken to be zero.

Results reported by Tsao and Vignola [1977] tend to confirm this conclusion using data drawn from the weekly T-bill auction.

An important general intuition lies behind Proposition 10 that will shortly enable us to generate a host of similar comparisons. The key insight is best seen by abstracting from the particular rules of the auction and representing a bidder's choice problem in a new way. In each auction game that we have studied, the bidders' strategies were increasing functions of their types, and by bidding $\beta(x)$, any bidder, regardless of his actual type, could arrange to win whenever $\max(x^*, \mathbf{Y}_k) < x$. We may therefore think of a bidder as choosing x, rather than as choosing particular bids.

Consider the problem faced by bidder 1 when his type is z in some auction game "A". If he chooses some $x \geq x^*$ and wins, then conditional on winning the expected value received is $R(x, z) = E[V_1|X_1 = z, \mathbf{Y}_k < x]$ and the expected payment is some amount $W^A(x, z)$. The two sides of the inequality in Proposition 10 represent $W^A(x, x)$ for the discriminatory and Vickrey auctions, respectively.

When bidder 1 chooses x, his expected payoff is $[R(x, z) - W^A(x, z)] F_k(x|z)$. At a symmetric equilibrium, it must be optimal for the bidder to choose $x = z$, so the first-order necessary condition is

$$0 = [R(z, z) - W^A(z, z)]f_k(z|z) + [R_1(z, z) - W_1^A(z, z)]F_k(z|z),$$

where subscripts on R and W^A denote partial derivatives. Solving for W_1^A, one can compute the total derivative of W^A.

$$\frac{d}{dz} W^A(z, z) = W_1^A(z, z) + W_2^A(z, z)$$

$$= R_1(z, z) + [R(z, z) - W^A(z, z)] \frac{f_k(z, z)}{F_k(z|z)} + W_2^A(z, z).$$

$$(**)$$

In each of the auctions studied, $W^A(x^*, x^*) = r$, and that boundary condition plus the differential equation (**) completely determine the $W^A(z, z)$ function. The differential equations corresponding to different auctions are identical, except for the W_2^A term.

It now follows that the winner's expected payment across different auctions can be compared by comparing the partial derivatives W_2^A. When the bidders' types are statistically independent, W_2^A is necessarily zero for all auction games. This fact can be used to derive Proposition 2, the revenue equivalence principle. More generally, different auction games yield different average revenues. The key to comparing games is the *linkage principle*, which is a consequence of equation (**).

The linkage principle: Let A and B be two auction games with symmetric equilibrium at which (1) units are awarded to all bidders with types $z > \max(x^*, \mathbf{X}_{(k+1)})$ and (2) bidders with types $z \leq x^*$ have expected payoff zero. If $W_2^A(z, z) \geq W_2^B(z, z)$ for all $z \geq x^*$, then $W^A(z, z) \geq W^B(z, z)$ for all $z \geq x^*$.

The function W_2^A summarizes the effect of the bidder's unobserved type on the amount he expects to pay. That effect arises only when the variables of the model are statistically dependent. As the winning bidder's actual type z rises, he expects the types of others to rise as well. If the price he pays depends on those types, then he expects the price to rise; that is, $W_2^A > 0$.

In the discriminatory auction, $W^D(x, z) = \beta^D(x)$ and $W_2^D = 0$: the equilibrium price is determined exclusively by the winner's type, so there is no linkage at all. In the Vickrey auction, $W^V(x, z) = E[\max(r, v_k(\mathbf{Y}_k, \mathbf{Y}_k))|X_1 = z, \mathbf{Y}_k < x]$. The Vickrey price depends on $\mathbf{Y}_k$ which is statistically linked to $\mathbf{X}_1$. By Proposition 6, $W_2^V \geq 0$. These observations and the linkage principle establish Proposition 10.

A second application of the linkage principle arises in connection with analyzing whether the seller, if he has information $\mathbf{X}_0$ of his own, should establish a policy of revealing that information, or whether he would be better off concealing it. A key word here is "policy": the idea is that the seller must commit himself to revealing information according to some rule. For example, the U.S. Congress could instruct the Department of Interior to conduct geologic surveys before offering the mineral rights on any piece of property. It could also order the Department to adopt a policy of always reporting the survey in detail, or summarizing it, or reporting it only if the information is favorable. In this last case, however, the bidders would "hear the silence" − withholding the report would be a sure sign of an unfavorable survey.

When $\mathbf{X}_0$ is reported, the set of bidders willing to bid at least r will be changed. However, the seller can choose to use the survey data to set an appropriate reserve price. We shall say that the seller has adopted a *fixed screening-level* policy at x^* if, upon reporting his information $\mathbf{X}_0$, he sets the reserve price $r = r(\mathbf{X}_0)$ to attract exactly those bidders whose types are at least x^*. When the seller reports all of his information and adopts a fixed screening-level policy at x^*, it can be shown that the conditions of the linkage principle are satisfied. That leads to the following result.

Proposition 11 (Milgrom and Weber [1982a]): *In a discriminatory auction, a policy of revealing $\mathbf{X}_0$ and fixing the screening level at x^* results in greater expected revenue than withholding the information and setting the screening level at x^*.*

Adopting the prescribed policy links the price to X_0, and X_0 is affiliated with the winning bidder's estimate. That linkage results in W_2^A being positive for the auction with X_0 announced. Proposition 11 follows as a consequence.

If the seller reports only a summary statement about X_0 – for example if he reports only that X_0 lies in some set T_0 – then conditional on that information, the variables $X_0, X_1, \ldots, X_n$ are still affiliated. Hence, by Proposition 11, reporting the remaining details of X_0 and fixing the screening level would further raise expected revenues. This observation leads to Proposition 12.

Proposition 12 (Milgrom and Weber [1982a]): *In a discriminatory auction, the expected-revenue maximizing policy for revealing information and setting a reserve price involves reporting X_0 precisely and in full detail.*

In the Vickrey auction, there is already some linkage of the price to variables other than the winner's type, but one can sometimes raise revenues further by introducing additional linkages. For example, the seller can raise revenues by reporting his information X_0.

Proposition 13 (Milgrom and Weber [1982a]): *In a Vickrey auction, a policy of revealing X_0 and fixing the screening level at x^* results in greater expected revenues than withholding the information and setting the screening level at x^*.*

Proposition 14 (Milgrom and Weber [1982a]): *In a Vickrey auction, the expected-revenue maximizing policy for revealing information and setting a reserve price involves reporting X_0 precisely and in full detail.*

In a discriminatory auction, revealing information has two effects. First, if $X_0, \ldots, X_n$ are strictly affiliated, then the seller's information tells each bidder something about his competitor's type. As a result, the bidders with lower types will, on average, raise their assessments of their competitors' bids. They will then bid more aggressively, and that will tend to make the higher types raise their bids, too. This effect is present even in a private-values model if types are affiliated. The next effect appears only in models involving the winner's curse. In such models, bidders tend to shade their bids to avoid the curse, and the lower types, who are overly pessimistic, shade their bids excessively. When the seller provides public information, he alleviates the winner's curse, allowing lower types to bid more aggressively on average, which in turn causes everyone to bid more aggressively. This raises revenues.

In contrast to the discriminatory auction, revealing information has no effect in the Vickrey auction game with private values, since the bidders all follow their dominant strategy ($\beta^V(x) = x$) regardless of the content of the seller's information. But if the private-values assumption does not hold and a winner's curse effect is present, then revealing affiliated information alleviates the winner's curse and causes the average price to rise: the inequality in Proposition 13 becomes strict.

Recall that in any private-values model, the Vickrey and English auctions are equivalent. In the general model, this equivalence may not hold. The equivalence or lack thereof depends on how much of the bidding behavior of the $n - 2$ lowest types can be observed during the auction by the two highest types. If none of their bidding can be observed, then the Vickrey and English auctions are strategically equivalent. Milgrom and Weber [1982a] have computed equilibrium strategies for the case where all of the bidding behavior can be observed. Observing those bids passes information to the last two bidders, with much the same effect (at equilibrium) as if the seller had revealed his information: Prices become linked monotonically to the types of $n - 2$ lowest bidders as well as to the types of the second highest bidder. Then, three new propositions follow, using the linkage principle.

Proposition 15 (Milgrom and Weber [1982a]): *The expected price paid by a winning bidder in the English auction is as high as, or higher than, that paid in the Vickrey auction.*

Proposition 16 (Milgrom and Weber [1982a]): *In an English auction, a policy of revealing $\mathbf{X}_0$ and fixing the screening level at x^* results in greater expected revenue than withholding the information and setting the screening level at x^*.*

Proposition 17 (Milgrom and Weber [1982a]): *In an English auction, the expected-revenue maximizing policy for revealing information and setting a reserve price involves reporting $\mathbf{X}_0$ precisely and in full detail.*

Some work has been done studying the incentives of bidders to gather information in a common value model. In a detailed example, Schweizer and von Ungern-Sternberg [1980] show that it may not pay a bidder to acquire information if his competitors will learn that he has done so. Lee [1982] notes that the seller can, by providing information, discourage bidders from gathering their own information (if such is costly). That policy tends to raise the expected price in a discriminatory auction.

Milgrom [1981] has studied the bidders' incentives to acquire information in a Vickrey auction and has proved the following result.

Proposition 18: *In a common-value model for a single object, let bidders* $1, \ldots, n$ *adopt the equilibrium strategies given in Proposition 7. Let there be an* $(n + 1)$*st bidder whose information* $\mathbf{X}_{n+1}$ *is a garbling of that of bidder 1 (i.e., the joint distribution of* $\mathbf{S}, \mathbf{X}_0, \ldots, \mathbf{X}_n$ *given both* $\mathbf{X}_1$ *and* $\mathbf{X}_{n+1}$ *does not depend on the value of* $\mathbf{X}_{n+1}$*). Then there is no strategy for bidder* $n + 1$ *that yields a positive expected payoff. Hence, an equilibrium of* $(n + 1)$*-bidder game ensues if bidders* $1, \ldots, n$ *use* β^V *and bidder* $n + 1$ *always bids zero.*

Following a different line of thought, Wilson [1977] and Milgrom [1979a,b] have studied how the price resulting from a first-price (discriminatory) auction aggregates the information of the many bidders. It might seem that the price could not reflect more information than was available to the winning bidder, since his bid sets the price. However, this reasoning is not correct. The winning bidder's type is a maximum order statistic from a (possibly large) sample, and such a statistic can sometimes reveal quite a lot of information.

In one version of the Wilson–Milgrom model, the bidder's types are independent estimates of the common value $\mathbf{S}_1$, drawn from a distribution with density $f(\cdot|\mathbf{S}_1)$, where the family of densities $\{f(\cdot|s)\}$ has the monotone likelihood ratio property. The upshot of their investigations is the following theorem.

Proposition 19: *Let a subscript of* n *denote the number of bidders in an auction. The following three statements are equivalent.*

(1) *The winning bid* $\beta_n^D(\mathbf{X}_{(1)})$ *is a consistent estimator*[6] *of* $\mathbf{S}_1$.
(2) *There exists some functions* g_n *such that* $g_n(\mathbf{X}_{(1)})$ *is a consistent estimator of* $\mathbf{S}_1$.
(3) *For any* $s < s'$, $\inf_x [f(x|s)/f(x|s')] = 0$.

The equivalence of the first two statements means that the first-price auction generates consistent estimates of $\mathbf{S}_1$ whenever any consistent estimator based on the maximum order statistic exists. The third statement makes it easy to check which distributions lead to consistency; in particular, if the types are normally distributed with mean $\mathbf{S}_1$ and fixed variance, or if they are uniformly distributed on $[0, \mathbf{S}_1]$, consistency does

---

[6] In other words, if $\mathbf{W}_n = \beta_n^D(\mathbf{X}_{(1)})$ denotes the winning bid in an auction with n bidders, then $\mathbf{W}_n$ converges in probability to $\mathbf{S}_1$.

follow, but if they are exponentially distributed with mean S_1, it does not.

When the winning bid is not a consistent estimator of S_1 in this model, there are two other possibilities. The first is that there is a degeneracy: there are two values s' and s'' such that for all $s \in (s', s'')$, $f(\cdot|s) \equiv f(\cdot|s')$. This case can be eliminated by reformulating the problem, replacing S_1 by its expected value conditional on the whole sequence $\{X_k\}$. The resulting game has the same normal form as the original game, and the degeneracy noted previously does not arise.

If the degeneracy described previously has been ruled out and the winning bid still does not consistently estimate S_1, then there is often a nonnegligible difference between the highest and second highest bidders' "estimates" of S_1, where the bidder's estimate is made conditional on his observed X_i and the hypothesis that X_i is the maximum observation. In that case, the bidder will attempt to earn nonnegligible positive profits. He will often succeed. Indeed, it can be shown for this case that as the number of bidders grows large, the bidders' total expected profits remain bounded away from zero and the seller's expected revenue remains bounded away from $E[S_1]$. The asymptotic expected profits depend only on the asymptotic likelihood ratios: $\inf_x f(x|s)/f(x|s')$.

5   Incentives for gathering information

It is well known that in any formal decision problem, information has nonnegative value. Effectively, information enlarges a decision maker's set of strategies because it permits basing a decision on more variables. In multiperson settings, the issues become subtler, because *if a decision maker is known to have gathered additional information*, the other agents may choose to revise their strategies. Such changes may either benefit or harm the decision maker. It is always true, however, that if a decision maker can costlessly gather information without letting anyone else become aware of that fact (use "covertly gathered information"), then he or she would benefit from (or at least not be harmed by) doing so.

To study the incentives of the bidders and the seller in an auction game to gather information, we shall deal with a simple model of asymmetrically informed bidders. This model was introduced by Wilson [1967] in response to a description by Woods [1965] of a competition between two oil companies bidding for oil and gas rights on U.S. government-owned territory. One company owned the rights on an adjacent tract and had been able to explore the new tract by drilling at an angle. The other company had access only to publicly available geologic data.

To model this situation, let V be the common value of the rights. Assume that $V > 0$ and $E[V]$ is finite. Let the random variable X represent the private information of the better-informed bidder whom we call bidder A. No assumptions about $\mathbf{X}$ are necessary; its values may lie in any measurable space. We assume the reserve price set by seller is zero.

Bidder A's decision problem actually depends on $\mathbf{X}$ only through the resulting estimate of $\mathbf{V}$: let $\mathbf{H} = H(\mathbf{X}) = E[\mathbf{V}|\mathbf{X}]$ denote that estimate. Let $\mathbf{U}$ denote a random variable, independent of $(\mathbf{V}, \mathbf{X})$, that is uniformly distributed on $(0,1)$. We assume that A observes $\mathbf{U}$ and uses it whenever he needs to randomize. A strategy for A is then a function $\beta: R_+ \times (0,1) \to R_+$, where $\beta(h, u)$ represents the bid made when $(\mathbf{H},\mathbf{U}) = (h,u)$. There is no loss of generality in restricting β to be nondecreasing in u.

A randomized strategy for the uninformed bidder B is simply a probability distribution function G on R_+. The auction is a discriminatory auction, and its equilibrium is given below.

Proposition 20 (Weverburgh [1979], Engelbrecht-Wiggans, Milgrom, and Weber [1981]): *In the asymmetric common-value model described previously, there is a unique Nash equilibrium point of the first-price auction game. The equilibrium strategies are*

$$\beta(h, u) = E[\mathbf{H}|\{\mathbf{H} < h \text{ or } (\mathbf{H} = h \text{ and } \mathbf{U} \leqslant u)\}]$$
$$G(b) = P\{\beta(\mathbf{H}, \mathbf{U}) \leqslant b\}.$$

To analyze how the seller's revenues and the bidders' profits depend on the better-informed bidder's information, let F denote the distribution of $\mathbf{H}$. Then, profits and revenues at the unique equilibrium are as follows.

Proposition 21 (Engelbrecht-Wiggans, Milgrom and Weber [1981]): *At equilibrium the expected profit of the better-informed bidder conditional on $\mathbf{H} = h$ is*

$$\int_0^h F(s) \, ds$$

and unconditionally it is

$$\int_0^\infty F(s) \, (1 - F(s)) \, ds.$$

The expected profit of the worse-informed bidder is zero. The seller's expected revenue is

$$\int_0^\infty (1 - F(s))^2 \, ds.$$

A host of conclusions flow from Proposition 21. First, consider what would happen to bidder B if he acquired some of A's information. If he could do so *covertly*, there would be no competitive response, and B would clearly benefit. If, however, it were common knowledge that B had gathered that information, Proposition 21 would apply, and B's profit would still be zero. Thus, as Milgrom and Weber [1982] have observed, B cannot gain by overtly collecting some of A's information.

If A could observe some additional variable $\mathbf{Z}$, his new estimate would be $\mathbf{H}' = E[\mathbf{V}|\mathbf{X}, \mathbf{Z}]$. If B believed that A had observed only $\mathbf{X}$, he would bid according to G. Then, if $\mathbf{H}' = h$, bidder A's maximal expected profit would be $\int_0^h F(s)\ ds$, by Proposition 21. (Notice that this profit depends only on B's strategy and on A's estimate; it does not matter whether A based his estimate on much information or on little.) If, on the other hand, B knew that A had observed both $\mathbf{X}$ and $\mathbf{Z}$, then A's maximal expected profit would be $\int_0^h F'(s)\ ds$, where F' is the distribution of $\mathbf{H}'$. Which of these two scenarios does A prefer?

Proposition 22 (Milgrom and Weber [1982]): *For any realizations of* $\mathbf{X}$ *and* $\mathbf{Z}$, *bidder A prefers that B know that A has observed both variables over having B believe that A has observed only* $\mathbf{X}$; *that is, for every h,*

$$\int_0^h F'(s)\ ds > \int_0^h F(s)\ ds.$$

In summary, the better-informed bidder prefers to do his information gathering *overtly*. When B knows that A has observed $\mathbf{Z}$, he realizes that he has become more vulnerable to the winner's curse, so he shades his bids, and A benefits from that response. On the other hand, if B can gather some of A's information, he would choose to do so *covertly*, because A's response to B's better information would be to bid more aggressively when the rights are relatively valuable, thereby depriving B of his best opportunity for earning a profit.

Notice that, in view of Proposition 21, the seller's interests and A's are strictly opposed. The sum of A's expected profit and the seller's expected revenue is $E[\mathbf{V}]$. Thus, if the seller has some information $\mathbf{Z}$, it may pay him to report it to reduce A's informational advantage.

We consider two cases. First, suppose A already knows $\mathbf{Z}$. For example, A might be better informed from his drillings on an adjacent tract and $\mathbf{Z}$ might be the royalty report that A filed for that tract.

Proposition 23 (Milgrom and Weber [1982]): *If A knows* ($\mathbf{X}$, $\mathbf{Z}$), *then a policy of announcing* $\mathbf{Z}$ *reduces bidder A's expected profit and raises the* *seller's expected revenue. Moreover, no policy of summarizing, garbling, or sometimes withholding* **Z** *results in greater expected revenue than the policy of reporting it precisely and in full detail.*

If A does not already know the seller's information, the matter becomes somewhat trickier. It is possible that the seller's information, though useless to B, is very useful to the better informed bidder A, much as half of a treasure map is most useful to the holder of the other half. A statistical example capturing this idea has been given by Milgrom and Weber [1981]. There is, however, an important class of models in which this problem can never arise.

Proposition 24 (Milgrom and Weber [1982]): *Let* **X** *and* **Z** *be real valued and suppose* (**V**, **X**, **Z**) *is affiliated. Then revealing* **Z** *raises the seller's expected revenue. Moreover, no policy of summarizing, garbling, or sometimes withholding* **Z** *results in greater expected revenue than the policy of reporting it precisely and in full detail.*

Proposition 24 is yet another consequence of the linkage principle.

6   Miscellaneous topics: collusion, sequencing, and bundling

The theory surveyed in the preceding sections deals with only a few of the many interesting and important questions concerning the conduct of auctions. Certainly, the assumption that bidders behave noncooperatively cannot be taken uncritically, especially in auctions like those for timber rights where the few buyers in each region may all be members of a single trade association (cf. Mead [1967]). Nor is the assumption that the bidders compete against one another once and for all a particularly appealing one. If bidders do bid against each other repeatedly, then they may attempt to infer something about their competitors' characteristics from their bidding history.

An interesting analysis that captures this learning feature has been given by Ortega-Reichert [1968]. In his model, two manufacturers compete for supply contracts in two periods. The cost of production of each manufacturer in each period is drawn from an exponential distribution with unknown mean **t**. The unknown mean has a gamma distribution.

In the first period, each bidder i offers a supply contract for a price $p_{i1} = p_{i1}(\mathbf{C}_{i1})$. The low bidder wins and earns a profit of $p_{i1} - \mathbf{C}_{i1}$. At the end of the first period, the bids are announced and the supply contract is awarded.

In the second period, the bids are again tendered, but this time each bidder has more information to use

$$p_{i2} = p_{i2}(\mathbf{C}_{i2} \mid \mathbf{C}_{i1}, p_{i1}, p_{j1})$$

where j denotes the other bidder. Ortega-Reichert found that, at equilibrium, p_{i2} is independent of $\mathbf{C}_{i1}$, but is increasing in its other arguments. In particular, by placing higher bids in the first period, a firm could induce its competitor to place higher bids in the second period. In effect, the competitor views the firm's bid as a statistic providing relevant information about the "technology" $\mathbf{t}$.

The result of the bidders' attempts to influence their competitors' beliefs is that the prices bid at the first round are higher than they would otherwise be. In modern parlance, this is a "signaling equilibrium," because each firm tries to signal to its competitors that its future costs will be high. At equilibrium, however, each bidder recognizes the others' incentive to signal and no one is fooled.

Although it would be risky to draw any general inferences from this two-period model, the nature of the analysis does at least suggest that equilibrium in repeated contests moves away from the competitive theory in the direction of a collusive theory. This seems to hold here even in a finitely repeated game model at a symmetric Nash equilibrium. The results reported by Kreps et al. [1982] suggest that frequent interaction among the bidders may quite generally enhance incentives to collude.

All of the auction theory that we have so far considered rests on the implicit assumption that preferences have a special additive structure so that auctions for single goods can be considered in isolation. This assumption is perhaps most clearly violated in sales of the assets of bankrupt of manufacturing firms, where the value of the land, plant, and equipment together may, for some buyers, exceed the sum of their individual values. To cope with that complementarity, an institution called "entirety bidding" has emerged. In one version, the entirety bids are made before the piecemeal auction begins, and the individual objects are awarded to the winning bidders only if their sum exceeds the highest entirety bid (Cassady [1967]). In another variation, entirety bidding occurs after the piecemeal auction. At this level, auction theory merges into the general theory of resource allocation.

7   Conclusion and postscript

Auctions represent an important institution used for conducting trade. The results that have been described in this survey give a good idea of why English auctions are more popular among sellers than sealed bids and other auction designs, and why auction houses adopt the practice of revealing their own estimates of worth for the items being offered.

Still, the received theory is far from complete: it does not consider entirety bidding and problems of complementary goods; it does not deal adequately with collusion, or repeated bidding, or the nature of competition when there are many sellers as well as many buyers; it does not treat competitive bidding in connection with procurement, where suppliers often have differentiated products so that the evaluation of bids is not so straightforward. Finally, the received theory has little to say about when auctions are more appropriate than other arrangements for conducting trade. These open questions are part of the agenda for future research.

Since this survey was written in October 1981, a great deal more has been learned about the economics of auctions. Specific predictions of the theory have been tested (sometimes confirmed, sometimes not) using both empirical data and a series of laboratory experiments. The independent private-values model has been extended to models with multiple buyers and sellers and to situations where two parameters of individual preference — such as the bidder's valuation and relative risk aversion — are both unknown. The theory of optimal auctions has been modified to include the case of risk-averse buyers. And the affiliated–monotone-value model has been generalized to accommodate the sequential sale of several identical items.

It is interesting to contrast the research achievements in auction theory of the last few years with the research agenda I proposed in 1981. Little has been learned about collusion in auctions; that topic certainly deserves more attention. Less has been learned about comparisons of alternative modes of transaction: When should a purchaser bargain with individual suppliers and when should he seek bids? Too much recent research effort in auctions has been simply applying the latest techniques (principally "mechanism design") to ever more complicated models; too little has been devoted to the very real and important economic questions that auctions raise.

REFERENCES

Brimmer, A. [1962]. "Price Determination in the United States Treasury Bill Market." *Review of Economics and Statistics*, *44*:178–183.
Brown, K. [1975]. "A Note on Optimal Fixed-Price Bidding with Uncertain Production Cost." *Bell Journal of Economics*, *6*:695–697.
Capen, E. C., R. V. Clapp, and W. M. Campbell [1971]. "Competitive Bidding in High-Risk Situations." *Journal of Petroleum Technology*, *23*:641–653.
Carson, D. [1959]. "Treasury Open Market Operations." *Review of Economics and Statistics*, *41*.

Cassady, R., Jr. [1967]. *Auctions and Auctioneering*. Berkeley: University of California Press.

Cox, J., B. Roberson, and V. Smith [In press]. "Theory and Behavior of Single Object Auctions," in *Research in Experimental Economics*, vol 2, edited by V. Smith.

Engelbrecht-Wiggans, R., P. R. Milgrom, and R. J. Weber [Forthcoming]. "Competitive Bidding and Proprietary Information." *Journal of Mathematical Economics*.

Friedman, M. [1960]. *A Program for Monetary Stability*. New York: Fordham University Press.

Goldstein, H. [1962]. "The Friedman Proposal for Auctioning Treasury Bills." *Journal of Political Economy*, 70:386−392.

Griesmer, J., R. Levitan, and M. Shubik [1967]. "Toward a Study of Bidding Processes, Part IV: Games with Unknown Costs." *Naval Research Logistics Quarterly*, 14:415−433.

Harris, M., and A. Raviv [1981]. "A Theory of Monopoly Pricing Schemes with Demand Uncertainty." *American Economic Review*, 71:347−365.

Harris, M., and A. Raviv [1982]. "Allocation Mechanisms and the Design of Auctions," *Econometrica*, 49:1477−1499.

Holt, C. A., Jr. [1980]. "Competitive Bidding for Contracts under Alternative Auction Procedures." *Journal of Political Economy*, 88:433−445.

Kreps, D., P. Milgrom, J. Roberts, and R. Wilson [1982]. "Rational Cooperation in the Finitely Repeated Prisoners' Dilemma." *Journal of Economic Theory*, 27:245−252.

Lee, T. [1982]. "Resource Information Policy and Federal Resource Leasing." *Bell Journal of Economics*, 13:561−568.

Maskin, E., and J. Riley [1980]. "Auctioning an Indivisible Object." JFK School of Government, Discussion Paper no. 87D, Harvard University, Cambridge, Mass.

Maskin, E., and J. Riley [1981]. "Multi-unit auctions, Price Discrimination and Bundling." Economics Discussion Paper no. 201, University of California at Los Angeles.

Matthews, S. [1979]. "Risk Aversion and the Efficiency of First- and Second-Price Auctions." CCBA Working Paper no. 586, University of Illinois.

Mead, W. J. [1967]. "Natural Resource Disposal Policy − Oral Auction Versus Sealed Bids." *Natural Resource Planning Journal*, M:194−224.

Milgrom, P. R. [1979a]. *The Structure of Information in Competitive Bidding*. New York: Garland.

Milgrom, P. R. [1979b]. "A Convergence Theorem for Competitive Bidding with Differential Information." *Econometrica*, 47:679−688.

Milgrom, P. R. [1981]. "Rational Expectations, Information Acquisition, and Competitive Bidding." *Econometrica*, 49:921−943.

Milgrom, P. R. [1981a]. "Good News and Bad News: Representation Theorems and Applications." *Bell Journal of Economics*, 12:380−391.

Milgrom, P. R., and R. J. Weber [1982]. "The Value of Information in a Sealed-Bid Auction." *Journal of Mathematical Economics*, 10:105−114.

Milgrom, P. R., and R. J. Weber [1982a]. "A Theory of Auctions and Competitive Bidding." *Econometrica*, 50:1089−1122.

Milgrom, P. R., and R. J. Weber [1982b]. "Sequential Auctions." Unpublished notes, Northwestern University, Evanston, Ill.

Myerson, R. [1981]. "Optimal Auction Design." *Mathematics of Operations Research*, 6:58–73.

Ortega-Reichert, A. [1968]. "Models for Competitive Bidding under Uncertainty." Department of Operations Research Technical Report no. 8 (Ph.D. dissertation), Stanford University, Stanford, Calif.

Reece, D. K. [1978]. "Competitive Bidding for Offshore Petroleum Leases." *Bell Journal of Economics*, 9:369–384.

Rieber, M. [1964]. "Collusion in the Auction Market for Treasury Bills." *Journal of Political Economy*, 72:509–512.

Riley, J., and R. Zeckhauser [1983]. "Optimal Selling Strategies: When to Haggle, When to Hold Firm." *Quarterly Journal of Economics*, 98:267–290.

Riley, J., and W. Samuelson [1981]. "Optimal Auctions." *American Economic Review*, 71:381–392.

Rothkopf, M. [1969]. "A Model of Rational Competitive Bidding." *Management Science*, 15:362–373.

Schweizer, U., and T. von Ungern-Sternberg [1980]. "Sealed Bid Auctions and the Search for Better Information." Department of Economics, University of Bonn.

Smith, V. [1966]. "Bidding Theory and the Treasury Bill Auction: Does Price Discrimination Increase Bill Prices?" *Review of Economics and Statistics*, 48:141–146.

Tsao, C., and A. Vignola [1977]. "Price Discrimination and the Demand for Treasury's Long Term Securities." Preliminary Report, U.S. Department of Treasury.

Weverburgh, M. [1979]. "Competitive Bidding with Asymmetric Information Reanalysed." *Management Science*, 25:291–294.

Wilson, R. [1967]. "Competitive Bidding with Proprietary Information." *Management Science*, 13:A816–A820.

Wilson, R. [1977]. "A Bidding Model of Perfect Competition." *Review of Economic Studies*, 4:511–518.

Woods, D. [1965]. "Decision Making under Uncertainty in Hierarchical Organizations." D.B.A. dissertation, Harvard University, Cambridge, Mass.

Vickrey, W. [1961]. "Counterspeculation, Auctions, and Competitive Sealed Tenders." *Journal of Finance*, 16:8–37.

Vickrey, W. [1962]. "Auctions and Bidding Games." In *Recent Advances in Game Theory* (conference proceedings), pp. 15–27. Princeton University, Princeton, N.J.

PART II
SIX PAPERS BY ELISHA A. PAZNER

CHAPTER 10

A difficulty in the concept of fairness

Elisha A. Pazner and David Schmeidler

This note raises a new difficulty concerning the possibility of satisfying equity and Pareto efficiency objectives simultaneously. When interpersonal comparisons of utility are ruled out, which is the case considered here, there is no natural way to define the concept of equity. An appropriate criterion for equity discussed in the literature seems to be that of fairness. An allocation is said to be fair (equitable) if no individual in the society prefers the bundle allocated to anyone else over the bundle allocated to him (Dubins and Spanier [2], Foley [3] and Sen [5]).

We present here two examples of economies in which no Pareto optimal allocation is fair, even in the absence of externalities, non convexities or other deviations from the classical Arrow–Debreu environment. In the first example there are two consumers, one consumption good and two kinds of labour (one for each consumer). The production possibilities of the economy are characterized by the constant returns to scale technology set $\{(x, y, z) \in R^3 \,|\, x \leq 0,\, y \leq 0 \text{ and } x + y/10 + z \leq 0\}$. Each consumer is endowed with one unit of his labour, $(1, 0, 0)$ and $(0, 1, 0)$ respectively. The preferences of the consumers can be represented by utility functions on R^3_+: $u_1(x, y, z) = x + 11z/10$ and $u_2(x, y, z) = y + 2z$. Each consumer is thus assumed to derive utility from the consumption good and from his leisure.

Let (x_1, y_1, z_1), (x_2, y_2, z_2) be a Pareto optimal allocation; hence it satisfies $y_1 = 0$, $x_2 = 0$ and $1 - x_1 + (1 - y_2)/10 = z_1 + z_2$. In addition, Pareto optimality implies $x_1 = 0$ since $u_1(0, 0, z_1 + x_1) > u_1(x_1, 0, z_1)$ for $x_1 > 0$ and $(0, 0, z_1 + x_1)$, $(0, y_2, z_2)$ is also feasible. Similarly, $y_2 < 1$ together with $z_2 > 0$ is incompatible with Pareto

First version received December 1972; final version accepted September 1973 (Eds.).
This research was supported (in part) by the Foerder Institute for Economic Research at Tel-Aviv University and by a grant from the National Science Foundation.

optimality because $u_2(0, y_2 + \varepsilon, z_2 - \varepsilon/10) > u_2(0, y_2, z_2)$ for any $0 < \varepsilon \leq \min\{10z_2, 1 - y_2\}$ and $(x_1, 0, z_1), (0, y_2 + \varepsilon, z_2 - \varepsilon/10)$ is feasible too. In case that $z_2 = 0$, any Pareto optimal allocation is of the form $(0, 0, z_1)$ $(0, y_2, 0)$ which is clearly not fair since $u_2(0, 0, z_1) > u_2(0, y_2, 0)$ as $z_1 \geq 1 \geq y_2$. We are left with the case of $y_2 = 1$ where any Pareto optimal allocation is of the form $(0, 0, z_1)$, $(0, 1, z_2)$ and $z_1 + z_2 = 1$. Noting that the definition of fairness means that each consumer evaluates the bundles of other consumers from his own point of view, the first individual will look at the bundle $(0, 1, z_2)$ of the second as involving the consumption of one unit of leisure and z_2 units of the consumption good (i.e., as though it were $(1, 0, z_2)$). Therefore, in order for the allocations under consideration to be fair from the point of view of the first individual, it must be true that $11z_1/10 \geq 1 + 11z_2/10$. Similarly, fairness from the point of view of the second individual requires $1 + 2z_2 \geq 2z_1$. These two inequalities are incompatible (as they imply $1/2 + z_2 \geq z_1 \geq 10/11 + z_2$). This completes our first counterexample.

In our second example, in order to illustrate that the result does not depend on permuting commodities when applying the fairness criterion, utility is assumed to depend only on consumption goods. Leisure as such does not yield direct utility but as the consumption (as well as the production) process is time-consuming, leisure time is a necessary input to the welfare of consumers. There are now five commodities: time, two types of labour services and two different consumption goods. Along the lines of the previous example, there are two individuals, the first having the initial endowment $(1, 1, 0, 0, 0)$ and the second having $(1, 0, 1, 0, 0)$. The units of the four last commodities (labour services and consumption goods) are defined so that k units of any commodity involve the use of k units of time. Denoting a point in the commodity space by (x, y, z, v, w), the fact that each activity consumes time restricts the consumption of each individual to be included in a hyperplane defined by the equality $y + z = v + w$. The technology is described by the following two activities: k units of the first labour service can produce k_1 units of the first consumption good and k_2 units of the second so that $k_1 + k_2 = k$. For the second type of labour service, the corresponding equality is $10 k_1 + k_2 = k$. The utility functions are $u_1(x_1, y_1, z_1, v_1, w_1) = 3v_1 + w_1$ and $u_2(x_2, y_2, z_2, v_2, w_2) = 4v_2 + w_2$. Clearly, in any Pareto optimal allocation $w_1 = 0$, since if $w_1 > 0$ the first individual would be better off devoting $w_1/2$ units of time and his labour service to the production of $w_1/2$ units of the first consumption good, thus increasing his utility level by $3/2w_1 - w_1 = w_1/2$. The same line of reasoning implies that in any Pareto optimal allocation the second individual will not produce the first commodity for his own consumption. If he consumes $v_2 > 0$, this quantity is provided to him by the work of the first individual; in this case, the bundle of the first individual will be $(1, (1 - v_2)/2, 0, (1 - v_2)/2, 0)$ and that of the second

$$(1, 0, (1 + v_2)/2, v_2, (1 - v_2)/2).$$

Applying the fairness criterion (without having to permute commodities) we get the two inequalities $3(1 - v_2)/2 \geqq 3v_2 + (1 - v_2)/2$ and $4v_2 + (1 - v_2)/2 \geqq 4(1 - v_2)/2$ which are incompatible as they imply $1/4 \geqq v_2 \geqq 3/11$ (i.e. $11 \geqq 12$). Obviously, the inequality $v_2 \geqq 3/11$ which is the fairness requirement of the second individual rules out any Pareto optimal allocation in which some of the fruits of his labour are transferred to the first individual. This completes our second counterexample.

What our examples suggest is that the goals of Pareto optimality and fairness may be mutually incompatible, i.e. that there is a trade-off between them. This is reminiscent of the familiar trade-off between efficiency and equity arising in the context of second-best situations (explored, for example, by Diamond and Mirrlees [1]). But here the conflict arises even in the absence of second-best restrictions on the feasibility of lump-sum redistributive devices (and does not presume interpersonal comparisons of utility). In other words, if one is strongly committed to fairness as a criterion for equity, Pareto optimality may have to be given up and vice versa. When Pareto optimality is deemed too important to be given up, a different criterion for equity (possibly less satisfactory than fairness) has to be used. In another paper by the authors [4], a Pareto optimal allocation is called equitable if at the prices supporting this allocation the value of the commodity bundle (including leisure) is the same for each consumer. In the first example, the resulting allocation would be $(0, 0, 55/100)$, $(0, 1, 45/100)$ (since the supporting prices have to be multiples of $(10, 1, 10)$) which clearly is not fair.

Finally we note that while our examples have been drawn from linear economies, it is easy to see that counterexamples can be obtained when either or both the technology and the preferences are strictly convex. In addition, for an economy in which there are many consumers and many commodities, we advance the following conjecture: if the labours of at least two individuals command different prices in any technologically efficient production plan, it is possible to define the preferences so that no Pareto-optimal allocation will be fair.

REFERENCES

Diamond, Peter A. and Mirrlees, James A. "Optimal Taxation and Public Production", Parts I and II, *American Economic Review*, *61*(1971).

Dubins, L. E. and Spanier, E. H. "How to Cut a Cake Fairly", *American Mathematical Monthly*, *68* (1961), pp. 1–17.

Foley, Duncan K. "Resource Allocation in the Public Sector", *Yale Economic Essays*, 7 (1967), especially pp. 73–76.

Pazner, Elisha A. and Schmeidler, David. "Decentralization, Income Distribution and the Role of Money in Socialist Economies", Foerder T.R. 8, Tel-Aviv University (September 1972).

Sen, Amartya K. *Collective Choice and Social Welfare* (San Franciso: Holden-Day, Inc., 1970), especially Chapter 9.

CHAPTER 11

Recent thinking on economic justice

Elisha A. Pazner

The exchange between economics and neighboring disciplines on the subject of distributive justice has been greatly facilitated by Phelps' (1973) *Economic Justice*. To further this dialogue, I present here in a nontechnical manner some recent developments in the pure theory of economic equity.

In light of space limitation, I confine this essay to a branch of the equity literature which has developed rapidly since the publication of Phelps' collection. Thus, rather than surveying interesting developments that are taking place within the traditional approaches, I review in the next few pages what I believe to be an interesting new way to confront the problem of economic justice.

Distributive justice has many dimensions. In particular, questions of procedural justice are certainly no less relevant than those relating to the quest for an independent criterion for a just distribution. For the importance of this distinction, we are in debt both to Rawls' *A Theory of Justice* and to Nozick's treatment of distributive justice in *Anarchy, State and Utopia*. The present review, though, is confined primarily to recent attempts to define plausible end-state criteria for assessing the justice of a distribution of resources. Except for occasional remarks, procedural justice is ignored. The reason for this lacuna is that while research efforts are currently addressed to questions of procedural justice as well, concrete results are yet to be obtained. It is to be hoped that in the not too distant future, interesting developments in this area will warrant a careful report.

The plan of the article is this: In Section 1 some standard economic terms are briefly recalled. Section 2 reviews the recent economic theory of fairness. In Section 3 some further concepts of economic equity are discussed. Finally, Section 4 presents some clarifying comments of a policy-oriented nature. A short Bibliographical Addendum concludes the article.

1   The economic framework

To avoid terminological ambiguities, let me briefly review some standard economic terms.

Each member of society in his capacity as consumer is assumed to have preferences over the set of possible consumption bundles. Each individual is assumed to derive "utility" from his consumption activities; the standard assumption is that more consumption is preferred to less. By an *economy* is meant a description of the society involving the set of individuals, their preferences and the society's aggregate consumption possibilities. When the aggregate consumption possibilities are fixed, i.e. when no production processes are available, the economy is said to be an *exchange economy*. The initial holdings of commodities prior to possible trading are also specified for each individual.

When production is possible, each individual's leisure-time is considered to be part of his consumption bundle. Time not spent as leisure is, by definition, spent as labor on production activities. The technological possibilities of an economy in which production is allowed are taken into account in the description of the set of aggregate consumption possibilities (including leisure) which are part of the definition of an economy. An economy in which production is possible is called a *production economy*.

The term *allocation* means a list of consumption bundles, one for each individual, satisfying the feasibility (scarcity) constraints imposed by the aggregate consumption possibilities. In the case of production economies, it is worth reminding that an allocation includes a full description of the consumption of leisure by each individual in addition to his consumption of "ordinary" consumer goods.

An allocation is said to be *Pareto-efficient* if it is impossible to make one individual better off by reshuffling consumption and/or production activities among individuals without making at least one other individual worse off. Pareto-efficiency is a minimal normative requirement, satisfaction of which is agreed to be desirable by virtually every modern welfare economist.

It is important to note that at any Pareto-inefficient allocation there exist mutually beneficial trading opportunities (i.e. opportunities of exchanging holdings which increase the utility of each individual trader-consumer) in both the exchange economy and production economy cases. A well-established result in welfare economics is that given any initial allocation there exist prices such that trading at these prices leads to a

Pareto-efficient allocation at which each market is cleared. The initial allocation is usually referred to as the *initial endowments* (i.e. a list of initial holdings of commodities by each consumer). This result holds only under a set of standard assumptions on the nature of the economic environment (i.e. preferences and technology). On the understanding that each trader makes a utility maximizing trading decision (subject to his budget or income constraint defined by the value of his initial endowment at the prevailing prices), and on the assumption that each is unable to influence the prevailing prices (which are the same as those faced by every other trader), the underlying market structure is said to be *perfectly competitive*. The market clearing allocation is called a *competitive equilibrium*.

The next two sections are a review of recent attempts at defining allocations that are both just and efficient. Such direct attempts at assessing the equity of allocations in terms of their intrinsic properties is what distinguishes the theories reviewed here from the traditional approaches to distributive justice.

2 The theory of fairness

A society in which nobody would prefer to be in anybody else's shoes is likely to display a kind of stability which conforms to our intuitive vision of the good society. The theory of fairness which I briefly review here is concerned with the question of economic envy. An allocation is said to be *fair* if it is envy-free. If every consumer is at least as pleased with the consumption bundle assigned to him as compared to that assigned to any other consumer, the corresponding allocation is said to be fair. To the extent that one's intuitive notion of the good society is that of an envy-free society the notion of fairness as a basic yardstick for equity will seem appropriate.

The first question that arises is whether envy-free allocations are always possible. Noting that any egalitarian allocation (in which every consumer is assigned an identical consumption bundle) is obviously envy-free, the answer to this first question is affirmative. The next question of interest to any economist raised in the tradition of modern Paretian welfare economics relates to whether among all fair allocations at least one can be found that is also Pareto-efficient. On the assumption that Pareto-efficiency is a normatively appealing desideratum, an affirmative answer to this second question would establish the possibility of satisfying the equity requirement of fairness without having to give up the separate objective of economic efficiency.

At this point it is important to distinguish between exchange and production economies. Considering first the case of an exchange economy in which the aggregate economic resources are available in fixed amounts, the answer is affirmative. This can easily be seen by noting that if each consumer is assigned an identical initial endowment of commodities and is allowed to trade in perfectly competitive markets, the resulting competitive equilibrium allocation (which always exists under the standard assumptions on consumers' preferences and is Pareto-efficient) must be envy-free. This follows from the fact that at such an allocation every consumer faces the same prices, has the same income, and competitive behavior implies that each consumer's utility is maximized subject to his budget constraint. There can be no envy at the equal income competitive equilibrium since each consumer's options are identical and each chooses a consumption bundle which is most preferred by him. Since all have the same income, each could have bought the bundle of any other but chose not to. Note that in this case, not only is the end-state criterion of fairness and efficiency achieved but there also exists a fair procedure leading to it.

The situation, however, is drastically changed when production is allowed and when it is realistically assumed that individuals are not identically endowed with innate productivity skills so that different individuals contribute differently to social product per unit of time input of their labor skills. The first problem in such a setting is whether there can be found a meaningful definition of identical initial endowments since the starting point is clearly one of inherent inequality because each person's endowment of "time" represents a different economic endowment reflecting productivity differences. In particular, the existence of a Pareto-efficient allocation "supported" by equal income budgets is generally in doubt since the efficiency-price (wage) of a person's labor (which is also the consumption price of a unit of leisure-time) reflects his marginal productivity and the latter will differ across individuals according to their skills. This implies that the argument used above for exchange economies cannot be advanced in the case of production economies. While this does not preclude the existence of allocations that are both envy-free and Pareto-efficient, it certainly indicates the complications introduced by the presence of differential productivity skills. And indeed it is now known that production economies satisfying the standard assumptions of economic theory can be constructed in such a manner that among all Pareto-efficient allocations none can be found that is envy-free. This is a disturbing result insofar as the equity notion of fairness is concerned since economic efficiency is the normative criterion upon which the foundations of modern welfare economics are laid. Virtually every economist will agree that the normative appeal of any equity notion that stands in conflict with Pareto-efficiency should be doubted.

Thus, while the notion of envy-free allocations is consistent with Pareto-efficiency in the case of exchange economies, it is not so in the case of production economies. It might be argued that the difficulty in the case of production economies is perhaps less serious than it first appears. For even if one's values conform to the desire of minimizing envy in some sense, this does not mean that individual productivity differences could not be adequately reflected in some modified version of the fairness criterion.

After all, the intuitive appeal of the fairness criterion in the case of exchange economies derives in large part from the fact that it treats symmetrically individuals that, by definition, are also symmetric insofar as their contribution to total product is concerned (since in the manna-from-heaven type of situation postulated in the exchange economy case, resources are assumed to be available without anybody having contributed to their formation). In the case of production economies, it might be argued, asymmetries in individual contributions to the social product ought to be reflected in corresponding asymmetries in the envy requirement. For instance, it has been suggested that individuals can raise complaints on grounds of envy against other individuals if and only if they also are willing and able to match their output. In other words, rather than basing the fairness evaluation on consumption bundles alone, one could (should?) base it on consumption-output configurations. In such a case, it can be shown that Pareto-efficient allocations always exist that have the property that each individual prefers his consumption-output bundle to that of any other individual. That is, he prefers his consumption-leisure bundle, with its implied contribution to output, to that of any other individual the contribution to output of which he would also be required to match whenever contemplating switching positions with him.

Implicit in this modified consumption-output fairness criterion is the notion that one has a property right in one's own labor and hence in the fruits of one's labor as well. Such an implicit value judgment seriously limits at the outset the kinds of redistributive measures that one will see as legitimate, and expresses the underlying value judgment of many libertarian approaches to distributive justice. If, as in the Rawlsian conception of distributive justice, it is agreed to regard differences in innate skills and abilities as irrelevant from a moral perspective, then the consumption-output fairness criterion will likewise seem to be lacking on ethical grounds.

The polar extreme to the view that one has an inherent right to the fruits of one's own labor is the position that individual productivity skills belong to no one in particular and ought to be regarded as a common pool of valuable resources which belongs to society as a whole. Everybody shares an equal property right in everybody's "time" (including one's "own"). In other words, if the total available "time" endowments in the economy were devoted in their entirety to production activities, individuals ought to get an equal share of total output. An envy complaint by A against B will be justified under this viewpoint if and only if it were true that if both A and B would spend their entire time working and retain the fruits of their extra labor, A would still be envious of B. Again, it can be shown that Pareto-efficient allocations having this modified fairness property always exist. We may want to call allocations having this property *potentially-fair allocations*.

In terms of the coordination of economic activity by means of a market-like mechanism capable of achieving potentially-fair and efficient allocations, a good way to think about this is the following. Imagine that the state "collects" everybody's initial endowment of time and every other available resource in the society. In compensation, each individual gets the same amount of abstract purchasing power by means of which he can buy resources from the state at competitive prices. Importantly, each individual is allowed to buy back whatever amount of leisure-time he wishes at the prevailing market price for his leisure, which will be equal to the wage set by the state for his labor services. If no individual chooses to buy back any leisure time, then each will possess precisely the same purchasing power over the remaining consumption commodities in the system provided the state charges each individual the same price for the same consumption commodity. The resulting allocation will therefore satisfy the potential-fairness requirement. In addition, if the state behaves competitively and seeks to maximize profits from production at its set prices, the equilibrium outcome of this market-socialism procedure will be Pareto-efficient as well.

It is interesting to spell out by analogy to our earlier discussion of the original fairness criterion in the exchange economy case the notion of equal endowments implicit in each of the two modified fairness criteria. In case of the consumption-output fairness criterion, if all the non-time resources available in the economy prior to production are distributed in a perfectly egalitarian manner and if each individual is in addition allowed to retain ownership over his entire "time-endowment," then letting individuals trade in perfectly competitive markets leads to an allocation that is Pareto-efficient and consumption-output fair. Such an allocation has been termed wealth-fair (and efficient) since the initial distribution of wealth (excluding time) is equal. Regarding potentially-fair allocations, it is easy to see from the discussion in the previous paragraph that the initial resources of the economy, including the implicit ownership rights in individual "times," are effectively distributed equally and when individu-

als trade to a corresponding competitive equilibrium the resulting allocation is Pareto-efficient and potentially-fair. Since the value at equilibrium
prices of every individual's consumption-cum-leisure bundle (with leisure
evaluated at the competitive wage) will be equal at the competitive
allocation in question, such an allocation has been termed income-fair
(and efficient). It probably would have been more suitable to label it
potential-income-fair.

Note that the wealth-fairness case is diametrically opposed to the
income-fairness case in that the initial endowments are effectively equalized only if each individual were to spend his entire time on leisure as
opposed to the full-time work which would make actual incomes equal in
the income-fairness case. This last comment further clarifies the precise
nature of the ownership rights in one's and others' "time" endowment
that are implicit in each of these two modified fairness criteria. Note also
that the fairness of the competitive procedure used in either case is now in
doubt; for unlike the exchange economy case, the competitive prices for
leisure (labor) differ now across individuals, a procedure that need not be
considered just even when the final outcome may.

One problem with both of the above-mentioned (modified) fairness
criteria is that each systematically discriminates among individuals in line
with their respective productive abilities. In the case of the consumption-
output fairness criterion, it is clear that, other things equal (in particular
preferences), the more able a person is the better he will be treated by the
socioeconomic system. It will always be the relatively unable that will
envy (according to the original fairness criterion) the more able in any
Pareto-efficient allocation satisfying the consumption-output fairness
criterion. In case of the potential-fairness criterion, the situation is
reversed. It will always be the more able that will envy (in the original
sense) the less able at any Pareto-efficient allocation satisfying the potential fairness criterion. It is dissatisfaction with these kinds of systematic
discrimination-according-to-ability that motivates the approach to the
equity problem discussed in the next section.

3   Equivalence criteria of equity

Agree to call two societies equivalent if every individual is equally well off
whether he lives in one or in the other. In particular, if it is agreed on an
equity norm and if this norm is satisfied by a certain society, it seems
plausible to suggest that the norm will be considered to be satisfied by any
society which displays the property that every individual is indifferent
between living in it and living in the good society (i.e. in the society
satisfying the equity norm). This approach underlies what may be termed

the *equivalence theory of equity*. This emerging theory is illustrated by two equity concepts:

1. Consider a society in which perfect equality is valued as such, i.e. a society whose underlying equity norm is one of perfect egalitarianism. The problem from the viewpoint of Paretian welfare economics is that perfectly egalitarian allocations (where each individual is assigned the same consumption bundle) are in general Pareto-inefficient. This fact confronts us with the most fundamental version of the oft-mentioned tradeoff between equality and efficiency. An intuitively appealing way to overcome this tradeoff is the following.

Let us agree to call an allocation *egalitarian-equivalent* if its underlying welfare distribution could have been generated by an egalitarian economy (i.e. an economy in which all consumers are assigned identical consumption bundles). In other words an allocation of consumption (cum-leisure) bundles is egalitarian-equivalent if even though it is not egalitarian in itself, it is considered individual-by-individual to be indifferent to the egalitarian allocation in some perfectly egalitarian economy.

Importantly, it is the case that egalitarian-equivalent allocations that are Pareto-efficient can always be found in economies satisfying the standard assumptions on individual preferences and technology. Thus, unlike the original fairness criterion, the egalitarian-equivalence concept is consistent with Pareto-efficiency, an important property. In fact, a good way to look at the general efficiency-equity problem is the following.

Consider the set of possible allocations, i.e. the set of all lists of consumption-cum-leisure bundles (one for each individual in the society) that the economy under consideration can provide. Out of the set of all possible allocations the efficiency criterion chooses those that are Pareto-efficient. Thus, the Pareto-efficiency criterion induces a restriction on the set of allocations we are willing to admit from a normative point of view. Likewise, any equity requirement restricts the set of normatively admissible allocations to those satisfying the equity requirement in question. The equity-efficiency problem relates primarily to the logical question whether the subset of allocations that are Pareto-efficient and the subset that satisfies the prescribed equity property have any common elements. If this obtains under general conditions on the economic environment (i.e. preferences, resource endowments and technology) then the particular equity notion under consideration is consistent with Pareto-efficiency. As noted above, allocations that are both egalitarian-equivalent and Pareto-efficient can always be found.

2. Consider now a society in which fairness in the original sense of freedom from envy is an accepted ethical norm. As explained in the

previous section, the problem from the viewpoint of Paretian welfare economics is that among all Pareto-efficient allocations none might be found that is envy-free. As in the case of the egalitarian norm, there is a troublesome equity-efficiency tradeoff. Consider then the following way to overcome this tradeoff.

Let us agree to call an allocation *fair-equivalent* if its underlying welfare distribution could have been generated by an envy-free allocation in some conceivable economy. That is, an allocation of consumption-cum-leisure bundles is said to be fair-equivalent if, even though it is not fair in itself, it is considered individual-by-individual to be indifferent to a fair allocation in some conceivable economy.

Again, it turns out that the fairness-equivalence criterion is consistent with Pareto-efficiency, a desired property. Fair-equivalent allocations that are Pareto-efficient can always be found in the standard kinds of economic environments considered in economic theory. While the fairness criterion is inconsistent with Pareto-efficiency, the fairness-equivalence requirement which is based on the same ethical notion of the desirability of the lack of envy can be invoked to overcome the efficiency shortcoming of the original fairness concept.

A moment's reflection should convince the reader that any egalitarian-equivalent allocation is in particular fair-equivalent (since there is no envy at the egalitarian reference allocation). Thus, the restrictive power of the egalitarian-equivalence criterion is stronger in the sense of ruling out more allocations as being inequitable since the set of egalitarian-equivalent allocations is a subset of those that are fair-equivalent. Now, whether or not sharpness (restrictive power) is a desirable attribute insofar as an equity concept is concerned is a debatable question. On the one hand, we certainly want an equity notion to have some degree of restrictive power since otherwise nothing could be ruled out as being inequitable. On the other hand, the more restrictive an equity notion is the more likely it becomes that it will generate objections for the simple reason that the likelihood increases that it will conflict with someone's values. Therefore, it should not necessarily be concluded that egalitarian-equivalence is more desirable a criterion since it is more restrictive. Actually, a good way to look at this issue is to remark simply that if one's basic conception of the good society is lack of envy, fairness-equivalence will seem to be more basic. And those who are egalitarian-minded can restrict themselves to egalitarian-equivalence since it does not conflict with the fairness-equivalence requirement anyway.

It is important to note also that unlike the modified fairness criteria mentioned in the previous section the two equivalence criteria do not discriminate among individuals on the basis of productive ability. This is because the definition of either equivalence criteria being based — as is the original fairness criterion — solely on properties of individual preference implies the criteria are neutral with respect to individual skills. While this reflects a particular value judgment, it is important to note that it is precisely the implicit value judgment underlying all of modern welfare economics. I, for one, incentive questions notwithstanding, am perfectly willing to follow the logic of such a value judgment to its ultimate consequences.

Finally, it is interesting to note that both the original fairness criterion and the two equivalence criteria can be rationalized in terms of the Rawlsian original position (provided individuals in the original position display some aversion to risk). To the extent that the original position is deemed to be a morally relevant experiment, this lends additional appeal to these new concepts of economic justice.

4   Concluding remarks

As the ultimate test of any theory of economic justice is doubtless its implications for social organization, I wish to conclude with some brief remarks on the way the approaches reported here might shed light on some major issues of social policy.

It is worth emphasizing that any notion of economic justice must be based on, or start from, an underlying notion of individual rights in the social sphere. In the case of the original fairness criterion and the equivalence criteria discussed above the starting point is that "rational" individuals have an inviolable right to their preferences. The problem of social justice is then viewed as searching for an equitable way to "aggregate" individual preferences to overcome the fundamental conflict of interest arising from the fact that economic resources are scarce relative to individuals' wants. In this sense, the approaches discussed here are consistent with the mainstream of modern welfare economics and its underlying sanction of individual preferences. Their contribution ought to be judged in light of the known difficulties involved in the search for a "good" aggregation procedure. I will attempt now to elucidate briefly the precise sense in which individuals are considered here to have a right to their preferences and to illustrate thereby how the present approach might be translated into concrete social policy recommendations.

To sharpen the issues, suppose that all individuals have exactly identical preferences. If it is agreed that each individual has an equal right to pursue satisfaction of his preferences to the maximum feasible extent (so long as all other individuals' rights to do likewise are not infringed) then social institutions ought to be designed to ensure that each individual will be able to achieve the same level of individual welfare (i.e. to reach the same level of "indifference" in this preference ordering; note the inescapable implicit interpersonal comparison of welfare here). In particular, if it happens that individuals have not been equally fortunate in the natural lottery of innate ability and skills, this morally arbitrary event (under the present set of values) should not interfere with the symmetric way in which levels of welfare ought to be distributed. The only meaning that any notion of fairness or equality of opportunity can have in this case relates to enabling individuals to achieve the same level of welfare. In terms of the proper distribution of educational and vocational resources among individuals, this will under normal circumstances imply that more resources ought to be spent on the least able. Only in those rare instances where everybody could be made better off by following different policy will a different educational policy be called for on grounds of Pareto-efficiency. Such might be the case when the technology translating educational inputs into the capability of producing consumption goods is such that educational inputs devoted to the more able are much more productive. But even in this case a tax-transfer mechanism ought to be designed so that everybody ultimately is made to enjoy the same level of welfare. Similar remarks apply to the provision of health services if innate ability is replaced by health level.

Note that both the original fairness criterion and the two equivalence criteria discussed above are consistent with this equal treatment property of individuals who have identical preferences. The two modified fairness criteria, on the other hand, are inconsistent with this principle as their implicit notion of individual rights also includes a specification of such rights over individual abilities. Whether or not this is a shortcoming depends upon one's value system.

Consider now the case where individuals have identical innate abilities but different preferences. Under the standard assumptions on the economic environment, if each is allowed to retain his initial time-endowment and if the ownership over other existing resources is also distributed equally, a competitive equilibrium will be both Pareto-efficient and envy-free. In this case, even though individual preferences differ (a fact that makes it difficult to define a norm for the equalization of individual welfare levels), the equity-efficiency objectives can be achieved by means of the market mechanism. Equality of opportunity in this instance is meaningfully satisfied whenever educational options are available at the same price for each individual. Even though people will choose to follow alternative options in line with their differing preferences, the ultimate outcome will be envy-free since market options are identical. Again, similar remarks apply to the health area with initial level of health replacing innate ability. There is absolutely no need for a tax-transfer mechanism in this instance on equity grounds if the original notion of fairness is accepted. If on the other hand satisfaction of the egalitarian equivalence criterion is sought, a tax-transfer scheme will be required even in this case.

The more difficult case is that where individuals differ in both preferences and abilities. In this case tax-subsidy schemes will generally be required even for the attainment of Pareto-efficient and envy-free allocations (whenever such exist). A similar remark applies to satisfaction of either of the equivalence criteria. Note also that the notion of equality of opportunity is more difficult to define in this general case as there is no solid yardstick of equality to start with since individuals are different in every relevant dimension. These difficult issues are the subject of current research.

I conclude by noting that it is my belief that the main contribution of the recent developments reported here might ultimately prove to lie in their enabling the discussion of policy issues within a well defined conceptual framework. Legitimate differences in opinions will then properly reflect differences in underlying values as opposed to methodological disagreement on the proper way to approach the policy dilemma in the first place. It is on, and only on, this latter aspect that professional agreement ought to be sought.

Bibliographical addendum

The notion of fairness discussed here has its roots in the mathematical problem of fair division analyzed by Steinhaus (1948) and by Dubins and Spanier (1961). The economic definition of fairness is due to Foley (1967). The question of the consistency of fairness and Pareto-efficiency in exchange economies was first posed and answered by Schmeidler and Yaari (who never wrote up their results). A minor flaw in their general proof of consistency was corrected by Varian (1974). Turning their attention to the special problems of fairness in production economies, Pazner and Schmeidler (1974) proved that allocations that are fair and Pareto-efficient may not exist in this case. The criterion of potential-fairness and establishing its consistency with Pareto-efficiency is due to Pazner and Schmeidler (1972); that of consumption-output-fairness and establishing its consistency with Pareto-efficiency is due to Varian (1974). The concept and analysis of egalitarian-equivalent allocations is due to Pazner and Schmeidler (1975); that of fair-equivalent allocations is due to Pazner (forthcoming). Other contributions to the theory of fairness include Vind

(1971), Schmeidler and Vind (1972), Feldman and Kirman (1974), Pazner and Schmeidler (1976), Varian (1975), and Daniel (1975) (who incorrectly attributes to Varian (1974) results due to others. These misattributions are rectified in Varian (forthcoming)).

Finally, as mentioned in the introduction, the present review is confined to new approaches to the problem of economic justice. For a more balanced survey of recent developments in the area the reader is referred to Phelps (1976).

REFERENCES

Daniel, T. E. [1975]. A revised concept of distributional equity. *Journal of Economic Theory 11*:94−109.

Dubins, L. and E. Spanier. [1961]. How to cut a cake fairly. *American Mathematical Monthly 68*:1−17.

Feldman, A. and A. Kirman. [1974]. Fairness and envy. *American Economic Review 64*:995−1005.

Foley, D. [1967]. Resource allocation in the public sector. *Yale Economic Essays 7*:73−6.

Nozick, R. [1974]. *Anarchy, state, and utopia*. Basic Books.

Pazner, E. Forthcoming. Pitfalls in the theory of fairness. *Journal of Economic Theory*.

Pazner, E. and D. Schmeidler. [1972]. Decentralization, income distribution, and the role of money in socialist economies. TR-8. Foerder Inst. for Econ. Res., Tel-Aviv University.

    [1974]. A difficulty in the concept of fairness. *Review of Economic Studies 41*:441−3.

    [1975]. Egalitarian equivalent allocations: A new concept of economic equity. Discussion Paper 174, Center for mathematical Studies in Economics and Management Science, Northwestern University.

    [1976]. Social contract theory and ordinal distributive equity. *Journal of Public Economics 5*.

Phelps, E. [1973]. *Economic justice*. Penguin.

    [1976]. Recent developments in welfare economics: justice et equité. In M. Intriligator, *Frontiers of Quantitative Economics*, Vol. *III*, North Holland.

Rawls, J. [1971]. *A theory of justice*. Harvard.

Schmeidler, D. and K. Vind. [1972]. Fair net trades. *Econometrica 40*:637−42.

Steinhaus, H. [1948]. The problem of fair division. *Econometrica 16*:101−4.

Varian, H. [1974]. Equity, envy, and efficiency. *Journal of Economic Theory 9*:63−91.

    [1975]. Distributive justice, welfare economics, and the theory of fairness. *Philosophy and Public Affairs 4*:223−47.

    [Forthcoming]. On the history of concepts of fairness. *Journal of Economic Theory*.

Vind, K. [1971]. Lecture notes for Economics 228, Stanford University.

CHAPTER 12

Social contact theory and ordinal distributive equity

Elisha A. Pazner and David Schmeidler

1   Introduction

The search for rules of social justice and distributive equity, a seemingly eternal conundrum of moral philosophy, has attracted the attention of normative economists for quite some time. Recurrent difficulties in the various attempts to incorporate such notions into economic analysis have to do with the cardinality of the individual utility functions used for such purposes and with the related problem of interpersonal comparisons of utilities whenever these are being made. These features are prominent throughout the classical utilitarian literature, are implicit in much of modern welfare economics and are in sharp contrast to the thoroughly ordinal nature of most of the economic theory of efficiency.

In this paper, inspired by Rawls' *A Theory of Justice*, we use the conceptual framework of social contract theory to show that the choice of distributive rules can be analyzed within an ordinal setting devoid of interpersonal comparisons of utilities; furthermore the analysis leads to determinate normative implications regarding distributive equity. The

Received April 1974, revised version received December 1974.

The concept of the original position, implicit in some of Lerner's and Harsanyi's works, lies at the heart of Rawls' contractarian approach to the theory of justice. This conceptual framework is used here to analyze the problem of distributive equity. It is shown that in a standard pure exchange economy, a social contract specifying the egalitarian distribution of economic resources might be expected to emerge in the original position. This result holds for any number of individuals and any number of commodities. The analysis does not involve interpersonal welfare comparisons and can be carried out within a purely ordinal framework of individual preferences.

The research of both authors has been supported by a grant from the Ford Foundation. An earlier version of this paper appeared as working paper no. 27 (July, 1973) of the Foerder Institute for Economic Research at Tel-Aviv University. The authors wish to thank the Editor and an anonymous referee for their helpful suggestions.

ordinal nature of the present discussion may be contrasted with the cardinality underlying the related works by Harsanyi (1953, 1955) and Lerner (1944) and the interpersonal comparisons of utilities present in the latter. Regarding the theory of social choice pioneered by Arrow (1963), the unanimously agreed upon social contract ('constitution') emerging from the present analysis may be an indication that the contractarian approach might offer a way out of some of the disturbing difficulties raised by Arrow's inquiry.

2   The contractarian framework

The analysis here is Rawlsian in the sense that we are concerned with types of institutional choices that rational individuals may be expected to adopt in an 'original position' in which a 'veil of ignorance' may cover both their personal features (say preferences) and their placing in the socioeconomic system (in terms, say, of the particular bundle to be assigned to them in any given distribution of bundles).

We depart however from Rawls in at least one important respect. Rawls' fundamental moral principle that society ought to maximize the welfare of the least well off we understand as meaning that this (the maximum function) is the social welfare function which Rawls' rational individuals are expected to accept ex ante (i.e. in the 'original position') as the guiding device in deciding about resource (bundles) allocation ex post (i.e. when individuals already know who they are). Without going into the question of whether the acceptance of this principle is as compelling as Rawls wishes to suggest [see Harsanyi (1973) for a critical examination of this issue], the operational meaning of this criterion in terms of the resulting distribution(s) of economic resources is dubious since it will depend on the particular (arbitrary?) way in which interpersonal comparisons of welfare (needed in order to determine who in any particular allocation is the worst off individual) will eventually have to be made [see also Arrow (1973)].

The point of view taken by us here differs from Rawls' in that we seek to determine ex-ante a *determinate distribution of economic resources* (rather than an agreed upon social welfare function) on which rational individuals can be expected to agree unanimously in the original position. We show in the context of a standard pure-exchange economy that individuals in an 'original position' in which they are faced by distributions of bundles, without knowing the particular bundle to be assigned to them in any particular distribution, will always unanimously choose the egalitarian distribution independently of whether or not their preferences are known to them.

It is also shown that the unanimous consensus on the egalitarian distribution of endowments is an extremely robust result. Indeed, it obtains for any of the standard criteria of decision making under complete ignorance (i.e. the maximin criterion, the minimax regret criterion and the principle of insufficient reason) which rational individuals may be expected to follow in the original position. The inherent risk-aversion underlying the above-mentioned decision criteria, coupled with the fundamental symmetry of the original position, turns out to dictate unequivocally a perfectly egalitarian outcome.

As is well known, maximization of any symmetric strictly quasiconcave and monotone increasing function over a convex and symmetric domain leads to a symmetric solution. Applying this reasoning to the problem of distributing a fixed aggregate endowment of commodities across the members of the society, the egalitarian distribution is optimal under any 'social welfare function' satisfying the above conditions (over the domain of individual consumption bundles). This is easily seen to be the link explaining the identical results obtained under the seemingly different approaches considered here.

In addition, it also turns out that both the maximin and the minimax regret criteria are ordinal in the present problem as the egalitarian distribution turns out to be invariant under any positive monotone transformations of the utility function(s) when either of these decision criteria is followed. This invariance also implies the absence of interpersonal comparisons of utilities, an important result.

It is also worthwhile emphasizing that the egalitarian distribution will be agreed upon unanimously even in the case where the individuals have 'vested interests' in the original position in terms of knowing already then what their precise utility function is; the fact that the bundles are not named in the original position turns out to be enough for the egalitarian result.

Finally, we wish to emphasize that the analysis is conducted throughout within the framework of timeless pure exchange economies in which distributional issues arise in their most primitive form. The question of possible extensions of the approach to production economies and to problems of resource distribution over time will be mentioned in the final section of the paper.

3   The egalitarian social contract

In the 'original position' suppose that there are H individuals who have to decide unanimously on the initial distribution of whatever aggregate economic resources the society may have at its disposal. The distinctive feature of the social contract under consideration lies in its informational structure as it is assumed that what any particular individual will actually get in the decided distribution cannot be known to him at the time of signing of the contract.

Consider first the case where each individual knows his (economic) preferences. To be more specific, assume that there are N commodities in our exchange economy, the aggregate endowment being a vector, say ω, in R^N_+ – the non-negative orthant of the N-dimensional Euclidean space – and the preferences of the hth individual ($h = 1, \ldots, H$) (assumed here to be known by the individual) are given by a continuous strictly quasiconcave, monotone increasing function, say u_h, from R^N_+ to the real numbers. A distribution of ω is an H-list of bundles $\mathbf{x} = (x_1, \ldots, x_H)$ in R^N_+ s.t. $\Sigma^H_{h=1} x_h = \omega$; note that $\mathbf{x}$ being a distribution means that x_h is not (necessarily) the bundle assigned to individual h. Indeed, the essence of this case lies in the assumption that each individual knows only that one bundle in $\mathbf{x}$ will accrue to him, but does not know in advance which bundle this is going to be.

3.1   The maximin social contract

Assuming that each individual $h(h = 1, \ldots, H)$ applies (separately) the maximin criterion in ranking the distributions, it is readily seen that

$$\underset{x}{\text{Max}} \, \underset{h'}{\text{Min}} \, u_h(x_{h'}) = u_h(\omega/H),$$

where $\mathbf{x}$ runs over all distributions and $h' = 1, \ldots, H$. In other words, the maximin criterion leads every individual to select the egalitarian distribution as his best choice. Using the terminology of Hurwicz (1973), we can say that the application of the maximin criterion under the informational assumptions stated above gives rise to a mechanism that assigns equal endowments to every individual in the society.

Note further that while we assumed each individual to know his u_h, all he has to know actually is that his u_h is one of H given utility functions, each one of which will eventually accrue to one of the H individuals. We shall now prove that this is indeed so. The problem faced in the 'original position' by each individual is now to find a distribution for which

$$\underset{x}{\text{Max}} \, \underset{u}{\text{Min}} \, \underset{h'}{\text{Min}} \, u(x_{h'})$$

is obtained, where $\mathbf{x}$ varies over all distributions, u runs over H given continuous, strictly quasiconcave and monotone increasing real valued functions on R^N_+, and $h' = 1, \ldots, H$. Suppose, by contradiction, that the maximinmin is obtained at the distribution $\mathbf{y}$, utility u_0 and bundle h_0, i.e.

$$\underset{x}{\text{Max}} \; \underset{u}{\text{Min}} \; \underset{h'}{\text{Min}} \; u(x_{h'}) = u_0(y_{h_0}) > \underset{u}{\text{Min}} \; u(\omega|H) = u_1(\omega/H).$$

The left-hand side of the inequality is clearly smaller than or equal to $\text{Min}_{h'}u_1(y_h)$. Thus we have for all $h'(h' = 1, \ldots, H)$ that $u_1(y_{h'}) > u_1(\omega|H)$, which is impossible since ω/H is a Pareto optimal allocation for the economy in which all the individuals have the same utility, namely u_1. It follows that the social contract will specify egalitarian endowments when the structure of information, as in Rawls, is such that in the original position the individuals are not only ignorant of their own placing in the social system but are ignorant of their personal features (preferences) as well.

In other words, a true state of primordial equality, where each individual may in the full sense of the term be any of the members of the society for which the social contract has to be signed, implies unanimous agreement on the egalitarian distribution of resources when each individual insists on getting at least his maximin.

We conclude the present discussion by noting that since the egalitarian distribution that results from the maximin(min) procedure is invariant under any monotone positive transformations of the utility functions, the apparent presence of interpersonal comparisons of utility is misleading and the procedure is truly devoid of any such comparisons.

3.2   *The minimax regret social contract*

One might also wish to consider the following problem in the original position. Suppose that all that the individuals know about their preferences is that they are going to be continuous, strictly quasiconcave and monotone increasing. The question then is whether application of the maximin criterion by each individual will again lead to a meaningful social contract regarding the distribution of economic resources. Formally, the optimization problem faced by each individual is now

$$\underset{x}{\text{Max}} \; \underset{u}{\text{Min}} \; \underset{h'}{\text{Min}} \; u(x_{h'}),$$

where $\mathbf{x}$ varies as before on all distributions, u now runs over the entire class of continuous, strictly quasiconcave and monotone increasing utility functions, and $h' = 1, \ldots, H$ as before. Noting that now Min_u has to be replaced by Inf_u and that

$$\underset{u}{\text{Inf}} \; \underset{h'}{\text{Min}} \; u(x_{h'}) = -\infty$$

independently of **x**, the distributive result is indeterminate in this case as maximization of this function will imply that each distribution is as desirable as any other under the maxinf(min) criterion.

This shows that one has to place explicit informational restrictions on the structure of knowledge supposed to prevail in the original position in order for the maximin criterion to lead to a meaningful (determinate) social contract. We saw above that it is enough for each individual to be faced by H (in fact, any finite number of) utility functions one of which will eventually be his, in order for the (maximin) procedure to lead to a determinate (egalitarian) distribution. It seems however that the spirit of Rawls' 'veil of ignorance' in the original position is more in line with the case where all the individual knows is that his preferences will be drawn from the entire above-mentioned class of utility functions, rather than from an a priori given finite subset therefrom. In order to solve this kind of problem, another criterion for decision-making under ignorance has to be applied since the maximin criterion leads to indeterminate results.

This also brings us to a more fundamental question that can be addressed to Rawls' analysis, namely why confine attention solely to the maximin criterion in the first place? In particular, Savage's minimax regret criterion seems on a priori grounds to be no less plausible a criterion, except perhaps for the cardinal notions usually involved in it. As we shall show that in the specific context considered here cardinality is not really required in applying the minimax regret criterion, this certainly enhances the appeal of this criterion in the present context.

Applying the minimax regret criterion, with regrets measured by the maximin procedure, the problem faced by each individual is to find the distribution where

$$\underset{x}{\text{Min}}\ \underset{u}{\text{Sup}}\ [\underset{y}{Max}\ \underset{h'}{\text{Min}}\ u(y_{h'}) - \underset{h'}{\text{Min}}\ u(x_{h'})]$$

obtains. From our earlier discussion we know that

$$\underset{y}{\text{Max}}\ \underset{h'}{\text{Min}}\ u(y_{h'}) = u(\omega/H),$$

and that whenever $\mathbf{x} \neq \omega/\mathbf{H}$,

$$u(\omega/H) > \underset{h'}{\text{Min}}\ u(x_{h'}).$$

Thus whenever $\mathbf{x} \neq \omega/\mathbf{H}$ the regret is positive independently of u and the minimal regret, which is zero, is obtained at the egalitarian distribution $\omega/\mathbf{H}$ once more. Since u runs over the entire class of strictly quasiconcave, continuous and monotone increasing utility functions, there is no operational meaning to a possible claim that interpersonal comparisons of utilities are involved in the present use of this criterion, and the procedure is truly ordinal.

3.3 *The insufficient reason social contract*

Another possible criterion, used in a similar context by Lerner (1944) and Harsanyi (1953, 1955), is that based on the principle of insufficient reason. Assuming first that each individual knows his strictly concave utility function u but does not know in advance the bundle $x_{h'}$ to be allocated to him in the selected distribution, it is easily seen that the social contract would lead once more to the egalitarian distribution (if he assigns the equal probability $1/H$ to each bundle). This is so since the strict concavity of u immediately implies that

$$\underset{x}{\text{Max}} \; \frac{1}{H} \sum_{h'=1}^{H} u(x_{h'}) = u(\omega/H).$$

The egalitarian result continues to hold (under the same, subjective, equiprobability assignment) if in addition the individual is to be assigned his utility function by a random process independent of the assignment of the bundle to him [see Sen (1973) and references therein for the case of one-dimensional commodity bundles]. However, an arbitrary monotone (continuous and increasing) transformation of the utility function(s) will not always preserve the egalitarian result (as strict concavity is required for the egalitarian result). This procedure *is* therefore cardinal (although interpersonal comparisons of utilities still need not be involved).

4 Concluding remarks

(1) The egalitarian social contract shown here to arise spontaneously for any of the standard decision criteria under ignorance, which any rational individual might use in ranking social states, illustrates the power of the concept of the original position insofar as equity analysis is concerned. In the case of a pure exchange economy, where no one can have any prior claims on the social dividend, the analysis shows that it is possible to advocate the intuitively appealing egalitarian distribution of resources without having recourse to problematic interpersonal utility comparisons (and without having to give up the cherished ordinal framework of standard economic theory). It should, however, be stressed that the assumption of risk-aversion in the original position is essential for the egalitarian result.

(2) The fact that the egalitarian distribution of resources will usually fail to be Pareto optimal can, in principle, easily be remedied. After the

social contract has been signed, and hence the veil of ignorance lifted, individuals may be permitted to trade in competitive markets so as to ensure the absence of a social dead weight loss. As they start with equal endowments, any competitive equilibrium will also be fair (in the sense that each individual will prefer his competitive bundle to that of any other individual), since the problems raised in Pazner and Schmeidler (1974a) and Varian (1974) do not apply to the 'classical environment' of the pure exchange economy under consideration. Hence, the intuitively appealing criterion of fair and Pareto efficient allocations can also be rationalized in terms of some kind of sequential contractarian situation. But note that from the viewpoint of the original position proper, the notion of fairness (i.e. absence of envy) precedes any efficiency considerations. Also, turning to the viewpoint of incentive compatibility, while the competitive mechanism is not cheatproof [in the sense of Hurwicz (1973)] – and hence the efficiency result of the 'sequential' allocative mechanism is actually in doubt – note that the egalitarian social contract is clearly incentive compatible (from the viewpoint of each individual in the original position). Finally note that in the original position, individuals should not be made aware of the possibility of recontracting out of the egalitarian distribution via the competitive mechanism; for if they knew this the problem might well have no solution at all (i.e. no social contract might be reached).

(3) Finally, we mention that the approach presented here can be used in the case of production economies. However, while it is possible to show that a variant of the egalitarian result obtains in this case as well (in the sense that each individual will be given a bundle lying on the boundary of an 'egalitarian' production set) the efficiency problems become acute indeed. For, depending upon the veil of ignorance one might want to impose, it may even be impossible to define efficient production plans (e.g. when it is not known in the original position which utility functions are associated with which particular labor service). It might however be worth mentioning that in the context of the problem of resource allocation over infinite time we have been able to show (for rational individuals in an original position in which they are left ignorant of the particular generation in which they are going to live) that while maximin behavior is inefficient, minimax regret consumption plans are consistent with the golden rule of saving [see Pazner and Schmeidler (1974b)].

REFERENCES

Arrow, K. J. [1963]. Social choice and individual values, 2nd edition (Wiley, New York).

Arrow, K. J. [1973]. Some ordinalist−utilitarian notes on Rawls's theory of justice, Journal of Philosophy 70, 245−263.

Harsanyi, J. C. [1953]. Cardinal utility in welfare economics and in the theory of risk taking, Journal of Political economy 61, 434−435.

Harsanyi, J. C. [1955]. Cardinal welfare, individualistic ethics and interpersonal comparison of utility, Journal of Political Economy 63, 309−321.

Harsanyi, J. C. [1973]. Can the maximin principle serve as a basis for morality? A critique of John Rawls's theory, Working paper no. cP−351 (Center for Research in Management Science, University of California, Berkeley).

Hurwicz, L. [1973]. The design of mechanisms for resource allocation, The American Economic Review, 63, 1−30.

Lerner, A. P. [1944]. The economics of control (Macmillan, New York).

Pazner, E. A. and D. Schmeidler. [1974a]. A difficulty in the concept of fairness, The Review of Economic Studies 41, 441−443.

Pazner, E. A. and D. Schmeidler. [1974b]. Just saving and the golden rule, Working paper no. 38 (The Foerder Institute for Economic Research, Tel-Aviv University).

Rawls, J. [1971]. A theory of justice (Harvard University Press, Cambridge, MA).

Sen, A. K. [1973]. On ignorance and equal distribution, American Economic Review 63, 1022−1024.

Varian, H. L. [1974]. Equity, envy, and efficiency, Journal of Economic Theory 9, 63−91.

CHAPTER 13

Pitfalls in the theory of fairness

Elisha A. Pazner

1   Introduction

Egalitarian allocations are in general Pareto-inefficient; likewise, fair (envy-free) allocations that are Pareto-efficient need not exist under the standard assumptions on the economic environment. Thus, if one's values conform to either egalitarianism or to freedom of envy an inescapable first-best equity-efficiency trade-off has to be confronted. The concept of egalitarian-equivalent allocations, recently advanced in [7], provides a possible way out of this trade-off for egalitarian oriented societies. This paper is concerned with mitigating the first-best equity-efficiency trade-off for value systems based on the desirability of freedom of envy.

2   The theory of fairness

An allocation is said to be fair if no person in the economy prefers anyone else's consumption bundle over his own (see [2]). In other words, a fair allocation is free of envy. The individualistic nature of the fairness idea is attractive and spiritwise consistent with Paretian welfare economics. The appealing features of the fairness criterion from a distributional equity viewpoint are that it treats economic agents symmetrically (in an obvious sense), is ordinal in nature, and is devoid of interpersonal welfare comparisons (since only intrapersonal utility comparisons are involved). It should be mentioned that from the viewpoint of political philosophy it is not entirely clear whether a concept of equity based on envy relationships can be morally acceptable (see [8, pp. 530−514]). Be that as it may, the concept of fairness is certainly interesting enough to warrant investigation of its analytical properties.

Received: November 21, 1975. Revised: July 6, 1976.

From the viewpoint of welfare economics, the major drawback of the fairness criterion lies in its being inconsistent with the Pareto-efficiency principle. Specifically, due to Pazner and Schmeidler [5], it is now known that even under the classical convexity and selfishness assumptions on the economic environment, allocations that are both fair and Pareto efficient will not always exist in economies with production. In light of the general acceptance of the Pareto criterion this presents a fundamental difficulty with the concept of fairness.

This fact prompted several attempts at modifying the concept of fairness in the hope of arriving at a reasonable equity criterion which would be consistent with Pareto efficiency. I turn now to a critical evaluation of the attempts made so far.

3   Existing concepts of fairness

(1) The first concept I wish to discuss is Varian's [10] interesting notion of *wealth-fair* allocations (called fair* in [9]). An allocation is said to be *wealth-fair* if no individual prefers the consumption–output bundle of anyone else over his own. In other words, a wealth-fair allocation is envy free in the sense that no person envies the complete position (defined as including the goods and leisure consumed *and* output produced) of any other person. As shown in [9], wealth-fair allocations are consistent with Pareto efficiency under the standard assumptions on the economic environment.

The problem of course is that unless the production technology is additively separable in each agent's labor time inputs, it is impossible to impute output according to individual productivity. In other words, production processes are more often than not of such a joint nature as to make it impossible to disentable individual contributions to total (observed) output. But in linear production• economies, for instance, the concept is well defined and the efficiency result of interest.

Confining our attention to those very special cases in which the wealth-fairness concept is well defined, it becomes of interest to discuss its normative significance. As noted by Varian himself [10], if one agent cannot possibly produce what another agent produces then no envy complaint can ever be raised by the first agent against the second. This example illustrates nicely the implicit sanctification of productivity (a morally irrelevant characteristic in itself)[1] underlying the wealth-fairness

---

[1] One may, or perhaps even should, distinguish here between differential productivities that are due to differential "innate abilities" (or, more generally, differential productivities

criterion. In other words, it is first and foremost a "to each according to productivity" kind of slogan. It somewhat mitigates this near-libertarian precept by requiring that those consumption commodities that are not resultant upon production should (loosely speaking) be divided in a fair manner (according to the original definition of fairness). In any case, ceteris paribus, this criterion penalizes the unable (in the productive sense). Horizontal equity (Musgrave's [3] suggestive term for the equal treatment of equals) is taken to mean under it that only persons who are identical both in preferences and in productivity will be treated equally. Persons who are identical only in preferences, on the other hand, will be treated differentially to an extent entirely dependent upon their differential productivities. If it is agreed that the subject matter of economic equity relates to preferences only (i.e., if it is agreed that the proper axiom of horizontal equity states that people with identical preferences ought to enjoy the same welfare level in the sense of being assigned a bundle lying on the same indifference surface)[2] then the wealth-fairness concept ought to be rejected on ethical grounds. Also, it would seem that wealth-fair allocations can under no circumstances be rationalized in terms of hypothetical contractual agreements in Rawls' [8] original position.

(2) The second concept of interest is that of *income-fairness* suggested by Pazner and Schmeidler [6] and further discussed by Varian [9, 10]. An allocation is said to be *income-fair* if at the efficiency prices supporting this allocation the value of each person's consumption-cum-leisure bundle is equal. In other words, an income-fair allocation calls for the perfect equalization of potential income (sometimes called implicit income).

---

that are essentially resultant upon a random act of nature) and those that are attributable to self-chosen actions by individuals (schooling, self-study, specialization, etc.). For the second category, under (hard to define) conditions of equal opportunity, the wealth-fairness concept has a certain normative significance. But I fail to see any possible moral justification for this concept in the case of innate (or, more generally, exogenous) productivity differentials.

[2] It might be appropriate at this point to correct a minor error by Varian [10, p. 246], who says that when all agents have the same tastes but different abilities, an equal division of goods and labor leads to a fair and Pareto-efficient allocation. Actually, the only inference that can be made in this instance is that at an allocation that is both fair and Pareto-efficient (such indeed exists in this case and is unique under the standard assumptions) the individuals get consumption−leisure bundles that all lie on the same indifference surface. Since abilities differ, the equal division is generally not Pareto-efficient (due to the leisure margin).

Unlike the wealth-fairness concept, under which each person has a full ownership right over his "natural" endowment of time, under the income-fairness criterion each person is thus effectively assigned an equal property right (or share) in everybody's endowment of time (including his own). The distribution of skills is thus viewed as a common pool of productive resources to be shared, in a sense, equally among all members of the society. Unlike the purely private good nature of individual productive skills implied by the wealth-fairness criterion (under which redistribution of the fruits of labor is prohibited), the income-fairness criterion is thus consistent with the general Rawlsian viewpoint.

As shown in [6], under the standard assumptions on the economic environment the income-fairness criterion is always consistent with Pareto efficiency, a desirable property. There is, however, one major drawback with the income-fairness concept. It does not satisfy horizontal equity as defined above, i.e., at an income-fair allocation two persons with identical preferences will not, in general, be assigned bundles that lie on the same indifference surface whenever their productivities differ (see [6]; for a clear illustration of this fact see [4, footnote 11, pp. 630−631]). In general, the more able a person, ceteris paribus, the more penalized he is relative to an unable one. Income-fair allocations therefore discriminate among people in a manner that is diametrically opposed to the discrimination taking place at wealth-fair allocations. In any event, as I consider the property of horizontal equity to be of importance, its violation under the income-fairness criterion is troublesome in my opinion.

(3) The last existing concept of fairness is that recently suggested by Daniel, who offers the following definitions. If the number of people who envy a person is equal to the number of people that he envies, then he will be said to be *balanced* with respect to envy at that allocation. An allocation is said to be *balanced* if everyone is balanced at it. He then goes on to prove that under the standard assumptions on the economic environment (to which a so-called nondegeneracy assumption is added) there always exist Pareto-efficient allocations that are balanced (see [1], some misattributions in which are rectified in [11]).

Thus the balancedness criterion of fairness is consistent with the Pareto-efficiency requirement, a result of some interest in itself. The question, however, is how normatively appealing is the balancedness requirement in the first place. Consider the extreme case of a large society in which every individual envies every other at some (Pareto-efficient) allocation. This allocation clearly satisfies the balancedness requirement. Yet, in such a large society what every individual can at most know is that he envies every other individual. There is really no way (if we want to be reasonable about it) for him to know that every other individual also envies him unless he is told so (say by an "ethical observer"). Thus the very spirit of the fairness idea (according to which each person can evaluate his position relative to others without any outside help) is lost. Furthermore, it is dubious whether the individual would feel much better even if he were told about this mysterious property of universal mutual envy. True it is a phenomenon that treats all agents symmetrically in a sense; but, it would seem to me that it would very likely give rise to the no less symmetrical situation in which everybody is at everybody else's throat. Hardly a stable social situation, and certainly not one in agreement with our intuitive vision of the good society. In brief, it is hard for me to take seriously the balancedness requirement as a plausible distributional equity criterion.

4   New concepts of fairness

In the light of the above discussion, the question arises whether one could advance new concepts of fairness which are free of the difficulties associated with earlier attempts. I shall now present two new concepts, the second of which I believe to deserve special attention.

   (1) In the light of the tremendous informational requirements in large societies placed upon any individual who has to perform the intrapersonal envy comparisons called by all the previous fairness criteria,[3] one could think it operationally meaningful to advance the following simplified fairness test. Let each person at any allocation determine whether he is better off with his bundle as compared to the average bundle in the economy. The informational requirements here are minimal in the sense that all that each agent has to know is his own bundle, the aggregate bundle,[4] and the number of agents in the economy. An allocation at

---

[3] The original fairness criterion requires for its application that each person knows at any allocation the consumption−leisure bundle that every other consumer gets. The wealth-fairness criterion requires in addition that each person know every other person's productivity (when the latter is well defined)! The income-fairness criterion requires each person to know every other person's actual ("market") income, consumption of leisure, and efficiency wage. The balancedness criterion requires each person to know every other person's consumption−leisure bundle and the preferences of every other person! Of all these, the income-fairness criterion is the least demanding from the informational viewpoint, but even it is extremely informationally demanding in a large society.

[4] Including of course the aggregate number of hours worked (and hence the aggregate amount of leisure). This datum is available in virtually every country.

which no individual prefers the average bundle over his own will be said to be *per-capita-fair*. In terms of the information likely to be (costlessly) available to any individual, this fairness requirement is very sensible.

Do per-capita-fair allocations exist? Of course. Simply give to each person an identical (egalitarian) consumption-cum-leisure bundle.[5] Will this egalitarian bundle be Pareto efficient? Generally not. In fact, the major difficulty with the concept of per-capita-fair allocations is that, like the original fairness criterion, it is inconsistent with the Pareto-efficiency requirement. To see that, simply observe that in any standard two-person production economy in which no fair and Pareto-efficient allocation exists, there can exist no per-capita-fair and Pareto-efficient allocation. For, under convex preferences, the fact that at every Pareto-efficient allocation in such an economy at least one of the individuals envies the other implies that the average bundle is also preferred to the bundle that he has. So no Pareto-efficient and per-capita-fair allocation can exist in such an economy and this simple counterexample is enough to rule out the interesting notion of per-capita-fairness on grounds of inconsistency with the Pareto principle.

(2) The second novel fairness concept which comes to mind is motivated by the concept of *egalitarian-equivalence* recently introduced by Pazner and Schmeidler [7]. An allocation will be said to be *fair-equivalent* if there exists a fair allocation in some hypothetical economy in which each person enjoys the same welfare level as that enjoyed by him at the allocation under consideration. In other words, an allocation is *fair-equivalent* if and only if its underlying welfare distribution could have been generated by a fair allocation in some hypothetical economy.[6] If such an allocation exists and if our conception of the "good society" is that of an envy-free society, the normative significance of any fair-equivalent allocation derives from the fact that each person is indifferent between living in the actual economy (at the said allocation) and living in the "good" (envy-free) reference economy.

---

[5] Note that in a production economy assigning to everybody the average bundle may not be feasible (as for instance will be the case when the "able" work more hours than the "unable"). But in order to apply the per-capita-fairness criterion, the feasibility problem is of no concern; each person asks himself whether he is better off with his bundle as compared to the (possibly infeasible) average bundle. Observe also that the same feasibility problem already arises with the original fairness criterion.

[6] Hypothetical because, again, feasibility (in the actual economy) of the fair allocation (in the reference economy) is not guaranteed. What is guaranteed, however, is that the underlying welfare distribution is feasible in the actual economy.

Regarding the question of whether or not the fairness-equivalence criterion is consistent with the Pareto-efficiency principle, recall first the following definition. An allocation is said to be *egalitarian-equivalent* if its underlying welfare distribution could have been generated by an egalitarian economy. Clearly, any egalitarian-equivalent allocation is also fair-equivalent. As shown in [7], Pareto-efficient and egalitarian-equivalent allocations always exist under (even weaker than) the standard assumptions on either exchange or production economies. This establishes the consistency of the fairness-equivalence requirement with the Pareto-efficiency criterion, an important property. No less important, horizontal equity is also satisfied.

It clearly is the case that the set of fair-equivalent allocations will always contain the set of egalitarian-equivalent allocations. Therefore, the restriction imposed on the Pareto set by the egalitarian-equivalence criterion is more discriminating (i.e., rule out more Pareto-efficient allocations as being normatively admissible on equity grounds). This might be considered by some as a distinct advantage of this criterion. But if one's view of the good society is that of freedom of envy, the fairness-equivalence criterion will seem more basic. And since those who are egalitarian-minded can always restrict their attention to the egalitarian-equivalent subset of the set of fair-equivalent allocations, I think it wisest to let the reader decide for himself which of these two concepts (if any) better conforms to his own values. The fact that they both satisfy the horizontal equity requirement is in my mind an important property when comparing either of them with the modified fairness criteria discussed in Section 3.

Like the modified fairness criteria discussed in Section 3, the two equivalence criteria are however much more informationally demanding than the original fairness criterion. The appealing simplicity with which each individual could perform his envy comparisons under the original notion of fairness is thus lost. In this sense, it would seem that the original theory of fairness may have reached a dead end. From the viewpoint of the omniscient-planner approach to Paretian welfare economics, though, the two equivalence criteria seem to offer a promising avenue out of what I like to think of as being the disturbing problem of the *first-best equity-efficiency trade-off*.

Mathematical appendix to Section 4

Since the concepts and propositions of this section are new, the following mathematical treatment intends to make precise the ideas and statements presented in the text. The notation is consistent with that in [7].

Let T denote the finite set of economic agents and let R^l_+ denote the nonnegative orthant of the Euclidean space of dimension l, the set of consumption commodity bundles. Each t in T has a preference relation $\gtrsim t$ on R^l_+ which is assumed to be *strongly connected, transitive, continuous, monotonic, and convex* (i.e., for all x, y, z in R^l_+, the following hold: $x \gtrsim_t y$ or $y \gtrsim_t x$; $x \gtrsim_t y$ and $y \gtrsim_t z$ imply $x \gtrsim_t z$; the sets $\{x' \in R^l_+ | x' \gtrsim_t x\}$ and $\{x' \in R^l_+ | x \gtrsim_t x'\}$ are closed in R^l_+; $x \gtrsim_t y$ implies $\lambda x + (1 - \lambda)y >_t y$ for $0 < \lambda < 1$; and $x > y$ implies $x >_t y$, where inequalities between vectors in R^l_+ hold coordinatewise by definition, and the relations $>_t$ and $\sim_t$ are induced by $\gtrsim_t$ in the usual way).

The set of technologically feasible production plans is denoted by K ($K \subset R^l$). As usual, if $z \in K$ then the negative coordinates of z denote inputs and the positive coordinates of z denote outputs. Let $W = \{\omega + K\} \cap R^l_+$, where $\omega \in R^l_+$ is an aggregate initial commodity vector, denote the feasible aggregate final consumption vectors. It is assumed that W is a compact and convex set with nonempty interior. Free disposal is also assumed, i.e., $x \leq y \in W$ implies $x \in W$.

The *economy* is formally defined as the vector $(T, R^l_+, \{\gtrsim_t\}_{t\in T}, W)$. An *allocation* is a T list of elements of R^l_+ whose sum belongs to W. An *assignment* is a T list of elements of R^l_+ (whose sum does not necessarily belong to W). In other words, while an allocation is a feasible T list of consumption (cum-leisure) bundles, an assignment is a T list of such bundles which is not necessarily feasible. An assignment is denoted by $\{z_t\}_{t\in T}$ or simply $\{z_t\}$. An allocation $\{x_t\}$ is *Pareto efficient* if for any other allocation $\{y_t\}$ the implication $(\forall t \in T, y_t \gtrsim_t x_t) \rightarrow (\forall t \in T, y_t \sim_t x_t)$ holds. An allocation $\{x_t\}$ is *fair* if for all t and t' in T: $x_t \gtrsim_t x_{t'}$.

Definition 1: An allocation $\{x_t\}$ is said to be *per-capita-fair* if for all t in T: $x_t \gtrsim_t \bar{x}$, where $\bar{x} = (\Sigma_{t\in T}x_t / |T|)$.

Proposition 1: *There exist economies as defined above in which no Pareto-efficient allocation is per-capita-fair.*

Proof: By counterexample. Consider a two-person economy as in [5], where no Pareto-efficient allocation is fair. At any Pareto-efficient allocation $\{x_1, x_2\}$ in such an economy, either $x_2 >_1 x_1$ and/or $x_1 >_2 x_2$. Suppose without loss of generality that $x_2 >_1 x_1$. By the convexity of preferences, $\bar{x} = (x_1 + x_2)/2 >_1 x_1$.   Q.E.D.

Definition 2: An allocation $\{x_t\}$ is said to be *fair-equivalent* if there exists an assignment $\{z_t\}$ such that for all t and t' in T: $x_t \sim_t z_t$ and $z_t \gtrsim_t z_{t'}$.

Thus a fair-equivalent allocation $\{x_t\}$ is agentwise indifferent to a fair allocation in an economy in which the assignment $\{z_t\}$ is feasible.

Proposition 2: *In an economy as defined above there always exist Pareto-efficient allocations that are fair-equivalent.*

For the proof of Proposition 2 we need a definition and a lemma.

Definition 3: An allocation $\{x_t\}$ is said to be *egalitarian-equivalent* if there is a bundle z in R^l_+ such that for all t in T: $x_t \sim_t z$.

Lemma: *If an allocation $\{x_t\}$ is egalitarian-equivalent then it is fair-equivalent.*

Proof: By the definition of an egalitarian-equivalent allocation, there exists a constant assignment $\{z\}_{t \in T}$ such that $x_t \sim_t z$, for all t in T. Since $z \gtrsim_t z$ for all t in T, $\{x_t\}$ is fair-equivalent.   Q.E.D.

Proof of Proposition 2: As shown in [7], in an economy as defined above there always exist Pareto-efficient allocations that are egalitarian-equivalent. By the Lemma, Proposition 2 then follows.   Q.E.D.

REFERENCES

1. T. E. Daniel, A revised concept of distributional equity, *J. Econ. Theory 11* [1975], 94–109.
2. D. K. Foley, Resource allocation in the public sector, *Yale Econ. Essays 7* [1967], 73–76.
3. R. A. Musgrave, "The Theory of Public Finance," p. 160, McGraw-Hill, New York, 1959.
4. R. A. Musgrave, Maximin, uncertainty and the leisure trade-off, *Quart. J. Econ. 88*[1974], 625–632.
5. E. Pazner and D. Schmeidler, A difficulty in the concept of fairness, *Rev. Econ. Studies 41* [1974], 441–443.
6. E. Pazner and D. Schmeidler, Decentralization, income distribution and the role of money in socialist economies, T.R. 8, The Foerder Institute for Economic Research, Tel-Aviv University, 1972, *Economic Inquiry*, to appear.
7. E. Pazner and D. Schmeidler, Egalitarian equivalent allocations: A new concept of economic equity, Discussion Paper No. 174, The Center for Mathematical Studies in Economics and Management Science, Northwestern University, September 1975.
8. J. Rawls, "A Theory of Justice," Harvard Univ. Press, Cambridge, Mass., 1971.
9. H. R. Varian, Equity, envy and efficiency, *J. Econ. Theory 9* [1974], 63–91.
10. H. R. Varian, Distributive justice, welfare economics, and the theory of fairness, *Philos. Public Affairs 4* [1975], 223–247.
11. H. R. Varian, On the history of concepts of fairness, Letter to the Editor, *J. Econ. Theory 13* [1976], 486–487.

CHAPTER 14

Cheatproofness properties of the plurality rule in large societies

Elisha A. Pazner and Eugene Wesley

1 Introduction

Vickrey [11] and Dummet and Farquharson [2] conjectured and Gibbard [5], Satterthwaite [9] and Schmeidler and Sonnenschein [10] proved that when the number of social alternatives is at least three, any non-imposed and non-dictatorial voting scheme is manipulable (in the sense of it being profitable for some voter at some profile to misrepresent his preferences in order to secure a social outcome preferred by him to that resulting in the event his vote reflects his true preferences). This manipulability (or non-cheatproofness) result was obtained by the above-mentioned authors under the (implicit) assumption that the number of individuals (voters) is finite. In the case of an infinite set of individuals the impossibility of a cheatproof social choice function no longer holds. This is shown in [8].

The concept of individual-cheatproofness can be extended quite naturally to the notion of coalitional-cheatproofness: Let a be a finite set of at least three distinct objects, called alternatives, and let Σ be the set of total, transitive, asymmetric (preference) orderings over a. Let V be a non-empty set of individuals. The elements in Σ^V are referred to as preference profiles. A social choice function (SCF) is a function $f\colon \Sigma^V \to a$. An SCF f is coalitionally-manipulable if for some preference profile $p = \{p_1\}_{i \in V}$ in Σ^V and some (non-empty) coalition $A \subset V$ there exists a preference profile $p' = \{p'_i\}_{i \in V}$ in Σ^V such that $p'_j = p_j$ for $j \notin A$ and $f(p')p_i f(p)$ for every $i \in A$. If f is not coalitionally-manipulable, f is said to be coalitionally-cheatproof.

In the case where V, the set of voters, is infinite it is shown in Pazner and Wesley [8] that there exists a coalitionally-cheatproof non-imposed

First version received July 1975; final version accepted September 1976 (Eds.).

and non-dictatorial SCF. Yet, while the existence of a coalitionally-cheatproof social choice function is rigorously proven in [8], the essentially non-constructive method of proof used there does not make it possible actually to present any concrete example of such a cheatproof method of social choice.

In this paper we turn to the constructive aspects of the problem of designing a coalitionally-cheatproof social choice function for large societies. One would like, if possible, to exhibit a coalitionally-cheatproof, non-imposed, non-dictatorial SCF in some explicit fashion.[1] It appears, however, that this cannot be done. If $V = \{1, 2, \ldots\}$ and has at least three alternatives, then the existence of an SCF $f: \Sigma^V \to a$ having these properties cannot be proven unless one uses some form of the axiom of choice.[2] Since every explicitly describable function is, in all likelihood, "constructible" within ZF (the Zermelo−Fraenkel axioms of set theory excluding the axiom of choice), a plausible conclusion is that no "definable" SCF exists bearing these properties.

The object of this work is to consider constructibly definable SCF's which, in some sense, very nearly satisfy the conditions (coalitionally-cheatproof, non-imposed, non-dictatorial). The social choice functions we consider are essentially variations of the plurality rule. The paper is divided into two parts. Section 2 deals with individual cheatproofness. We produce a limit theorem which asserts that when the number of voters is large (but finite) the plurality rule is individually-cheatproof most of the time. The coalitional aspects of the problem are the subject matter of Section 3.

2   A limit theorem on the plurality rule

Let $a = \{a_1, \ldots, a_k\}$ be a set of alternatives and let $V_n = \{v_1, \ldots, v_n\}$ be a set of individuals. Let Σ denote the set of all strong orderings (i.e. the set of total, asymmetric and transitive binary relations) on a. Each element $p = (p_1, \ldots, p_n)$ in Σ^{V_n} (the set of functions from V_n to Σ), where $p_i \in \Sigma$ for all i, $1 \le i \le n$, is called a preference profile. A function f from Σ^{V_n} to a is called a social choice function (SCF). An SCF f is said

---

[1] This problem does not arise if only individual-cheatproofness is required; for an explicit example, see [8].

[2] If $F: \Sigma^V \to a$ is a coalitionally-cheatproof, non-dictatorial, non-imposed SCF, then using F one can construct a non-principal ultrafilter over V (see [8]). It is shown in [3], however, that the existence of a non-principal ultrafilter over V cannot be proven in ZF alone. ($ZF \equiv$ the Zermelo−Fraenkel axioms of set theory without the axiom of choice.)

to be individually-manipulable at $p = (p_1, \ldots, p_n) \in \Sigma^{V_n}$ if there exist $p_i' \in \Sigma$ and an i_0, $1 \leq i_0 \leq n$ such that

$$f(p_i', p_2', \ldots, p_n')p_{i_0}f(p_1, p_2, \ldots, p_n)$$

where $p_i' = p_i$ for all $i \neq i_0$. f is individually-cheatproof at p if it is not individually-manipulable at that profile.

For every $p = (p_1, \ldots, p_n)$ in Σ^{V_n} and every i, $1 \leq i \leq k$, let $C(p, i) = \{v_j | v_j \in V_n$ and $a_i p_j a_l$ for all a_l in a such that $a_l \neq a_i\}$, i.e. $C(p, i)$ is the set of individuals who most prefer a_i under the profile p. Let $|C(p, i)|$ be the number of individuals in $C(p, i)$. In conformance with this notation, let $|V_n|$ be the number of individuals in V_n, i.e. $|V_n| = n$. We define the plurality rule $F: \Sigma^{V_n} \to a$ as follows:

Let $p = (p_1, \ldots, p_n)$ be a preference profile in Σ^{V_n}. If for some i, $1 \leq i \leq k$,

$$|C(p, i)| > |C(p, l)|$$

for all l, $1 \leq l j k$, $l \neq i$, then let $F(p) = a_i$. If not, let $F(p) = a_{j_1}$ where j_1 is the smallest index such that $|C(p, j_1)| \geq |C(p, l)|$ for all l, $1 \leq l \leq k$.

Let $\mathcal{D}_n$ be the set of preference profiles in Σ^{V_n} for which F is individually-cheatproof.

Let $|\mathcal{D}_n|$, $|\Sigma^{V_n}|$ be the number of elements in $\mathcal{D}_n$ and Σ^{V_n}, respectively.

Theorem 1:

$$\lim_{n \to \infty} \frac{|\mathcal{D}_n|}{|\Sigma^{V_n}|} = 1.$$

To prove the theorem, two auxiliary lemmas will be utilized. In order to formulate them, we introduce some additional notation.

For any $\varepsilon > 0$ and any natural number n, and any i, j, $1 \leq i \leq k$, $1 \leq j \leq k$, $i \neq j$, let

$$T(n, \varepsilon, i, j) = \left\{ p | p \in \Sigma^{V_n}, \frac{|C(p, i) - C(p, j)|}{\sqrt{2n/k}} < \varepsilon \right\}.$$

Let $|T(n, \varepsilon, i, j)|$ be the number of preference profiles in $T(n, \varepsilon, i, j)$. Then:

Lemma 1:

$\lim_{n \to \infty} |T(n, \varepsilon, i, j)|/|\Sigma^{V_n}| \leq 2\varepsilon/\sqrt{2\pi}$ for any i, j, $1 \leq i \leq k$, $1 \leq j \leq k$, $i \neq j$.

Proof: In proving the Lemma we make use of the central limit theorem in probability theory ([6, p. 290]). We assume that a probability measure P is defined over Σ so that all preference orders in Σ are equally likely to occur when random choices are made[3] (i.e. we assume that all possible profiles are equally probable for the society under consideration).

Suppose that each $v_m \in V_n$ randomly chooses a preference ordering p_m in accordance with the probability measure P. A randomly selected preference profile $p = (p_1, \ldots, p_n)$ is thereby obtained. The probabilities are then such that given any $a_{i_1}, a_{i_2} \in a$, where $a_{i_1} \neq a_{i_2}$, we have $P(a_{i_1} p_m a_{i_2}) = P(a_{i_2} p_m a_{i_1})$. Let $i, j, i \neq j$, be any fixed natural numbers between 1 and k, inclusive. Define in the following manner the random variables $\xi_1, \xi_2, \ldots$, over the set of infinite sequences of preference orders:

$$\xi_l \overset{\text{def}}{=} \xi_l(p_1, p_2, \ldots) = \begin{cases} 1 & \text{if under } p_l, a_i \text{ is preferred over all other} \\ & \text{elements in } a \\ -1 & \text{if under } p_l, a_j \text{ is preferred over all other} \\ & \text{elements in } a \\ 0 & \text{otherwise.} \end{cases} \tag{2.1}$$

Each ξ_l then depends only on the lth element, p_l, of the infinite sequence, i.e. $\xi_l(p) = \bar{\xi}_l(p_l)$ where $\bar{\xi}_l$ is defined in obvious fashion. It is thus easily seen that

$$\left\{ p = (p_1, \ldots, p_n) \mid p \in \Sigma^{V_n}, \frac{|\Sigma_{l=1}^{i=n} \xi_l(p_l)|}{\sqrt{2n/k}} < \varepsilon \right\} = T(n, \varepsilon, i, j)$$

and that consequently

$$P\left(\frac{|\Sigma_{l=1}^{l=n} \xi_l|}{\sqrt{2n/k}} < \varepsilon \right) = \frac{|T(n, \varepsilon, i, j)|}{|\Sigma^{V_n}|}.$$

Therefore, it is sufficient to prove that

$$\lim_{n \to \infty} P\left(\frac{|\Sigma_{l=1}^{l=n} \xi_l|}{\sqrt{2n/k}} < \varepsilon \right) \leq 2\varepsilon/\sqrt{2\pi}. \tag{2.2}$$

For each random variable ξ_l, let $\bar{a}_l = E(\xi_l)$, the expectation of ξ_l. Then $\bar{a}_l = 0$ for all l. Let $\bar{b}_l^2 = E(\xi_l - E(\xi_l))^2 = 2/k$. Let

$$B_n^2 = \Sigma_{l=1}^{l=n} \bar{b}_l^2 = 2n/k$$

---

[3] Note that throughout, the lower-case p and p_l stand for preference profiles and orderings respectively while capital P denotes the probability measure.

Let F_l be the distribution function of the random variable ξ_l. Then for any $\tau > 0$

$$\lim_{n \to \infty} \frac{1}{B_n^2} \Sigma_{l=1}^{l=n} \int_{|x - \bar{a}_l| > \tau B_n} (x - \bar{a}_l)^2 dF_l(x) = \lim_{n \to \infty} (k/2n) \Sigma_{l=1}^{l=n} \int_{x > \tau B_n} x^2 dF_l(x) = 0.$$

Hence, the Lindeberg condition (Gnedenko [6, p. 289]) is satisfied. Then by the central limit theorem (Gnedenko [6, p. 290]), as $n \to \infty$

$$P\left\{ \frac{1}{B_n} \Sigma_{k=1}^{k=n} (\xi_k - \bar{a}_k) < x \right\} \to \frac{1}{\sqrt{2\pi}} \int_{-\infty}^{x} \exp[-z^2/2] dz$$

uniformly in x. Thus

$$P\left(-\varepsilon < \frac{1}{B_n} \Sigma_{l=1}^{l=n} \xi_l < \varepsilon \right) \to \frac{1}{\sqrt{2\pi}} \int_{-\varepsilon}^{\varepsilon} \exp[-z^2/2] dz < \frac{2\varepsilon}{\sqrt{2\pi}}$$

or

$$\lim_{n \to \infty} P\left(\frac{|\Sigma \xi_l|}{\sqrt{2n/k}} < \varepsilon \right) \leqq \frac{2\varepsilon}{\sqrt{2\pi}},$$

from which the truth of the lemma follows. ‖

Lemma 2: *Given any $\varepsilon > 0$ and any positive integer n, let*

$$T(n, \varepsilon) = \bigcup_{1 \leqq i, \, j \leqq k, \, i \neq j} T(n, \varepsilon, i, j).$$

Then

$$\lim_{n \to \infty} \frac{|T(n, \varepsilon)|}{|\Sigma^{V_n}|} \leqq k^2 \frac{2\varepsilon}{\sqrt{2\pi}}.$$

Proof: Let $P(T(n, \varepsilon))$ be the probability that a randomly chosen preference profile in Σ^{V_n} occurs in $T(n, \varepsilon)$. Then $P(T(n, \varepsilon)) = |T(n, \varepsilon)|/|\Sigma^{V_n}|$. However,

$$P(T(n, \varepsilon)) = P\left(\bigcup_{1 \leqq i, \, j \leqq k, \, i \neq j} T(n, \varepsilon, i, j) \right) \leqq \sum_{1 \leqq i, \, j \leqq k, \, i \neq j} P(T(n, \varepsilon, i, j)),$$

which for sufficiently large n is equal to or less than $k^2 2\varepsilon/\sqrt{2\pi}$. Then

$$\lim_{n \to \infty} \frac{|T(n, \varepsilon)|}{|\Sigma^{V_n}|} = \lim_{n \to \infty} (P(Tn, \varepsilon)) \leqq k^2 \frac{2\varepsilon}{\sqrt{2\pi}},$$

which completes the proof of the lemma. ‖

Now, consider $\Sigma^{V_n} \backslash T(n, \varepsilon)$. It follows from Lemma 2 that

$$\lim_{n \to \infty} \frac{|\Sigma^{V_n} \backslash T(n, \, \varepsilon)|}{|\Sigma^{V_n}|} \gtrsim 1 - \frac{k^2 2\varepsilon}{\sqrt{2\pi}}.$$

However, given any fixed $\varepsilon > 0$, for all sufficiently large n

$$\Sigma^{V_n} \backslash T(n, \, \varepsilon) \subset \mathscr{D}_n.$$

Thus, given any fixed $\varepsilon > 0$

$$\lim_{n \to \infty} \frac{|\mathscr{D}_n|}{|\Sigma^{V_n}|} \gtrsim 1 - \frac{k^2 2\varepsilon}{\sqrt{2\pi}},$$

from which the theorem follows. ||

Theorem 1 proved here indicates that the plurality rule (cum a reasonable tie-breaking device) is approximately cheatproof in large finite societies. More exactly, we have shown that as the number of individuals tends to infinity the proportion of profiles at which the plurality rule is individually-cheatproof tends to one. This means that the issue of preference misrepresentation by any single voter in a large society can be ignored for all practical purposes when social choices are made according to the plurality rule. This of course should have been expected on purely intuitive grounds as any isolated individual does not really count when society is sizeable. Somewhat less intuitive is Theorem 2 in the next section in which it is stated that a variant of the plurality rule is almost coalitionally-cheatproof in societies in which there is a countable infinity of voters.

3   Coalitional aspects

Regarding limit theorems for coalitional-cheatproofness, Stephen J. Nickell pointed out to us that it directly follows from the proof of Theorem 1 above that for coalitions of size n^α or less (with $0 \leqq \alpha < \frac{1}{2}$) the proportion of cheatproof profiles tends to 1 as n tends to infinity whenever $\varepsilon \sqrt{2n}/k > n^\alpha$. In other words, under the plurality rule most profiles are cheatproof for small coalitions. In light of the cost of coalition formation, this is an interesting property.

It might also be worth while mentioning that this result can in some instances be extended to large coalitions as well. For example, if A is any infinite set of integers and A_n is the set of integers belonging to A that are less than n, then it is true that for large n, most profiles in Σ^{V_n} are cheatproof for the coalition A_n. The reason for that is that for most profiles there will be at least one member of A_n whose best element coincides with the social choice obtaining under the plurality rule. He will therefore not collaborate with others in bringing about a change. The presence of even one such recalcitrant destroys the unity of interests required for A_n to manipulate the outcome. While additional examples of types of coalitions (even large ones) that are most of the time unable to manipulate the outcome can readily be advanced, a full characterization of all such coalitions has proved to be beyond our ability at this point.

Also of interest is the question whether constructive coalitional-cheatproofness results can be advanced for the case of an infinite set of voters. We therefore turn now to the problem of formulating a variant of the plurality rule for infinitely sized societies which is almost always cheatproof with respect to a well defined class of coalitions.

Let $V = \{1, 2, \ldots\}$ be a countably infinite set of voters, $a = \{a_1, \ldots, a_m\}$ a finite set of alternatives, Σ the set of total, transitive, asymmetric (preference) orders over a. The elements $p = (p_1, p_2, \ldots) \in \Sigma^V$ are referred to as preference profiles. We would like to define a social choice function $f: \Sigma^V \to a$ which chooses the alternative favoured by a "plurality" of the voters. Since there are likely to be an infinite set of voters favouring each alternative we cannot determine plurality simply by counting.

We are therefore led to settle for a social choice function which falls short of being a plurality rule in the strict sense. For any integer $1 \leq n \leq \infty$ and any natural i, $1 \leq i \leq m$ and any $p \in \Sigma^V$, let $C_n(p, i) = \{j \mid 1 \leq j \leq n$ and $a_i p_j a_k$ for all $a_k \neq a_i$, $a_k \in a\}$. Let $|C_n(p, i)|$ be the number of j's in $C_n(p, i)$. We consider the following SCF, $F: \Sigma^V \to a$: For any $p \in \Sigma^V$, if $\lim_{n \to \infty} |C_n(p, j)|/n$ exists for all j, $1 \leq j \leq m$ and if for some k, $1 \leq k \leq m$,

$$\lim_{n \to \infty} |C_n(p, k)|/n > \lim_{n \to \infty} |C_n(p, l)|/n$$

for all $l \neq k$, $1 \leq l \leq m$, then let $F(p) = a_k$. Otherwise, let $F(p) = a_1$. We note that for almost all p in Σ^V, $F(p) = a_1$. Thus F is very nearly an imposed regime. In those rare instances where a significant proportion of the population is unified against the regime's policy, the regime yields (the alternative a_1 may be thought to be the status-quo).

In presenting this SCF, our purpose is not to assert that it is an ideal one. Our contention, rather, is that in spite of the fact that the SCF, F, is less than ideal, it nevertheless illustrates the possibility of a workable democracy since it is in some sense coalitionally-cheatproof and hence conducive to social stability (without being fully imposed or dictatorial).

It is not difficult to show that F is not coalitionally-cheatproof in the strict sense. We shall claim, however, that for almost every profile $p \in \Sigma^V$, $F(p)$ is coalitionally-cheatproof for practically all of the important coalitions. By important coalitions we mean the following:

In dealing with large populations, the coalitions of significance are usually definable by some simple phrase in the English language, e.g. upper middle class, New Yorkers, coal miners, etc. Coalitions that are not easily definable are likely to be too complicated to be formed. If we carry this principle over to the case of an infinite population $V = \{1, 2, \ldots\}$, we would conclude that the coalitions of significance are those that may be defined by a phrase in the English language, e.g., the set of even numbers, the set of primes less than 1500, etc. Although there are $2^{\aleph_0}$ subsets of V, only $\aleph_0$ are definable by sentences of finite length. Thus a substantial restriction is imposed on the coalitions of interest.

We would like to assert the following: If $\mathcal{A}$ is the set of coalitions definable in the English language, then for almost all p in Σ, F is coalitionally-cheatproof for all $A \in \mathcal{A}$. Although there seems to be no reason why such a result cannot be obtained, it is somewhat difficult to formulate this mathematically; we know of no adequate mathematical description of what constitutes a set which is definable in English. (What is and is not English?) We would prefer instead to consider a more mathematically precise language — the language of set theory. This language possesses a very small vocabulary — the symbols $\epsilon, \equiv, \forall, \exists, \sim$ (not), $\wedge$ (and), $\vee$ (or), and some rigidly defined syntactical rules for forming sentences. In spite of its meagreness, the language is nevertheless sufficiently powerful to formulate all of the familiar concepts in classical analysis — limits, irrationals, π, e, Bessel functions, etc. If we assume that classical concepts are adequate tools for forming models of social behaviour, we would conclude that the language of set theory is also satisfactory for this purpose. Thus in many situations the assumption that the admissible coalitions are those that can be described in the language of set theory seems to be quite acceptable. Let $\mathcal{A}$ be the set of coalitions (subsets of V) that are describable in the language of set theory. We then have the following result:

Theorem 2: *For almost all $p \in \Sigma^V$, the SCF F: $\Sigma^V \to a$ described above is cheatproof for all coalitions in $\mathcal{A}$.*[4]

Proof: We make use of the fact that $\mathcal{A}$ is countably infinite. Let $\bar{\mathcal{A}} = \{A_1, A_2, \ldots\}$ be a sequence (an enumeration) of infinite coalitions in

---

[4] By this we mean: For almost every $p \in \Sigma^V$ no $A \in \mathcal{A}$ exists such that for some

$$p' = (p'_1, p'_2, \ldots) \in \Sigma^V,$$

where $p'_i = p_i$ for $i \in A$, $F(p')p_j F(p)$ for all $j \in A$. We also wish to point out that this result generalizes to the case where the set of allowable coalitions is any countable number of subsets of V.

$\mathcal{A}$, whereby every infinite subset of V is indexed in the sequence. For every natural k let

$Q_k = \{p \mid p = \{p_1, p_2, \ldots\} \in \Sigma^V$ and for every natural j between 1 and m (where m is the number of alternatives in a) there are an infinite number of i's in A_k who favour a_j (under p) above all other alternatives$\}$.

By virtue of the Borel−Cantelli lemma ([6, p. 247]) we find that the probability that a randomly selected profile $p \in \Sigma^V$ will belong to Q_k is 1, given any natural number k. Thus if we let $Q = \cap_{k=1}^{k=\infty} Q_k$, it follows that prob $(\{p \mid p \in Q\})$, the probability that a randomly selected $p \in \Sigma^V$ will belong to Q, is also equal to 1. Let

$R \stackrel{\text{def}}{\equiv} \{p \mid p = (p_1, p_2, \ldots) \in \Sigma^V$ and for every natural j between 1 and m, $\lim_{n \to \infty} |C_n(p, j)|/n$ exists and is equal to $1/m\}$.

As a result of the strong law of large numbers, prob $(\{p \mid p \in R\}) = 1$. Letting $S = R \cap Q$, we receive that prob $(\{p \mid p \in S\}) = 1$. Clearly $F(p) = a_1$ for every $p \in S$. Moreover, given any $p \in S$, $F(p)$ is coalitionally-cheatproof with respect to every coalition $A \in \mathcal{A}$. This is because for any $A \in \mathcal{A}$ and all $p \in S$, an infinite number of voters in A will prefer a_1 to all other alternatives.

It should be noted that there are coalitions of interest which are not included in $\mathcal{A}$. For example, consider an arbitrary preference profile $p = (p_1, p_2, \ldots) \in \Sigma^V$ and let $A_p^{a_2}$ be the set of voters who most prefer a_2 under the profile p, i.e. $A_p^{a_2} = \{j \mid a_2 p_j a_i$ for all $a_i \neq a_2$, $a_i \in A\}$. For almost all p in Σ^V, $A_p^{a_2} \notin \mathcal{A}$. We can argue, however, that in many practical cases, coalitions like $A_p^{a_2}$ cannot actually arise. Completely free communication among the voters with regard to their true preferences would be required in order for this group to form. When existing conditions do not permit free communication, these coalitions are not likely to arise. In such situations, the formable coalitions are only those belonging to $\mathcal{A}$. With these underlying considerations of the costs of coalition formation, we believe the present result to be of some practical interest.

REFERENCES

1. Bourbaki, N. *Elements of Mathematics: General Topology*, Part 1 (Reading, Massachusetts: Addison-Wesley, 1966).
2. Dummet, M. and Farquharson, R. "Stability in Voting", *Econometrica*, 29 [1961], especially p. 34.
3. Feferman, S. "Some applications of the Notions of Forcing and Generic Sets

(Summary)", *The Theory of Models* (Proceedings of the 1963 International Symposium at Berkeley, North Holland Publishing, 1965, 89–95).

4. Fishburn, P. C. "Arrow's Impossibility Theorem: Concise Proof and Infinite Voters", *Journal of Economic Theory*, 2 [1970], 103–106.
5. Gibbard, A. "Manipulation of Voting Schemes: A General Result", *Econometrica*, *41* (1973), 587–601.
6. Gnedenko, B. V. *The Theory of Probability* (Chelsea, New York, 1963).
7. Kirman, A. P. and Sondermann, D. "Arrow's Theorem, Many Agents, and Invisible Dictators", *Journal of Economic Theory*, 5 [1972], 267–277.
8. Pazner, E. A. and Wesley, E. "Stability of Social Choices in Infinitely Large Societies", *Journal of Economic Theory*, *14* [1977], 252–262.
9. Satterthwaite, M. "Strategy Proofness and Arrow's Conditions: Existence and Correspondence Theorems for Voting Procedures and Social Welfare Functions", *Journal of Economic Theory*, *10* [1975], 187–217.
10. Schmeidler, D. and Sonnenschein, H. "The Possibility of a Cheat-Proof Social Choice Function: A Theorem of A. Gibbard and M. Satterthwaite" (Discussion Paper No. 89, Revised, The Center for Mathematical Studies in Economics and Management Science, Northwestern University, Evanston, Illinois, May 1974).
11. Vickrey, W. "Utility, Strategy, and Social Decision Rules", *Quarterly Journal of Economics*, *74* [1960], especially p. 518.

Egalitarian equivalent allocations: a new concept of economic equity

Elisha A. Pazner and David Schmeidler

Foreword

The conceptual difficulties involved in the quest for a normative criterion for social choice are well-known. Arrow's celebrated impossibility theorem has taught us to be more modest in our search for such a criterion than earlier pioneers of the new welfare economics had been hoping for. In the context of assessing the relative social desirability of alternative economic allocations, the concept of Pareto efficiency still stands out as the central cornerstone of normative economics. However, since it is recognized that some Pareto allocations may be rather inequitable from some intuitive distributional viewpoint, one would like to supplement the Pareto condition with some notion of economic justice. If possible, attempts should be made to design notions of distributive justice that, like the Pareto criterion itself, are ordinal in nature and do not involve questionable interpersonal utility comparisons. This paper presents such an attempt.

1   Introduction

While a systematic review of the vast literature on normative economics is beyond the scope of this paper, some brief remarks regarding the present state of the art will help put the problem of economic equity in proper perspective.

When one rereads such classics of the new welfare economics as Bergson (1938), Samuelson (1947, 1950, 1956), and Graaff (1957), one

Pazner's research was done while he visited Northwestern University. Schmeidler's research was done partly in Tel-Aviv and partly while he visited the University of Illinois. The research in Tel-Aviv was supported by the Foerder Institute for Economic Research.

cannot help but feel how disturbing for normative economics Arrow's (1963) general impossibility theorem really is. If Bergsonian social welfare functions had been able to satisfy Arrow's minimal conditions on such functions, a very powerful analytical concept would indeed have become available. Significant insights to normative economics have nevertheless been provided by the social welfare function approach. But the explicit underlying (ordinal) interpersonal welfare comparisons (effectively ruled out by Arrow's result) imply that a robust equity criterion, normatively compelling for any possible economy, cannot be derived from this particular approach.

The question that suggests itself therefore is whether any reasonable equity criterion, the normative significance of which is equally valid in any particular society (economy), can be advanced.

A few years ago Foley (1967) advanced the concept of fair (or envy-free) allocations as a reasonable equity criterion. An allocation is said to be fair if nobody prefers anybody else's bundle over his own. The concept of fairness is appealing from an equity viewpoint in that it treats economic agents symmetrically, is ordinal in nature, and is free of interpersonal comparisons of utility. However, as shown by Pazner and Schmeidler (1974), standard Arrow–Debreu production economies may display the disturbing feature that among all Pareto-efficient allocations none can be found that is fair. In light of the general acceptance of the Pareto criterion, it would be desirable to have a concept of equity that never conflicts with Pareto efficiency (under the standard assumptions on the economic environment). Since the fairness criterion does not possess this property and since there is also the question of whether an equity concept based on envy can be morally acceptable in the first place (see Rawls, 1971), the issue of defining an adequate criterion is still open.

The present paper introduces a concept of economic equity that, as fairness, possesses an appealing symmetry property, is ordinal in nature, and is free of interpersonal welfare comparisons. Specifically, an allocation is said to be egalitarian-equivalent if there exists a fixed commodity bundle (the same for each agent) that is considered by each agent to be indifferent to the bundle that he actually gets in the allocation under consideration. In other words, an egalitarian-equivalent allocation has the special property that its underlying welfare distribution could have been generated by an egalitarian economy. It is shown that Pareto-efficient and egalitarian-equivalent allocations always exist under (even weaker than) the standard conditions on the economic environment. When supplemented by the egalitarian-equivalence criterion, the set of Pareto-efficient allocations is thus restricted to those allocations having the property that there exists an egalitarian economy (i.e., an economy in which everybody gets an identical bundle) in which every agent enjoys precisely the same welfare level as that experienced by him at the Pareto allocation under consideration. Another equivalent way of characterizing the set of Pareto allocations that are admissible according to the egalitarian-equivalence criterion is to visualize those for which all the underlying indifference surfaces have at least one point of intersection (when drawn in the same commodity space with respect to the same origin).

Two remarks on our approach are called for at this point. First, note that the normative significance of an egalitarian-equivalent allocation derives from its being agent-wise indifferent to the egalitarian distribution of commodities in some hypothetical economy. This may bring to mind the hypothetical compensation tests of Kaldor (1939), Hicks (1939), Scitovsky (1941), and Samuelson (1950) in some of which a state of the economy was said to be better than another if in the first state everybody could be made better off than in the second by suitable lump-sum transfers (without requiring actual compensation to be effected). But note that in our case the welfare distribution is *not* hypothetical (only the reference egalitarian economy conducive to the same welfare distribution is). Since our interest here is precisely in the distributional aspects of any allocation, the distribution of welfare is all-important; in the compensation tests, efficiency was the issue so that the actual distribution of welfare was essentially ignored. Potential welfare was the issue there; actual welfare is the issue here.

The second remark we wish to make deals with the horizontal and vertical equity aspects of any egalitarian-equivalent allocation (see Musgrave, 1959, for the concepts of horizontal and vertical equity). Any two individuals having identical preferences will enjoy precisely the same welfare level in any egalitarian-equivalent allocation (since the egalitarian reference economy assigns to everybody an identical bundle that is preference-wise indifferent for each individual to his actual bundle). Hence horizontal equity is satisfied; that is, equal treatment of equals is assured. For any two individuals having different preferences, the inequality in their actual bundles in any egalitarian-equivalent allocation is limited by the requirement that their underlying indifference curves (surfaces) contain at least one common bundle (since they must meet precisely at the egalitarian allocation of the hypothetical reference economy). Hence a particular notion of vertical equity is implicit in the egalitarian-equivalence criterion; an egalitarian economy exists that would assign to each individual the same welfare level as in the actual allocation.

The main results in the present paper are as follows. The new concept of equity is shown to be consistent with Pareto efficiency in both pure exchange and production economies (Sections 2 and 5). In the case of two-person economies, it is shown that any fair allocation is also egalitarian-equivalent (Section 3). In the case of n-person economies this relationship no longer holds, but it is seen that the larger becomes the number of agents, the smaller becomes the set of Pareto-efficient and egalitarian-equivalent allocations in relation to the set of Pareto allocations (Section 2). It is also interesting to note that some very natural maximin interpretations (justifications?) can be given to the set of Pareto-efficient and egalitarian-equivalent allocations (Section 4).

The precise plan of the paper is as follows. In Section 2 the concept of egalitarian-equivalent allocation is further explained, and its consistency with the Pareto criterion established. Section 3 relates the new concept to that of fairness and presents an arbitration scheme for allocations based on the new concept. Section 4 discusses some maximin interpretations of the results and relates the present approach to Rawls's theory of justice. While Sections 2 through 3 deal mainly with pure exchange economies, it is made explicit in Section 5 that the results carry over to production economies.

The Mathematical Appendices at the end of the paper contain the relevant definitions and statements for each section. A section containing the proofs concludes the appendices. The text and the appendices have been designed to make it possible for them to be read independently. Both the text and the appendices are self-contained, but the reader of the appendices should consult the text for interpretive purposes.

2   The concept of Pareto-efficient-egalitarian-equivalent allocations (PEEEA)

Consider a standard pure exchange economy in which externalities are absent and where each consumer has preferences over the nonnegative orthant of the (Euclidean) commodity space that can be represented by a continuous and monotone-increasing utility function .Given any vector of aggregate endowments, modern welfare economics has singled out the set of Pareto-efficient allocations (the contract curve) as the relevant set of allocations from the viewpoint of normative social choice.

The problem of course is that the contract curve (more generally, the Pareto set) contains some rather unappetizing allocations (for instance all those at which one individual gets everything, or more generally those in which one or some individuals do not get anything). The subject matter of the theory of economic equity, as we see it, is to supplement the Pareto criterion by an ethically appealing distributional criterion, the role of which should essentially be to restrict the set of admissible Pareto-efficient allocations. As the theoretical justification for any equity criterion depends heavily on its being consistent with the existing conceptual framework of modern economic theory, our objective is to present an equity criterion that does not presume interpersonal welfare comparisons and that does not stand in conflict with the ordinal nature of Pareto-efficiency.

For the sake of expositional simplicity, consider the case where there are two consumers and two commodities (but note that every step in the argument carries over to any number of agents and commodities; see the Mathematical Appendix to this section). Suppose that each consumer is given precisely half the total endowments. This egalitarian distribution will in general not be Pareto-efficient. Consider the ray in commodity space that goes from the origin through the vector of aggregate endowments. The egalitarian distribution is represented by each man being given the same bundle along this ray. If the egalitarian distribution is not Pareto-efficient, then (by monotonicity and continuity of preferences) moving each man slightly up along the ray yields distributions of utilities that are still feasible, since the starting utility distribution is in the interior of the utility possibility set. In particular, if we simultaneously move each man up along the commodity ray in precisely the same manner, we eventually shall hit a utility distribution that lies on the utility possibility frontier. This means that there exists a Pareto-efficient allocation that is equivalent from the viewpoint of each consumer to the hypothetical (nonfeasible) distribution along the ray that would give to each consumer the same bundle (which, by being strictly greater than the egalitarian distribution of the aggregate endowments, is itself not feasible). This Pareto-efficient allocation is thus equivalent to the egalitarian distribution in the hypothetical (larger than the original) economy.

It is now clear that we can repeat this experiment along any positive direction in the commodity space and by so doing generate the set of Pareto-efficient allocations, each of them having the following property: there is an egalitarian allocation in some hypothetical economy (in which the preferences of the agents are identical to those of the economy under consideration and the aggregate endowments of some or all commodities are larger than those of the original economy), so that the welfare levels in the hypothetical economy are agent-wise equal to those of the allocation under consideration.

The resulting set of allocations is what we call the set of Pareto-efficient and egalitarian-equivalent allocations (PEEEA in the sequel). It is a restriction of the Pareto set of the economy to those allocations having the specified equity property that their underlying utility levels distribution could have been generated by some egalitarian economy.

That this method indeed restricts the set of admissible Pareto-efficient allocations is clear, since, for instance, under strictly monotone preferences the "end-points" of the utility possibility frontier (in which some consumers get nothing) are excluded. How substantial the restriction is in fact depends of course on the precise form of the preference orderings. However, it is obvious that, under strict convexity of preferences when the number of agents is much greater than that of commodities, the restriction is significant — a desirable result.

From the viewpoint of the ethical appeal of the concept, observe that it is equivalent to restricting the set of admissible Pareto-efficient allocations to those for which the underlying indifference surfaces all meet at least once at a bundle common to all. Since each man is indifferent between having his actual bundle and a given bundle, that is also indifferent from the viewpoint of every other consumer, the concept treats agents symmetrically in this sense.

3   PEEEA as a fair arbitration scheme for allocations

In this section we relate the concept of Pareto-efficient-egalitarian-equivalent allocations to that of fair and Pareto-efficient allocations. We do so by confining most of the discussion to two-person economies. The special interest of this case stems from its applicability to the well-known two-person bargaining problem. We note in passing that the search for plausible arbitration schemes is very closely related to the quest for an acceptable normative criterion for the division of economic resources; in either case we are looking for solution concepts that will be deemed "fair" when all possible social environments (preferences, resources, etc.) are considered at the outset. The bargaining problem is usually formulated in terms of cardinal utilities and admits of a number of interesting solutions (e.g., Harsanyi−Zeuthen, 1956; Nash, 1950; and the recent work of Kalai−Smorodinsky, 1975). The case of ordinal preferences, on which so much of economic theory is based, presents special difficulties and does not yet lead to comparable solution concepts. The notion of a fair allocation can be thought of as presenting a plausible way of restricting the set of admissible solutions in the ordinal case. Before discussing the relevance of the PEEEA concept in the present context, it thus seems appropriate to review briefly some results of the fairness literature.

Recall the definition of a fair allocation. An allocation is said to be fair (equitable) if no individual prefers the bundle of any other individual in the allocation over his own. In other words, a fair allocation is an allocation in which there is no envy; no individual would like to switch bundles with any other. A Pareto-efficient allocation that is fair is called a fair and Pareto-efficient allocation. Fair and Pareto-efficient allocations have been the subject of some recent literature (Foley, 1967; Pazner and Schmeidler, 1974; and Varian, 1974). The main result in the present context is that while fair and Pareto-efficient allocations always exist in standard pure exchange economies, they may fail to exist in standard production economies (Pazner and Schmeidler, 1974). This failure is not restricted to the two-person case; we shall come back to this matter later on. Hence the need for a different normative criterion which one would like, as in the case of fairness, to be ordinal in nature and free of interpersonal welfare comparisons.

As argued below, a major appeal of the concept of PEEEA in the two-person case lies in its including all fair and efficient allocations whenever they exist and importantly in its consistency in the general n-person case (in the sense that Pareto-efficient-egalitarian-equivalent allocations always exist) even when fair and efficient allocations fail to exist.

For the sake of expositional simplicity we shall conduct the discussion in this section in terms of two commodities. As shown in the Mathematical Appendix to this section, the results carry over to any number of commodities.

Note first that if the indifference curves of the two individuals (each drawn with respect to the same origin and passing through the corresponding agent's bundle) do not intersect, then the allocation under consideration cannot be fair, for, in such a case the indifference curve of one of the agents must lie below that of the other, implying that the first agent envies the second. Since the PEEEA restriction of the Pareto set is precisely via the exclusion of all Pareto-efficient allocations for which the indifference curves do not intersect, we conclude that this method does not rule any fair and Pareto-efficient allocation.

Second, observe that while the intersection of the underlying indifference curves is necessary for any allocation to be fair, it is by no means sufficient. It is easy to see that if each agent's bundle lies on the same side of the intersection point (when the latter is unique), it must be the case that one agent envies the other.

We conclude thus that the set of Pareto-efficient-egalitarian-equivalent allocations (PEEEA) includes the set of Pareto-efficient and fair allocations, and that the latter is usually a proper subset of the former.

Coming back to the bargaining problem, consider the following proposed solution. Suppose that the preferences in a two-person exchange economy are convex. The suggested solution is the PEEEA, which is equivalent to the egalitarian reference bundle lying on the ray through the aggregate endowment. The choice of this ray is motivated by the fact that the particular PEEEA induced by it is fair. To see this, note that the average bundle for this allocation must lie at or below the egalitarian reference bundle, both being on the same ray. This fact coupled with the convexity (toward the origin) of the indifference curves precludes the possibility of envy.

It is easy to see that for any other ray, one can find convex preferences such that the resulting PEEEA is not fair.

Thus the choice of the ray through the aggregate endowment yields a well-defined, fair, and canonic arbitration scheme for two-person exchange economies with convex preferences. This scheme (i.e., selecting the PEEEA corresponding to this canonic ray) can be applied to any number of agents and commodities. In the case of more than two agents, the resulting PEEEA need not be fair; however, the scheme still yields a determinate distribution of welfare levels even when the preferences are not convex (in which case fair and efficient allocations may fail to exist altogether). An additional justification for the concept of PEEEA with an arbitrary number of agents is provided in the next section that discusses its natural maximin interpretations. There again, the special role of the ray through aggregate endowments will be brought out.

Finally, note also that the arbitration scheme presented here remains well defined when considering economies with production; the resulting PEEEA, however, need not be fair even in the two-person case, since fair and efficient allocations may not exist in production economies.

4   Maximin properties of PEEEA

In light of the interest in the maximin criterion for social welfare generated by Rawls's *A Theory of Justice* (1971), we turn now to some natural maximin interpretations of the notion of PEEEA.

Consider a ray in commodity space. For each individual choose the utility function representing his preferences so that the utility level of a point on the ray is equal to its Euclidean distance from the origin. Due to our assumptions on preferences (total, transitive, reflexive, continuous, and monotonic binary relations over the commodity space), this is a well-defined utility function. Applying the Rawlsian maximin social welfare function to these particular utility representations yields a Pareto-efficient allocation (which is unique if strict convexity of preferences is also assumed). This allocation is egalitarian-equivalent; all the individuals obtain equal utility levels, and a corresponding egalitarian bundle is located on the ray at a distance from the origin equal to the common utility level. Thus, the application of Rawls's maximin principle leads to a Pareto-efficient allocation that for each individual is indifferent preference-wise to the egalitarian allocation in some hypothetical economy. Stated somewhat differently, the PEEEA notion is consistent with the maximin principle.

A different way to relate the concept of PEEEA to Rawls's theory of justice is the following. Suppose that individuals in a Rawlsian original position have to decide about the distribution of some vector of aggregate endowments. As shown in Pazner and Schmeidler (1976), these individuals will unanimously agree on the egalitarian distribution of resources. One problem with this solution is that it usually will not be Pareto efficient. But if it is assumed that people in the original position accept the principle of Pareto efficiency, the egalitarian contract can be taken to mean that only Pareto-efficient allocations that could have been generated utility-wise by egalitarian economies (i.e., only PEEEA) are admissible. This suggests that the notion of PEEEA is consistent with social choices in the original position. We shall return to this point later on.

Returning to the method of calibrating the utilities in order to apply the maximin criterion, we believe that some remarks seem appropriate. First, whenever a particular ray is considered, the choice of the Euclidean distance as a measure of utility is immaterial, since if the same monotone-increasing transformation is applied to all the utility functions, the maximin solution remains the same. The essential restriction is that given a consumption bundle along this ray, all the agents are supposed to assign an identical utility level to this consumption bundle. Thus, the choice of a ray, together with this "common utility" supposition, implies a particular method of interpersonal utility comparisons. It should be clear that the entire set of PEEEA is generated by letting the ray along which utilities are calibrated vary across all positive directions. So, the choice of the ray dictates the final outcome.

The ray passing through the aggregate endowment is of particular significance as it also passes through the average (egalitarian) bundle in any allocation. In view of the previously mentioned result that individuals in a Rawlsian original position will agree on the egalitarian distribution where each gets the vector of average endowments, the choice of the ray passing through this vector can be rationalized in terms of the revealed preferences of individuals in the original position. The welfare expectations of all the parties to the social contract being precisely reflected by the vector of average endowments makes it appropriate to calibrate preferences in this particular way. Agreeing on the PEEEA corresponding to this choice of ray (i.e., applying the maximin criterion to this specific way of comparing utilities) is then a natural solution from the viewpoint of the Rawlsian framework. This also completes our discussion of the previous section where we suggested this particular arbitration scheme for general n-person economies.

It may be worthwhile to note that the argument of the previous paragraph regarding the calibration of utilities by the average bundle can be used to rationalize the common practice to base welfare evaluations on economic indexes (cost of living, per capita consumption, or income, etc.) that are constructed on the basis of average economic bundles. To the pragmatic reasons underlying this implicit choice of "utility numéraire" one can add the analytical justification provided above.

We conclude this section by noting that while the maximin criterion cannot by itself rule out any particular Pareto-efficient allocation on a priori grounds, the major appeal of the PEEEA concept lies in its doing so in a plausible way. In the absence of explicit interpersonal utility comparisons, the maximin criterion is entirely inoperative. The notion of PEEEA, on the other hand, is devoid of any such comparisons, since the set of allocations induced by it is invariant under any admissible representation of the agents' preferences. This last remark should not be confused with the fact illustrated above that under a particular method of interpersonal comparisons any PEEEA can be generated by means of the maximin criterion.

5   PEEEA in economies with production

As mentioned earlier, the present paper is partly motivated by the fact that fair and Pareto-efficient allocations may fail to exist in standard Arrow–Debreu production economies. Since Pareto efficiency is too convincing a criterion to be given up lightly, the basic purpose of the paper is to present a new notion of equity that does not conflict with efficiency in production economies as well. In this section our sole intention is to show that the concept of PEEEA is well defined even in the presence of production. All the results that were presented for exchange economies (with the obvious exception of the fairness result of Proposition 6 in the Mathematical Appendix to Section 3) carry over to production economies.

As usual, describe the production possibilities of the economy by the set of technologically feasible production plans. This set, combined with the aggregate initial endowments (including labor services, capital goods, etc.) defines the set of feasible final aggregate bundles (assumed to be closed and bounded). Due to the presence of different labor (leisure) services and nonfinal-consumption goods, it is customary and reasonable to weaken the monotonicity assumption of preferences to weak mono-tonicity (and local nonsatiation). However, we add an assumption of utility connectedness across the agents. Specifically, we assume that whenever an agent is not at his minimum welfare position, it is possible to increase the level of welfare of any other agent (by direct transfer of commodities or indirectly via production). Thus, existence and maximin properties of the PEEEA are maintained.

Two special points concerning the choice of a ray are worth noting. First, rays along which the labor services (leisure) are not in equal proportions could be excluded. This may be rationalized by the implicit assumption that each agent derives utility only from his own labor ser-vices (which is interpreted as leisure) so that the quantities of the labor services with which he is not endowed are immaterial to him; (this observation is also part of the reason for dropping the strict monotonicity assumption on preferences). And if we want the egalitarian-reference-bundles to be truly egalitarian, we would like them to contain equal amounts of labor services (i.e., equal consumption of leisure) as well as equal amounts of final commodities.

The second point concerning the choice of a ray is the following. If we choose a ray passing through a particular feasible final aggregate bundle, the average bundle of a corresponding PEEEA need not lie on the same ray. Thus the existence of a canonic ray (i.e., a ray passing through both the egalitarian-reference-bundle and the average bundle of a correspond-ing PEEEA) is not obvious. However, an application of a fixed point argument (as shown in the Appendix) yields the existence of the desired canonic ray. But if only rays along which labor services are in equal proportions are considered such a canonic ray may not exist.

Mathematical appendices

Mathematical appendix to Section 2

Let T denote the (finite) set of agents in the economy and let R^l_+ denote the nonnegative orthant of the Euclidean space of dimensions l, the set of commodity bundles. Each t in T has a preference relation $\geq_t$ on R^l_+, which is assumed to be *total*, *transitive*, *continuous*, and *monotonic* (i.e., for all x, y, z in R^l_+ the following hold: $x \geq_t y$ or $y \geq_t x$; $x \geq_t y$ and $y \geq_t z$ imply that $x \geq_t z$; the sets $\{x' \in R^l_+ | x' \geq_t x\}$ and $\{x' \in R^l_+ | x \geq_t x'\}$ are closed in R^l_+, and $x \geqq y$ and $x \neq y$ imply that $x >_t y$, where inequalities between vectors in R^l_+ hold coordinate-wise by definition, and the rela-tions $>_t$ and $\sim_t$ are induced by $\geq_t$ in the usual way).

The *economy* is formally defined as the vector $(T, R^l_+, \{\geq_t\}_{t \in T}, w)$

where w is an aggregate, initial commodity vector, $w > 0$, $w \in R_+^l$. The equity problem is that of dividing w among the members of T. An *allocation* is a T-list of elements of R_+^l whose sum is smaller than or equal to w. An allocation is denoted by $\{x_t\}_{t \in T}$ or simply $\{x_t\}$. An allocation $\{x_t\}$ is *Pareto-efficient* if for any other allocation $\{y_t\}$ the implication,

$$(\forall_t \in T, y_t \gtrsim_t x_t) \rightarrow (\forall_t \in T, y_t \sim_t x_t)$$

holds.

Definition: An allocation $\{x_t\}$ is said to be *egalitarian equivalent* if there is a bundle z in R_+^l so that for all t in T, $z \sim_t x_t$; such a vector z is called an *egalitarian-reference-bundle*.

In particular, the constant allocation $\{y_t\}$ where for all t, $y_t = w/|T|$ is egalitarian equivalent. First, the following results are established.

Proposition 1: *For every $\bar{x} > 0$ in R_+^l there is a positive real number $\bar{r}$ so that there exists a Pareto-efficient-egalitarian-equivalent allocation $\{x_t\}$ with $\bar{r}\bar{x}$ being the egalitarian-reference-bundle (i.e., for all t in T, $\bar{r}\bar{x} \sim_t x_t$).*

For the next result the *strict convexity* assumption is used: For all t in T, all x, $y \in R_+^l$ and all $0 < r < 1$, if $x \neq y$ and $x \gtrsim_t y$, then $rx + (1 - r)y >_t y$. We then have the straightforward result.

Proposition 2: *Under the assumption of strict convexity, for every egalitarian bundle there is at most one Pareto-efficient allocation.*

The following technical result is needed for the sequel:

Proposition 3: *Let there be given a convergent sequence $(\bar{x}_n)$ in R_+^l with a limit $\bar{x} > 0$ and suppose also that $\bar{x}_n > 0$ for all n. Denote by $\bar{r}_n$ (and $\bar{r}$) the real number corresponding to $\bar{x}_n$ (and $\bar{x}$) via Proposition 1. Then one has $\bar{r}_n \rightarrow \bar{r}$.*

Denote by P the set

$$\left\{ x \in R_+^l \,|\, x > 0 \text{ and } \sum_{i=1}^{l} x^i = 1 \right\}$$

and denote by RP the set of egalitarian-reference-bundles: $\{\bar{r}\bar{x} \in R_+^l \,|\, \bar{x} \in P$ and $\bar{r}$ corresponds to $\bar{x}$ via Proposition 1$\}$. As a simple consequence of Proposition 3, one has that RP is homeomorphic to P. Furthermore, if RP

is a bounded set, then the homeomorphism, as well as Propositions 1 and 3, can be extended to $\bar{P}$, the closure of P in R_+^l, and $\overline{RP}$ correspondingly. Next denote by ARP the set of allocations, each of them being Pareto-efficient and egalitarian-equivalent to some bundle in RP. By Propositions 1, 2, and 3 we have

Proposition 4: *Under the strict convexity assumption the correspondence that applies Pareto-efficient $\bar{x}$-equivalent allocations to each $\bar{x}$ in RP is a well-defined continuous function from RP onto ARP.*

However, note that the function of Proposition 4 is not one to one; one may have two distinct bundles in RP yielding the same Pareto-efficient-egalitarian-equivalent allocation in ARP. As an example, consider a two-person, two-commodity economy with aggregate initial endowment. (3, 3) and a Pareto-efficient allocation $\{(1, 1), (2, 2)\}$. The corresponding preferences are represented by symmetric utility functions, $u_1(x) = x^1 x^2$, $u_2(x) = x^1 + x^2$. The symmetry of the utility functions implies that any allocation with values on the diagonal is Pareto-efficient and that if two indifference curves meet off-diagonal, they meet twice. As the consequence of this example, it is not true that ARP is homeomorphic to P. Nevertheless, it is intuitively obvious that the set of Pareto-efficient-egalitarian-equivalent allocations is of dimension $l - 1$ at most, whereas the set of Pareto-efficient allocations is homeomorphic to the simplex in $R^{|T|}$ (i.e., of dimension $|T| - 1$). This last assertion appears in the book by Arrow–Hahn (1971, Ch. 5), which also includes all the technical tools needed for following the present discussion; the topological characterization of ARP is outside the scope of this paper. In any event, when the number of agents is large relative to the number of commodities, the restriction of the Pareto-set induced by the egalitarian-equivalent requirement is significant; relatively few Pareto-efficient allocations are not ruled out as being inequitable.

Mathematical appendix to Section 3

An allocation $\{x_t\}$ is *fair*, by definition, if for all t and t' in T:$x_t \gtrsim_t x_{t'}$. In the case of a two-person economy, the following results hold:

Proposition 5: *In a two-person economy a fair allocation is egalitarian equivalent.*

The preference relation of agent t is said to be *convex* if in the definition of strict convexity in the previous Mathematical Appendix, the relation $\gtrsim_t$ is substituted for by $>_t$.

Proposition 6: *In a two-person economy with convex preferences, if the egalitarian-reference-bundle lies on the ray through the aggregate endowment, the corresponding PEEEA is fair.*

Mathematical appendix to Section 4

Given $\bar{x} > 0$ in R^l_+ and t in T, we define the utility function u_t representing the preferences $\gtrsim_t$ of agent t as follows: for any x in R^l_+, let $s\bar{x}$ be the unique point on the ray through $\bar{x}$ indifferent to x according to the preferences of agent t(i.e., $s\bar{x} \sim_t x$). $u_t(x)$ is then equal, by definition, to the Euclidean norm of $s\bar{x}$. It is obvious that this u_t is a well-defined continuous utility function representing the preferences $\gtrsim_t$.

Proposition 7: *Given $\bar{x} > 0$ in R^l_+, let $\{u_t\}_{t\in T}$ be the list of utility functions defined above. The problem of maximizing over allocations $\{y_t\}$ the minimum over t in T of $u_t(y_t)$ has as the solution of PEEEA of Proposition 1.*

Mathematical appendix to Section 5

The set of technologically feasible production plans is denoted by K, $(K \subset R^l)$. As usual, if $z \in K$, then the negative coordinates of z denote inputs, and the positive coordinates of z denote outputs. Let $W = \{w + K\} \cap R^l_+$ denote the feasible aggregate final consumption vectors. It is assumed that W is a compact set with a nonempty interior. As previously, free disposal is also assumed; i.e., $x \leq y \in W$ implies that $x \in W$.

In this section we relax the monotonicity assumption on preferences, and it is only assumed that for all t in T and for all x, y in R^l_+: $x > y$ implies that $x >_t y$.

We further assume that the economy satisfies a so-called *utility connectedness* assumption: for any allocation $\{x_t\}$ and agent t' in T, if $x_{t'} \neq 0$, then there is an allocation $\{y_t\}$ so that for all $t \neq t'$, $y_t >_t x_t$.

Proposition 8: *Propositions 1, 2, 3, 4, 5, and 7 carry over to an economy with production as defined above; strict convexity for an economy with production means strict convexity of the set W in addition to strict convexity of preferences.*

Note that in Propositions 1 and 7 convexity of preferences is not assumed. Hence the corresponding results for an economy with production do not require convexity either.

Proposition 9: *If the preference relation of each agent t in T is convex and the set W is strictly convex, then there is a PEEEA for which the average bundle and the egalitarian-reference-bundle lie on the same ray.*

Remember that W is strictly convex in R_+^l if for all x and y in W, $x \neq y$, $(x + y)/2$ is in the interior of W (relative to R_+^l).

Mathematical appendix: The proofs

This section includes proofs, schemes of proofs, and hints for proofs of the propositions stated in the previous subsections. The notations are those of the previous appendices.

Proof of Proposition 1: Set $C = \{r > 0 |$ there is an $r\bar{x}$-equivalent allocation$\}$. The set C is nonempty, since $x_t = \bar{x}r/|T|$, for all t in T, defines an egalitarian-equivalent allocation whenever $r\bar{x} \leq w$ and $r > 0$. (Existence of such an r is obvious, since $w > 0$.) It is bounded, since monotonicity of preferences implies that there is no $r\bar{x}$-equivalent allocation when $r\bar{x} > w$. (Here the fact that $\bar{x} > 0$ is used to assert the existence of such an r.) Let $\bar{r}$ be the l.u.b. of C (sup C). Because of the compactness of the set of allocations and the continuity of preferences $\bar{r} \in C$.

To complete the proof, one has to show that an $\bar{r}x$-equivalent allocation is Pareto-efficient. Denote by $\{x_t\}$ an $\bar{r}x$-equivalent allocation, and suppose, per absurdum, that there is an allocation $\{y_t\}$ with $y_t \geq_t x_t$ for all t and $y_t >_t x_t$ for some t. Because of our monotonicity assumption there is another allocation, say $\{z_t\}$, so that $z_t >_t x_t$ for all t in T. By continuity (and monotonicity) there is, for each t in T, a positive number s_t so that $z_t \sim (\bar{r} + s_t)x$. Setting $\bar{s} = \min_t s_t$ and applying once again monotonicity and continuity, we get an $(\bar{r} + \bar{s})\bar{x}$-equivalent allocation – a contradiction. Q.E.D.

The proof of Proposition 2 is well-known. Existence of two distinct Pareto-efficient allocations that have identical utility representation (same reference bundle) contradicts strict convexity. The proof of Proposition 3 is similarly straightforward. It only requires the continuity of agents' preferences and the compactness of the set of allocations. As mentioned in the Mathematical Appendix to Section 2 the combination of Propositions 1, 2, and 3 yields Proposition 4.

The proof of Proposition 5 is also immediate. If the two indifference surfaces $\{x \in R_+^l \,|\, x \sim_i x_i\}i = 1, 2$ (where $\{x_1, x_2\}$ is the fair allocation of the Proposition) do not meet, then one is above the other – a contradiction to the assumption that $\{x_1, x_2\}$ is envy-free.

Proof of Proposition 6: Denote by x the reference point of the allocation (on the ray from the origin through w). Except in the trivial case when $x_1 = x_2 = x = w/2$ (which is fair) the inequality $x > w/2$ holds, which implies, in turn, the relations $x_i \sim_i x >_i w/2$ for $i = 1, 2$. If, per absurdum $x_1 >_2 x_2$ (or $x_2 >_1 x_1$), then by convexity we get $x_1/2 + x_2/2 = w/2 >_2 x_2$ (or $w/2 >_1 x_1$) – a contradiction.   Q.E.D.

The proofs of Propositions 7 and 8 are very simple and do not require any new ideas; hence, they are omitted.

Proof of Proposition 9: Set $S = \{\Sigma_{t \in T} x_t | \{x_t\}$ is a Pareto-efficient allocation$\}$, $\bar{S} = \{x/|x|| $ for some x in $S\}$, and S is the convex hull of $\bar{S}$. Since S is compact, so is $\hat{S}$ where $\bar{S}$ denotes the set of rays to which the average bundles of efficient allocations belong. We define an upper-semicontinuous correspondence $F: \hat{S} \to \hat{S}$ a fixed point of which is a ray that satisfies the conclusion of Proposition 9. For x in $\hat{S}$ we define $F(x)$ to be the set of average bundles corresponding to PEEEA's with reference-bundle on the ray through x. It is obvious that the existence of a fixed point of F concludes the proof of the Proposition. We shall check the conditions of Kakutani's fixed-point theorem. The set $\hat{S}$ is compact and convex and $F(\hat{S}) \subset \hat{S}$. It is equally obvious that $F(x)$ is a convex set for all $x \in \hat{S}$ and that Proposition 1 (and the corresponding part of Proposition 7) can be extended in our case to upper-semicontinuous correspondence instead of the continuous function in case of strictly convex preferences. (Again, Arrow and Hahn, 1971, Ch. 5, can be consulted for the technical details.)   Q.E.D.

REFERENCES

Arrow, K. J., *Social Choice and Individual Values*, second ed. (New Haven and London: Yale University Press, 1963).
    and F. Hahn, *General Competitive Analysis* (San Francisco: Holden-Day, Inc., 1971).
Bergson, A., "A Reformulation of Certain Aspects of Welfare Economics," *Quarterly Journal of Economics*, LII [1938], 310–34.
Foley, D. K., "Resource Allocation in the Public Sector," *Yale Economic Essays*, VII [1967], especially 73–76.
Graaff, J. de V., *Theoretical Welfare Economics* (Cambridge: Cambridge University Press, 1957).
Harsanyi, J. C., "Approaches to the Bargaining Problem Before and After the Theory of Games: A Critical Discussion of Zeuthen's, Hicks', and Nash's Theories," *Econometrica*, XXIV [1956], 144–57.
Hicks, J. R., "The Foundations of Welfare Economics," *Economic Journal*, XLIX [1939], 696–700, 711–12.

Kalai, E., and M. Smorodinsky, "Other Solutions to Nash's Bargaining Problem," *Econometrica*, XLIII [1975], 513–18.

Kaldor, N., "Welfare Propositions of Economics and Interpersonal Comparisons of Utility," *Economic Journal*, XLIX [1939], 549–52.

Musgrave, R. A., *The Theory of Public Finance* (New York: McGraw-Hill, 1959), p. 160.

Nash, J. F., "The Bargaining Problem," *Econometrica*, XVIII [1950], 155–62.

Pazner, E., and D. Schmeidler, "A Difficulty in the Concept of Fairness," *Review of Economic Studies*, XLI [1974], 441–43.

"Social Contract Theory and Ordinal Distributive Equity," *Journal of Public Economics*, V [1976], 246–57.

Rawls, J., *A Theory of Justice* (Cambridge: Harvard University Press, 1971). (On envy, see pp. 530–41.)

Samuelson, P. A., *Foundations of Econmic Analysis* (Cambridge: Harvard University Press, 1947), Ch. 8.

"Evaluation of Real National Income," *Oxford Economic Papers*, N.S. II [1950], 1–29.

"Social Indifference Curves," *Quarterly Journal of Economics*, LXX [1956], 1–22.

Scitovsky, T., "A Note on Welfare Propositions in Economics," *Review of Economic Studies*, IX [1941], 77–88.

Varian, H., "Envy, Equity and Efficiency," *Journal of Economic Theory*, IX [1974], 63–91.

Author index

Subject index

362